Learning Snowflake SQL and Scripting

Generate, Retrieve, and Automate Snowflake Data

Alan Beaulieu

Beijing · Boston · Farnham · Sebastopol · Tokyo

Learning Snowflake SQL and Scripting

by Alan Beaulieu

Published by O'Reilly Media, Inc., 1005 Gravenstein Highway North, Sebastopol, CA 95472.

O'Reilly books may be purchased for educational, business, or sales promotional use. Online editions are also available for most titles (*http://oreilly.com*). For more information, contact our corporate/institutional sales department: 800-998-9938 or *corporate@oreilly.com*.

Acquisitions Editor: Andy Kwan
Development Editor: Corbin Collins
Production Editor: Katherine Tozer
Copyeditor: nSight, Inc.
Proofreader: Tove Innis

Indexer: Ellen Troutman-Zaig
Interior Designer: David Futato
Cover Designer: Karen Montgomery
Illustrator: Kate Dullea

October 2023:   First Edition

Revision History for the First Edition

2023-10-03:   First Release

See *http://oreilly.com/catalog/errata.csp?isbn=9781098140328* for release details.

978-1-098-14032-8

LSI

Table of Contents

Preface

Welcome to *Learning Snowflake SQL and Scripting*. Perhaps you are brand new to databases and will need to run queries or reports against a Snowflake database. Or perhaps, like myself, you have been working with databases such as Oracle, SQL Server, or MySQL for years, and your company has begun transitioning to cloud-based platforms. Whatever the case, this book strives to empower you with a detailed understanding of Snowflake's SQL implementation so that you can be as effective as possible.

To help put things in context, I'll start with a brief history of databases, starting with the introduction of relational databases in the 1980s and leading up to the availability of cloud-based database platforms such as Snowflake. If you're ready to jump right into learning SQL, feel free to move on to Chapter 1, but you should read "Setting Up a Sample Database" on page xii if you want to create your own database with which to experiment.

Relational Database Primer

Computerized database systems have been around since the 1960s, but for the purposes of this book, let's start with the introduction of relational databases, which started hitting the market in the 1980s with products such as Oracle, Sybase, SQL Server (Microsoft), and Db2 (IBM). Relational databases are based on rows of data stored in tables, and related rows stored in different tables are linked using redundant values. For example, the ACME Wholesale customer can be identified using customer ID 123 in the `Customer` table, and any of ACME's orders in the `Orders` table would also be identified using customer ID 123.

A table, such as `Customer` or `Orders` mentioned above, is comprised of multiple columns, such as name, address, and telephone number. One or more of these columns is used to uniquely identify each row in the table (known as the *primary key*). For the example database used for this book, there is a `Customer` table whose primary key consists of a single column named `custkey`, and every row in the `Customer` table must have a unique `custkey` value. There is also an `Orders` table that includes the column `custkey` to reference the customer who placed the order. The `Orders.custkey` column is referred to as a *foreign key* to the `Customer` table and must contain a value that exists in the `Customer.custkey` column. Table P-1 shows a quick recap of the terminology introduced so far.

Table P-1. Terms and definitions

Column	An individual piece of data
Row	A set of related columns
Table	A set of rows
Primary key	One or more columns that can be used as a unique identifier for each row in a table
Foreign key	One or more columns that can be used together to identify a single row in another table

So far, we've discussed the use of redundant column values to link tables via primary and foreign keys, but there are rules regarding the storage of redundant values. For example, it is perfectly fine for the `Orders` table to include a column to hold values of `Customer.custkey`, but it is not okay to include other columns from the `Customer` table, such as the name or address columns. If you were looking at a row in the `Orders` table and wanted to know the name and address of the customer who placed the order, you should go get these values from the `Customer` table rather than storing the customer's name and address in the `Orders` table. The process of designing a database to ensure that each independent piece of information is in only one place (except for foreign keys) is known as *normalization.*

Normalization rules also apply to individual columns, in that a column should hold only a single independent value. One common example would be a mailing address, which is comprised of multiple elements, such as street, city, state, and zip code. A normalized design would therefore include multiple columns, as demonstrated in Table P-2.

Table P-2. Sample address columns

Address1	3 Maple Street
Address2	Suite 305
City	Anytown
State	TX
Zip code	12345

Companies often have multiple databases used for different purposes, and the degree of normalization can vary greatly. A database used exclusively by a company's shipping department, for example, may include a single address column used to print shipping labels, which for the example above might contain the value "3 Maple Street, Suite 305, Anytown, TX 12345." It may also be the case that the shipping database is refreshed daily from a central, normalized database.

Snowflake

First launched in 2014, Snowflake is a cloud-based, full-featured, relational database. Snowflake databases can be hosted on any of the three major cloud platforms (Amazon AWS, Microsoft Azure, and Google Cloud), which allows customers with existing cloud deployments to stick with what they know. Both storage and compute engines can be scaled on demand, and Snowflake's software as a service (SaaS) model frees companies from the need to hire legions of network, server, and database administrators, allowing organizations to focus on their core business.

There are many ways to interact with Snowflake, but for the purposes of this book I suggest you use Snowflake's browser-based graphical tool named Snowsight, which is an excellent tool and is regularly updated and enhanced. Read Snowsight's online documentation (*https://oreil.ly/TxWhI*) for an overview of its capabilities.

What Is SQL?

Structured query language (SQL) is the language originally developed for querying and manipulating data in relational databases. The SQL language has evolved to handle complex data, such as JavaScript Object Notation (JSON) documents, allowing easier integration between SQL and procedural languages, such as Java.

The SQL language is comprised of several groups of commands, as shown in Table P-3.

Table P-3. SQL command categories

Category	Usage	Examples
Schema statements	Creating and modifying database structures	Create table, Create index, Alter table
Data statements	Querying and manipulating data	Select, Insert, Update, Delete, Merge
Transaction statements	Creating and ending transactions	Commit, Rollback

You may also see schema statements classified as data definition language (DDL), and data statements classified as data manipulation language (DML). The schema statements are used to create or alter tables, indexes, views, and various other database structures. Once these structures are in place, you will use the data statements to insert, modify, and delete rows in your tables, and to retrieve data.

While you will see some schema statements used in this book, the vast majority of examples cover the data statements, which, though few in number, are rich and powerful statements worthy of in-depth study.

SQL is a *nonprocedural language*, meaning that you define what you want done, but not how to do it. For example, if you are running a report that lists the top ten customers per geographic region, you would write a `select` statement that sums sales for each customer, but it would be up to the database server to determine how best to retrieve the data. There are generally multiple ways to generate a particular set of results, and some are more efficient than others, so it is left to the database server to determine how to pull data from multiple tables in an efficient manner.

What Is SQL Scripting?

If you have programmed with a procedural language such as Java, C#, or Go, you are familiar with such programming constructs as looping, if-then-else, and exception handling. SQL, being a nonprocedural language, has none of these constructs. To bridge this gap, most database platforms provide both a nonprocedural SQL implementation along with a procedural language that includes both the SQL data statements such as `select` and `insert` along with all of the usual procedural programming constructs. Oracle, for example, provides the PL/SQL procedural language, while Microsoft provides the Transact-SQL language.

Snowflake provides the Snowflake Scripting language, which allows you to declare variables, incorporate looping and if-then-else statements, and detect and handle exceptions. Snowflake Scripting language will be covered in Chapters 15, 16, and 17 of this book.

Setting Up a Sample Database

The nice people at Snowflake have provided several sample databases so that potential customers can gain experience with their SQL implementation. One of the sample databases, TPCH_SF1, is used for the majority of the examples in this book. However, since the TPCH_SF1 database is quite large (over 8.7 million rows of data), I chose to use a small subset (about 330,000 rows) of TPCH_SF1. You will have two options for setting up your own sample database (see "Sample Database Setup" on page xiv), which will depend on whether the TPCH_SF1 sample database is still being made available by Snowflake.

The sample database contains eight tables containing information about customer orders of a set of parts provided by a set of suppliers, a real-life example of which might be a company that sells automobile parts made by other companies. Appendix A contains a visual representation of these tables along with the relationships between the tables.

If you want to run the example queries in this book, setting up a free 30-day Snowflake account is very easy. Once your account is active, you can follow my instructions for setting up your sample database.

Setting Up a Snowflake Account

One of the great things about SaaS is that there is generally nothing that needs to be installed locally. All of your interactions with Snowflake will be through a standard browser of your choice. Here are the steps needed to create your own account:

1. Go to *www.snowflake.com* and click the START FOR FREE button on the top right of the page.

2. Enter your first name, last name, email, company name, role, and country. Click CONTINUE.

3. Choose the Standard edition and choose one of the three cloud providers. A drop-down will appear allowing you to choose the closest cloud node. Check the box to agree to the terms and conditions and click GET STARTED.

4. An email will be sent asking you to activate your account. Click on CLICK TO ACTIVATE in the email.

5. A tab will open in your browser asking you to choose a username and password. After choosing, you will be asked to log in.

6. Your account page will appear in your browser.

That's all there is to it. You will have 30 days to experiment, after which you will need to provide a credit card to continue. You can track your costs under Admin>Usage so you don't have any unwanted surprises. If you exceed the 30-day trial period and want to continue, here are a couple tips to help keep the costs down:

1. When working in Snowflake, the set of compute resources attached to your session is referred to as the *virtual warehouse*. You have your choice of anything from a very small warehouse (X-Small) all the way up to the 4X-Large warehouse. Make sure you choose the X-Small warehouse when working with the sample database for this book.

2. After a configurable period of inactivity, your warehouse will be shut down. The default setting is 10 minutes, but you can reduce it to as little as 1 minute. I suggest setting it 3 to 4 minutes.

Both the warehouse size and auto-suspend period can be modified by choosing the Admin>Warehouses menu, clicking on your warehouse name (which is named COMPUTE_WH by default), and then clicking the Edit menu option in the top right corner, as shown in Figure P-1.

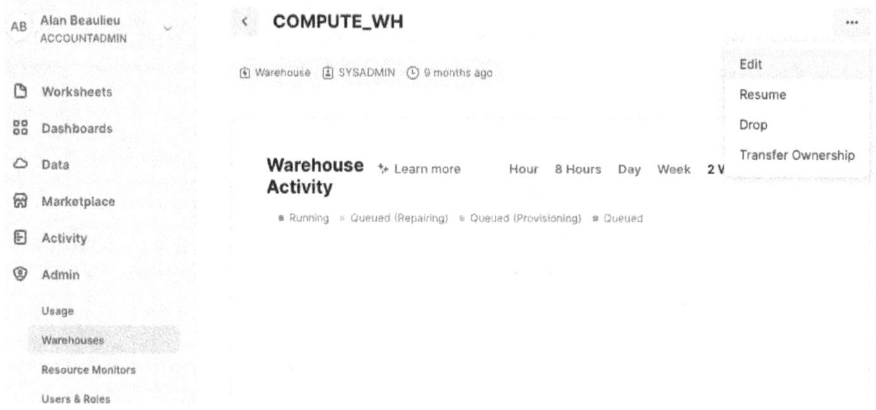

Figure P-1. Editing warehouse settings

Sample Database Setup

No matter which of the options you choose for creating your sample database tables, there are a couple of things you will need to do first.

Create a worksheet

In Snowsight, worksheets are where you will interact with your database. You can create different worksheets for different purposes, so let's create a worksheet called *Learning_Snowflake_SQL*. To do so, click Worksheets in the left-hand menu, then click the "+" button at the top right and choose SQL Worksheet. A new worksheet tab will appear and will be given a default name based on the current date/time. You can click the menu next to the worksheet name and choose Rename, at which point you can name it **LEARNING_SNOWFLAKE_SQL**, as shown in Figure P-2.

You can use this worksheet to run your SQL commands, starting with the `create database` statement in the next section.

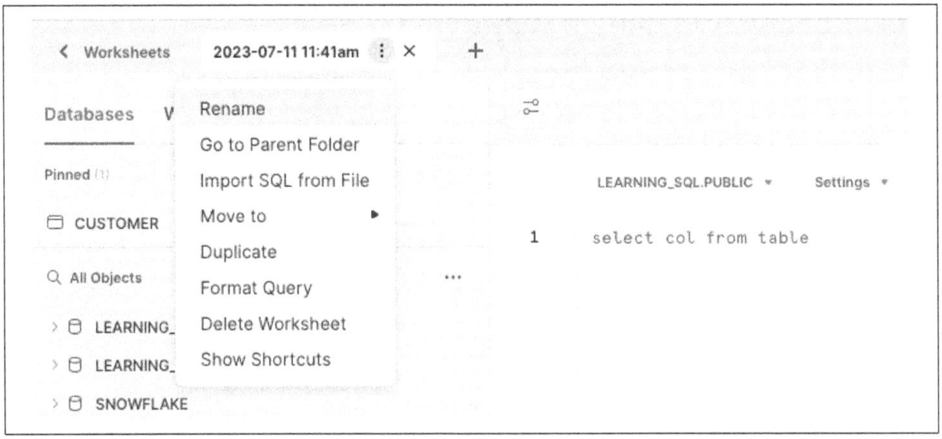

Figure P-2. Renaming a worksheet

Create your database

Now that you have a worksheet, you can start entering commands. The first task will be creating your sample database, as shown in Figure P-3.

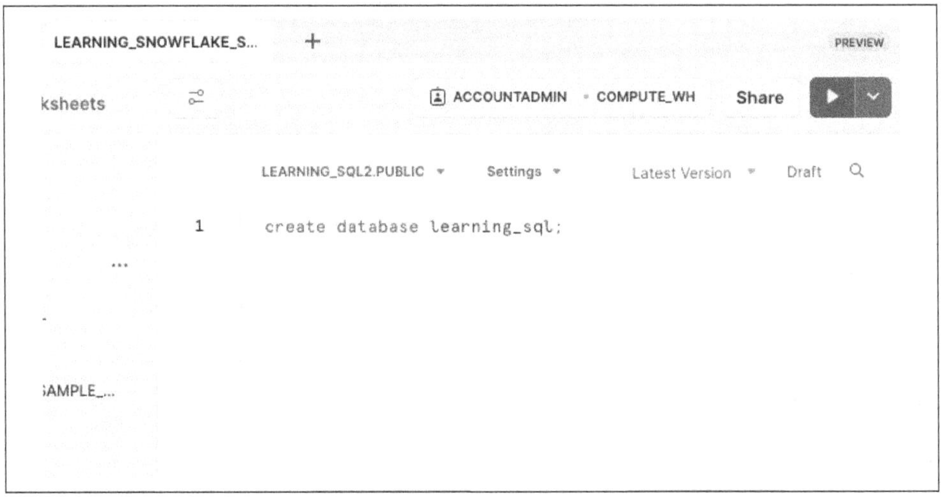

Figure P-3. Create a new database

After typing **create database learning_sql** into your worksheet, click the Run button (the white arrow with a blue background at the top right) to execute your command. Your database will be created and a schema named *Public* will be created by default. This is where the tables for your sample database will be created.

Sample Database Option #1: Copy from TPCH_SF1

In order to choose this option, which is the simpler of the two methods, you must first check to see which Snowflake sample databases are available. To do so, choose the Data>Databases menu option to see the list of available databases. If you see TPCH_SF1 under the *SNOWFLAKE_SAMPLE_DATA* database, you're in luck, as shown in Figure P-4.

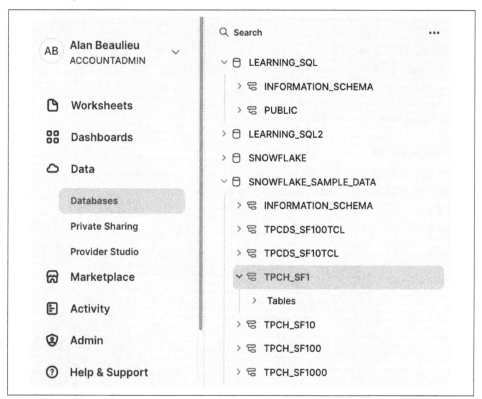

Figure P-4. Sample database listing

The next section describes how to copy the data from TPCH_SF1 into your own database.

Create and populate the tables

Before executing the commands to create your tables, you will need to specify the database and schema in which you will be working, as shown in Figure P-5.

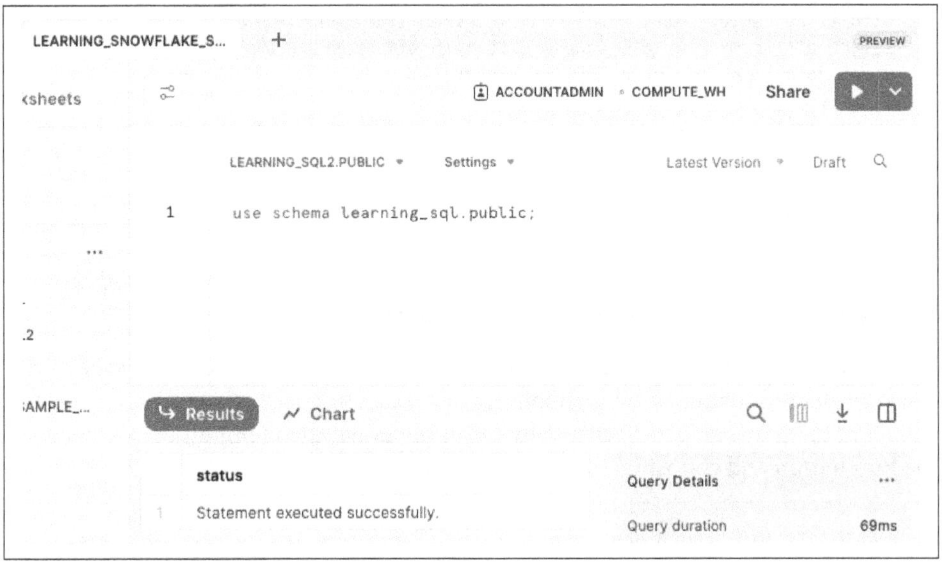

Figure P-5. Setting the database and schema

After entering the use schema command and pressing the Run button, you're ready to create your tables. Here's the set of commands:

```
create table region
as select * from snowflake_sample_data.tpch_sf1.region;

create table nation
as select * from snowflake_sample_data.tpch_sf1.nation;

create table part as
select * from snowflake_sample_data.tpch_sf1.part
where mod(p_partkey,50) = 8;

create table partsupp as
select * from snowflake_sample_data.tpch_sf1.partsupp
where mod(ps_partkey,50) = 8;

create table supplier as
with sp as (select distinct ps_suppkey from partsupp)
select s.* from snowflake_sample_data.tpch_sf1.supplier s
inner join sp
on s.s_suppkey = sp.ps_suppkey;

create table lineitem as
select l.* from snowflake_sample_data.tpch_sf1.lineitem l
inner join part p
on p.p_partkey = l.l_partkey;

create table orders as
```

```
with li as (select distinct l_orderkey from lineitem)
select o.* from snowflake_sample_data.tpch_sf1.orders o
inner join li on o.o_orderkey = li.l_orderkey;

create table customer as
with o as (select distinct o_custkey from orders)
select c.* from snowflake_sample_data.tpch_sf1.customer c
inner join o on c.c_custkey = o.o_custkey;
```

This script can also be found at my GitHub page (*https://github.com/alanbeau/lear ningsnowflakesql/blob/main/Copy_Sample_Database.sql*).

Once you have loaded these eight `create table` commands into your worksheet, you can run them individually by highlighting and executing each statement, or you can run all of them in a single execution by dropping down the menu on the right side of the Run button and choosing Run All, as shown in Figure P-6.

Figure P-6. Choosing Run All option from Run menu

Whether you run them one at a time or all together, the end result should be eight new tables in the *Public* schema of your Learning_SQL database. If you run into problems, you can simply start again by re-creating the database via `create or replace database learning_sql`, which will drop any existing tables.

Sample Database Option #2: Load Data from GitHub Files

You will need to use this option if the TPCH_SF1 sample database is no longer available from Snowflake (or if you were unable for any reason to use option #1). For this option, you will need to create eight tables in the *learning_sql.public* schema, and then load each table using CSV files available from my GitHub page. The following sections will lead you through the process.

Creating sample database tables

Load the *Learning_Snowflake_SQL_Schema.sql* file from GitHub (*https://github.com/alanbeau/learningsnowflakesql/blob/main/Learning_Snowflake_SQL_Schema.sql*) into your worksheet. Figure P-7 shows what it looks like.

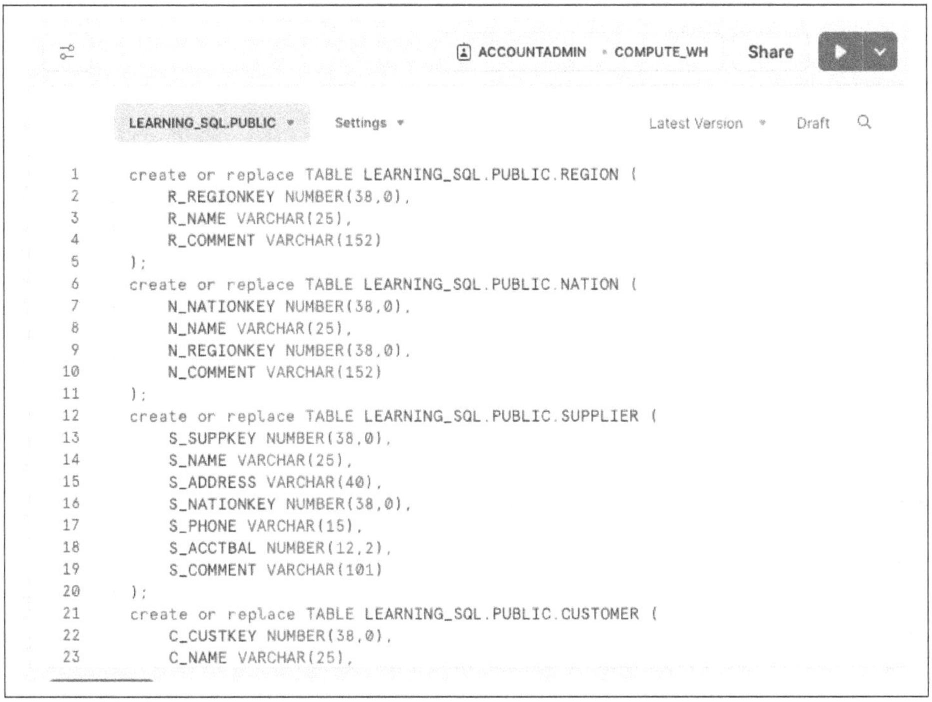

Figure P-7. Create table statements

You can highlight each `create table` statement and click the Run button, or you can use the drop-down menu next to the Run button to choose the Run All option, which will execute all eight statements. After executing, you should be able to see all eight tables under Database>LEARNING_SQL>PUBLIC>Tables, as shown in Figure P-8.

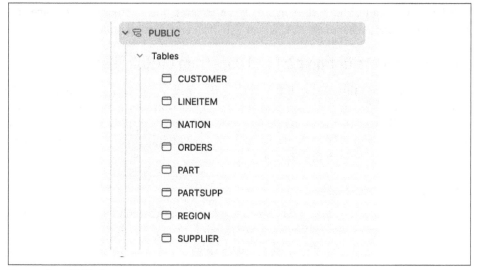

Figure P-8. Table listing

Once again, if you run into problems, you can simply start again by recreating the database via `create or replace database learning_sql`, which will drop any existing tables.

Load files into tables

Now that the tables are in place, you can load each one individually using CSV files available from my GitHub page. Each table has a similarly named file; for example, you will load the `Customer` table using the *customer.csv.gz* file, the `Region` table using the *region.csv.gz* file, etc. Table P-4 shows the files for each of the eight tables.

Table P-4. CSV file assignment

Table name	GitHub file
Customer	*https://github.com/alanbeau/learningsnowflakesql/blob/main/customer.csv.gz*
Lineitem	*https://github.com/alanbeau/learningsnowflakesql/blob/main/lineitem.csv.gz*
Nation	*https://github.com/alanbeau/learningsnowflakesql/blob/main/nation.csv.gz*
Orders	*https://github.com/alanbeau/learningsnowflakesql/blob/main/orders.csv.gz*
Part	*https://github.com/alanbeau/learningsnowflakesql/blob/main/part.csv.gz*
Partsupp	*https://github.com/alanbeau/learningsnowflakesql/blob/main/partsupp.csv.gz*
Region	*https://github.com/alanbeau/learningsnowflakesql/blob/main/region.csv.gz*
Supplier	*https://github.com/alanbeau/learningsnowflakesql/blob/main/supplier.csv.gz*

To download all eight files from GitHub (*https://github.com/alanbeau/learningsnow flakesql*), select each file individually and use the "Download raw file" option.

To load the Customer table, find the table in the Database>LEARNING_ SQL>
PUBLIC>Tables menu and click the Load Table menu option, as shown in Figure P-9.

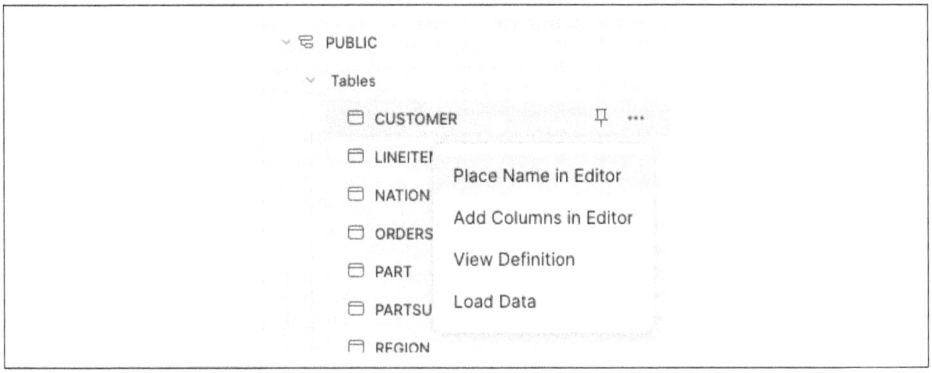

Figure P-9. Load Data menu option

Figure P-10 shows the pop-up window that is launched from the Load Data menu
option.

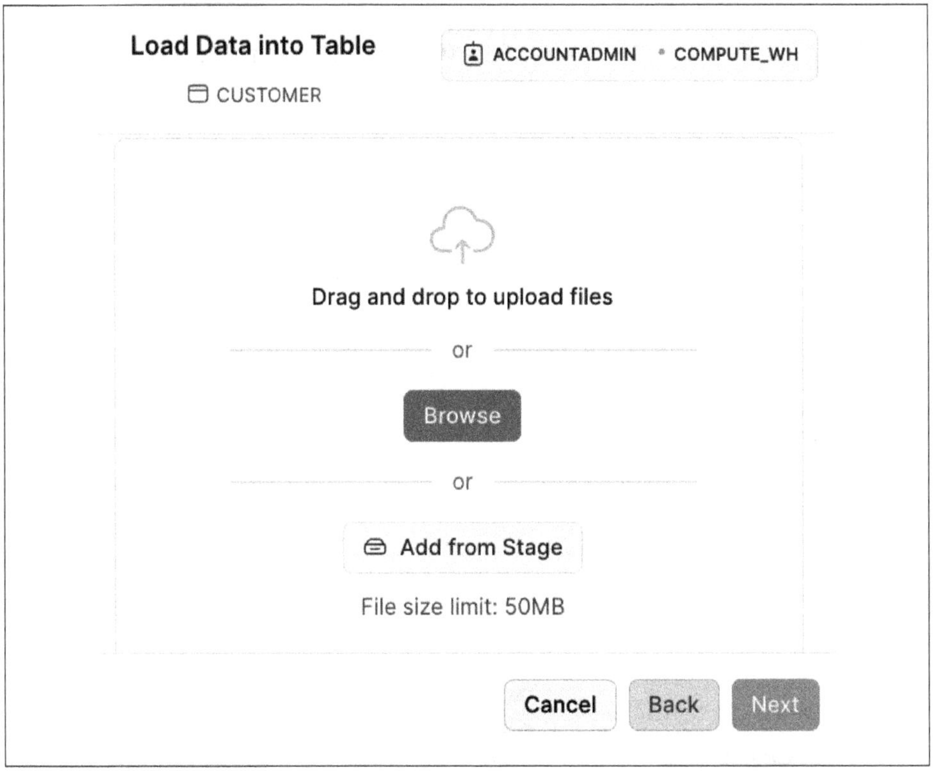

Figure P-10. Load Data pop-up window

Click Browse and choose the appropriate GitHub file, as shown in Figure P-11.

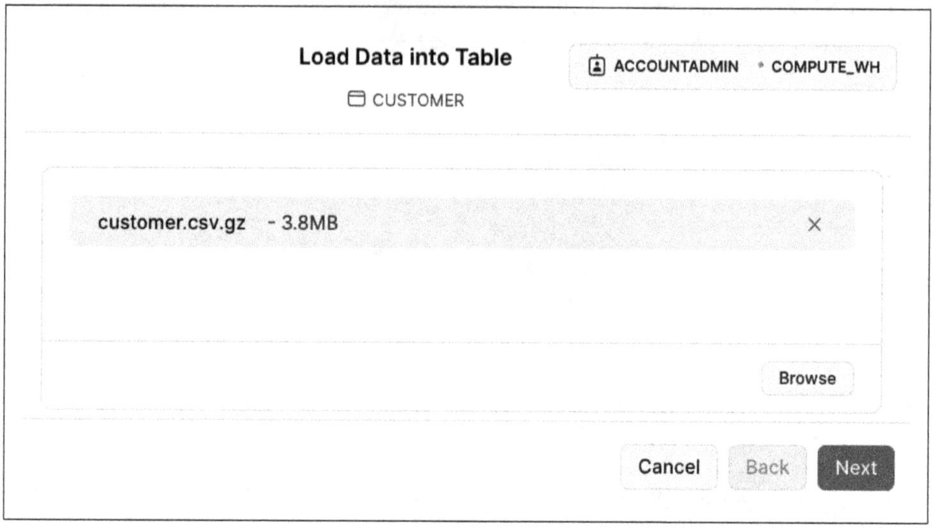

Figure P-11. Choose CSV file

Click Next and choose the "Delimited Files (CSV or TSV)" option under the File Format drop-down, as shown in Figure P-12.

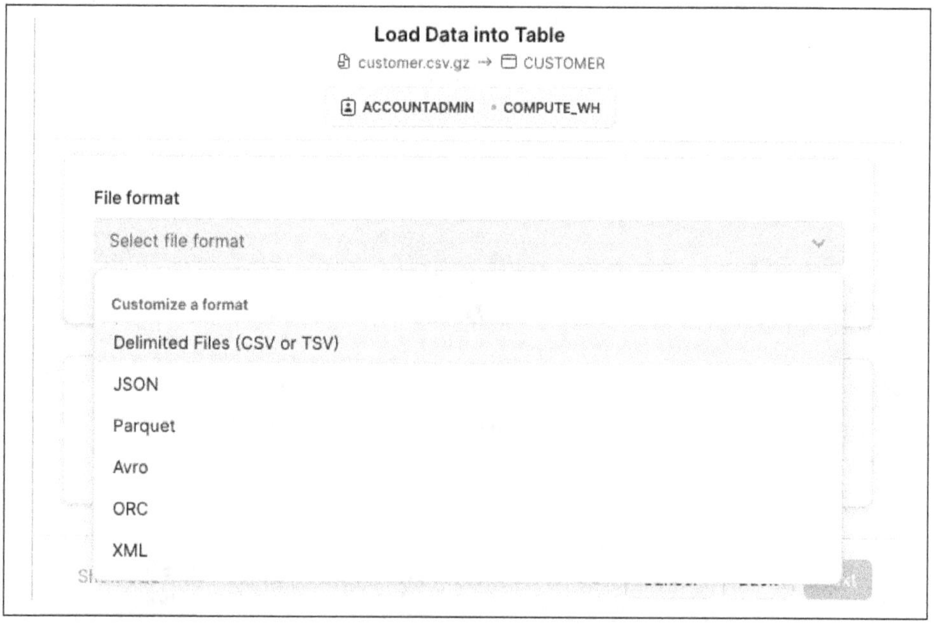

Figure P-12. Choosing delimited file option

Leave all the other fields as is (default options) and click Next. After completing, you should see a window similar to Figure P-13.

Figure P-13. Successful data load

Click Done and move on to the next table. Be careful to choose the appropriate file for each of the other seven tables.

Conventions Used in This Book

The following typographical conventions are used in this book:

Italic
> Indicates new terms, URLs, email addresses, filenames, and file extensions.

`Constant width`
> Used for program listings, as well as within paragraphs to refer to program elements such as variable or function names, databases, data types, environment variables, statements, and keywords.

`Constant width bold`
> Shows commands or other text that should be typed literally by the user, as well as code of particular interest to the present discussion.

`Constant width italic` or `<constant width in angle brackets>`
> Shows text that should be replaced with user-supplied values or by values determined by context.

This element signifies a general note.

This element indicates a warning or caution.

Using Code Examples

Supplemental material (code examples, exercises, etc.) is available for download at *https://github.com/alanbeau/learningsnowflakesql*.

If you have a technical question or a problem using the code examples, please send an email to *bookquestions@oreilly.com*.

This book is here to help you get your job done. In general, if example code is offered with this book, you may use it in your programs and documentation. You do not need to contact us for permission unless you're reproducing a significant portion of the code. For example, writing a program that uses several chunks of code from this book does not require permission. Selling or distributing examples from O'Reilly books does require permission. Answering a question by citing this book and quoting example code does not require permission. Incorporating a significant amount of example code from this book into your product's documentation does require permission.

We appreciate, but generally do not require, attribution. An attribution usually includes the title, author, publisher, and ISBN. For example: "*Learning Snowflake SQL and Scripting* by Alan Beaulieu (O'Reilly). Copyright 2024 Alan Beaulieu, 978-1-098-14032-8."

If you feel your use of code examples falls outside fair use or the permission given above, feel free to contact us at *permissions@oreilly.com*.

O'Reilly Online Learning

O'REILLY® For more than 40 years, *O'Reilly Media* has provided technology and business training, knowledge, and insight to help companies succeed.

Our unique network of experts and innovators share their knowledge and expertise through books, articles, and our online learning platform. O'Reilly's online learning platform gives you on-demand access to live training courses, in-depth learning paths, interactive coding environments, and a vast collection of text and video from O'Reilly and 200+ other publishers. For more information, visit *http://oreilly.com*.

How to Contact Us

Please address comments and questions concerning this book to the publisher:

> O'Reilly Media, Inc.
> 1005 Gravenstein Highway North
> Sebastopol, CA 95472
> 800-889-8969 (in the United States or Canada)
> 707-829-7019 (international or local)
> 707-829-0104 (fax)
> *support@oreilly.com*
> *https://www.oreilly.com/about/contact.html*

We have a web page for this book, where we list errata, examples, and any additional information. You can access this page at *https://oreil.ly/learning-snowflake-and-sql*.

For news and information about our books and courses, visit *https://oreilly.com*.

Find us on LinkedIn: *https://linkedin.com/company/oreilly-media*.

Follow us on Twitter: *https://twitter.com/oreillymedia*.

Watch us on YouTube: *https://youtube.com/oreillymedia*.

Acknowledgments

I would like to thank several people at O'Reilly Media for helping bring this book to life, including Andy Kwan for helping with various technical issues, Corbin Collins for his excellent advice and editing skills, and Katherine Tozer and Carol Keller for the final push to get us to the finish line. I would also like to thank my tech reviewers, including Ed Crean and Joyce Kay Avila, whose expertise with the Snowflake ecosystem helped make this book much more detailed. Also, thanks to Pankaj Gupta and Nadir Doctor, both of whom saw the book at the early release time and enthusiastically volunteered to review the book. Lastly, thanks to my wife Nancy for encouraging me through not just this book but the five editions of *Learning SQL* and *Mastering Oracle SQL* over the past 20 years.

CHAPTER 1

Query Primer

Let's roll up our sleeves and look at some queries using the `select` statement, which is the SQL statement used to execute queries.

Query Basics

If you followed the steps listed in the Preface, then you have created a Snowflake account and have created your sample database. To enter queries using Snowsight, create a new worksheet by selecting the Worksheets button on the left side of the screen, and then click the "+" button at the top right. Your new worksheet will appear in the left pane with a name using the current date and time, but you can rename it to `Learning_Snowflake_SQL` to use for the examples in this book. Before running any queries in your new worksheet, set the schema to the *Public* schema in the Learning_SQL database: `use schema learning_sql.public;`.

After entering this command into your worksheet, click on the right arrow at the top right of the screen to execute the command, as shown in Figure 1-1.

Every time you log in to Snowsight, you will want to execute this `use schema` statement before executing queries against the sample database.

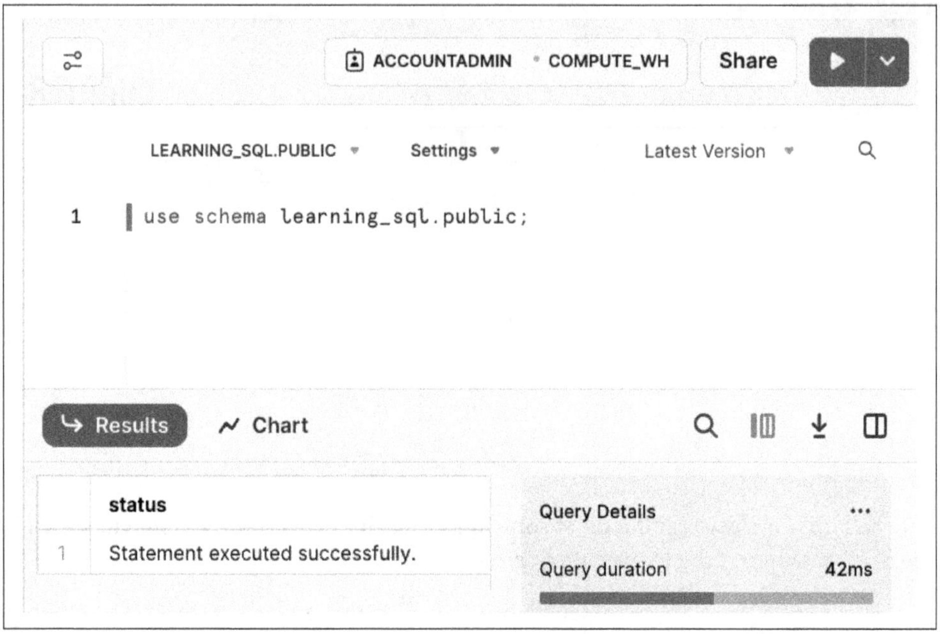

Figure 1-1. Setting the schema using Snowflake's web interface (Snowsight)

Snowflake Web Interface Versus SnowSQL CLI

For most examples shown in this book, I will be using Snowflake's CLI, known as SnowSQL, rather than the Snowsight web interface. This allows the SQL statements in the examples to be copied from the book (assuming you are using an online copy) and also eliminates unnecessary clutter. I recommend that you use Snowsight, however, since it is a powerful tool that can be run from any device, but if you would like to use SnowSQL, you can follow these installation and usage instructions (*https://oreil.ly/KKTcq*).

When using SnowSQL, always add a semicolon to the end of your SQL statement, then hit Enterto execute the statement. Also, along with setting the current schema with the use schema command, I also set the prompt in SnowSQL using the following statement:

```
!set prompt_format=[schema]>;
```

This is why all of my examples will show the prompt PUBLIC>, but you can use the default prompt format if you prefer.

Next, let's begin with a simple query to return the current date:

```
PUBLIC>select current_date;
+--------------+
| CURRENT_DATE |
|--------------|
| 2023-03-19   |
+--------------+
```

This query calls the built-in function `current_date()`, which by default returns the date in YYYY-MM-DD format (4-digit year, 2-digit month, 2-digit day). Select statements return a *result set*, which is a set of one or more rows having one or more columns. For this first example, the result set consists of a single row having a single column.

A database table also consists of one or more rows having one or more columns, so a result set returned by a `select` statement could be the entire contents of a table. Here's what that would look like using the smallest table in the sample database, `Region`, which contains the following data:

```
PUBLIC>select *
       from region;
+-------------+-------------+------------------------------------+
| R_REGIONKEY | R_NAME      | R_COMMENT                          |
|-------------+-------------|------------------------------------+
|           0 | AFRICA      | lar deposits. blithely final pac...|
|           1 | AMERICA     | hs use ironic, even requests. s    |
|           2 | ASIA        | ges. thinly even pinto beans ca    |
|           3 | EUROPE      | ly final courts cajole furiously...|
|           4 | MIDDLE EAST | uickly special accounts cajole c...|
+-------------+-------------+------------------------------------+
```

Here are a couple of things to consider concerning this query:

- `select *` is shorthand for "return every column."
- This query includes both a `select` clause and a `from` clause. A `from` clause is used to specify the table(s) from which to retrieve data.

And here are a couple of things to consider about the result set:

- The `Region` table has 5 rows and 3 columns.
- The comments in the third column of the result set are randomly generated. This is true for all descriptive columns in the sample database.
- SnowSQL automatically formats the result set to include the column names, and uses the +, -, and | characters to make borders around each column and row.

If you are using Snowsight rather than SnowSQL, the result set will look something like what is shown in Figure 1-2.

```
LEARNING_SQL.PUBLIC  ▾

1   select *
2   from region;
```

🖰 Objects   ☰ Editor   ↳ Results   ⤳ Chart

	R_REGIONKEY	R_NAME	R_COMMENT
1	0	AFRICA	lar deposits. blithely final packages cajole. regular waters are final reques
2	1	AMERICA	hs use ironic, even requests. s
3	2	ASIA	ges. thinly even pinto beans ca
4	3	EUROPE	ly final courts cajole furiously final excuse
5	4	MIDDLE EAST	uickly special accounts cajole carefully blithely close requests. carefully fi

Figure 1-2. Querying Region table using Snowsight

If you'd like to see what columns are available in a table, you can use Snowflake's describe statement. Here's what it returns for the Region table:

```
PUBLIC>describe table region;
+-------------+---------------+--------+-------+---------+...
| name        | type          | kind   | null? | default |...
|-------------+---------------+--------+-------+---------+...
| R_REGIONKEY | NUMBER(38,0)  | COLUMN | N     | NULL    |...
| R_NAME      | VARCHAR(25)   | COLUMN | N     | NULL    |...
| R_COMMENT   | VARCHAR(152)  | COLUMN | Y     | NULL    |...
+-------------+---------------+--------+-------+---------+...
```

The Region table has a numeric column named r_regionkey to hold a unique numeric value for each row, and two character columns (varchar stands for *variable character*) to hold the region's name and comments about the region.

Command Parameters

Many of Snowflake's built-in commands, such as the show tables command shown in the previous example, include multiple optional parameters affecting how the command should be executed. In this case, I used the terse parameter to specify that only 5 of the 18 possible columns be included in the result set. If you want to see the full set of parameters available for any of Snowflake's commands, you can peruse Snowflake's SQL Command Reference (*https://oreil.ly/ZZ8FH*).

To see information about all of the tables available in a database, use the `show tables` command (using the `terse` option to limit the number of columns):

```
PUBLIC>show terse tables in PUBLIC;
+-------------------------------+----------+-------+...
| created_on                    | name     | kind  |...
|-------------------------------+----------+-------+...
| 2023-02-28 06:55:21.382 -0800 | CUSTOMER | TABLE |...
| 2023-02-28 06:51:41.226 -0800 | LINEITEM | TABLE |...
| 2023-02-28 06:43:46.739 -0800 | NATION   | TABLE |...
| 2023-02-28 06:53:19.090 -0800 | ORDERS   | TABLE |...
| 2023-02-28 06:44:35.450 -0800 | PART     | TABLE |...
| 2023-02-28 06:45:20.267 -0800 | PARTSUPP | TABLE |...
| 2023-02-28 06:42:32.322 -0800 | REGION   | TABLE |...
| 2023-02-28 06:49:39.242 -0800 | SUPPLIER | TABLE |...
+-------------------------------+----------+-------+...
```

One thing to consider is that the output of `show tables` will only include tables that you've been given the privilege to see, so keep this in mind when you begin working with other databases. The eight tables returned by the `show tables` command will be used for most of the examples in this book. Appendix A shows a diagram of these tables, including all columns and the relationships between tables.

Query Clauses

Queries are comprised of multiple components, or *clauses*. Two of the clauses, `select` and `from`, were introduced in the previous section, but there are eight different clauses that can be added to a Snowflake query, as shown in Table 1-1.

Table 1-1. Query clauses

Clause name	Purpose
select	Specifies the columns to be included in the result set
from	Identifies the tables from which to retrieve data and how the tables should be joined
where	Removes unwanted rows in the result set
group by	Groups rows together by common values
having	Removes unwanted rows in the result set based on groupings
qualify	Removes unwanted rows in the result set based on results of windowing functions (see Chapter 14)
order by	Sorts the result set by one or more columns
limit	Restricts the number of rows in the result set

Of the eight clauses listed in Table 1-1, only `select` is required, and some are used in tandem (for example, you wouldn't use the `having` clause without first specifying a `group by` clause). All of these clauses are covered in this book, with some of the more advanced ones left for later chapters. The following sections outline the uses of each of these clauses.

The select Clause

As demonstrated earlier in the chapter, a query can consist of just a `select` clause. Here's an example that returns a result set consisting of a single column:

```
PUBLIC>select 'Welcome to Snowflake SQL!';
+----------------------------+
| 'WELCOME TO SNOWFLAKE SQL!' |
|----------------------------|
| Welcome to Snowflake SQL!  |
+----------------------------+
```

The `select` clause is the only required clause in a query, but it isn't particularly useful by itself. To make things more interesting, let's write a query to retrieve some of the columns from the `Nation` table, which looks as follows:

```
PUBLIC>describe table nation;
+-------------+-------------+--------+-------+---------+...
| name        | type        | kind   | null? | default |...
|-------------+-------------+--------+-------+---------+...
| N_NATIONKEY | NUMBER(38,0) | COLUMN | N     | NULL    |...
| N_NAME      | VARCHAR(25)  | COLUMN | N     | NULL    |...
| N_REGIONKEY | NUMBER(38,0) | COLUMN | N     | NULL    |...
| N_COMMENT   | VARCHAR(152) | COLUMN | Y     | NULL    |...
+-------------+-------------+--------+-------+---------+...
```

The next query retrieves the first three columns from `Nation`:

```
PUBLIC>select n_nationkey, n_name, n_regionkey
       from nation;
+-------------+--------------------+-------------+
| N_NATIONKEY | N_NAME             | N_REGIONKEY |
|-------------+--------------------+-------------|
|           0 | ALGERIA            |           0 |
|           1 | ARGENTINA          |           1 |
|           2 | BRAZIL             |           1 |
|           3 | CANADA             |           1 |
|           4 | EGYPT              |           4 |
|           5 | ETHIOPIA           |           0 |
|           6 | FRANCE             |           3 |
|           7 | GERMANY            |           3 |
|           8 | INDIA              |           2 |
|           9 | INDONESIA          |           2 |
|          10 | IRAN               |           4 |
|          11 | IRAQ               |           4 |
|          12 | JAPAN              |           2 |
|          13 | JORDAN             |           4 |
|          14 | KENYA              |           0 |
|          15 | MOROCCO            |           0 |
|          16 | MOZAMBIQUE         |           0 |
|          17 | PERU               |           1 |
|          18 | CHINA              |           2 |
|          19 | ROMANIA            |           3 |
```

```
|                 20 | SAUDI ARABIA   |            4 |
|                 21 | VIETNAM        |            2 |
|                 22 | RUSSIA         |            3 |
|                 23 | UNITED KINGDOM |            3 |
|                 24 | UNITED STATES  |            1 |
+--------------------+----------------+--------------+
```

There are four columns in the Nation table, but the query retrieves just three of them. The purpose of the select clause in this query, therefore, is to specify which of all possible columns should be included in the result set. A select clause isn't just limited to columns in a table, however, but can contain any of the following:

- Literals, such as the number 99 or the string 'Welcome to Snowflake SQL!'
- Expressions, such as n_nationkey * 100
- Built-in function calls, such as concat(n_nationkey, ':', n_name)
- User-defined function calls built with Java, Python, JavaScript, or the Snowflake Scripting language

Built-in and user-defined functions will be covered in detail in later chapters.

Column aliases

While the database server will assign column names for you, you may want to specify your own names by using *column aliases*. This is especially helpful for any literals, expressions, or function calls included in your select clause. Here's an example with the column aliases shown in bold:

```
PUBLIC>select 'Welcome to Snowflake SQL!' as welcome_message,
       5 * 3.1415927 as circle_circumference,
       dayname(current_date) as day_of_week;
+---------------------------+----------------------+-------------+
| WELCOME_MESSAGE           | CIRCLE_CIRCUMFERENCE | DAY_OF_WEEK |
|---------------------------+----------------------+-------------|
| Welcome to Snowflake SQL! |           15.7079635 | Fri         |
+---------------------------+----------------------+-------------+
```

Column aliases may be preceded by the as keyword, which improves readability.

Removing duplicates

In some cases, a query may return duplicate values. For example, the following query returns the values in the n_regionkey column of the Nation table:

```
PUBLIC>select n_regionkey from nation;
+-------------+
| N_REGIONKEY |
|-------------|
|           0 |
```

```
|           1 |
|           1 |
|           1 |
|           4 |
|           0 |
|           3 |
|           3 |
|           2 |
|           2 |
|           4 |
|           4 |
|           2 |
|           4 |
|           0 |
|           0 |
|           0 |
|           1 |
|           2 |
|           3 |
|           4 |
|           2 |
|           3 |
|           3 |
|           1 |
+-------------+
```

As you can see, there are only five different values for n_regionkey across the 25 rows of the Nation table. If you wanted to retrieve only the unique set of values in the n_regionkey column, you can use the distinct keyword:

```
PUBLIC>select distinct n_regionkey from nation;
+-------------+
| N_REGIONKEY |
|-------------|
|           0 |
|           1 |
|           3 |
|           2 |
|           4 |
+-------------+
```

Adding distinct to your select clause will instruct the server to sort the values and remove any duplicates.

The from Clause

Earlier in this chapter, examples retrieve data from a single table, but the from clause can reference multiple tables. When there are two or more tables in the from clause, its role expands to include not just a list of tables, but the means by which the tables should be linked. To illustrate, let's say you want to retrieve data from the Nation table, but rather than retrieving the n_regionkey column, you want to use the n_regionkey value to retrieve the region's name from the Region table. Here's what that query would look like:

```
PUBLIC>select n_nationkey, n_name as nation_name,
          r_name as region_name
       from nation join region
       on nation.n_regionkey = region.r_regionkey;
+--------------+----------------+-------------+
| N_NATIONKEY  | NATION_NAME    | REGION_NAME |
|--------------+----------------+-------------|
|            0 | ALGERIA        | AFRICA      |
|            1 | ARGENTINA      | AMERICA     |
|            2 | BRAZIL         | AMERICA     |
|            3 | CANADA         | AMERICA     |
|            4 | EGYPT          | MIDDLE EAST |
|            5 | ETHIOPIA       | AFRICA      |
|            6 | FRANCE         | EUROPE      |
|            7 | GERMANY        | EUROPE      |
|            8 | INDIA          | ASIA        |
|            9 | INDONESIA      | ASIA        |
|           10 | IRAN           | MIDDLE EAST |
|           11 | IRAQ           | MIDDLE EAST |
|           12 | JAPAN          | ASIA        |
|           13 | JORDAN         | MIDDLE EAST |
|           14 | KENYA          | AFRICA      |
|           15 | MOROCCO        | AFRICA      |
|           16 | MOZAMBIQUE     | AFRICA      |
|           17 | PERU           | AMERICA     |
|           18 | CHINA          | ASIA        |
|           19 | ROMANIA        | EUROPE      |
|           20 | SAUDI ARABIA   | MIDDLE EAST |
|           21 | VIETNAM        | ASIA        |
|           22 | RUSSIA         | EUROPE      |
|           23 | UNITED KINGDOM | EUROPE      |
|           24 | UNITED STATES  | AMERICA     |
+--------------+----------------+-------------+
```

The from clause contains two tables, Nation and Region, and also includes the on subclause to specify that the regionkey columns (n_regionkey in the Nation table and r_regionkey in the Region table) should be used to join the tables. In simpler terms, the query specifies that for every row in the Nation table, use the n_region key value to look up the region's name in the Region table. Multitable joins are covered extensively in Chapter 3.

Generating Data Sets Using Values

Along with retrieving data from tables, Snowflake allows you to generate data on the fly using the values subclause of the from clause. This can be very handy for creating small data sets that aren't found in any of your tables. For example, if you need a list of month names and numbers, but there are no tables in your database containing calendar information, you could use the following query:

```
PUBLIC> select *
        from (values
        ('JAN',1),
        ('FEB',2),
        ('MAR',3),
        ('APR',4),
        ('MAY',5),
        ('JUN',6),
        ('JUL',7),
        ('AUG',8),
        ('SEP',9),
        ('OCT',10),
        ('NOV',11),
        ('DEC',12))
        as months (month_name, month_num);
+------------+-----------+
| MONTH_NAME | MONTH_NUM |
|------------+-----------|
| JAN        |         1 |
| FEB        |         2 |
| MAR        |         3 |
| APR        |         4 |
| MAY        |         5 |
| JUN        |         6 |
| JUL        |         7 |
| AUG        |         8 |
| SEP        |         9 |
| OCT        |        10 |
| NOV        |        11 |
| DEC        |        12 |
+------------+-----------+
```

This query generates a twelve-row data set named Months with columns month_name and month_num. I will be using values in a number of examples in the book.

The where Clause

While there are cases when you want to retrieve all rows from a table, it is common to retrieve only a subset of the rows, which is the job of the where clause. For example, you may only want to retrieve rows from the Nation table that have a name starting with the letter *U*:

```
PUBLIC>select n_name
        from nation
        where n_name like 'U%';
+----------------+
| N_NAME         |
```

```
|----------------|
| UNITED KINGDOM |
| UNITED STATES  |
+----------------+
```

The job of the where clause is *filtering*, or the removal of unwanted rows. Each element in the where clause is called a *condition*, which for the previous example is:

```
n_name like 'U%'
```

There can be multiple conditions in a where clause, as shown by the next example, which retrieves the names of nations starting with either *U* or *A*:

```
PUBLIC>select n_name
       from nation
       where n_name like 'U%'
       or n_name like 'A%';
+----------------+
| N_NAME         |
|----------------|
| ALGERIA        |
| ARGENTINA      |
| UNITED KINGDOM |
| UNITED STATES  |
+----------------+
```

The previous query includes two conditions, separated by or, which specifies that any row satisfying either condition should be included in the result set. Chapter 2 covers filtering in detail.

The group by Clause

As suggested by the name, the group by clause is used for grouping rows. Grouping rows of data is a very common practice, especially for reporting and data analysis. To illustrate, the next example counts the number of countries in the Nation table for each row in the Region table:

```
PUBLIC>select r_name as region_name,
       count(*) as number_of_countries
       from nation join region
       on nation.n_regionkey = region.r_regionkey
       group by r_name;
+-------------+---------------------+
| REGION_NAME | NUMBER_OF_COUNTRIES |
|-------------+---------------------|
| AFRICA      |                   5 |
| AMERICA     |                   5 |
| MIDDLE EAST |                   5 |
| EUROPE      |                   5 |
| ASIA        |                   5 |
+-------------+---------------------+
```

This query groups the rows in Nation by their regions, and then uses the built-in count() function to determine the number of nations in each region. Chapter 7 covers grouping.

The having Clause

I introduced the concept of filtering when discussing the role of the where clause (see "The where Clause" on page 10), but there are actually three different query clauses that play this role. The second one is the having clause, but its role is to filter rows based on grouped data. Let's use another table, Supplier, to demonstrate how this works. Here's the definition of Supplier:

```
PUBLIC>describe table supplier;
+--------------+--------------+--------+-------+---------+...
| name         | type         | kind   | null? | default |...
+--------------+--------------+--------+-------+---------+...
| S_SUPPKEY    | NUMBER(38,0) | COLUMN | N     | NULL    |...
| S_NAME       | VARCHAR(25)  | COLUMN | N     | NULL    |...
| S_ADDRESS    | VARCHAR(40)  | COLUMN | N     | NULL    |...
| S_NATIONKEY  | NUMBER(38,0) | COLUMN | N     | NULL    |...
| S_PHONE      | VARCHAR(15)  | COLUMN | N     | NULL    |...
| S_ACCTBAL    | NUMBER(12,2) | COLUMN | N     | NULL    |...
| S_COMMENT    | VARCHAR(101) | COLUMN | Y     | NULL    |...
+--------------+--------------+--------+-------+---------+...
```

The Supplier table includes the s_nationkey column, which is a link to the primary key of the Nation table (n_nationkey). The next query counts up the number of suppliers in each nation:

```
PUBLIC>select n_name as nation_name,
       count(*) as number_of_suppliers
    from supplier join nation
    on supplier.s_nationkey = nation.n_nationkey
    group by n_name;
+-----------------+---------------------+
| NATION_NAME     | NUMBER_OF_SUPPLIERS |
+-----------------+---------------------+
| PERU            |                 421 |
| ETHIOPIA        |                 380 |
| ARGENTINA       |                 413 |
| MOROCCO         |                 373 |
| IRAQ            |                 438 |
| UNITED KINGDOM  |                 390 |
| UNITED STATES   |                 393 |
| CANADA          |                 412 |
| RUSSIA          |                 401 |
| ROMANIA         |                 398 |
| BRAZIL          |                 397 |
| EGYPT           |                 415 |
| INDONESIA       |                 405 |
```

```
| ALGERIA        |                 420 |
| VIETNAM        |                 399 |
| JORDAN         |                 362 |
| JAPAN          |                 377 |
| SAUDI ARABIA   |                 411 |
| KENYA          |                 376 |
| CHINA          |                 407 |
| GERMANY        |                 396 |
| FRANCE         |                 402 |
| IRAN           |                 393 |
| INDIA          |                 415 |
| MOZAMBIQUE     |                 406 |
+----------------+---------------------+
```

There are suppliers in each of the 25 nations, with Jordan having the fewest suppliers (362), and Iraq having the most (438). If you want to retrieve only those nations having more than 400 suppliers, you could add a having clause containing a filter condition on the results of the count() function. Here's what that would look like:

```
PUBLIC>select n_name as nation_name,
        count(*) as number_of_suppliers
      from supplier join nation
      on supplier.s_nationkey = nation.n_nationkey
      group by n_name
      having count(*) > 400;
+---------------+---------------------+
| NATION_NAME   | NUMBER_OF_SUPPLIERS |
|---------------+---------------------|
| PERU          |                 421 |
| ARGENTINA     |                 413 |
| IRAQ          |                 438 |
| CANADA        |                 412 |
| RUSSIA        |                 401 |
| EGYPT         |                 415 |
| INDONESIA     |                 405 |
| ALGERIA       |                 420 |
| SAUDI ARABIA  |                 411 |
| CHINA         |                 407 |
| FRANCE        |                 402 |
| INDIA         |                 415 |
| MOZAMBIQUE    |                 406 |
+---------------+---------------------+
```

You can have both where and having clauses in the same query, but any conditions in the where clause are evaluated *prior* to grouping rows, whereas the conditions in the having clause are evaluated *after* the rows have been grouped. Here's an example with multiple filters:

```
PUBLIC>select n_name as nation_name,
        count(*) as number_of_suppliers
      from supplier join nation
      on supplier.s_nationkey = nation.n_nationkey
```

```
        where n_name like '%A'
        group by n_name
        having count(*) > 400;
+----------------+----------------------+
| NATION_NAME    | NUMBER_OF_SUPPLIERS  |
|----------------+----------------------|
| ARGENTINA      |                  413 |
| CHINA          |                  407 |
| INDIA          |                  415 |
| CANADA         |                  412 |
| RUSSIA         |                  401 |
| INDONESIA      |                  405 |
| SAUDI ARABIA   |                  411 |
| ALGERIA        |                  420 |
+----------------+----------------------+
```

This query first finds suppliers in nations whose name ends in *A*, sums the number of suppliers for each nation, and then discards any rows for which the number of suppliers is less than or equal to 400. The `having` clause is covered along with the `group by` clause in Chapter 7.

The qualify Clause

So far, you've seen two different clauses used for filtering; `where` and `having`. The third clause used for filtering is `qualify`, but it is a special-purpose clause used only for filtering rows based on the results of *windowing functions*, which are used for multiple purposes including assigning rankings. To illustrate, the next example assigns a rank to every row in the `Nation` table based on the number of characters in the name, using the built-in `length()` function:

```
PUBLIC>select n_name,
         rank() over (order by length(n_name) desc) as length_rank
       from nation;
+----------------+-------------+
| N_NAME         | LENGTH_RANK |
|----------------+-------------|
| UNITED KINGDOM |           1 |
| UNITED STATES  |           2 |
| SAUDI ARABIA   |           3 |
| MOZAMBIQUE     |           4 |
| ARGENTINA      |           5 |
| INDONESIA      |           5 |
| ETHIOPIA       |           7 |
| MOROCCO        |           8 |
| ALGERIA        |           8 |
| VIETNAM        |           8 |
| ROMANIA        |           8 |
| GERMANY        |           8 |
| JORDAN         |          13 |
| FRANCE         |          13 |
```

```
| CANADA        |          13 |
| RUSSIA        |          13 |
| BRAZIL        |          13 |
| JAPAN         |          18 |
| KENYA         |          18 |
| EGYPT         |          18 |
| CHINA         |          18 |
| INDIA         |          18 |
| IRAQ          |          23 |
| PERU          |          23 |
| IRAN          |          23 |
+---------------+-------------+
```

The rank() function is used to generate a ranking for each row, yielding the top ranking to United Kingdom with 14 characters, and the lowest rankings for Iraq, Peru, and Iran, each having only 4 characters. Without going into much detail on the rank() function (which is covered in Chapter 14), let's modify the previous query to return only those rows with a ranking of 5 or less by adding a qualify clause:

```
PUBLIC>select n_name,
          rank() over (order by length(n_name) desc) as length_rank
       from nation
       qualify length_rank <= 5;
+---------------+-------------+
| N_NAME        | LENGTH_RANK |
|---------------+-------------|
| UNITED KINGDOM |          1 |
| UNITED STATES |           2 |
| SAUDI ARABIA  |           3 |
| MOZAMBIQUE    |           4 |
| ARGENTINA     |           5 |
| INDONESIA     |           5 |
+---------------+-------------+
```

This version of the query returns 6 rows since both Argentina and Indonesia tie for 5th place with 9 characters each. The qualify clause is covered in Chapter 14.

The order by Clause

In general, result sets retuned by queries are not in any particular order. If you want your results to be sorted, such as alphabetically, numerically, or chronologically, you can add an order by clause at the end of your query. The order by clause can include one or more of the elements in your select clause and can reference each either by name or position.

The Supplier table includes the s_acctbal column, which presumably contains an amount owed to each supplier. The next example sorts the results by s_acctbal in descending order:

```
PUBLIC>select s_name, s_acctbal
       from supplier
       order by s_acctbal desc;
+--------------------+-----------+
| S_NAME             | S_ACCTBAL |
|--------------------+-----------|
| Supplier#000006343 |   9998.20 |
| Supplier#000002522 |   9997.04 |
| Supplier#000000892 |   9993.46 |
| Supplier#000002543 |   9992.70 |
| Supplier#000001833 |   9992.26 |
| Supplier#000009966 |   9991.00 |
| Supplier#000002892 |   9989.02 |
| Supplier#000008875 |   9984.69 |
| Supplier#000002331 |   9984.20 |
| Supplier#000007895 |   9977.32 |
... <7,380 rows omitted>
| Supplier#000003627 |   -986.14 |
| Supplier#000001907 |   -987.45 |
| Supplier#000001654 |   -988.37 |
| Supplier#000001870 |   -989.05 |
| Supplier#000008224 |   -989.86 |
| Supplier#000001764 |   -990.13 |
| Supplier#000005298 |   -990.16 |
| Supplier#000008927 |   -995.53 |
| Supplier#000007259 |   -997.61 |
| Supplier#000009795 |   -998.22 |
+--------------------+-----------+
```

The Supplier table has 7,400 rows, so I omitted most of them, but you can see how the s_acctbal value decreases over the rows in the result set. The column used for sorting could also be specified by its position in the select clause, which in this case would be 2:

```
PUBLIC>select s_name, s_acctbal
       from supplier
       order by 2 desc;
+--------------------+-----------+
| S_NAME             | S_ACCTBAL |
|--------------------+-----------|
| Supplier#000006343 |   9998.20 |
| Supplier#000002522 |   9997.04 |
| Supplier#000000892 |   9993.46 |
| Supplier#000002543 |   9992.70 |
| Supplier#000001833 |   9992.26 |
| Supplier#000009966 |   9991.00 |
| Supplier#000002892 |   9989.02 |
| Supplier#000008875 |   9984.69 |
| Supplier#000002331 |   9984.20 |
| Supplier#000007895 |   9977.32 |
... <7,390 rows omitted>
+--------------------+-----------+
```

You can specify the sort order as either descending (desc) or ascending (asc). While there is no chapter specifically for the order by clause, you will see it used in various examples in this book.

The limit Clause

The result set from the previous example contained 7,400 rows; wouldn't it be great if you could specify that only a subset be returned? This is where the limit clause comes in, and it allows you to specify how many rows to return, starting either at the first row or at a specified offset. Here's the query from the previous section, but with a limit clause to specify that only the first 10 rows be returned:

```
PUBLIC>select s_name, s_acctbal
       from supplier
       order by s_acctbal desc
       limit 10;
+--------------------+----------+
| S_NAME             | S_ACCTBAL |
|--------------------+----------|
| Supplier#000006343 |   9998.20 |
| Supplier#000002522 |   9997.04 |
| Supplier#000000892 |   9993.46 |
| Supplier#000002543 |   9992.70 |
| Supplier#000001833 |   9992.26 |
| Supplier#000009966 |   9991.00 |
| Supplier#000002892 |   9989.02 |
| Supplier#000008875 |   9984.69 |
| Supplier#000002331 |   9984.20 |
| Supplier#000007895 |   9977.32 |
+--------------------+----------+
```

In this example, the server sorts all 7,400 rows as specified by the order by clause, and then returns only the first 10. You can also use the optional offset subclause to tell the server to start at a particular row. Since I know that there are 7,400 rows in the Supplier table, I can specify an offset of 7,390 to see the last 10 rows in the result set:

```
PUBLIC>select s_name, s_acctbal
       from supplier
       order by s_acctbal desc
       limit 10 offset 7390;
+--------------------+----------+
| S_NAME             | S_ACCTBAL |
|--------------------+----------|
| Supplier#000003627 |   -986.14 |
| Supplier#000001907 |   -987.45 |
| Supplier#000001654 |   -988.37 |
| Supplier#000001870 |   -989.05 |
| Supplier#000008224 |   -989.86 |
| Supplier#000001764 |   -990.13 |
| Supplier#000005298 |   -990.16 |
```

```
| Supplier#000008927 |   -995.53 |
| Supplier#000007259 |   -997.61 |
| Supplier#000009795 |   -998.22 |
+--------------------+----------+
```

While it would be great if you could specify `limit -10` to see the last 10 rows in the result set without knowing the total number of rows, that functionality isn't available at this time. However, you can always sort in the opposite direction and choose the first 10 rows:

```
PUBLIC>select s_name, s_acctbal
           from supplier
           order by s_acctbal asc
           limit 10;
+--------------------+----------+
| S_NAME             | S_ACCTBAL |
|--------------------+----------|
| Supplier#000009795 |   -998.22 |
| Supplier#000007259 |   -997.61 |
| Supplier#000008927 |   -995.53 |
| Supplier#000005298 |   -990.16 |
| Supplier#000001764 |   -990.13 |
| Supplier#000008224 |   -989.86 |
| Supplier#000001870 |   -989.05 |
| Supplier#000001654 |   -988.37 |
| Supplier#000001907 |   -987.45 |
| Supplier#000003627 |   -986.14 |
+--------------------+----------+
```

Limit Versus Top

Along with the `limit` clause, Snowflake provides the `top` keyword, which you can specify in the `select` clause to limit the number of rows a query returns. To see the top 10 suppliers ranked by account balance, you could use the following query:

```
PUBLIC>select top 10 s_name, s_acctbal
         from supplier
         order by s_acctbal desc;
+--------------------+----------+
| S_NAME             | S_ACCTBAL |
|--------------------+----------|
| Supplier#000006343 |   9998.20 |
| Supplier#000002522 |   9997.04 |
| Supplier#000000892 |   9993.46 |
| Supplier#000002543 |   9992.70 |
| Supplier#000001833 |   9992.26 |
| Supplier#000009966 |   9991.00 |
| Supplier#000002892 |   9989.02 |
| Supplier#000008875 |   9984.69 |
| Supplier#000002331 |   9984.20 |
```

```
| Supplier#000007895 |   9977.32 |
+--------------------+-----------+
```

Using `top 10` is equivalent to adding a `limit 10` clause after `order by`, but the `top` functionality doesn't allow for an offset, so it is not as flexible.

Wrap-Up

The `select` statement certainly seems simple at first, but as you combine more and more of the eight clauses demonstrated in this chapter, queries can become quite sophisticated. Things become even more interesting when you start including subqueries (Chapter 8), conditional logic (Chapter 10), and window functions (Chapter 14). Chapters 5 and 6 introduce some of the other SQL data statements, such as `insert` and `update`, some of which will utilize some of the same clauses used to construct `select` statements.

Test Your Knowledge

The following exercises are designed to strengthen your understanding of the `select` statement. Please see "Chapter 1" in Appendix B for solutions.

Exercise 1-1

Write a query to retrieve the `n_nationkey` and `n_name` columns from the `Nation` table. Sort the rows by `n_name` values.

Exercise 1-2

Write a query to retrieve the `n_nationkey` and `n_name` columns from the `Nation` table, but only for those rows with a value of 3 for `n_regionkey`.

Exercise 1-3

Write a query to retrieve the `n_nationkey` and `n_name` columns from the `Nation` table and join to the `Region` table (using the `r_regionkey` column) to retrieve only those nations belonging to the Africa region (`r_name = 'AFRICA'`).

Exercise 1-4

Retrieve the `s_name` and `s_acctbal` columns from the `Supplier` table. Sort by `s_acctbal` in descending order and retrieve only the first 10 rows (which will be the 10 suppliers with the highest `s_acctbal` values).

CHAPTER 2

Filtering

There are cases when you will want to deal with every row in a table, such as:

- Removing all rows from a table used for nightly data loads
- Modifying all rows in a table after adding a new column
- Retrieving all rows from a message-queue table

Most of the time, however, you will want to focus on a *subset* of the rows in a table by including a `where` clause. Along with the `select` statement used for querying data, several other SQL data statements, including `update` and `delete`, include a `where` clause consisting of one or more *filter conditions* used to narrow the statement's focus. As shown in Chapter 1, `select` statements can also perform filtering in the `having` and `qualify` clauses, making filtering one of the most common activities when writing SQL data statements. This chapter explores the many different types of conditions available for filtering data.

Condition Evaluation

The `where` clause consists of one or more *conditions* separated by the `and` and `or` operators. If there is a single condition, it must evaluate as `true` in order for a row to be included in the result set. If there are two or more conditions, there are multiple possible outcomes:

- If the conditions are separated by the `and` operator, then all of the conditions must evaluate as `true`.
- When the `or` operator is used, only one condition must evaluate as `true`.

Let's say you are querying a directory to look up an old friend and use the following where clause:

```
where last_name = 'SMITH' and state = 'CA'
```

The where clause consists of two conditions separated by the and operator. Your query would return rows for all people having both the last name Smith and who reside in California, which would likely yield a result set in the thousands. Next, let's consider what would happen if you used or to separate the two conditions instead of using and:

```
where last_name = 'SMITH' or state = 'CA'
```

For this case, any person *either* having the last name Smith *or* residing in California will be included, which will yield a result set in the millions. Here are all the possible ways a person could be included in the result set:

- Last name is Smith and lives in California
- Last name is Smith and lives in any state
- Lives in California and has any last name

As you can see, the choice of operator used to separate multiple conditions can have a big impact on the number of rows returned.

Using Parentheses

Let's expand on the conditions from the previous example:

- Your friend's last name might still be Smith, but they may have gotten married and changed their last name to Jackson.
- Your friend may still live in California, but has possibly moved to Washington.

Your query should return everyone with a last name of Smith or Jackson, and who lives either in California or Washington. This is getting complicated, and the best way to build your where clause is to use parentheses to separate the different conditions:

```
where (last_name = 'SMITH' or last_name = 'JACKSON')
   and (state = 'CA' or state = 'WA')
```

The two groups of conditions within each set of parentheses must evaluate as true to be included in the result set. You should always use parentheses to make your logic clear to the database server and to any person who may look at your queries.

Using the not Operator

If you are interested in retrieving rows for everyone *except* those found in the previous example, there are multiple ways to construct your where clause. The simplest way would be to add the `not` operator with another set of parentheses around the entire set of conditions:

```
where not ((last_name = 'SMITH' or last_name = 'JACKSON')
    and (state = 'CA' or state = 'WA'))
```

One way to interpret this would be "return all rows except those that evaluated as true in the previous query," or "return only those rows that were excluded last time." In any case, using the `not` operator can sometimes be the simplest way to formulate a `where` clause, and sometimes the use of `not` can tie your brain in knots (pun intended).

There are usually multiple ways to express the same logic, and some are easier than others for people to understand. Here's another way to write the previous example without using the `not` operator:

```
where last_name <> 'SMITH' and last_name <> 'JACKSON'
    and state <> 'CA' and state <> 'WA'
```

In this case, no parentheses are needed because the `and` operator is used between each condition.

Condition Components

Now that you understand how conditions are evaluated, let's take a look at how to build conditions. A condition is made up of one or more *expressions* combined with one or more *operators*. An expression can be any of the following:

- A column in a table
- A number or date
- A string literal, such as `'New York City'`
- A built-in function, such as `concat('Snowflake',' Rules!')`
- A subquery
- A list of expressions, such as `('New York City','Dallas','Chicago')`

The operators used within conditions include:

- Comparison operators, such as =, <, >, !=, <>, `like`, `in`, and `between`
- Arithmetic operators, such as +, −, *, and /

The following sections show how expressions and operators can be combined to create various types of conditions.

Equality Conditions

Many of the conditions you come across will be of the form column = expression, such as:

- c_custkey = 12345

- s_name = 'Acme Wholesale'

- o_orderdate = to_date('02/14/2022', 'MM/DD/YYYY')

Conditions such as these are called *equality conditions* because they equate one expression to another. Equality conditions are commonly used for filtering in a query's where clause, but are also commonly found in the from clause, in which case it is called a *join condition*. Here's an example with equality conditions in both the from and where clauses :

```
PUBLIC>select n_name, r_name
       from nation join region
       on nation.n_regionkey = region.r_regionkey
       where r_name = 'ASIA';
+-----------+--------+
| N_NAME    | R_NAME |
|-----------+--------|
| INDIA     | ASIA   |
| INDONESIA | ASIA   |
| JAPAN     | ASIA   |
| CHINA     | ASIA   |
| VIETNAM   | ASIA   |
+-----------+--------+
```

While join conditions are usually equality conditions, conditions used for filtering can take many forms.

Inequality Conditions

Another common type of condition is the *inequality condition*, which evaluates as true when two expressions are *not* the same. Here's how the previous example would look using an inequality condition in the where clause:

```
PUBLIC>select n_name, r_name
       from nation join region
       on nation.n_regionkey = region.r_regionkey
       where r_name <> 'ASIA';
+----------------+-------------+
| N_NAME         | R_NAME      |
|----------------+-------------|
| ALGERIA        | AFRICA      |
| ARGENTINA      | AMERICA     |
| BRAZIL         | AMERICA     |
| CANADA         | AMERICA     |
```

```
| EGYPT          | MIDDLE EAST |
| ETHIOPIA       | AFRICA      |
| FRANCE         | EUROPE      |
| GERMANY        | EUROPE      |
| IRAN           | MIDDLE EAST |
| IRAQ           | MIDDLE EAST |
| JORDAN         | MIDDLE EAST |
| KENYA          | AFRICA      |
| MOROCCO        | AFRICA      |
| MOZAMBIQUE     | AFRICA      |
| PERU           | AMERICA     |
| ROMANIA        | EUROPE      |
| SAUDI ARABIA   | MIDDLE EAST |
| RUSSIA         | EUROPE      |
| UNITED KINGDOM | EUROPE      |
| UNITED STATES  | AMERICA     |
+----------------+-------------+
```

This query returns rows for every nation that is not in the Asia region. When building inequality conditions, you may choose to use either the != or <> operator.

Range Conditions

In some cases, you will want to determine if an expression falls within a specified range. Known as *range conditions*, these are commonly used with numeric or date columns and utilize the between operator. Here's an example using a numeric column:

```
PUBLIC>select s_suppkey, s_name
       from supplier
       where s_suppkey between 1 and 10;
+-----------+--------------------+
| S_SUPPKEY | S_NAME             |
|-----------+--------------------|
|         1 | Supplier#000000001 |
|         4 | Supplier#000000004 |
|         7 | Supplier#000000007 |
|         9 | Supplier#000000009 |
|        10 | Supplier#000000010 |
+-----------+--------------------+
```

Ranges are *inclusive*, meaning that both end points (1 and 10 here) are included. Here's another example of a range condition using a date column in the Orders table:

```
PUBLIC>select o_orderkey, o_custkey, o_orderdate
       from orders
       where o_orderdate between
         to_date('29-JAN-1998','DD-MON-YYYY')
         and to_date('30-JAN-1998','DD-MON-YYYY');
+------------+-----------+-------------+
| O_ORDERKEY | O_CUSTKEY | O_ORDERDATE |
|------------+-----------+-------------|
```

```
|    4909378 |      63949 | 1998-01-29 |
|    4951490 |      92749 | 1998-01-30 |
|    4952614 |      65761 | 1998-01-30 |
|    5027238 |      76006 | 1998-01-30 |
|    5242726 |      10808 | 1998-01-30 |
|    5273254 |      48983 | 1998-01-30 |
|    5293440 |     102916 | 1998-01-29 |
|    5368644 |      86063 | 1998-01-30 |
|    5412320 |      88709 | 1998-01-29 |
|    5496775 |     145853 | 1998-01-30 |
... (72 rows omitted)
|    1625990 |      63979 | 1998-01-29 |
|     640257 |      65215 | 1998-01-30 |
|     723141 |      12304 | 1998-01-29 |
|     741702 |      57932 | 1998-01-29 |
|     788864 |      91507 | 1998-01-29 |
|     806916 |      26027 | 1998-01-29 |
|     830405 |     149674 | 1998-01-29 |
|     884417 |     109099 | 1998-01-29 |
|     934885 |     102566 | 1998-01-29 |
|    1077319 |      87767 | 1998-01-30 |
+------------+-----------+------------+
```

While it is uncommon, you may also see range conditions used for character data, such as the following query that returns all nations whose name falls between the range 'GA' to 'IP':

```
PUBLIC>select n_name from nation
       where n_name between 'GA' and 'IP';
+-----------+
| N_NAME    |
|-----------|
| GERMANY   |
| INDIA     |
| INDONESIA |
+-----------+
```

While there are four nations that begin with the letter I, only two of them fall within the given range. If we want to include Iran and Iraq, the upper range can be extended to 'IS'.

Membership Conditions

In some cases, you will want to retrieve rows where a certain column matches a set of values. For example, the Customer table includes the column c_mktsegment, which contains the values AUTOMOBILE, MACHINERY, BUILDING, HOUSEHOLD, and FURNITURE. If you wanted to retrieve information about customers in the first three market segments, you could use three different conditions separated by the or operator:

```
where c_mktsegment = 'AUTOMOBILE' or c_mktsegment = 'MACHINERY'
or c_mktsegment = 'BUILDING'
```

While this may seem reasonable for this particular example, if you were looking for 10 or more values, building separate conditions for each value would become tedious. Instead, you can build a single *membership condition* using the in operator:

```
where c_mktsegment in ('AUTOMOBILE','MACHINERY','BUILDING')
```

Using the in operator, you can write a single condition no matter how many expressions are in the set. Additionally, you can use not in to retrieve rows for any values *not* contained in the set.

Matching Conditions

The last type of condition covered in this chapter concerns partial string matches. There are many situations where you will want to return rows where a character column starts with a particular letter or includes a set of letters anywhere within the string. These types of conditions are called *matching conditions* and use the like operator, as shown in the next example that retrieves all nations starting with *M*:

```
PUBLIC>select n_name
       from nation
       where n_name like 'M%';
+------------+
| N_NAME     |
|------------|
| MOROCCO    |
| MOZAMBIQUE |
+------------+
```

When searching for partial string matches, you might be interested in strings that:

- Begin/end with a certain character
- Begin/end with a substring
- Contain a certain character anywhere within the string
- Contain a substring anywhere within the string
- Follow a specific format, regardless of individual characters

You can build *search expressions* to identify these and many other partial string matches by using the wildcard characters shown in Table 2-1.

Table 2-1. Wildcard characters

Wildcard character	Matches
%	Any number of characters (0,1,..,N)
_	Exactly 1 character

The underscore character (_) matches a single character, while the percent sign (%) matches 0, 1, or more characters. Therefore, the search expression used in the previous example finds nations whose name starts with an *M* followed by any number of characters. Table 2-2 shows some other sample search expressions along with the interpretation.

Table 2-2. Sample search expressions

Search expression	Interpretation
'*I___*'	Exactly 4 characters long starting with *I*
'%E'	Any length, ends with *E*
'__A%'	3 or more characters in length, *A* in third position
'%ND%'	Any length, contains substring ND anywhere in string

Matching conditions can be relatively sophisticated, and you can use multiple matching conditions if it isn't possible to use a single search expression:

```
PUBLIC>select n_name
       from nation
       where n_name like 'M%'
       or n_name like 'U%';
+----------------+
| N_NAME         |
|----------------|
| MOROCCO        |
| MOZAMBIQUE     |
| UNITED KINGDOM |
| UNITED STATES  |
+----------------+
```

If you are familiar with *regular expressions*, you will be happy to know that Snowflake includes the `regexp_like()` function, which allows you to build complex search expressions. While not covered in this book, here's what the previous example would look like using `regexp_like`:

```
PUBLIC>select n_name
       from nation
       where regexp_like(n_name, '^[MU].*');
+----------------+
| N_NAME         |
|----------------|
| MOROCCO        |
| MOZAMBIQUE     |
| UNITED KINGDOM |
| UNITED STATES  |
+----------------+
```

This regular expression looks for strings starting with *M* or *U* followed by any number of characters.

Null Values

When inserting data into a database, there are multiple situations in which a value cannot be supplied for a particular column. There are several cases where this might be true, including:

- A value may be supplied at a later date but is not known when the row is first created. This would be the case for the termination date of a new employee.
- The column does not apply for a particular row. One example might be a shipping provider for an ebook delivered electronically.

For these types of cases, relational databases assign a null value to the column. When building filtering conditions, you will need to be aware of whether a column allows null values (this is specified when a table is created) and consider whether you want rows with null values to be included or excluded from your result set. Here are two basic rules to keep in mind:

- An expression can *be* null, but it can never *equal* null.
- Two nulls are never equal to each other.

To illustrate, consider the following two queries:

```
PUBLIC>select 'YES' as is_valid where null = null;
+----------+
| IS_VALID |
|----------|
+----------+
0 Row(s) produced.
PUBLIC>select 'YES' as is_valid where null is null;
+----------+
| IS_VALID |
|----------|
| YES      |
+----------+
1 Row(s) produced.
```

The first query uses the filter condition null = null, which will always evaluate as false, whereas the second query uses the is null operator, which in this case evaluates as true.

Table Creation in Snowflake

Snowflake's `create table` statement will be discussed in Chapter 5, but over the preceding chapters there will be a number of times where I will create simple tables to use across a set of examples. There are several flavors of `create table`, and the one that I use looks as follows:

```
create table <table_name>
as select ...;
```

This form of `create table` will create a table using the columns defined in the `select` statement, and will also populate the table with the result set returned by the query. I like this method because it is easier than creating an empty table and then executing multiple `insert` statements to populate the table.

To illustrate further, the next few examples use a simple table named `null_example` to demonstrate how to handle `null` values in your filter conditions:

```
PUBLIC>create table null_example
       (num_col number, char_col varchar(10))
       as select *
       from (values (1, 'ABC'),
                    (2, 'JKL'),
                    (null, 'QRS'),
                    (3, null));
+------------------------------------------+
| status                                   |
|------------------------------------------|
| Table NULL_EXAMPLE successfully created. |
+------------------------------------------+

PUBLIC>select * from null_example;
+---------+----------+
| NUM_COL | CHAR_COL |
|---------+----------|
|       1 | ABC      |
|       2 | JKL      |
|    NULL | QRS      |
|       3 | NULL     |
+---------+----------+
```

Snowflake's `values` subclause is useful when you need to generate a small data set, either by itself or to join to other tables. As you can see, there are four rows in this data set, with `null` values for one of the numeric columns and one of the character columns. The next example adds a filter condition on the `num_col` column:

```
PUBLIC>select num_col, char_col
       from null_example
       where num_col < 3;
```

```
+---------+----------+
| NUM_COL | CHAR_COL |
|---------+----------|
|       1 | ABC      |
|       2 | JKL      |
+---------+----------+
```

This query returns the first two rows in the null_example table, which is certainly valid, but what about the third row, which has a null value for num_col? This row was not included because null cannot be equated to any value. If you want to include this row, you will need to add another filter condition:

```
PUBLIC>select num_col, char_col
        from null_example
        where num_col < 3
           or num_col is null;
+---------+----------+
| NUM_COL | CHAR_COL |
|---------+----------|
|       1 | ABC      |
|       2 | JKL      |
|    NULL | QRS      |
+---------+----------+
```

Because this is a common issue when writing filter conditions, all major databases, including Snowflake, provide multiple built-in functions used for dealing with null values. One such function is nvl(), which can be used to substitute a value for any nulls encountered. The next example uses a single filter condition using nvl() to replace both conditions in the previous example:

```
PUBLIC>select num_col, char_col
        from null_example
        where nvl(num_col,0) < 3;
+---------+----------+
| NUM_COL | CHAR_COL |
|---------+----------|
|       1 | ABC      |
|       2 | JKL      |
|    NULL | QRS      |
+---------+----------+
```

The nvl() function in this example will substitute the value 0 for any null values encountered while evaluating the filter condition. If you want the null value in the result set to be replaced as well, you will need to add the same nvl() function to the select clause:

```
PUBLIC>select nvl(num_col,0) as num_col, char_col
        from null_example
        where nvl(num_col,0) < 3;
+---------+----------+
| NUM_COL | CHAR_COL |
```

```
|---------+----------|
|       1 | ABC      |
|       2 | JKL      |
|       0 | QRS      |
+---------+----------+
```

When working with a database that you are not familiar with, it is a good idea to find out which columns in a table allow null values so that you can add the appropriate filter conditions to keep data from slipping through the cracks.

Filtering Using Snowsight

While the previous examples in this chapter demonstrate different filters used in SQL statements, if you are using Snowsight there are some additional useful filtering tools. When filtering on a date column, for example, you can use the built-in :daterange expression, which allows you to run the same query using different dates or date ranges. Figure 2-1 shows an example from earlier in the chapter, but this time executed from Snowsight and using :daterange.

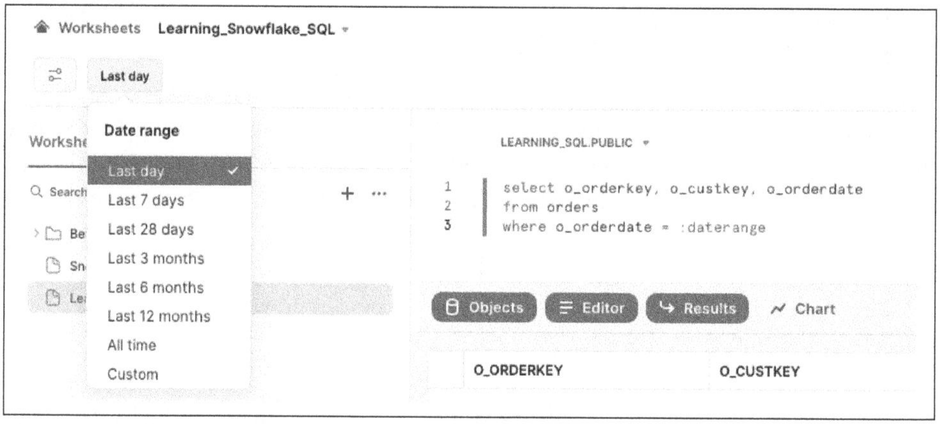

Figure 2-1. Filtering on date columns using Snowsight

As soon as you add :daterange to your where clause (and before you execute the query), Snowsight adds a menu to the top left of the pane with the default of "Last day." You can choose from any of the defaults, or you can choose Custom and build your own date range, as shown in Figure 2-2.

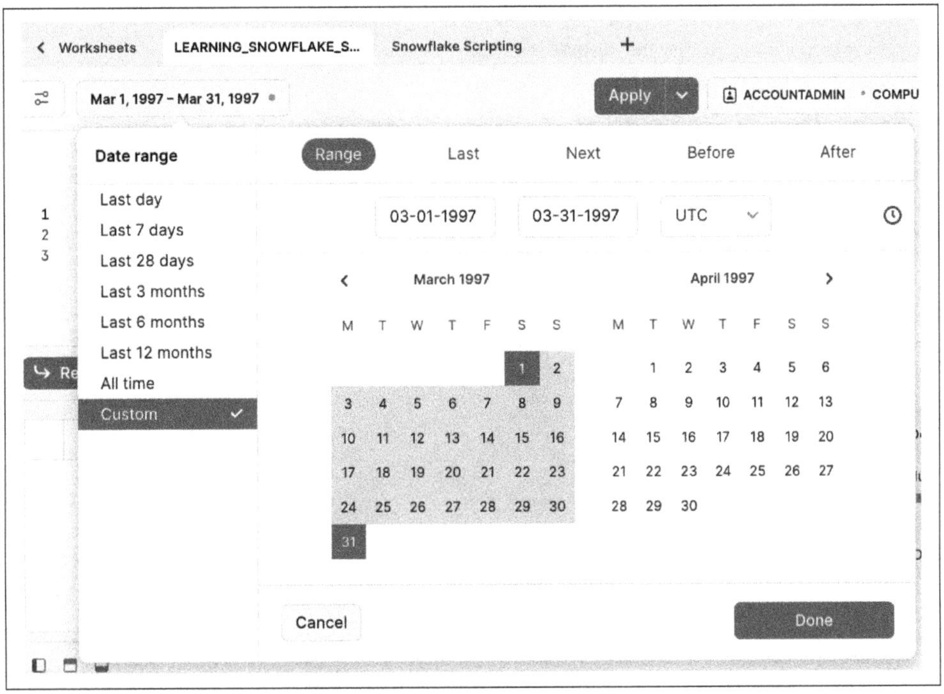

Figure 2-2. Building a custom date filter using Snowsight

After you've chosen your date range, you can click Apply to execute the query, and the chosen date range will be applied, as shown in Figure 2-3.

If you want to change the date range, you can click the same menu on the top left, modify the dates, and execute the query again. This allows you to retrieve different result sets without changing the SQL statement, which can be very useful when doing data analysis.

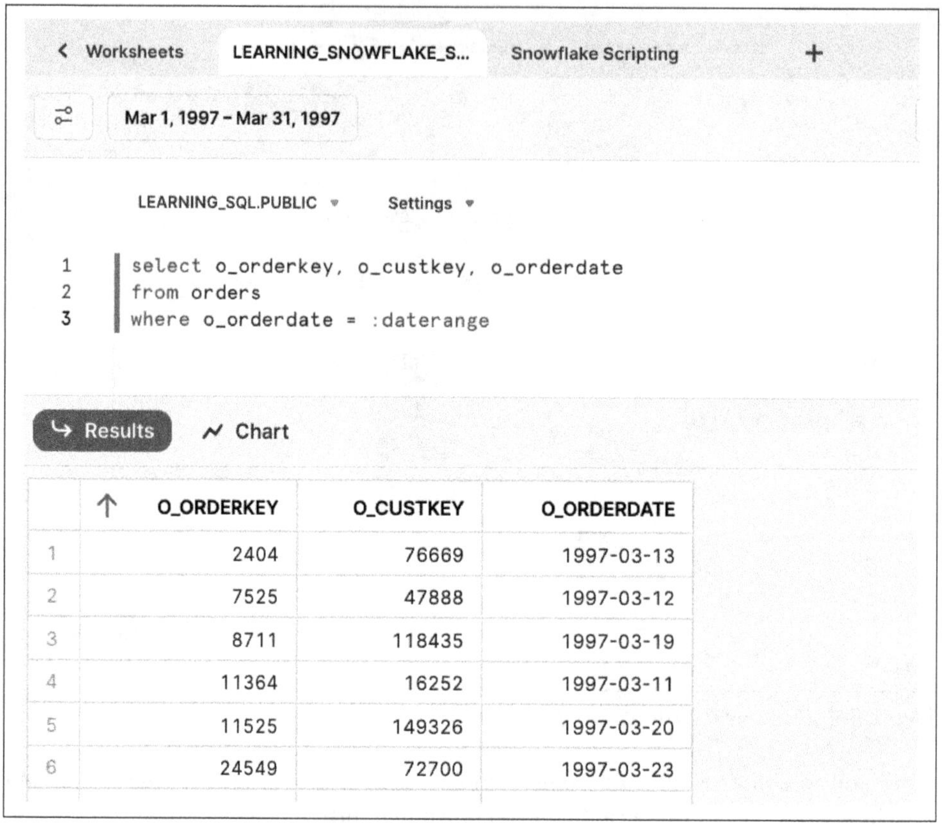

Figure 2-3. Executing query in Snowsight using custom date range

Along with the built-in `:daterange` filter, you can build your own custom filters using Snowsight and utilize them across multiple queries. To build a new filter, click the menu on the top left and choose Manage Filters, as shown in Figure 2-4.

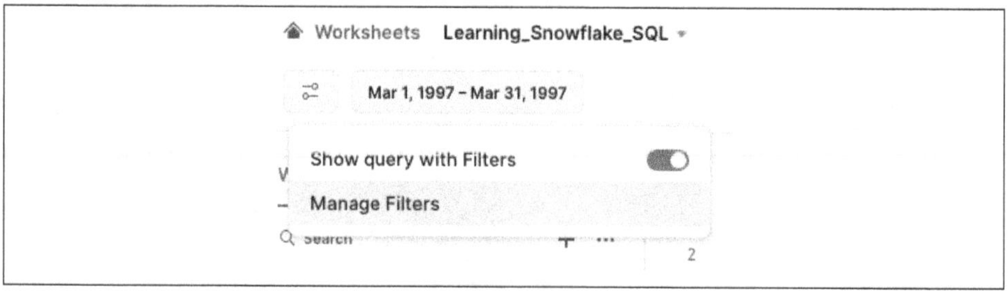

Figure 2-4. Managing filters in Snowsight

Figure 2-5 shows the Filters window, which will initially show the two default filters :daterange and :datebucket (the :datebucket filter will be covered in Chapter 7).

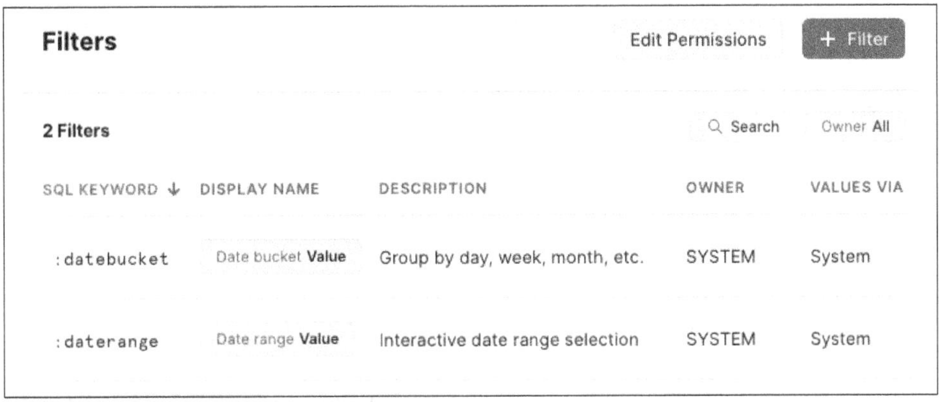
Filters
Edit Permissions
+ Filter
2 Filters
Search
Owner All
SQL KEYWORD
DISPLAY NAME
DESCRIPTION
OWNER
VALUES VIA
:datebucket
Date bucket Value
Group by day, week, month, etc.
SYSTEM
System
:daterange
Date range Value
Interactive date range selection
SYSTEM
System

Figure 2-5. Filter management window

Click the "+ Filter" button at the top right to add a new filter. Figure 2-6 shows the window used to add a new filter.

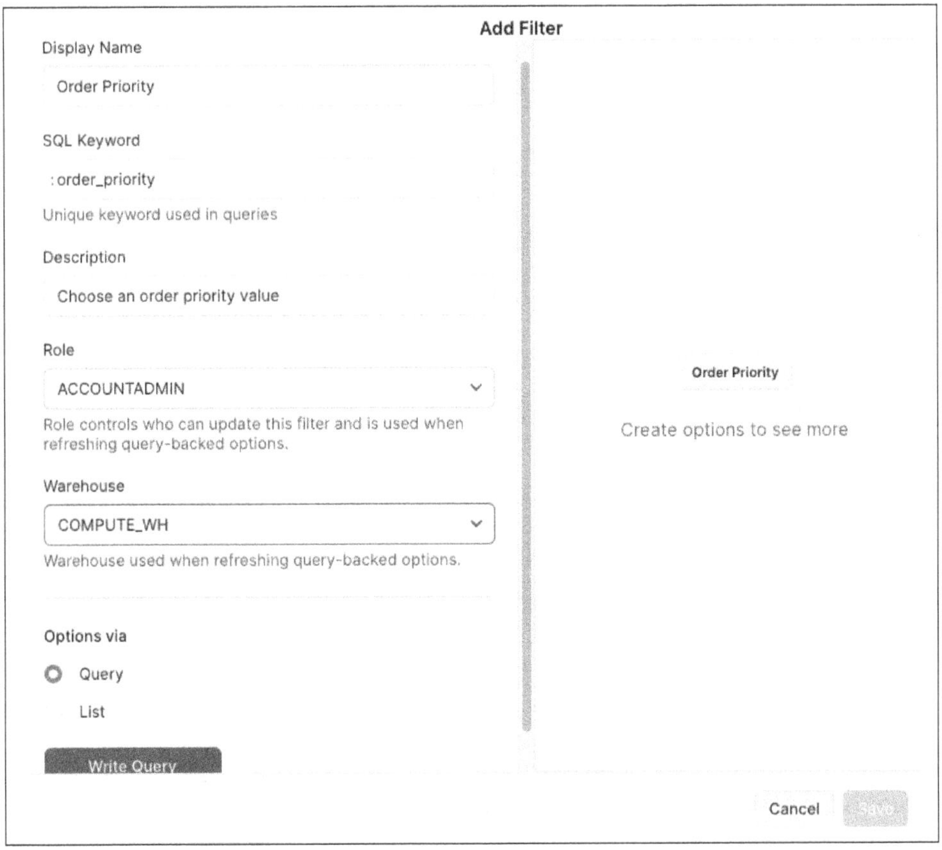
Add Filter
Display Name
Order Priority
SQL Keyword
:order_priority
Unique keyword used in queries
Description
Choose an order priority value
Role
ACCOUNTADMIN
Role controls who can update this filter and is used when refreshing query-backed options.
Warehouse
COMPUTE_WH
Warehouse used when refreshing query-backed options.
Options via
Query
List
Write Query
Order Priority
Create options to see more
Cancel

Figure 2-6. Adding a custom filter

I have decided to create my custom filter for the o_orderpriority column in the Orders table, which has the following values:

```
PUBLIC>select distinct o_orderpriority from orders;
+------------------+
| O_ORDERPRIORITY  |
|------------------|
| 4-NOT SPECIFIED  |
| 2-HIGH           |
| 3-MEDIUM         |
| 1-URGENT         |
| 5-LOW            |
+------------------+
```

I can add these values to the filter by clicking Write Query and pasting the query used to generate the values, as shown in Figure 2-7.

Figure 2-7. Associating query with custom filter

After clicking the Done button and saving the filter, I can use it in my query to choose a specific order priority, as shown in Figure 2-8.

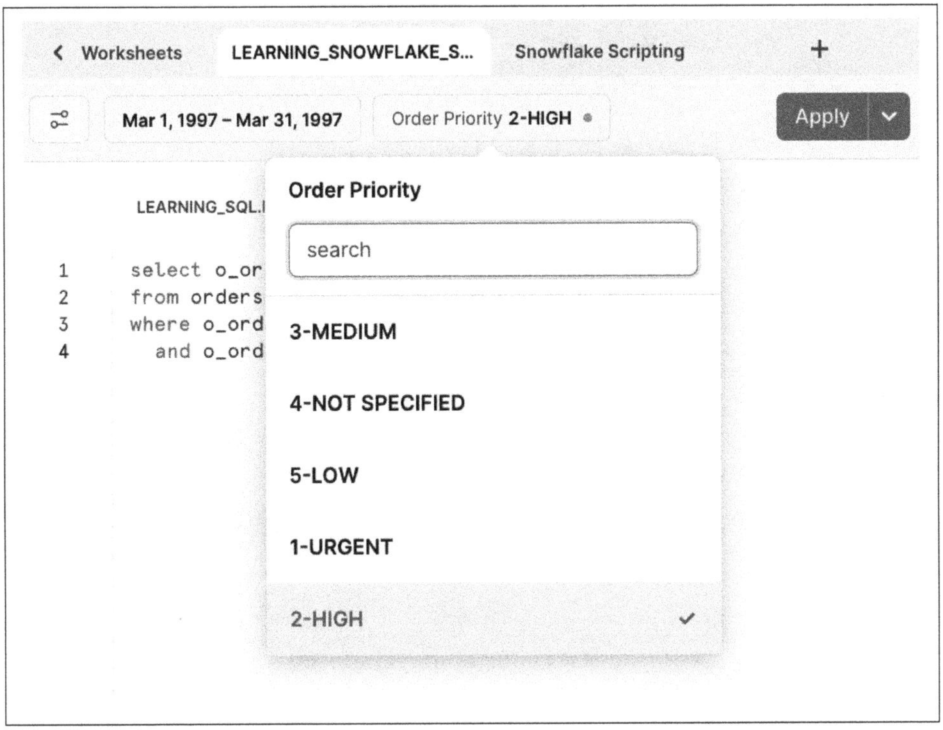

Figure 2-8. Using custom filter

After choosing a value, click Apply to execute the query using the chosen filter value. Figure 2-9 shows the results for the value 2-High.

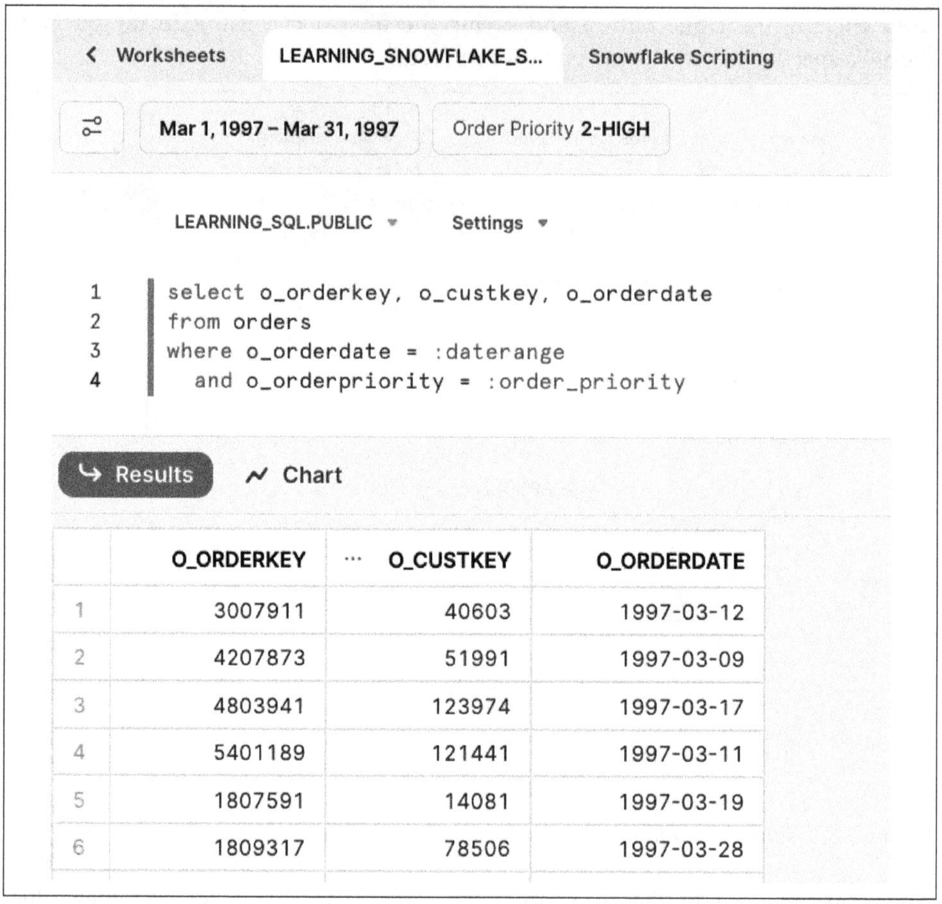

Figure 2-9. Executing query using custom filter

You can change the values for either filter and rerun the query without the need to modify the query. If you want to see the actual query that is executed, you can find it under Activity>Query History from the main Snowsight menu, as shown in Figure 2-10.

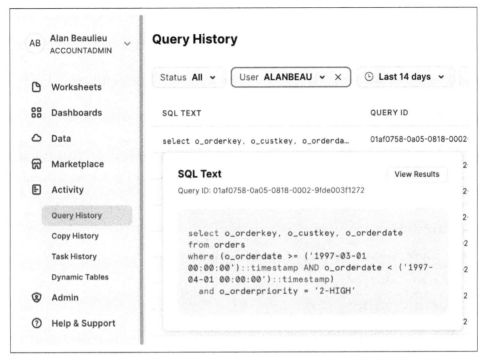

Figure 2-10. Snowsight query history showing applied filter values

If you will be working with the same database for a while, you can build a library of custom filters to assist with your data analysis and data mining.

Wrap-Up

This chapter introduced you to various ways in which to restrict the rows retrieved by a query using filter conditions. You were also introduced to null values and shown how they can be handled in queries. You will see filter conditions used in many examples in later chapters, including for other SQL statements such as delete and update.

Test Your Knowledge

The following exercises are designed to test your understanding of filter conditions. Please see "Chapter 2" in Appendix B for solutions.

Exercise 2-1

Retrieve the c_name and c_acctbal (account balance) columns from the Customer table, but only for those rows in the Machinery segment (c_mktsegment = 'MACHINERY') and with an account balance greater than 9998.

Exercise 2-2

Retrieve the c_name, c_mktsegment (market segment), and c_acctbal (account balance) columns from the Customer table, but only for those rows in either the Machinery or Furniture market segments with an account balance between –1 and 1.

Exercise 2-3

Retrieve the c_name, c_mktsegment (market segment), and c_acctbal (account balance) columns from the Customer table, but only for those rows where *either* the market segment is Machinery and the account balance is 20, *or* the market segment is Furniture and the account balance is 334.

Exercise 2-4

Given a table named Balances with the following data:

Acct_Num	Acct_Bal
1234	342.22
3498	9.00
3887	(null)
6277	28.33

Write a query that retrieves all rows that do *not* have a value of 9 for the acct_bal column.

Joins

The first two chapters introduced the `from` clause and showed a number of examples with two tables joined together. This chapter delves deeper into multitable joins, including the use of the join types `inner`, `outer`, and `cross`.

What Is a Join?

Some people find joins to be confusing, so I find it helpful to start with a very brief overview of database design. The sample database used for many of the examples in this book includes data about customers submitting orders for a set of parts available from a number of suppliers. Such a database might be used by an online car parts or appliance repair business. If you were the database architect charged with designing the database for one of these businesses, you would likely start with the business definition (customers submitting orders for a set of parts available from a number of suppliers) and break it into a number of *business entities*, such as:

- Customer
- Part
- Supplier
- Orders

Your next step would be to determine all the things you need to know about each of these entities, create columns to hold this data, and build database tables for each entity. Some of these columns would be informational, such as a supplier's name and address, and other columns would be used for traversal between tables, such as the `custkey` column in the `Orders` table to link to the corresponding row in the `Customer` table.

Now let's say that you have been hired by the business and your first task is to write a report showing all of the orders for the current day. The report should include information about each order, including the order date, order priority, and the name of the customer who submitted the order. The query that you write to retrieve the data for this report will therefore need to bring together, or *join*, the Orders and Customer tables in order to retrieve data from both tables.

The first step is to look at the definitions of the two tables:

```
PUBLIC>describe table customer;
+---------------+--------------+--------+-------+---------+...
| name          | type         | kind   | null? | default |...
|---------------+--------------+--------+-------+---------+...
| C_CUSTKEY     | NUMBER(38,0) | COLUMN | N     | NULL    |...
| C_NAME        | VARCHAR(25)  | COLUMN | N     | NULL    |...
| C_ADDRESS     | VARCHAR(40)  | COLUMN | N     | NULL    |...
| C_NATIONKEY   | NUMBER(38,0) | COLUMN | N     | NULL    |...
| C_PHONE       | VARCHAR(15)  | COLUMN | N     | NULL    |...
| C_ACCTBAL     | NUMBER(12,2) | COLUMN | N     | NULL    |...
| C_MKTSEGMENT  | VARCHAR(10)  | COLUMN | Y     | NULL    |...
| C_COMMENT     | VARCHAR(117) | COLUMN | Y     | NULL    |...
+---------------+--------------+--------+-------+---------+...

PUBLIC>describe table orders;
+----------------+--------------+--------+-------+---------+...
| name           | type         | kind   | null? | default |...
|----------------+--------------+--------+-------+---------+...
| O_ORDERKEY     | NUMBER(38,0) | COLUMN | N     | NULL    |...
| O_CUSTKEY      | NUMBER(38,0) | COLUMN | N     | NULL    |...
| O_ORDERSTATUS  | VARCHAR(1)   | COLUMN | N     | NULL    |...
| O_TOTALPRICE   | NUMBER(12,2) | COLUMN | N     | NULL    |...
| O_ORDERDATE    | DATE         | COLUMN | N     | NULL    |...
| O_ORDERPRIORITY| VARCHAR(15)  | COLUMN | N     | NULL    |...
| O_CLERK        | VARCHAR(15)  | COLUMN | N     | NULL    |...
| O_SHIPPRIORITY | NUMBER(38,0) | COLUMN | N     | NULL    |...
| O_COMMENT      | VARCHAR(79)  | COLUMN | N     | NULL    |...
+----------------+--------------+--------+-------+---------+...
```

Every row in the Customer table has a unique numeric identifier stored in the c_cust key column, and every row in the Orders table has a column, o_custkey, that holds the customer's unique identifier. Therefore, Customer.c_custkey and Orders.o_cust key will be the columns used to join the two tables. Here's how the query would look:

```
PUBLIC>select o_orderkey, o_orderstatus, o_orderdate, c_name
       from orders join customer
       on orders.o_custkey = customer.c_custkey
       limit 10;
+------------+---------------+-------------+--------------------+
| O_ORDERKEY | O_ORDERSTATUS | O_ORDERDATE | C_NAME             |
|------------+---------------+-------------+--------------------|
|     600006 | O             | 1996-09-16  | Customer#000083098 |
|     600037 | F             | 1994-06-26  | Customer#000107722 |
|     600064 | O             | 1997-11-04  | Customer#000089008 |
|     600065 | F             | 1993-09-15  | Customer#000146441 |
|     600132 | O             | 1998-01-08  | Customer#000131644 |
```

```
|      600165 | F              | 1992-12-08 | Customer#000139328 |
|      600228 | F              | 1992-03-01 | Customer#000046379 |
|      600262 | O              | 1997-03-03 | Customer#000011323 |
|      600327 | O              | 1997-02-25 | Customer#000133094 |
|      600484 | O              | 1997-08-11 | Customer#000120598 |
+-------------+----------------+------------+--------------------+
```

The from clause lists the tables to be joined, and the on subclause contains the join condition(s) needed to traverse from one table to the other. Now that you are comfortable with the concept of table joins, we'll dive a little deeper.

Table Aliases

Chapter 1 introduced you to column aliases, which give you the ability to provide a name of your choosing to the columns in the select clause. Here's the example again:

```
PUBLIC>select 'Welcome to Snowflake SQL!' as welcome_message,
        5 * 3.1415927 as circle_circumference,
        dayname(current_date) as day_of_week;
+---------------------------+----------------------+-------------+
| WELCOME_MESSAGE           | CIRCLE_CIRCUMFERENCE | DAY_OF_WEEK |
|---------------------------+----------------------+-------------|
| Welcome to Snowflake SQL! |           15.7079635 | Fri         |
+---------------------------+----------------------+-------------+
```

You can also provide aliases for the tables in the from clause, which is useful for enhancing the readability of your queries and can also be required in certain cases. Let's take the query from the previous section and add the alias o for the Orders table and c for the Customer table:

```
PUBLIC>select o.o_orderkey, o.o_orderstatus, o.o_orderdate,
        c.c_name
    from orders as o
    join customer as c
    on o.o_custkey = c.c_custkey
    limit 10;
+------------+---------------+------------+--------------------+
| O_ORDERKEY | O_ORDERSTATUS | O_ORDERDATE | C_NAME            |
|------------+---------------+------------+--------------------|
|     600006 | O             | 1996-09-16 | Customer#000083098 |
|     600037 | F             | 1994-06-26 | Customer#000107722 |
|     600064 | O             | 1997-11-04 | Customer#000089008 |
|     600065 | F             | 1993-09-15 | Customer#000146441 |
|     600132 | O             | 1998-01-08 | Customer#000131644 |
|     600165 | F             | 1992-12-08 | Customer#000139328 |
|     600228 | F             | 1992-03-01 | Customer#000046379 |
|     600262 | O             | 1997-03-03 | Customer#000011323 |
|     600327 | O             | 1997-02-25 | Customer#000133094 |
|     600484 | O             | 1997-08-11 | Customer#000120598 |
+------------+---------------+------------+--------------------+
```

The table aliases are provided in the `from` clause (using `as o` and `as c`), and they are also referenced in the `select` clause and in the `on` subclause of the `from` clause. While it is not required that table aliases be used everywhere, it is a good practice to do so, especially when multiple tables are referenced in the `from` clause. Table aliases will be used for all remaining examples in this book that include two or more tables.

Inner Joins

Looking at the previous example, if a value exists for the `custkey` column in one table but not the other, then the join from `Orders` to `Customers` doesn't exist, and those rows are excluded from the result set. For example, if a row in the `Orders` table has a value of 1234 in the `o_custkey` column, but there is no row in the `Customer` table having a value of 1234 for the `c_custkey` column, then that order would not appear in the result set.

This type of join is known as an *inner join*, and it is the most commonly used type of join. Inner joins are the default type of join, and you are not required to specify the `inner` keyword in the `from` clause. Here's the previous example again, but this time using a fully specified join type:

```
PUBLIC>select o.o_orderkey, o.o_orderstatus, o.o_orderdate,
       c.c_name
    from orders as o
    inner join customer as c
    on o.o_custkey = c.c_custkey
    limit 10;
+-------------+---------------+-------------+--------------------+
| O_ORDERKEY  | O_ORDERSTATUS | O_ORDERDATE | C_NAME             |
|-------------+---------------+-------------+--------------------|
|      600006 | O             | 1996-09-16  | Customer#000083098 |
|      600037 | F             | 1994-06-26  | Customer#000107722 |
|      600064 | O             | 1997-11-04  | Customer#000089008 |
|      600065 | F             | 1993-09-15  | Customer#000146441 |
|      600132 | O             | 1998-01-08  | Customer#000131644 |
|      600165 | F             | 1992-12-08  | Customer#000139328 |
|      600228 | F             | 1992-03-01  | Customer#000046379 |
|      600262 | O             | 1997-03-03  | Customer#000011323 |
|      600327 | O             | 1997-02-25  | Customer#000133094 |
|      600484 | O             | 1997-08-11  | Customer#000120598 |
+-------------+---------------+-------------+--------------------+
```

Let's explore this concept in a bit more detail, but this time using a couple of small tables named `Customer_simple` and `Orders_simple`:

```
PUBLIC>create table customer_simple (custkey, custname)
    as select *
    from (values (101, 'BOB'), (102, 'KIM'), (103, 'JIM'));
+-----------------------------------------------+
| status                                        |
```

```
|---------------------------------------------|
| Table CUSTOMER_SIMPLE successfully created. |
+---------------------------------------------+

PUBLIC>select * from customer_simple;
+---------+----------+
| CUSTKEY | CUSTNAME |
|---------+----------|
|     101 | BOB      |
|     102 | KIM      |
|     103 | JIM      |
+---------+----------+
PUBLIC>create table orders_simple (ordernum, custkey)
       as select *
       from (values (990, 101), (991, 102),
                    (992, 101), (993, 104));
+------------------------------------------+
| status                                   |
|------------------------------------------|
| Table ORDERS_SIMPLE successfully created.|
+------------------------------------------+

PUBLIC>select * from orders_simple;
+----------+---------+
| ORDERNUM | CUSTKEY |
|----------+---------|
|      990 |     101 |
|      991 |     102 |
|      992 |     101 |
|      993 |     104 |
+----------+---------+
```

Looking at the data, there are three rows in Customer_simple with custkey values of
101, 102, and 103. There are four rows in Orders_simple, three of which reference
custkey 101 and 102, but another that references custkey 104, which does not exist
in the Customer_simple table. Here's what happens if we join these two tables using
custkey:

```
PUBLIC>select o.ordernum, o.custkey, c.custname
       from orders_simple as o
       inner join
       customer_simple as c
       on o.custkey = c.custkey;
+----------+---------+----------+
| ORDERNUM | CUSTKEY | CUSTNAME |
|----------+---------+----------|
|      990 |     101 | BOB      |
|      991 |     102 | KIM      |
|      992 |     101 | BOB      |
+----------+---------+----------+
```

The result set includes only those rows for which there is a valid join between the two tables, which leaves out `ordernum` 993. There are cases when you don't want to include these mismatched rows, but there are other cases when you *will* want all the rows from one of the tables regardless of whether a join exists. This latter case is explored in the next section.

Outer Joins

The next most common type of join is the *outer join*, which will return all of the rows from table A regardless of whether a join exists to table B. Here's what the previous example returns when the `inner` join is changed to be `outer`:

```
PUBLIC>select o.ordernum, o.custkey, c.custname
       from orders_simple as o
       left outer join
       customer_simple as c
       on o.custkey = c.custkey;
+----------+---------+----------+
| ORDERNUM | CUSTKEY | CUSTNAME |
|----------+---------+----------|
|      990 |     101 | BOB      |
|      991 |     102 | KIM      |
|      992 |     101 | BOB      |
|      993 |     104 | NULL     |
+----------+---------+----------+
```

The result set now includes the fourth row from the `orders_simple` table (`ordernum` 993), but the `custname` column is `null`, since there is no row in the `Customer_simple` table for `custkey` 104. The join was specified to be *left outer*, meaning that all rows from the table on the left side of the join (`Orders_simple`) should be included. If you're wondering whether you can specify a *right outer* join, the answer is yes, but you will rarely ever see it used. Here's what the previous query would look like using a `right outer` join:

```
PUBLIC>select o.ordernum, o.custkey, c.custname
       from orders_simple as o
       right outer join
       customer_simple as c
       on o.custkey = c.custkey;
+----------+---------+----------+
| ORDERNUM | CUSTKEY | CUSTNAME |
|----------+---------+----------|
|      990 |     101 | BOB      |
|      991 |     102 | KIM      |
|      992 |     101 | BOB      |
|     NULL |    NULL | JIM      |
+----------+---------+----------+
```

While the first three rows in the result set look exactly the same as the `inner join` example, the fourth row now contains the extra row from the `Customer_simple` table (`custkey` 104, `custname` JIM), with `null` values for the two `Orders_simple` columns.

Cross Joins

The last type of join to be covered in this chapter is the *cross join*, which is a bit of a misnomer because no actual join is happening. Rather, the two tables are merged together, which is known as the *cartesian product* of the two tables. If I perform a `cross` join on a table with 50 rows to another table with 150 rows, the result set would contain 7,500 rows (50 × 150).

There aren't generally a lot of valid reasons for using `cross` joins with your tables, but I use them all the time to construct data on the fly. For example, let's say you are asked to generate a quarterly report spanning the years 2020, 2021, and 2022, but there isn't any table in the database that contains information about quarters. You can generate a result set to use for your query that includes the 12 needed rows (3 years × 4 quarters/year) by building two data sets and merging them using `cross join`. Here's what that might look like:

```
PUBLIC>select years.yearnum, qtrs.qtrname, qtrs.startmonth,
       qtrs.endmonth
    from
    (values (2020), (2021), (2022))
    as years (yearnum)
    cross join
    (values ('Q1',1,3), ('Q2',4,6), ('Q3',7,9),('Q4',10,12))
    as qtrs (qtrname, startmonth, endmonth)
    order by 1,2;
+---------+---------+------------+----------+
| YEARNUM | QTRNAME | STARTMONTH | ENDMONTH |
|---------+---------+------------+----------|
|    2020 | Q1      |          1 |        3 |
|    2020 | Q2      |          4 |        6 |
|    2020 | Q3      |          7 |        9 |
|    2020 | Q4      |         10 |       12 |
|    2021 | Q1      |          1 |        3 |
|    2021 | Q2      |          4 |        6 |
|    2021 | Q3      |          7 |        9 |
|    2021 | Q4      |         10 |       12 |
|    2022 | Q1      |          1 |        3 |
|    2022 | Q2      |          4 |        6 |
|    2022 | Q3      |          7 |        9 |
|    2022 | Q4      |         10 |       12 |
+---------+---------+------------+----------+
```

You can use this data set to join to your Orders table to sum the total sales for each quarter. One thing to keep in mind is that the cross join does not include the on subclause, since there is no join being specified.

Joining Three or More Tables

All of the examples so far in this chapter have joined exactly two tables, but there is no upper limit on the number of tables in a from clause. Let's expand on the first example in this chapter, which returned a row for each order along with the customer's name, to also include the part names included in each order.

This query will require the Lineitem and Part tables. Here are the table definitions:

```
PUBLIC>describe table lineitem;
+------------------+---------------+--------+-------+---------+...
| name             | type          | kind   | null? | default |...
|------------------+---------------+--------+-------+---------+...
| L_ORDERKEY       | NUMBER(38,0)  | COLUMN | N     | NULL    |...
| L_PARTKEY        | NUMBER(38,0)  | COLUMN | N     | NULL    |...
| L_SUPPKEY        | NUMBER(38,0)  | COLUMN | N     | NULL    |...
| L_LINENUMBER     | NUMBER(38,0)  | COLUMN | N     | NULL    |...
| L_QUANTITY       | NUMBER(12,2)  | COLUMN | N     | NULL    |...
| L_EXTENDEDPRICE  | NUMBER(12,2)  | COLUMN | N     | NULL    |...
| L_DISCOUNT       | NUMBER(12,2)  | COLUMN | N     | NULL    |...
| L_TAX            | NUMBER(12,2)  | COLUMN | N     | NULL    |...
| L_RETURNFLAG     | VARCHAR(1)    | COLUMN | N     | NULL    |...
| L_LINESTATUS     | VARCHAR(1)    | COLUMN | N     | NULL    |...
| L_SHIPDATE       | DATE          | COLUMN | N     | NULL    |...
| L_COMMITDATE     | DATE          | COLUMN | N     | NULL    |...
| L_RECEIPTDATE    | DATE          | COLUMN | N     | NULL    |...
| L_SHIPINSTRUCT   | VARCHAR(25)   | COLUMN | N     | NULL    |...
| L_SHIPMODE       | VARCHAR(10)   | COLUMN | N     | NULL    |...
| L_COMMENT        | VARCHAR(44)   | COLUMN | N     | NULL    |...
+------------------+---------------+--------+-------+---------+...

PUBLIC>describe table part;
+------------------+---------------+--------+-------+---------+...
| name             | type          | kind   | null? | default |...
|------------------+---------------+--------+-------+---------+...
| P_PARTKEY        | NUMBER(38,0)  | COLUMN | N     | NULL    |...
| P_NAME           | VARCHAR(55)   | COLUMN | N     | NULL    |...
| P_MFGR           | VARCHAR(25)   | COLUMN | N     | NULL    |...
| P_BRAND          | VARCHAR(10)   | COLUMN | N     | NULL    |...
| P_TYPE           | VARCHAR(25)   | COLUMN | N     | NULL    |...
| P_SIZE           | NUMBER(38,0)  | COLUMN | N     | NULL    |...
| P_CONTAINER      | VARCHAR(10)   | COLUMN | N     | NULL    |...
| P_RETAILPRICE    | NUMBER(12,2)  | COLUMN | N     | NULL    |...
| P_COMMENT        | VARCHAR(23)   | COLUMN | Y     | NULL    |...
+------------------+---------------+--------+-------+---------+...
```

The `Lineitem` table includes the `l_orderkey` column to link to the `Orders` table, and also includes the `l_partkey` column to link to the `Part` table. Here are all of the joins needed for this query:

Orders *to* Customer

    Gets the customer's name (`Orders.o_custkey` = `Customer.c_custkey`)

Orders *to* Lineitem

    Gets the components of each order (`Orders.o_orderkey` = `Lineitem.l_order key`)

Lineitem *to* Part

    Gets the part name (`Lineitem.l_partkey` = `Part.p_partkey`)

Here's what the query would look like:

```
PUBLIC>select o.o_orderkey, o.o_orderdate, c.c_name, p.p_name
       from orders as o
       inner join customer as c
       on o.o_custkey = c.c_custkey
       inner join lineitem as l
       on o.o_orderkey = l.l_orderkey
       inner join part p
       on l.l_partkey = p.p_partkey
       limit 10;
+------------+------------+---------------------+----------------+
| O_ORDERKEY | O_ORDERDATE | C_NAME             | P_NAME         |
|------------+------------+---------------------+----------------|
|    1800003 | 1992-01-29 | Customer#000142558 | orange sandy...|
|    1800003 | 1992-01-29 | Customer#000142558 | midnight nav...|
|    1800069 | 1996-01-05 | Customer#000069002 | midnight chi...|
|    1800099 | 1993-12-17 | Customer#000136330 | honeydew moc...|
|    1800102 | 1994-10-16 | Customer#000024164 | orange olive...|
|    1800128 | 1993-12-30 | Customer#000028465 | wheat thistl...|
|    1800134 | 1994-11-21 | Customer#000055042 | tomato blanc...|
|    1800163 | 1996-07-28 | Customer#000116533 | turquoise co...|
|    1800230 | 1993-04-30 | Customer#000109345 | drab black f...|
|    1800259 | 1992-02-21 | Customer#000110386 | sienna white...|
+------------+------------+---------------------+----------------+
```

Looking at the results, you can see that orderkey 1800003 covers two rows in the result set, which is because there are two rows in `Lineitem` for that order. This query looks quite a bit more complex, but nothing new is being introduced; it's just an expansion of the two-table join to include four tables. Each join includes its own `on` subclause to define the appropriate join condition.

The sequence of the tables in the `from` clause makes no difference. Here's the same query but with the join order flipped to start with the `Part` table and end with `Customer`:

```
PUBLIC>select o.o_orderkey, o.o_orderdate, c.c_name, p.p_name
       from part as p
       inner join lineitem as l
       on l.l_partkey = p.p_partkey
       inner join orders as o
       on o.o_orderkey = l.l_orderkey
       inner join customer as c
       on o.o_custkey = c.c_custkey
       limit 10;
```

Keep in mind that the Snowflake server will determine how best to execute your queries and will not necessarily access the tables in the order specified in your from clause.

Joining a Table to Itself

Every once in a while, you will come across a case where you need to join a table to itself. This might seem a bit odd, but there are valid reasons for doing so. Some tables include a *self-referencing foreign key*, which means that it includes a column that references the primary key within the same table. While the sample database doesn't include such a relationship, let's build a simple table name employee using the values subclause:

```
PUBLIC>create table employee
       (empid number, emp_name varchar(30), mgr_empid number)
       as select *
       from (values
           (1001, 'Bob Smith', null),
           (1002, 'Susan Jackson', 1001),
           (1003, 'Greg Carpenter', 1001),
           (1004, 'Robert Butler', 1002),
           (1005, 'Kim Josephs', 1003),
           (1006, 'John Tyler', 1004));
+---------------------------------------------+
| status                                      |
|---------------------------------------------|
| Table EMPLOYEE_SIMPLE successfully created. |
+---------------------------------------------+

PUBLIC>select * from employee;
+-------+----------------+-----------+
| EMPID | EMP_NAME       | MGR_EMPID |
|-------+----------------+-----------|
|  1001 | Bob Smith      |      NULL |
|  1002 | Susan Jackson  |      1001 |
|  1003 | Greg Carpenter |      1001 |
|  1004 | Robert Butler  |      1002 |
|  1005 | Kim Josephs    |      1003 |
|  1006 | John Tyler     |      1004 |
+-------+----------------+-----------+
```

This table includes the employee's ID and name, along with the employee ID of the employee's manager. For this example, Bob Smith has no manager, and Susan Jackson and Greg Carpenter both report to Bob Smith. John Tyler reports to Robert Butler, who reports to Susan Jackson, and Kim Josephs reports to Greg Carpenter.

Next, let's write a query that returns the name and ID of each employee, along with the name of the employee's manager. To do so, the Employee table will need to be joined to itself, using the mgr_empid column to join back to the empid column. Here's what that looks like:

```
PUBLIC>select e.empid, e.emp_name, mgr.emp_name as mgr_name
       from employee as e
       inner join employee as mgr
       on e.mgr_empid = mgr.empid;
+-------+----------------+----------------+
| EMPID | EMP_NAME       | MGR_NAME       |
|-------+----------------+----------------|
|  1002 | Susan Jackson  | Bob Smith      |
|  1003 | Greg Carpenter | Bob Smith      |
|  1004 | Robert Butler  | Susan Jackson  |
|  1005 | Kim Josephs    | Greg Carpenter |
|  1006 | John Tyler     | Robert Butler  |
+-------+----------------+----------------+
```

Here are a few things to consider:

- Table aliases are required in this query because you need to refer to each table in the from clause using a unique name.

- The self-join is necessary here because each row in the result set contains values from two different rows in the Employee table.

- There is no row in the result set for Bob Smith.

Regarding this last point, Bob Smith has a null value for the mgr_empid column, which implies that Bob is the highest-level manager in the company.

To include Bob in the results, the previous query needs to be modified to use an outer join:

```
PUBLIC>select e.empid, e.emp_name, mgr.emp_name as mgr_name
       from employee e
       left outer join employee mgr
       on e.mgr_empid = mgr.empid;
+-------+----------------+----------------+
| EMPID | EMP_NAME       | MGR_NAME       |
|-------+----------------+----------------|
|  1002 | Susan Jackson  | Bob Smith      |
|  1003 | Greg Carpenter | Bob Smith      |
|  1004 | Robert Butler  | Susan Jackson  |
|  1005 | Kim Josephs    | Greg Carpenter |
```

```
| 1006 | John Tyler    | Robert Butler |
| 1001 | Bob Smith     | NULL          |
+------+---------------+---------------+
```

Because Bob Smith has a null value for mgr_empid, using an inner join will exclude him from the result set, but an outer join will include every row in the Employee table regardless of whether the self-join succeeds.

Joining the Same Table Twice

The previous section shows a special case where the same table is included twice in the from clause and joined to itself, but there are other cases where you will want the same table to be used twice but joined to different tables. To illustrate, let's modify the Employee table to include two new numeric columns, one to hold the employee's country of birth, and another to hold the employee's current location:

```
PUBLIC>alter table employee add column birth_nationkey integer;
+---------------------------------+
| status                          |
|---------------------------------|
| Statement executed successfully.|
+---------------------------------+

PUBLIC>alter table employee add column current_nationkey integer;
+---------------------------------+
| status                          |
|---------------------------------|
| Statement executed successfully.|
+---------------------------------+
```

Here's the revised definition of Employee showing the two new columns:

```
PUBLIC>describe employee;
+-------------------+-------------+--------+-------+---------+...
| name              | type        | kind   | null? | default |...
|-------------------+-------------+--------+-------+---------+...
| EMPID             | NUMBER(4,0) | COLUMN | Y     | NULL    |...
| EMP_NAME          | VARCHAR(14) | COLUMN | Y     | NULL    |...
| MGR_EMPID         | NUMBER(4,0) | COLUMN | Y     | NULL    |...
| BIRTH_NATIONKEY   | NUMBER(38,0)| COLUMN | Y     | NULL    |...
| CURRENT_NATIONKEY | NUMBER(38,0)| COLUMN | Y     | NULL    |...
+-------------------+-------------+--------+-------+---------+...
```

The next task is to populate the new columns for all six rows in the Employee table using values from the Nation table. Since the values of Nation.n_nationkey range from 0 (Algeria) to 24 (United States), I will assign values to birth_nationkey and current_nationkey somewhat randomly, by using empid - 1000 for birth_nation key, and empid - 999 for current_nationkey. Here's the update statement:

```
PUBLIC>update employee
      set birth_nationkey = empid - 1000,
      current_nationkey = empid - 999;
+--------------------------+---------------------------------------+
| number of rows updated | number of multi-joined rows updated |
|--------------------------+---------------------------------------|
|                      6 |                                    0 |
+--------------------------+---------------------------------------+
```

Here's what the Employee data looks like after the update statement:

```
PUBLIC>select empid, emp_name, birth_nationkey, current_nationkey
      from employee;
+-------+---------------+-----------------+-------------------+
| EMPID | EMP_NAME      | BIRTH_NATIONKEY | CURRENT_NATIONKEY |
|-------+---------------+-----------------+-------------------|
|  1001 | Bob Smith     |               1 |                 2 |
|  1002 | Susan Jackson |               2 |                 3 |
|  1003 | Greg Carpenter|               3 |                 4 |
|  1004 | Robert Butler |               4 |                 5 |
|  1005 | Kim Josephs   |               5 |                 6 |
|  1006 | John Tyler    |               6 |                 7 |
+-------+---------------+-----------------+-------------------+
```

Now that the data is set up, the final task is to write a query that returns each employee's ID, name, birth nation, and current nation. Since every row in Employee potentially references two different rows in the Nation table, the query needs to join Nation twice using two different table aliases. Here's what that would look like:

```
PUBLIC>select e.empid, e.emp_name,
         n1.n_name as birth_nation, n2.n_name as current_nation
      from employee e
      inner join nation as n1
      on e.birth_nationkey = n1.n_nationkey
      inner join nation as n2
      on e.current_nationkey = n2.n_nationkey;
+-------+---------------+--------------+----------------+
| EMPID | EMP_NAME      | BIRTH_NATION | CURRENT_NATION |
|-------+---------------+--------------+----------------|
|  1001 | Bob Smith     | ARGENTINA    | BRAZIL         |
|  1002 | Susan Jackson | BRAZIL       | CANADA         |
|  1003 | Greg Carpenter| CANADA       | EGYPT          |
|  1004 | Robert Butler | EGYPT        | ETHIOPIA       |
|  1005 | Kim Josephs   | ETHIOPIA     | FRANCE         |
|  1006 | John Tyler    | FRANCE       | GERMANY        |
+-------+---------------+--------------+----------------+
```

The birth_nation value is retrieved using the first join to Nation, which has table alias n1, and the current_nation value is retrieved using the second join to Nation with alias n2.

Wrap-Up

In this chapter, you learned about the different types of joins, including inner, outer, and cross joins. You were also exposed to some of the different ways in which multiple tables can be joined, including joining a table to itself and joining the same table multiple times in the same query. Understanding joins is crucial to writing queries, so you might spend a little extra time on this to get comfortable with the concepts.

In addition to the join types discussed here, Chapter 9 will explore several more advanced join types such as `full outer join` and `lateral join`.

Test Your Knowledge

The following exercises are designed to test your understanding of joins. Please see "Chapter 3" in Appendix B for solutions.

Exercise 3-1

Fill in the blanks (denoted by ❶ and ❷) in the query below to obtain the results that follow:

```
PUBLIC>select r.r_name as region_name, n.n_name as nation_name
    from region as r
    inner join nation ❶
        on ❷ = n.n_regionkey
    where n.n_name like 'A%';
+-------------+-------------+
| REGION_NAME | NATION_NAME |
|-------------+-------------|
| AFRICA      | ALGERIA     |
| AMERICA     | ARGENTINA   |
+-------------+-------------+
```

Exercise 3-2

Given the following data for the `Pet_Owner` and `Pet` tables, write a query that returns the `owner_name` and `pet_name` of every owner/pet match (same value for `owner_id` column). Don't include owners with no pets or pets with no owner:

```
Pet_Owner                         Pet
+----------+------------+         +--------+----------+----------+
| OWNER_ID | OWNER_NAME |         | PET_ID | OWNER_ID | PET_NAME |
|----------+------------|         +--------+----------+----------+
|        1 | John       |         |    101 |        1 | Fluffy   |
|        2 | Cindy      |         |    102 |        3 | Spot     |
|        3 | Laura      |         |    103 |        4 | Rover    |
|        4 | Mark       |         |    104 |     NULL | Rosco    |
+----------+------------+         +--------+----------+----------+
```

Exercise 3-3

Using the same data set from Exercise 3-2, write a query that returns every pet own-er's name along with the name of the matching pet if one exists. Results should include every row from Pet_Owner.

Exercise 3-4

Expanding on the owner/pet exercises, let's say that pets can have zero, one, or two owners:

```
Pet_Owner
+----------+------------+
| OWNER_ID | OWNER_NAME |
|----------+------------|
|        1 | John       |
|        2 | Cindy      |
|        3 | Laura      |
|        4 | Mark       |
+----------+------------+
Pet
+--------+-----------+-----------+----------+
| PET_ID | OWNER_ID1 | OWNER_ID2 | PET_NAME |
|--------+-----------+-----------+----------|
|    101 |         1 |      NULL | Fluffy   |
|    102 |         3 |         2 | Spot     |
|    103 |         4 |         1 | Rover    |
|    104 |      NULL |      NULL | Rosco    |
+--------+-----------+-----------+----------+
```

Return the name of each pet, along with the names of Owner #1 and Owner #2. The result set should have one row for each pet (4 total). Some of the owner names will be null.

Working with Sets

Although you can interact with your data one row at a time, relational databases are really all about *sets*. This chapter explores the use of *set operators*, which allow you to combine data from multiple result sets. I'll start with a quick overview of set theory and then move on to show how the set operators union, intersect, and except can be used to blend multiple data sets together.

Set Theory Primer

You may recall from an early math class seeing diagrams such as the one shown in Figure 4-1.

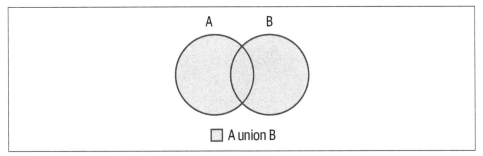

Figure 4-1. Union of two sets

The shaded area in Figure 4-1 represents the *union* of sets A and B, with the overlapping area included just once. Here's another way of illustrating the union operation, using two sets of integers:

```
A = {1, 2, 4, 7, 9}
B = {3, 5, 7, 9}
A union B = {1, 2, 3, 4, 5, 7, 9}
```

In this example, set A contains 5 integers, and set B contains 4 integers. Each set has a couple of unique values, but both sets share the values 7 and 9. The union of A and B yields a total of 7 values, with the integers 7 and 9 included just once.

Next, let's look at the area shared by two sets, known as the *intersection*. Figure 4-2 shows the graphical depiction of an intersection.

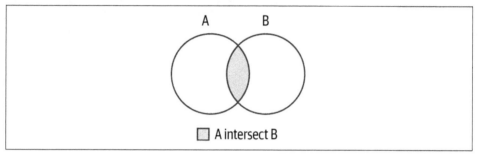

Figure 4-2. Intersection of two sets

Using the same sets of integers as the last example, you can see that the intersection of A and B contains only the numbers 7 and 9:

```
A = {1, 2, 4, 7, 9}
B = {3, 5, 7, 9}
A intersect B = {7, 9}
```

If there is no overlap between the two sets, the intersection would be empty, and intersect is the only set operator that can yield an empty set.

The third and last diagram shown in Figure 4-3 illustrates an operation where the contents of one set is returned *minus* any overlap with another set.

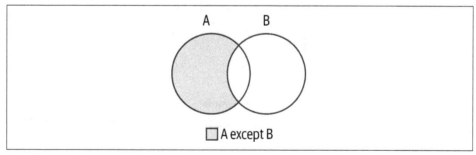

Figure 4-3. Minus of two sets

Known as the **except** operation (but you may also use **minus** interchangeably), this operation yields all of set A without any overlap with set B. Here's the same operation using the numeric sets:

```
A = {1, 2, 4, 7, 9}
B = {3, 5, 7, 9}
A except B = {1, 2, 4}
```

Of the three set operations, **except** is the only one that yields a different result if you switch the order of the sets. Here's the same example, but showing the result of B except A:

```
A = {1, 2, 4, 7, 9}
B = {3, 5, 7, 9}
B except A = {3, 5}
```

These three set operators cover many situations, but how might you describe the case shown in Figure 4-4?

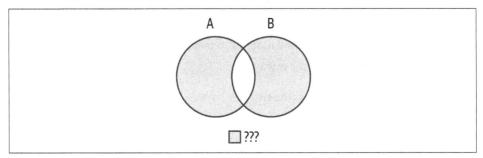

Figure 4-4. Mystery operation

The operation illustrated in Figure 4-4 cannot be achieved using one of the three set operators described previously. It can be achieved, however, by combining multiple set operators. Here are two different ways to generate the shaded area shown in Figure 4-4:

```
(A union B) except (A intersect B)
   -- or --
(A except B) union (B except A)
```

The next sections in this chapter will show you how to put these set operators to work.

The union Operator

The union operator allows you to combine two data sets. Here's a simple example:

```
PUBLIC>select 1 as numeric_col, 'ABC' as string_col
       union
       select 2 as numeric_col, 'XYZ' as string_col;
+-------------+------------+
| NUMERIC_COL | STRING_COL |
|-------------+------------|
|           1 | ABC        |
|           2 | XYZ        |
+-------------+------------+
```

This is about as simple as it gets: two single-row result sets, without any overlapping values, combining to make a two-row result set. This type of statement is known as a *compound query* because it contains two independent queries separated by a set operator. Before moving to more advanced examples, here are some restrictions related to the two sets being combined:

- Both sets must contain the same number of columns.
- The data types of the columns must match.

Here's how Snowflake responds if the two sets have a different column count:

```
PUBLIC>select 1 as numeric_col, 'ABC' as string_col
       union
       select 2 as numeric_col, 'XYZ' as string_col,
         99 as extra_col;
001789 (42601): SQL compilation error:
invalid number of result columns for set operator ...
```

In this case, you will see a very specific error message from Snowflake, but here's the error thrown if the column types don't match:

```
PUBLIC>select 1 as numeric_col, 'ABC' as string_col
       union
       select 'XYZ' as numeric_col, 2 as string_col;
100038 (22018): Numeric value 'ABC' is not recognized
```

This error message is more general in nature, but it tells you that given the data type used in the first column of the first query (the number 1), the value 'ABC' does not match.

As mentioned earlier, the union operator removes duplicates when constructing the result set, meaning that any overlaps are represented only once. Here are the same two sets used earlier ({1, 2, 4, 7, 9} and {3, 5, 7, 9}) built using the values subclause and then combined using union:

```
PUBLIC>select integer_val
       from (values (1), (2), (4), (7), (9))
       as set_a (integer_val)
       union
       select integer_val
       from (values (3), (5), (7), (9))
       as set_b (integer_val);
+-------------+
| INTEGER_VAL |
|-------------|
|           1 |
|           2 |
|           4 |
|           7 |
|           9 |
|           3 |
|           5 |
+-------------+
```

As you can see, both sets include 7 and 9, but these values only appear once in the result set because the union operator sorts the values and removes duplicates.

While this is the default behavior, there are cases when you *don't* want the duplicates to be removed, in which case you can use union all:

```
PUBLIC>select integer_val
       from (values (1), (2), (4), (7), (9))
       as set_a (integer_val)
       union all
       select integer_val
       from (values (3), (5), (7), (9))
       as set_b (integer_val);
+-------------+
| INTEGER_VAL |
|-------------|
|           1 |
|           2 |
|           4 |
|           7 |
|           9 |
|           3 |
|           5 |
|           7 |
|           9 |
+-------------+
```

The result set now includes nine rows instead of seven, with the duplicate 7s and 9s making up the extra two rows.

The sample database includes data from 1992 through 1998; here's a query that uses union to find all customers who placed orders greater than $350,000 in 1992 or 1993:

```
PUBLIC>select distinct o_custkey
       from orders
       where o_totalprice > 350000
         and date_part(year, o_orderdate) = 1992
       union
       select distinct o_custkey
       from orders
       where o_totalprice > 350000
         and date_part(year, o_orderdate) = 1993;
+-----------+
| O_CUSTKEY |
|-----------|
|    114856 |
|    116683 |
|      4334 |
|     61790 |
|     24275 |
|     20665 |
|    130745 |
|     70054 |
|    122047 |
|    123934 |
... <847 rows omitted>
|    102304 |
|    106813 |
|    109519 |
|    120437 |
|    131131 |
|    130987 |
|    108745 |
|      5330 |
|     95137 |
|     59665 |
+-----------+
```

This query could have been written with a single filter condition and without the union operator, but this form of the query will be useful to compare the results of intersect and except in the next two sections.

The intersect Operator

As described earlier in the chapter (see "Set Theory Primer" on page 57), the intersect operator is used to find the intersection between two data sets. Here's an example using the two numeric data sets from earlier:

```
PUBLIC>select integer_val
       from (values (1), (2), (4), (7), (9))
       as set_a (integer_val)
```

```
intersect
select integer_val
from (values (3), (5), (7), (9))
as set_b (integer_val);
+-------------+
| INTEGER_VAL |
|-------------|
|           7 |
|           9 |
+-------------+
```

The overlap of sets A and B are the values 7 and 9; all other values are unique to each set.

In the previous section, the query against the Orders table using union returned 867 rows. Let's see what happens when union is changed to intersect for the same query:

```
PUBLIC>select distinct o_custkey
       from orders
       where o_totalprice > 350000
         and date_part(year, o_orderdate) = 1992
       intersect
       select distinct o_custkey
       from orders
       where o_totalprice > 350000
         and date_part(year, o_orderdate) = 1993;
+-----------+
| O_CUSTKEY |
|-----------|
|    100510 |
+-----------+
```

While there are 867 different customers who placed orders over $350,000 in 1992 or 1993, only one of them placed such orders in both years.

The except Operator

The third and last of the set operators is except, which is used to return rows from set A without any overlap with set B. Here's an example using the two numeric data sets from earlier:

```
PUBLIC>select integer_val
       from (values (1), (2), (4), (7), (9))
       as set_a (integer_val)
       except
       select integer_val
       from (values (3), (5), (7), (9))
       as set_b (integer_val);
```

```
+-------------+
| INTEGER_VAL |
|-------------|
|           1 |
|           2 |
|           4 |
+-------------+
```

This operation yields the set {1, 2, 4}, which are the three values found in set A but not in set B. Switching the order of the two sets yields a different result:

```
PUBLIC>select integer_val
       from (values (3), (5), (7), (9))
       as set_b (integer_val)
       except
       select integer_val
       from (values (1), (2), (4), (7), (9))
       as set_a (integer_val);
+-------------+
| INTEGER_VAL |
|-------------|
|           3 |
|           5 |
+-------------+
```

Unlike union and intersect, which will yield the same results regardless of which set is above or below the set operator, keep in mind that A except B will usually yield different results than B except A.

Returning to the Orders query, here are the results when using except:

```
PUBLIC>select distinct o_custkey
       from orders
       where o_totalprice > 350000
         and date_part(year, o_orderdate) = 1992
       except
       select distinct o_custkey
       from orders
       where o_totalprice > 350000
         and date_part(year, o_orderdate) = 1993;
+-----------+
| O_CUSTKEY |
|-----------|
|    134878 |
|    125183 |
|     44240 |
|     79138 |
|     71119 |
... <444 rows omitted>
|     74929 |
|    149240 |
|     23587 |
|     79999 |
```

```
|     46490 |
+-----------+
```

This query returns 454 customers and when the order of the sets is reversed (orders from 1993 first), the query returns 412 rows.

Set Operation Rules

The following sections outline some rules to keep in mind when working with set operators.

Sorting Compound Query Results

If you want your results to be sorted when using set operators, you need to abide by the following rules:

- There may only be one order by clause, and it must be at the end of the statement.
- When specifying column names in the order by clause, you must use the column names/aliases from the first query.

Regarding the second point, the individual queries used as part of a compound statement may retrieve data from different tables having different column names, so the column names used in the first query determine what can be specified in the order by clause. Here's an example:

```
PUBLIC>select distinct o_orderdate from orders
       intersect
       select distinct l_shipdate from lineitem
       order by o_orderdate;
+-------------+
| O_ORDERDATE |
|-------------|
| 1992-01-03  |
| 1992-01-04  |
| 1992-01-05  |
| 1992-01-06  |
| 1992-01-07  |
... <2,394 rows omitted>
| 1998-07-29  |
| 1998-07-30  |
| 1998-07-31  |
| 1998-08-01  |
| 1998-08-02  |
+-------------+
```

In this example, the column used for sorting must be by o_orderdate rather than l_shipdate; here's what happens if you specify l_shipdate as the sort column:

```
PUBLIC>select distinct o_orderdate from orders
        intersect
        select distinct l_shipdate from lineitem
        order by l_shipdate;
000904 (42000): SQL compilation error: error line 4 at position 9
invalid identifier 'L_SHIPDATE'
```

To avoid confusion in these cases, you can specify matching column aliases for both queries and use the alias in your order by clause.

Set Operation Precedence

If your compound query contains more than two queries using different set opera-tors, you need to consider the order in which to place the queries in order to achieve the desired results. Figure 4-5 shows the "mystery operation" introduced earlier as Figure 4-4.

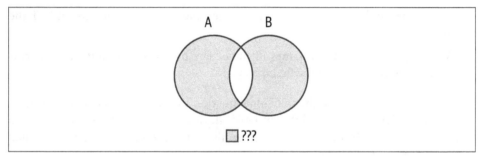

Figure 4-5. Mystery operation

Let's see how this could be accomplished using the two simple numeric sets used throughout this chapter:

```
PUBLIC>select integer_val
        from (values (1), (2), (4), (7), (9))
        as set_a (integer_val);
+-------------+
| INTEGER_VAL |
|-------------|
|           1 |
|           2 |
|           4 |
|           7 |
|           9 |
+-------------+

PUBLIC>select integer_val
        from (values (3), (5), (7), (9))
        as set_b (integer_val);
+-------------+
| INTEGER_VAL |
```

```
|-------------|
|           3 |
|           5 |
|           7 |
|           9 |
+-------------+
```

As mentioned earlier in the chapter, there are multiple ways to generate the shaded area in Figure 4-5, which in this case is the set {1, 2, 3, 4, 5}, but let's choose the second one:

```
(A except B) union (B except A)
```

Here's how that might be constructed for the two numeric sets:

```
PUBLIC>select integer_val
       from (values (1), (2), (4), (7), (9))
       as set_a (integer_val)
       except
       select integer_val
       from (values (3), (5), (7), (9))
       as set_b (integer_val)
       union
       select integer_val
       from (values (3), (5), (7), (9))
       as set_b (integer_val)
       except
       select integer_val
       from (values (1), (2), (4), (7), (9))
       as set_a (integer_val);
+-------------+
| INTEGER_VAL |
|-------------|
|           3 |
|           5 |
+-------------+
```

All the pieces seem to be in place and in the right order, but the results don't seem to be correct. The issue here is that the server is applying these operations from the top down, whereas these operations need to be grouped together. Specifically, the two except operations need to be done independently, and the two resulting sets can then be joined together using union. To do so, you must use parentheses:

```
PUBLIC>(select integer_val
       from (values (1), (2), (4), (7), (9))
       as set_a (integer_val)
       except
       select integer_val
       from (values (3), (5), (7), (9))
       as set_b (integer_val)
       )
       union
       (select integer_val
```

```
        from (values (3), (5), (7), (9))
        as set_b (integer_val)
        except
        select integer_val
        from (values (1), (2), (4), (7), (9))
        as set_a (integer_val)
        );
+--------------+
| INTEGER_VAL |
|--------------|
|            1 |
|            2 |
|            4 |
|            5 |
|            3 |
+--------------+
```

When building compound queries with three or more set operators, make sure you consider how the different operations may need to be grouped in order to achieve the desired results.

Wrap-Up

In this chapter, you learned how the set operators union, intersect, and except can be used to identify overlaps between multiple data sets. You were also introduced to strategies for combining these operations in order to identify complex relationships between data sets. While you may not see these set operators used in many examples in later chapters, keep these powerful tools in mind when performing data analysis or crafting reports.

Test Your Knowledge

The following exercises are designed to test your understanding of set operators. Please see "Chapter 4" in Appendix B for solutions.

Exercise 4-1

Given the following two sets:

A = {3, 5, 7, 9}

B = {4, 5, 6, 7, 8}

Which sets are generated by each of the following operations?

- A union B
- A union all B
- A intersect B

- A except B
- B except A

Exercise 4-2

Write a compound query that returns the names of all regions (`Region.r_name`) and nations (`Nation.n_name`) that start with the letter A.

Exercise 4-3

Modify the query from Exercise 4-2 to sort by name (the default sort is fine).

Exercise 4-4

Given the following three sets:

    A = {3, 5, 7, 9}

    B = {4, 5, 6, 7, 8}

    C = {8, 9, 10}

What set is returned by the following operation?

    (A except B) intersect C

Creating and Modifying Data

The first four chapters have been primarily concerned with the `select` statement. Now it's time to switch gears and look at table creation along with the rest of the SQL data statements, including `insert`, `update`, `delete`, and `merge`.

Data Types

This section explores the different data types that may be used to store data in Snowflake.

Character Data

Storing character data in Snowflake is refreshingly simple; there is a single variable-length data type named `varchar` that can store up to 16 MB of character data. Data is stored using the Unicode UTF-8 character set, so the upper limit on the number of characters that may be stored in a single `varchar` column depends on whether you are storing single-byte or multibyte characters. When defining a column as `varchar`, you may optionally specify a maximum number of characters, as in:

```
favorite_movie varchar(100)
```

For the `favorite_movie` column, Snowflake would store up to 100 bytes of data depending on the length of the string. If you do not specify a maximum length, the column will hold up to 16 MB.

In order to be compatible with other database systems, Snowflake allows character columns to be defined using any of the following:

- `char, character, char varying`
- `nchar, nchar varying`
- `nvarchar, nvarchar2`
- `string, text`

While you are free to use any of these synonyms, they are generally used for porting table definitions from other database servers. If you're building new tables in Snowflake, you should just use `varchar`.

Char Versus Varchar

In many database servers, the `char` data type is used to store fixed-length strings that are padded with spaces if the string length is less than the maximum length. Therefore, a column defined as char(5) would hold exactly 5 characters, right-padded with spaces if necessary, so the string "cat" would be stored as `'cat '`.

All character columns stored in Snowflake are variable-length, even if defined using `char`, and Snowflake will never add spaces to the end of a string. The only thing to keep in mind when defining a column as `char` in Snowflake is that the default length is 1 if you do not specify a length.

When providing values for character columns, you will need to use single quotes as delimiters:

```
PUBLIC>select 'here is a string' as output_string;
+------------------+
| OUTPUT_STRING    |
|------------------|
| here is a string |
+------------------+
```

If your string contains a single quote (usually as an apostrophe), you can use two single quotes together to tell Snowflake that it hasn't reached the end of the string, as in:

```
PUBLIC>select 'you haven''t reached the end yet' as output_string;
+------------------------------+
| OUTPUT_STRING                |
|------------------------------|
| you haven't reached the end yet |
+------------------------------+
```

For complex strings, you have the option of using two dollar signs ($$) as delimiters, in which case Snowflake will accept the string exactly as written, as in:

```
PUBLIC>select $$string with 4 single quotes ' ' ' '$$
       as output_string;
+------------------------------------+
| OUTPUT_STRING                      |
|------------------------------------|
| string with 4 single quotes ' ' ' ' |
+------------------------------------+
```

Depending on the type of data being stored in your database, you might find that the majority of your columns will be defined as `varchar`.

Numeric Data

Similar to character data, Snowflake has a single data type called number that will handle just about any type of numeric data. The values stored in a number column can include up to 38 digits, either with a decimal point (floating-point numbers) or without (integers). Therefore, a column defined as number could contain any of the following values:

- 0
- -1
- 99,999,999,999,999,999,999,999,999,999,999,999,999
- 0.00000000000000000000000000000000000001
- 1,234,567.12345678901234567890123456789

The total number of digits is known as the *precision*, and the maximum number of digits to the right of the decimal point (if there are any) is called the *scale*. The total number of digits must not exceed 38, and if you don't specify the precision and scale when defining your numeric columns, the default will be number(38,0). If you are storing data with a specific format, such as numbers between –999.99 and 999.99, you could define the column in this case to be number(5,2). The storage needed for numeric data is variable depending on the number of digits, so there is nothing wasteful about defining all of your numeric columns as number(38,0).

To simplify the porting of data from other database systems, Snowflake will accept any of the following data types:

- decimal, numeric, real
- tinyint, smallint, int, integer, bigint
- double, float, float4, float8

When defining new columns, however, you may want to stick with integer for integers and number for floating-point numbers.

Temporal Data

Along with strings and numbers, you will almost certainly be dealing with *temporal data*, which holds information about dates and/or times. Here are some examples:

- A person's birthday, which generally holds the month/day/year of a person's birth.
- The time of day at which a particular event happens, such as the start or end of a work shift.

- The exact time at which an automobile passed through an electronic tolling station, which requires the date, hour, minute, second, and partial second (thousandths).

- The time at which a reminder should be sent to a user of a calendar app, including the date, time of day, and the user's time zone.

Snowflake supports three different temporal data types, as shown in Table 5-1.

Table 5-1. Snowflake temporal data types

Data type	Allowable range
date	1582-01-01 to 9999-12-31
time	00:00:00 to 23:59:59.999999999
timestamp	1582-01-01 00:00:00 to 9999-12-31 23:59:59.999999999

Snowflake dates can range from the year 1582 to the year 9999, and times are comprised of hours, minutes, seconds, and partial seconds to 9 significant digits (nanoseconds). Timestamps are a combination of date and time and come in three flavors:

timestamp_ntz
    No specific time zone

timestamp_ltz
    Uses current session's time zone

timestamp_tz
    Allows time zone to be specified

You are usually aware of what time zone you are currently in (unless of course you are reading this while on an airplane), but you may not know the time zone setting in your database, which can be determined using the show parameters command:

```
PUBLIC>show parameters like 'timez%';
+----------+---------------------+---------------------+...
| key      | value               | default             |...
|----------+---------------------+---------------------+...
| TIMEZONE | America/Los_Angeles | America/Los_Angeles |...
+----------+---------------------+---------------------+...
```

If you would like to change the default time zone, you can do so using either the alter session command to change the time zone in your session, or the alter account command if you'd like to make the change permanent. Here's how you might change it at the session level:

```
PUBLIC>alter session set timezone='America/New_York';

+-----------------------------------+
| status                            |
```

```
|-----------------------------------|
| Statement executed successfully.  |
+-----------------------------------+

PUBLIC>show parameters like 'timez%';
+----------+------------------+---------------------+...
| key      | value            | default             |...
|----------+------------------+---------------------+...
| TIMEZONE | America/New_York | America/Los_Angeles |...
+----------+------------------+---------------------+...
```

Here's a query that returns the current date, time, and timestamp using some of Snowflake's built-in functions:

```
PUBLIC>select current_date, current_time, current_timestamp;
+--------------+--------------+------------------------------+
| CURRENT_DATE | CURRENT_TIME | CURRENT_TIMESTAMP            |
|--------------+--------------+------------------------------|
| 2022-10-12   | 12:59:41     | 2022-10-12 12:59:41.598 -0400 |
+--------------+--------------+------------------------------+
```

The -0400 designation at the end of the timestamp value tells me that my time zone is 4 hours behind Greenwich Mean Time (GMT). Keep in mind that the value may vary by an hour depending on whether your time zone is currently in daylight saving time.

Snowflake is very flexible regarding date literals and can handle many common formats. For example, Snowflake allowed all of the following string literals to be inserted into a date column:

- '24-OCT-2022'
- '2022-10-24'
- '10/24/2022'

However, there is a single default format for date values to be returned, which is found in the date_output_format parameter:

```
PUBLIC>show parameters like 'date_output%';
+--------------------+------------+------------+-------+...
| key                | value      | default    | level |...
|--------------------+------------+------------+-------+...
| DATE_OUTPUT_FORMAT | YYYY-MM-DD | YYYY-MM-DD |       |...
+--------------------+------------+------------+-------+...
```

When your query returns a date value, it will be shown using the date_output_format value:

```
PUBLIC>select current_date;
+--------------+
| CURRENT_DATE |
|--------------|
| 2022-10-24   |
+--------------+
```

If you'd prefer a different format, you can change the value of date_output_format in your session:

```
PUBLIC>alter session set date_output_format='MM/DD/YYYY';
+--------------------------------+
| status                         |
|--------------------------------|
| Statement executed successfully. |
+--------------------------------+

PUBLIC>select current_date;
+--------------+
| CURRENT_DATE |
|--------------|
| 10/24/2022   |
+--------------+
```

There is also a timestamp_output_format parameter, which defaults to 'YYYY-MM-DD HH24:MI:SS.FF3'.

Other Data Types

Along with the three major types of data (character, numeric, temporal), Snowflake includes some specialty data types, some of which are mainly used for semistructured data such as JSON documents.

Boolean

The boolean data type is known as a *logical data type* and can hold the values true and false. Snowflake is quite flexible when assigning a value to a boolean column or variable and will accept any of the following:

- Strings 'true', '1', 'yes', 't', 'y', 'on' for true
- Strings 'false', '0', 'no', 'f', 'n', 'off' for false
- Number 0 for false
- Any nonzero number for true

You can use true and false by themselves, or as part of an expression, as shown by the next example:

```
PUBLIC>select true, false, true = true, true = false;
+------+-------+-------------+--------------+
| TRUE | FALSE | TRUE = TRUE | TRUE = FALSE |
|------+-------+-------------+--------------|
| True | False | True        | False        |
+------+-------+-------------+--------------+
```

Like any other data type, boolean columns may also be null.

Variant

`Variant` is the Swiss Army knife of data types; it can hold any type of data. As you can imagine, this provides a great deal of flexibility when storing semistructured data. If you are inserting values into a `variant` column, you can use the `::` operator to cast a string, number, date, etc., to a `variant` type, as in:

```
PUBLIC>select 1::variant, 'abc'::variant, current_date::variant;
+------------+----------------+----------------------+
| 1::VARIANT | 'ABC'::VARIANT | CURRENT_DATE::VARIANT |
|------------+----------------+----------------------|
| 1          | "abc"          | "2022-10-13"         |
+------------+----------------+----------------------+
```

Snowflake provides the built-in function `typeof()` to tell you what type of data is being stored:

```
PUBLIC>select typeof('this is a character string'::variant);
+-------------------------------------------------+
| TYPEOF('THIS IS A CHARACTER STRING'::VARIANT)   |
|-------------------------------------------------|
| VARCHAR                                         |
+-------------------------------------------------+

PUBLIC>select typeof(false::variant);
+-----------------------+
| TYPEOF(FALSE::VARIANT) |
|-----------------------|
| BOOLEAN               |
+-----------------------+

PUBLIC>select typeof(current_timestamp::variant);
+-----------------------------------+
| TYPEOF(CURRENT_TIMESTAMP::VARIANT) |
|-----------------------------------|
| TIMESTAMP_LTZ                     |
+-----------------------------------+
```

You can also use the `variant` data type to store JSON documents (see Chapter 18).

Array

The `array` data type is a variable-length array of `variant` values. Arrays can be created with an initial length of 0 or greater and can be extended later; there is no upper limit on the number of elements in an array, but there is an overall size limit of 16 MB. The square brackets ([and]) are used as delimiters for array literals; here's an example of an array containing a number, a string, and a time value:

```
PUBLIC>select [123, 'ABC', current_time] as my_array;
+---------------+
| MY_ARRAY      |
|---------------|
```

```
| [            |
|    123,      |
|    "ABC",    |
|    "10:27:33" |
| ]            |
+-------------+
```

The result set is a single row containing a single column of type array. Arrays can be *flattened* into X rows (X = 3 in this case) by using a combination of the table() and flatten() functions:

```
PUBLIC>select value
         from table(flatten(input=>[123, 'ABC', current_time]));
+-------------+
| VALUE       |
|-------------|
| 123         |
| "ABC"       |
| "10:29:25"  |
+-------------+
```

The three-element array has now been flattened into three rows, each containing a single variant column, which the flatten command has labeled as value. The array type will be utilized in Chapters 16 and 18.

Object

Snowflake's object type stores an array of *key-value pairs*, with the keys being of type varchar and the values of type variant. Object literals are created using curly braces ({ and }), and keys are separated from values using colons. Here's an example using holiday definitions:

```
PUBLIC>select {'new_years' : '01/01',
               'independence_day' : '07/04',
               'christmas' : '12/25'}
         as my_object;
+--------------------------------+
| MY_OBJECT                      |
|--------------------------------|
| {                              |
|    "christmas": "12/25",       |
|    "independence_day": "07/04", |
|    "new_years": "01/01"        |
| }                              |
+--------------------------------+
```

This result set consists of a single row with a single column of type object, but you can use the flatten() and table() functions to transform this result set into three rows, each having a key and value column:

```
PUBLIC>select key, value
       from table(flatten(
         {'new_years' : '01/01',
          'independence_day' : '07/04',
          'christmas' : '12/25'}));
+------------------+---------+
| KEY              | VALUE   |
|------------------+---------|
| christmas        | "12/25" |
| independence_day | "07/04" |
| new_years        | "01/01" |
+------------------+---------+
```

With the object flattened, you can modify your query to retrieve a particular key value:

```
PUBLIC>select value
       from table(flatten(
         {'new_years' : '01/01',
          'independence_day' : '07/04',
          'christmas' : '12/25'}))
       where key = 'new_years';
+---------+
| VALUE   |
|---------|
| "01/01" |
+---------+
```

Objects will be discussed further in Chapter 18.

Creating Tables

Now that you have a good grasp of the different data types available in Snowflake, let's create a table to use for the remaining examples in this chapter. The table will be named Person and will contain the following information:

- First and last name
- Birth date
- Eye color

- Occupation
- Names of children
- Years of education

This table will have a mix of varchar, date, number, and even an array (for children's names). Here's the table definition:

```
PUBLIC>create table person
       (first_name varchar(50),
        last_name varchar(50),
        birth_date date,
        eye_color varchar(10),
        occupation varchar(50),
        children array,
```

```
        years_of_education number(2,0)
        );
+-----------------------------------+
| status                            |
|-----------------------------------|
| Table PERSON successfully created. |
+-----------------------------------+
```

The following sections in this chapter will use this table to demonstrate how to add and delete rows, as well as how to modify existing rows.

Populating and Modifying Tables

Since the `Person` table is empty, the first task is to add a few rows. Here's the first row, using the simplest form of the `insert` statement:

```
PUBLIC>insert into person (first_name, last_name, birth_date,
        eye_color, occupation, children, years_of_education)
        values ('Bob','Smith','22-JAN-2000','blue','teacher',
        null, 18);
+-------------------------+
| number of rows inserted |
|-------------------------|
|                       1 |
+-------------------------+
```

This statement lists the columns to be populated, and then uses a `values` subclause to provide values for each column. While you do not need to specify values for every column in a table, I did for this example, even though `null` was specified for the `children` column since Bob Smith has no children. Therefore, the previous example could have omitted the `children` column, as shown in the next example, which adds a row for Gina Peters:

```
PUBLIC>insert into person (first_name, last_name, birth_date,
        eye_color, occupation, years_of_education)
        values ('Gina','Peters','03-MAR-2001','brown',
        'student', 12);
+-------------------------+
| number of rows inserted |
|-------------------------|
|                       1 |
+-------------------------+
```

Snowflake allows multiple rows to be inserted in the same statement, using multiple sets of values separated by commas. The next example adds Tim, Kathy, and Sam to the table:

```
PUBLIC>insert into person (first_name, last_name, birth_date,
        eye_color, occupation, years_of_education)
        values
        ('Tim','Carpenter','09-JUL-2002','green','salesman', 16),
```

```
            ('Kathy','Little','29-AUG-2001','blue','professor', 20),
            ('Sam','Jacobs','13-FEB-2003','brown','lawyer', 18);
+-------------------------+
| number of rows inserted |
|-------------------------|
|                       3 |
+-------------------------+
```

There are now five rows in the Person table, but let's say that we were given the wrong eye color for all of them and want to start from scratch. Snowflake provides the overwrite option, which will first remove all rows from the table before inserting new rows. Here's a statement that will delete and re-add all five people:

```
PUBLIC>insert overwrite into person
        (first_name, last_name, birth_date,
         eye_color, occupation, years_of_education)
        values
        ('Bob','Smith','22-JAN-2000','brown','teacher', 18),
        ('Gina','Peters','03-MAR-2001','green','student', 12),
        ('Tim','Carpenter','09-JUL-2002','blue','salesman', 16),
        ('Kathy','Little','29-AUG-2001','brown','professor', 20),
        ('Sam','Jacobs','13-FEB-2003','blue','lawyer', 18);
+-------------------------+
| number of rows inserted |
|-------------------------|
|                       5 |
+-------------------------+
```

Along with using values, you can use a select statement to generate one or more rows to be inserted into a table. Let's say that Tim Carpenter has a twin sister named Sharon, so they share the same last name, eye color, and birth date. However, Sharon has more years of education, a different occupation, and has two children. The next statement retrieves Tim's row using a select statement, augments the necessary columns, and inserts the new row for Sharon:

```
PUBLIC>insert into person (first_name, last_name, birth_date,
        eye_color, occupation, children, years_of_education)
        select 'Sharon' as first_name,
        last_name, birth_date, eye_color,
        'doctor' as occupation,
        ['Sue'::variant, 'Shawn'::variant] as children,
        20 as years_of_education
        from person
        where first_name = 'Tim' and last_name = 'Carpenter';
+-------------------------+
| number of rows inserted |
|-------------------------|
|                       1 |
+-------------------------+
```

While the `select` statement in this example retrieves data from the same table named in the `insert` statement, your query can retrieve data from any table and can return more than one row.

Deleting Data

There are now six rows in the `Person` table:

```
PUBLIC>select first_name, last_name
        from person;
+------------+------------+
| FIRST_NAME | LAST_NAME  |
|------------+------------|
| Bob        | Smith      |
| Gina       | Peters     |
| Tim        | Carpenter  |
| Kathy      | Little     |
| Sam        | Jacobs     |
| Sharon     | Carpenter  |
+------------+------------+
```

If you'd like to remove Sam Jacobs from the table, you can execute a `delete` statement using a `where` clause to specify the row(s) to be removed:

```
PUBLIC>delete from person
        where first_name = 'Sam' and last_name = 'Jacobs';
+------------------------+
| number of rows deleted |
|------------------------|
|                      1 |
+------------------------+
```

Most of the time, you will probably use this simple form of the `delete` statement, but in some cases you might want to remove rows in one table based on rows in another table. For example, Bob Smith appears in both the `Person` and `Employee` tables:

```
PUBLIC>select first_name, last_name
        from person
        where last_name = 'Smith';
+------------+------------+
| FIRST_NAME | LAST_NAME  |
|------------+------------|
| Bob        | Smith      |
+------------+------------+

PUBLIC>select emp_name
        from employee
        where emp_name like '%Smith';

+------------+
| EMP_NAME   |
|------------|
```

```
| Bob Smith |
+-----------+
```

Let's say you want to remove any rows from `Person` where a row exists in `Employee` having the same name (Bob Smith happens to be the only case). For this type of operation, Snowflake provides the `using` subclause to join to another table:

```
PUBLIC>delete from person
       using employee
       where employee.emp_name =
           concat(person.first_name, ' ', person.last_name);
+------------------------+
| number of rows deleted |
|------------------------|
|                      1 |
+------------------------+
```

This example uses the `concat()` function to build a single string containing both the person's first and last names and uses this concatenated string to join to the `Employee` table. I needed to do this because the employee's name is stored as a single string in the `Employee` table, whereas the first and last names are in separate columns in the `Person` table.

Bob Smith is now gone from the `Person` table, although the other four rows are still there because there was no matching row in `Employee`:

```
PUBLIC>select first_name, last_name from person;
+------------+-----------+
| FIRST_NAME | LAST_NAME |
|------------+-----------|
| Gina       | Peters    |
| Tim        | Carpenter |
| Kathy      | Little    |
| Sharon     | Carpenter |
+------------+-----------+

PUBLIC>select emp_name from employee;
+----------------+
| EMP_NAME       |
|----------------|
| Bob Smith      |
| Susan Jackson  |
| Greg Carpenter |
| Robert Butler  |
| Kim Josephs    |
| John Tyler     |
+----------------+
```

As you can see, Bob Smith's row remains in the `Employee` table, which is to be expected since the `delete` statement can only remove rows from a single table.

Oops! Where's the Undo Button...

Let's say you just deleted some data, and immediately afterward realized that maybe you didn't want to delete it after all. If you were using a spreadsheet or word processing application, you could just use Edit>Undo to restore the deleted data, but you are using a database, and your delete statement has been committed (more about this in Chapter 11) and the data is gone.

Thankfully, Snowflake has a feature called Time Travel, which allows you to see the state of your data at a particular point in time. If you are using Snowflake Standard edition, you can see your data as it was up to 24 hours ago. With Snowflake Enterprise, you can configure the retention period to be up to 90 days in the past.

I'll cover Time Travel a bit more in Chapter 9, but here's a quick example showing you how to retrieve deleted data. Let's say you're Bob Smith, and your employee Greg Carpenter comes into your office, throws a letter of resignation on your desk, and storms out. Looks like it's time to remove Greg from the Employee table:

```
PUBLIC>delete from employee where emp_name = 'Greg Carpenter';
+------------------------+
| number of rows deleted |
|------------------------|
|                      1 |
+------------------------+
```

Five minutes later, Greg calls to apologize and ask for his job back. You agree, and now you need to put Greg's information back into the Employee table. You can query the Employee table as it was 10 minutes ago (travel –600 seconds into the past) by using the at subclause:

```
PUBLIC>select * from employee at(offset => -600)
       where emp_name = 'Greg Carpenter';
+-------+-----------------+-----------+-----------------+...
| EMPID | EMP_NAME        | MGR_EMPID | BIRTH_NATIONKEY |...
|-------+-----------------+-----------+-----------------+...
|  1003 | Greg Carpenter  |      1001 |               3 |...
+-------+-----------------+-----------+-----------------+...
```

You've traveled back in time 10 minutes to find Greg's data, and now you can add his data back into the Employee table by pairing the previous query with an insert statement:

```
PUBLIC>insert into employee
       select * from employee at(offset => -600)
       where emp_name = 'Greg Carpenter';
+-------------------------+
| number of rows inserted |
|-------------------------|
|                       1 |
+-------------------------+
```

Greg's data has been restored, maybe not as quickly as Edit>Undo, but certainly a lot easier than calling your database administrator to ask for the deleted data to be restored.

Modifying Data

If you want to modify existing data in a table, you use an update statement. Your statement will need to identify which row(s) you want to modify by specifying a where clause, and then describe the desired changes in a set clause. Here's an update statement that changes Kathy Little's occupation and eye color:

```
PUBLIC>update person
    set occupation = 'musician', eye_color = 'grey'
    where first_name = 'Kathy' and last_name = 'Little';
+-----------------------+-------------------------------------+
| number of rows updated | number of multi-joined rows updated |
|-----------------------+-------------------------------------|
|                     1 |                                   0 |
+-----------------------+-------------------------------------+
```

Snowflake's response tells us that one row was updated, but it also specifies that no multijoined rows were modified. This second piece of information isn't relevant if your statement uses a where clause, but you can optionally use a from clause if you want to apply changes from values in another table. To demonstrate, let's put Bob Smith back in the Person table:

```
PUBLIC>insert into person (first_name, last_name, birth_date,
    eye_color, occupation, years_of_education)
    values ('Bob','Smith','22-JAN-2000','blue','teacher', 18);
+------------------------+
| number of rows inserted |
|------------------------|
|                      1 |
+------------------------+
```

Similar to what was done in "Deleting Data" on page 82, where data from the Employee table was used to delete a row in the Person table, the next statement updates Bob's row in Person using data from his Employee row:

```
PUBLIC>update person as p
    set occupation = 'boss'
    from employee as e
    where e.emp_name =
     concat(p.first_name, ' ', p.last_name)
     and e.mgr_empid is null;
```

```
+------------------------------+------------------------------------------+
| number of rows updated | number of multi-joined rows updated |
|------------------------------+------------------------------------------|
|                            1 |                                        0 |
+------------------------------+------------------------------------------+
```

This statement sets the occupation to boss if there is a row in the Employee table with
the same first/last name and with a null value for mgr_empid (meaning that the person has no manager). The only row for which this is true is Bob Smith's row, so his
row now shows boss in the occupation column:

```
PUBLIC>select first_name, last_name, occupation
       from person;
+------------+-----------+------------+
| FIRST_NAME | LAST_NAME | OCCUPATION |
|------------+-----------+------------|
| Gina       | Peters    | student    |
| Tim        | Carpenter | salesman   |
| Kathy      | Little    | musician   |
| Sharon     | Carpenter | doctor     |
| Bob        | Smith     | boss       |
+------------+-----------+------------+
```

Similar to the prior update statement, there was one row updated and no multijoined
rows updated. What this second part means is that each updated row in Person
joined to exactly one row in Employee, which is generally what you want to see. However, the next statement shows what happens if rows in Person join to *multiple*
Employee rows:

```
PUBLIC>update person as p
       set p.years_of_education = e.empid - 1000
       from employee as e
       where e.empid < 1003;
+------------------------------+------------------------------------------+
| number of rows updated | number of multi-joined rows updated |
|------------------------------+------------------------------------------|
|                            5 |                                        5 |
+------------------------------+------------------------------------------+
```

For this statement, Snowflake tells us there were five multijoined rows updated,
which means that all five rows in Person joined to multiple rows in Employee. Looking at the where clause, you can see why; there are two rows in Employee with empid <
1003, so every row in Person joined to two rows in Employee. Let's see what the data
looks like after the update statement:

```
PUBLIC>select first_name, last_name, years_of_education
       from person;
+------------+-----------+--------------------+
| FIRST_NAME | LAST_NAME | YEARS_OF_EDUCATION |
|------------+-----------+--------------------|
```

```
| Gina       | Peters    |                  1 |
| Tim        | Carpenter |                  1 |
| Kathy      | Little    |                  1 |
| Sharon     | Carpenter |                  1 |
| Bob        | Smith     |                  1 |
+------------+-----------+--------------------+
```

For each of the five rows in Person, the years_of_education column was set to 1001 − 1000 = 1. There are two rows in Employee with a value of empid less than 1003 (Bob Smith with empid = 1001, and Susan Jackson with empid = 1002), but Bob Smith's row was the last one to be used for the update in this case. If you don't want to allow multijoined updates to succeed (and I can't think of why you would), you can set the error_on_nondeterministic_update parameter to true, after which Snowflake will throw an error:

```
PUBLIC>alter session set error_on_nondeterministic_update=true;
+--------------------------------+
| status                         |
|--------------------------------|
| Statement executed successfully. |
+--------------------------------+

PUBLIC>update person as p
       set p.years_of_education = e.empid - 1000
       from employee as e
       where e.empid < 1003;
100090 (42P18): Duplicate row detected during DML action
Row Values: ["Gina", "Peters", 11384, "green", "student", NULL, 1]
```

The error happened after the first multijoined row was encountered, which in this case happened to be Gina Peters.

Merging Data

Now that you understand how to use the insert, delete, and update statements, let's look at how you can do all three operations in a single statement. To see how this works, imagine that someone in human resources loaded data into a table called Person_Refresh and asks you to modify the Person table to match the new table. Here's how the data was loaded:

```
PUBLIC>create table person_refresh as
       select *
       from (values
       ('Bob','Smith','no','22-JAN-2000','blue','manager'),
       ('Gina','Peters','no','03-MAR-2001','brown','student'),
       ('Tim','Carpenter','no','09-JUL-2002','green','salesman'),
       ('Carl','Langford','no','16-JUN-2001','blue','tailor'),
       ('Sharon','Carpenter','yes',null,null,null),
       ('Kathy','Little','yes',null,null,null))
       as hr_list (fname, lname, remove, dob, eyes, profession);
```

```
+----------------------------------------------+
| status                                       |
|----------------------------------------------|
| Table PERSON_REFRESH successfully created.   |
+----------------------------------------------+

PUBLIC>select * from person_refresh;
+--------+-----------+--------+-------------+-------+------------+
| FNAME  | LNAME     | REMOVE | DOB         | EYES  | PROFESSION |
|--------+-----------+--------+-------------+-------+------------|
| Bob    | Smith     | no     | 22-JAN-2000 | blue  | manager    |
| Gina   | Peters    | no     | 03-MAR-2001 | brown | student    |
| Tim    | Carpenter | no     | 09-JUL-2002 | green | salesman   |
| Carl   | Langford  | no     | 16-JUN-2001 | blue  | tailor     |
| Sharon | Carpenter | yes    | NULL        | NULL  | NULL       |
| Kathy  | Little    | yes    | NULL        | NULL  | NULL       |
+--------+-----------+--------+-------------+-------+------------+
```

Here's a list of the people currently in the Person table:

```
PUBLIC>select first_name, last_name, birth_date,
        eye_color, occupation
      from person;
+------------+-----------+------------+-----------+------------+
| FIRST_NAME | LAST_NAME | BIRTH_DATE | EYE_COLOR | OCCUPATION |
|------------+-----------+------------+-----------+------------|
| Gina       | Peters    | 2001-03-03 | green     | student    |
| Tim        | Carpenter | 2002-07-09 | blue      | salesman   |
| Kathy      | Little    | 2001-08-29 | grey      | musician   |
| Sharon     | Carpenter | 2002-07-09 | blue      | doctor     |
| Bob        | Smith     | 2000-01-22 | blue      | boss       |
+------------+-----------+------------+-----------+------------+
```

Comparing these two sets, it looks like Kathy Little and Sharon Carpenter have a value of yes for the remove column (meaning that they should be removed from the Person table), and Carl Langford is a new row that needs to be added. Additionally, there are some changes to some of the values in the eye_color and occupation columns.

The easiest approach would be to delete all rows in the Person table and reload from the Person_Refresh table, but let's say that isn't an option because removing rows would cause unwanted changes in downstream systems. Instead, you can execute a single merge statement to add any new rows, remove rows no longer needed, and modify any existing rows. Here's what it looks like:

```
PUBLIC>merge into person as p
      using person_refresh as pr
      on p.first_name = pr.fname
        and p.last_name = pr.lname
      when matched and pr.remove = 'yes' then delete
      when matched then update set p.birth_date = pr.dob,
```

```
        p.eye_color = pr.eyes,
        p.occupation = pr.profession
    when not matched then insert
        (first_name, last_name, birth_date, eye_color, occupation)
    values (pr.fname, pr.lname, pr.dob,
        pr.eyes, pr.profession);
+-------------------+-------------------+-------------------+
| # of rows inserted | # of rows updated | # of rows deleted |
|-------------------+-------------------+-------------------|
|                 1 |                 3 |                 2 |
+-------------------+-------------------+-------------------+
```

There's a lot going on, so here's an overview:

- The target table (the table to be modified) is Person, and the source table (the table providing the new values) is Person_Refresh.

- The using clause names the source table, and the on subclause describes how the source table should be joined to the target table.

- For any rows common to both the target and source tables, the when matched clause describes how the rows in the target table should be modified.

- For any rows in the source table but not in the target table, the when not matched clause describes how rows should be inserted.

- The when clauses are evaluated from top to bottom, so matching rows will be deleted if the remove column = yes and updated otherwise.

After the statement has executed, Snowflake responds with the number of rows inserted, updated, and deleted. Here's what the Person table looks like after the merge statement:

```
PUBLIC>select first_name, last_name, birth_date,
        eye_color, occupation
        from person;
+------------+-----------+------------+-----------+------------+
| FIRST_NAME | LAST_NAME | BIRTH_DATE | EYE_COLOR | OCCUPATION |
|------------+-----------+------------+-----------+------------|
| Carl       | Langford  | 2001-06-16 | blue      | tailor     |
| Gina       | Peters    | 2001-03-03 | brown     | student    |
| Tim        | Carpenter | 2002-07-09 | green     | salesman   |
| Bob        | Smith     | 2000-01-22 | blue      | manager    |
+------------+-----------+------------+-----------+------------+
```

As you can see, Kathy Little and Sharon Carpenter have been removed, Carl Langford has been added, and the appropriate changes were made to Gina, Tim, and Bob's data.

Wrap-Up

This chapter covered topics that are central to relational databases: namely, the types of data that can be stored, how to create tables, and how to add, delete, and modify data in tables. Chapter 6 will expand upon the topics in this chapter by investigating many of the ways that you can generate, convert, and manipulate data.

Test Your Knowledge

The following exercises are designed to strengthen your understanding of how to create and modify data. Please see "Chapter 5" in Appendix B for solutions.

Exercise 5-1

Write a query that returns the string 'you can't always get what you want'.

Exercise 5-2

Write a query that returns an array containing the number 985, the string 'hello there', and the boolean value true.

Exercise 5-3

Write a query that uses the array generated in Exercise 5-2 as an input, and then flattens the array into three rows.

Exercise 5-4

Given the following data for the Pet_Owner and Pet tables, write an update statement that sets the Pet.Owner column to the name of the associated owner in the Pet_Owner.Owner_Name column:

```
Pet_Owner                     Pet
+----------+------------+     +--------+----------+----------+-------+
| OWNER_ID | OWNER_NAME |     | PET_ID | OWNER_ID | PET_NAME | OWNER |
|----------+------------|     +--------+----------+----------+-------+
|        1 | John       |     |    101 |        1 | Fluffy   | NULL  |
|        2 | Cindy      |     |    102 |        3 | Spot     | NULL  |
|        3 | Laura      |     |    103 |        4 | Rover    | NULL  |
|        4 | Mark       |     |    104 |     NULL | Rosco    | NULL  |
+----------+------------+     +--------+----------+----------+-------+
```

Data Generation, Conversion, and Manipulation

In Chapter 5, you learned about the different data types available in Snowflake, including numeric, temporal, and character. This chapter will explore Snowflake's many built-in functions used to generate, convert, and manipulate values for these data types.

Working with Character Data

Snowflake includes a wide array of functions used for handling character data, whether you need to concatenate strings, search for substrings, change to upper- or lowercase, or do just about anything else.

String Generation and Manipulation

Creating a string literal is a simple matter of enclosing your string in single quotes:

```
PUBLIC>select 'here is my string';
+--------------------+
| 'HERE IS MY STRING' |
|--------------------|
| here is my string  |
+--------------------+
```

If you have two strings that you want to concatenate, you can choose between using the || operator, or using the built-in concat() function:

```
PUBLIC>select 'string 1' || ' and ' || 'string2';
+-----------------------------------------
| 'STRING 1' || ' AND ' || 'STRING2' |
|-----------------------------------------|
| string 1 and string2                |
+-----------------------------------------+

PUBLIC>select concat('string1',' and ','string2');
+-----------------------------------------+
| CONCAT('STRING1',' AND ','STRING2') |
|-----------------------------------------|
| string1 and string2                 |
+-----------------------------------------+
```

If you need to include a character that doesn't appear on your keyboard, you can use the char() function if you know the character's ASCII value. For example, if you want to disclose how many euros you spent on a trip to Paris, you could do the following:

```
PUBLIC>select concat('I spent ',char(8364),'357 in Paris');
+-----------------------------------------------+
| CONCAT('I SPENT ',CHAR(8364),'357 IN PARIS') |
|-----------------------------------------------|
| I spent €357 in Paris                        |
+-----------------------------------------------+
```

There are also functions for changing a string to all lowercase, all uppercase, or uppercase for the first character of each word:

```
PUBLIC>select upper(str.val), lower(str.val), initcap(str.val)
       from (values ('which case is best?'))
         as str(val);
+--------------------+---------------------+--------------------+
| UPPER(STR.VAL)     | LOWER(STR.VAL)      | INITCAP(STR.VAL)   |
|--------------------+---------------------+--------------------|
| WHICH CASE IS BEST? | which case is best? | Which Case Is Best?|
+--------------------+---------------------+--------------------+
```

There's even a function to reverse the characters of a string:

```
PUBLIC>select reverse('?siht daer uoy nac');
+------------------------------+
| REVERSE( '?SIHT DAER UOY NAC') |
|------------------------------|
| can you read this?           |
+------------------------------+
```

Another common need is the removal of spaces from the beginning or ending of a string, or from both ends:

```
PUBLIC>select ltrim(str.val), rtrim(str.val), trim(str.val)
       from (values ('   abc   ')) as str(val);
+----------------+----------------+----------------+
| LTRIM(STR.VAL) | RTRIM(STR.VAL) | TRIM(STR.VAL) |
|----------------+----------------+----------------|
| abc            |    abc         | abc            |
+----------------+----------------+----------------+
```

While it can be difficult to tell by looking, the length() function can be used to show
that the ltrim() and trim() functions are returning different strings:

```
PUBLIC>select length(ltrim(str.val)) as str1_len,
       length(rtrim(str.val)) as str2_len,
       length(trim(str.val)) as str3_len
       from (values ('   abc   ')) as str(val);
+----------+----------+----------+
| STR1_LEN | STR2_LEN | STR3_LEN |
|----------+----------+----------|
|        7 |        7 |        3 |
+----------+----------+----------+
```

If you want to make sure that certain characters don't appear in a string, you can use
the translate() function to replace them with an empty string. For example, here's a
way to remove any formatting characters from a string containing a phone number:

```
PUBLIC>select translate('(857)-234-5678','()-','');
+------------------------------------+
| TRANSLATE('(857)-234-5678','()-','') |
|------------------------------------|
| 8572345678                         |
+------------------------------------+
```

Here's another example using the translate() function, this time to replace a set of
characters with a different set:

```
PUBLIC>select translate('AxByCz','ABC','XYZ');
+-------------------------------+
| TRANSLATE('AXBYCZ','ABC','XYZ') |
|-------------------------------|
| XxYyZz                        |
+-------------------------------+
```

The next section demonstrates other ways to find and replace or extract a set of
characters.

String Searching and Extracting

To find the position of a substring within a string, you can use the position() function, which returns the position at which the substring is found, or else 0 if the substring isn't found. Additionally, you can specify an optional starting position if you

don't want the search to start at the first character. Here's an example showing multiple uses of the `position()` function:

```
PUBLIC>select position('here',str.val) as pos1,
         position('here',str.val,10) as pos2,
         position('nowhere',str.val) as pos3
      from (values ('here, there, and everywhere')) as str(val);
+------+------+------+
| POS1 | POS2 | POS3 |
|------+------+------|
|    1 |   24 |    0 |
+------+------+------+
```

The substring `'here'` can be found at positions 1, 8, and 24, but the second call to `position()` specifies that the search start at position 10, which is why the function returns 24.

If you only want part of a string, you can use the `substr()` function, which takes a string, a starting position, and an optional number of characters:

```
PUBLIC>select substr(str.val, 1, 10) as start_of_string,
         substr(str.val, 11) as rest_of_string
      from (values ('beginning ending')) as str(val);
+-----------------+----------------+
| START_OF_STRING | REST_OF_STRING |
|-----------------+----------------|
| beginning       | ending         |
+-----------------+----------------+
```

The first call to `substr()` asks for the first 10 characters of the string, whereas the second call asks for the remainder of the string starting at the 11th character. You can also use the `position()` function as a parameter to the `substr()` function to determine the starting position, as in the following example:

```
PUBLIC>select substr(str.val, position('every',str.val))
      from (values ('here, there, and everywhere'))
         as str(val);
+----------------------------------------+
| SUBSTR(STR.VAL, POSITION('EVERY',STR.VAL)) |
|----------------------------------------|
| everywhere                             |
+----------------------------------------+
```

In this example, the `position()` function returns the value 18, and the `substr()` function then returns all characters starting at position 18.

Snowflake also has several functions that return a `boolean` value rather than a numeric position, which can be useful for filter conditions:

```
PUBLIC>select str.val
      from (values ('here, there, and everywhere')) as str(val)
         where startswith(str.val,'here');
```

```
+---------------------------+
| VAL                       |
|---------------------------|
| here, there, and everywhere |
+---------------------------+

PUBLIC>select str.val
       from (values ('here, there, and everywhere')) as str(val)
       where endswith(str.val,'where');
+---------------------------+
| VAL                       |
|---------------------------|
| here, there, and everywhere |
+---------------------------+

PUBLIC>select str.val
       from (values ('here, there, and everywhere')) as str(val)
       where contains(str.val,'there');
+---------------------------+
| VAL                       |
|---------------------------|
| here, there, and everywhere |
+---------------------------+
```

These examples show how you can determine if a string starts with, ends with, or contains a substring at any position.

Working with Numeric Data

Generating numeric data is fairly straightforward; you can type a number, retrieve a number from a column in a table, or use any of the arithmetic operators +, -, *, or / to perform calculations:

```
PUBLIC>select 10 as radius, 2 * 3.14159 * 10 as circumference;
+--------+---------------+
| RADIUS | CIRCUMFERENCE |
|--------+---------------|
|     10 |      62.83180 |
+--------+---------------+
```

You can also use parentheses in order to dictate calculation precedence:

```
PUBLIC>select (3 * 6) - (10 / 2);
+--------------------+
| (3 * 6) - (10 / 2) |
|--------------------|
|          13.000000 |
+--------------------+
```

For more complicated calculations, you will want to become familiar with the many built-in numeric functions available in Snowflake, some of which are demonstrated in the next section.

Numeric Functions

An earlier example showed the calculation of a circle's circumference, but if you also want to calculate the area (πr^2), you can use the power() function:

```
PUBLIC>select 10 as radius, 2 * 3.14159 * 10 as circumference,
       3.14159 * power(10,2) as area;
+--------+---------------+---------+
| RADIUS | CIRCUMFERENCE |    AREA |
|--------+---------------+---------|
|     10 |      62.83180 | 314.159 |
+--------+---------------+---------+
```

There is also a handy pi() function so you don't have to look up the value of π:

```
PUBLIC>select 10 as radius, 2 * 3.14159 * 10 as circumference,
       pi() * power(10,2) as area;
+--------+---------------+----------------+
| RADIUS | CIRCUMFERENCE |           AREA |
|--------+---------------+----------------|
|     10 |      62.83180 |    314.159265359 |
+--------+---------------+----------------+
```

If you need to calculate the remainder when one number is divided into another, you can use the mod() function:

```
PUBLIC>select mod(70, 9);
+------------+
| MOD(70, 9) |
|------------|
|          7 |
+------------+
```

When dealing with numbers that can be either negative or positive, you may want to use the sign() function to determine whether a number is negative (–1), zero (0), or positive (+1), and you can also use the abs() function to return the absolute value:

```
PUBLIC>select sign(-7.5233), abs(-7.5233);
+---------------+--------------+
| SIGN(-7.5233) | ABS(-7.5233) |
|---------------+--------------|
|            -1 |       7.5233 |
+---------------+--------------+
```

Finally, when dealing with noninteger values (real numbers), there are functions that can be used to remove the decimal portion (trunc()), round up to the nearest value (round()), or round to the nearest lower or higher integer (floor() and ceil()):

```
PUBLIC>select trunc(6.49), round(6.49, 1),
       floor(6.49), ceil(6.49);
+-------------+----------------+-------------+------------+
| TRUNC(6.49) | ROUND(6.49, 1) | FLOOR(6.49) | CEIL(6.49) |
|-------------+----------------+-------------+------------|
```

```
|            6 |          6.5 |        6 |        7 |
+-------------+--------------+----------+----------+
```

There are also a set of *aggregate functions*, which are performed across a set of numeric values and are used to compute averages, medians, and standard deviations, among other things. Aggregate functions will be covered in Chapter 7.

Numeric Conversion

If you need to convert a string to a number, there are several strategies: *explicit* conversion, where you specify that the string be converted to a number, and *implicit* conversion (also known as *coercion*), where Snowflake sees the need for the conversion and attempts to do so. Let's start with an example of implicit conversion:

```
PUBLIC>select 123.45 as real_num
       union
       select '678.90' as real_num;
+----------+
| REAL_NUM |
|----------|
|   123.45 |
|   678.90 |
+----------+
```

In this example, the first query defines the data type of real_num to be number, which necessitates the server to attempt to convert the string in the second query to type number as well. In this case, the conversion was a success, but if you recall from Chapter 4 (see "The union Operator" on page 60), Snowflake will throw an error if the conversion fails:

```
PUBLIC>select 123.45 as real_num
       union
       select 'AAA.BB' as real_num;
100038 (22018): Numeric value 'AAA.BB' is not recognized
```

Rather than leaving it up to Snowflake, you can explicitly request a data conversion using one of the following:

- The cast() function
- The cast operator ::
- A specific conversion function such as to_decimal()

Here's an example using all three options to convert a string into a decimal value of type number(7,2):

```
PUBLIC>select cast(str.val as number(7,2)) as cast_val,
          str.val::number(7,2) as cast_opr_val,
          to_decimal(str.val,7,2) as to_dec_val
       from (values ('15873.26')) as str(val);
```

```
+----------+---------------+------------+
| CAST_VAL | CAST_OPR_VAL | TO_DEC_VAL |
|----------+---------------+------------|
| 15873.26 |      15873.26 |   15873.26 |
+----------+---------------+------------+
```

All three conversions were successful in this case, but if `str.val` includes any nonnumeric characters, all three would fail:

```
PUBLIC>select cast(str.val as number(7,2)) as cast_val,
       str.val::number(7,2) as cast_opr_val,
       to_decimal(str.val,7,2) as to_dec_val
    from (values ('$15873.26')) as str(val);
100038 (22018): Numeric value '$15873.26' is not recognized
```

The change from the prior example is the addition of a dollar sign ($) to the beginning of `str.val`. While $ is indeed a nonnumeric character, it is actually quite common for a numeric string to include nonnumeric characters such as $, €, £, or parentheses surrounding the number to indicate a negative value. The `to_decimal()` function luckily includes an optional *formatting string*:

```
PUBLIC>select to_decimal(str.val,'$99999.99',7,2) as to_dec_val
            from (values ('$15873.26')) as str(val);
+------------+
| TO_DEC_VAL |
|------------|
|   15873.26 |
+------------+
```

In this example, the formatting string specifies that the string should consist of a dollar sign followed by five numbers followed by a decimal point followed by two more numbers. If you want to test the conversion of a string before actually doing so, you can use the `try_to_decimal()` function, which returns `null` if the conversion fails but does *not* throw an error:

```
PUBLIC>select try_to_decimal(str.val,'$99999.99',7,2) as good,
           try_to_decimal(str.val,'999.9',4,2) as bad
        from (values ('$15873.26')) as str(val);
+----------+------+
|     GOOD | BAD  |
|----------+------|
| 15873.26 | NULL |
+----------+------+
```

The first conversion succeeds and returns the converted value, whereas the second conversion fails and returns `null`.

Number Generation

For situations when you need to generate a set of numbers, such as for fabricating test data, Snowflake provides a number of handy built-in functions. The first step involves a call to the `generator()` function, which is a *table function* used to generate rows of data. Table functions are called in the `from` clause of a query and will be covered in Chapter 17, so for now just think of `generator()` as a function that returns a configurable number of rows. Here's an example that asks `generator()` to return five rows, and then calls the `random()` function to generate a random number for each row:

```
PUBLIC>select random()
        from table(generator(rowcount => 5));

+----------------------+
|             RANDOM() |
|----------------------|
| -3677757698388611270 |
| -3592261260448828970 |
|  3109671761060067515 |
|  9164189189028838701 |
|   254977226160947522 |
+----------------------+
```

If you want a sequence of numbers rather than a random set, you can use the `seq1()` function:

```
PUBLIC>select seq1()
        from table(generator(rowcount => 5));

+--------+
| SEQ1() |
|--------|
|      0 |
|      1 |
|      2 |
|      3 |
|      4 |
+--------+
```

Generating sequences can be very handy for fabricating all types of data. Here's an example that generates date values corresponding to the first day of the month for every month in 2023:

```
PUBLIC>select to_date('01/' ||
        to_char(seq1() + 1) ||
        '/2023','DD/MM/YYYY') as first_of_month
        from table(generator(rowcount => 12));

+----------------+
| FIRST_OF_MONTH |
|----------------|
| 2023-01-01     |
| 2023-02-01     |
| 2023-03-01     |
```

```
| 2023-04-01   |
| 2023-05-01   |
| 2023-06-01   |
| 2023-07-01   |
| 2023-08-01   |
| 2023-09-01   |
| 2023-10-01   |
| 2023-11-01   |
| 2023-12-01   |
+--------------+
```

In this example, the `seq1()` function will return values from 0 to 11, so the query adds 1 to each value to get values from 1 to 12, and then uses these values to build dates for each month of the year.

Working with Temporal Data

Temporal data is the most complex of the three data types explored in this chapter, largely because there are many ways in which a date can be described. Here are some of the ways I can format the date/time on which I wrote this chapter:

- 11/03/2022
- Thursday, November 3, 2022
- 2022-11-03 15:48:56.092 -0700
- 03-NOV-2022 06:48:56 PM EST
- Stardate 76307.5 (a little humor for you Trekkies out there)

As described in "Temporal Data" on page 73, Snowflake is quite forgiving regarding dates and will apply several common *formatting strings* (except Stardates...) to try to decipher your date literals. However, you can always specify a formatting string to tell Snowflake how to interpret your date or timestamp literal:

```
PUBLIC>select to_timestamp('04-NOV-2022 18:48:56',
        'DD-MON-YYYY HH24:MI:SS') as now;
+-------------------------+
| NOW                     |
|-------------------------|
| 2022-11-04 18:48:56.000 |
+-------------------------+
```

Notice that Snowflake uses your formatting string to interpret your timestamp literal, but it uses the format defined in parameter `timestamp_output_format` to return the timestamp, which in this case is the default setting of YYYY-MM-DD HH24:MI:SS.SSS. If you want to see the output format defined for your database, you can execute the following command:

```
PUBLIC>show parameters like 'timestamp_out%';
+------------------------+------------------------------------+...
| key                    | value                              |...
|------------------------+------------------------------------|...
| TIMESTAMP_OUTPUT_FORMAT | YYYY-MM-DD HH24:MI:SS.FF3 TZHTZM    |...
+------------------------+------------------------------------+...
```

You can use the `alter session` command to change the output format to whatever suits you:

```
PUBLIC>alter session set timestamp_output_format =
       'MM/DD/YYYY HH12:MI:SS AM TZH';
+-------------------------------+
| status                        |
|-------------------------------|
| Statement executed successfully. |
+-------------------------------+

PUBLIC>select current_timestamp;
+----------------------------+
| CURRENT_TIMESTAMP          |
|----------------------------|
| 11/03/2022 04:42:47 PM -0700 |
+----------------------------+
```

The next section describes other ways to generate date values.

Date and Timestamp Generation

When you need to generate a temporal value, you can provide a date literal and hope that Snowflake figures it out (via implicit conversion); you can supply a formatting string; or you can use one of the built-in functions to generate a date, time, or timestamp value. Here's an example showing how to use the `date_from_parts()` and `time_from_parts()` functions:

```
PUBLIC>select date_from_parts(2023, 3, 15) as my_date,
       time_from_parts(10, 22, 47) as my_time;
+------------+----------+
| MY_DATE    | MY_TIME  |
|------------+----------|
| 2023-03-15 | 10:22:47 |
+------------+----------+
```

For both functions, no formatting string is needed, because you specify the date/time components in a specified order (year/month/day for a date, hour/minute/second for a time). There is also a `timestamp_from_parts()` function, and it allows several different options, one of which is passing in calls from the `date_from_parts()` and `time_from_parts()` functions:

```
PUBLIC>select timestamp_from_parts(
       date_from_parts(2023, 3, 15),
```

```
        time_from_parts(10, 22, 47)) as my_timestamp;
+--------------------------+
| MY_TIMESTAMP             |
|--------------------------|
| 2023-03-15 10:22:47.000  |
+--------------------------+
```

The `date_from_parts()` function also allows zero or negative numbers for month or day, which allows you to move backward in time. Specifying 0 for the day value will move backward one day, specifying –1 day will move backward two days, etc. This is handy for finding month end dates without having to remember which months have 30 days and which have 31:

```
PUBLIC>select date_from_parts(2024, seq1() + 2, 0) as month_end
        from table(generator(rowcount => 12));
+------------+
| MONTH_END  |
|------------|
| 2024-01-31 |
| 2024-02-29 |
| 2024-03-31 |
| 2024-04-30 |
| 2024-05-31 |
| 2024-06-30 |
| 2024-07-31 |
| 2024-08-31 |
| 2024-09-30 |
| 2024-10-31 |
| 2024-11-30 |
| 2024-12-31 |
+------------+
```

This query generates numbers from 0 to 11 using the `generator()` and `seq1()` functions, adds 2 to each number to specify a month, and specifies 0 days to move back one day, resulting in the month end dates for every month in 2024. If you look at the second row of the result set, you can see that Snowflake figured out that 2024 is a leap year and returned February 29th.

Manipulating Dates and Timestamps

The following sections describe temporal functions that return dates, strings, and numbers.

Temporal functions that return dates

Snowflake has several built-in functions that accept one date value as a parameter and return a different date value. For example, you might retrieve a date from a column and then determine the beginning of the month, quarter, or year associated with that date. For these types of operations, you can use the `date_trunc()` function:

```
PUBLIC>select date_trunc('YEAR',dt.val) as start_of_year,
        date_trunc('MONTH',dt.val) as start_of_month,
        date_trunc('QUARTER',dt.val) as start_of_quarter
    from (values (to_date('26-MAY-2023','DD-MON-YYYY')))
        as dt(val);

+---------------+----------------+------------------+
| START_OF_YEAR | START_OF_MONTH | START_OF_QUARTER |
|---------------+----------------+------------------|
| 2023-01-01    | 2023-05-01     | 2023-04-01       |
+---------------+----------------+------------------+
```

While `date_trunc()` will move a date value backward, there are other occasions where you want to move forward. For example, the `dateadd()` function allows one or more increments of a given unit of time (such as day, month, year, hour, or minute) to be added to a date. Here's what happens when three different dates are moved forward in time by one month:

```
PUBLIC>select
        dateadd(month, 1,
            to_date('01-JAN-2024','DD-MON-YYYY')) as date1,
        dateadd(month, 1,
            to_date('15-JAN-2024','DD-MON-YYYY')) as date2,
        dateadd(month, 1,
            to_date('31-JAN-2024','DD-MON-YYYY')) as date3;
+------------+------------+------------+
| DATE1      | DATE2      | DATE3      |
|------------+------------+------------|
| 2024-02-01 | 2024-02-15 | 2024-02-29 |
+------------+------------+------------+
```

In this example, one month is added to three different dates, all of which are in January of 2024. The first two yield predictable results, but the third (`date3`) merits discussion: moving the date January 31, 2024, ahead by one month results in February 29, 2024, which is exactly one month in the future but is only 29 days. Therefore, the unit of time (a month in this case) can be somewhat fluid depending on the situation. Here's another example, this time moving backward in time by one year:

```
PUBLIC>select dateadd(year, -1,
        to_date('29-FEB-2024','DD-MON-YYYY')) new_date;
+------------+
| NEW_DATE   |
|------------|
| 2023-02-28 |
+------------+
```

In this case, moving backward from February 29, 2024, yields the value February 28, 2023, which is correct since 2024 is a leap year but 2023 is not.

Temporal functions that return strings

If you need to extract the name of a month or the day of the week, you can use the dayname() and monthname() functions:

```
PUBLIC>select dayname(current_date), monthname(current_date);
+-----------------------+-------------------------+
| DAYNAME(CURRENT_DATE) | MONTHNAME(CURRENT_DATE) |
|-----------------------+-------------------------|
| Sun                   | Nov                     |
+-----------------------+-------------------------+
```

Snowflake is rather light on functionality for extracting strings from dates, but the next section demonstrates several functions used to extract numeric values from dates.

Temporal functions that return numbers

The date_part() function can be used to extract various units of time. Here's an example that extracts the year, quarter, month, and week numbers for a given date:

```
PUBLIC>select date_part(year, dt.val) as year_num,
        date_part(quarter, dt.val) as qtr_num,
        date_part(month, dt.val) as month_num,
        date_part(week, dt.val) as week_num
    from (values(to_date('24-APR-2023','DD-MON-YYYY')))
        as dt(val);
+----------+---------+-----------+----------+
| YEAR_NUM | QTR_NUM | MONTH_NUM | WEEK_NUM |
|----------+---------+-----------+----------|
|     2023 |       2 |         4 |       17 |
+----------+---------+-----------+----------+
```

You can also extract hours, minutes, seconds, and partial seconds when working with a time or timestamp value:

```
PUBLIC>select date_part(hour, dt.val) as hour_num,
        date_part(minute, dt.val) as min_num,
        date_part(second, dt.val) as sec_num,
        date_part(nanosecond, dt.val) as nsec_num
    from (values(current_timestamp)) as dt(val);
+----------+---------+---------+----------+
| HOUR_NUM | MIN_NUM | SEC_NUM | NSEC_NUM |
|----------+---------+---------+----------|
|       18 |      33 |       9 | 87000000 |
+----------+---------+---------+----------+
```

Another function that returns a number is datediff(), which will return the number of time units (years, months, days, hours, etc.) between two different date values. Here's an example using two dates slightly more than one year apart:

```
PUBLIC>select datediff(year, dt.val1, dt.val2) num_years,
        datediff(month, dt.val1, dt.val2) num_months,
```

```
        datediff(day, dt.val1, dt.val2) num_days,
        datediff(hour, dt.val1, dt.val2) num_hours
    from (values (to_date('12-FEB-2022','DD-MON-YYYY'),
        to_date('06-MAR-2023','DD-MON-YYYY'))) as dt(val1, val2);
+-----------+------------+----------+----------+
| NUM_YEARS | NUM_MONTHS | NUM_DAYS | NUM_HOURS |
|-----------+------------+----------+----------|
|         1 |         13 |      387 |     9288 |
+-----------+------------+----------+----------+
```

The `datediff()` function returns an integer, so the value returned is approximate when asking for the number of years or months. The return value can be negative, however, as shown by the next example, which simply reverses the order of the dates from the previous example:

```
PUBLIC>select datediff(year, dt.val1, dt.val2) num_years,
        datediff(month, dt.val1, dt.val2) num_months,
        datediff(day, dt.val1, dt.val2) num_days,
        datediff(hour, dt.val1, dt.val2) num_hours
    from (values (to_date('06-MAR-2023','DD-MON-YYYY'),
        to_date('12-FEB-2022','DD-MON-YYYY'))) as dt(val1, val2);
+-----------+------------+----------+----------+
| NUM_YEARS | NUM_MONTHS | NUM_DAYS | NUM_HOURS |
|-----------+------------+----------+----------|
|        -1 |        -13 |     -387 |    -9288 |
+-----------+------------+----------+----------+
```

If you want to know the difference between two dates without regard to whether the first date comes before or after the second date, you can always wrap the call to `date diff()` in the `abs()` function, discussed in "Numeric Functions" on page 96.

Date Conversion

Snowflake provides several different functions used to convert from one data type to another. The examples in "Working with Temporal Data" on page 100 make use of the `to_date()` function, which converts a string to a date value using a formatting string (e.g., `DD-MON-YYYY`). This same conversion can be done using the `cast()` function:

```
PUBLIC>select cast('23-SEP-2023' as date) as format1,
        cast('09/23/2023' as date) as format2,
        cast('2023-09-23' as date) as format3;
+------------+------------+------------+
| FORMAT1    | FORMAT2    | FORMAT3    |
|------------+------------+------------|
| 2023-09-23 | 2023-09-23 | 2023-09-23 |
+------------+------------+------------+
```

In this example, I am using three different formats of the same date and once again Snowflake handles all three without a problem. If your format isn't recognized, however, you will receive an error:

```
PUBLIC>select cast('09-23-2023' as date);
100040 (22007): Date '09-23-2023' is not recognized
```

If you want Snowflake to attempt the conversion without raising an error, you can use the `try_cast()` function, which will return `null` if the conversion fails:

```
PUBLIC>select try_cast('09-23-2023' as date);
+------------------------------+
| TRY_CAST('09-23-2023' AS DATE) |
|------------------------------|
| NULL                         |
+------------------------------+
```

The `cast()` function can also be used to convert a string to a number, or to convert from a real number to an integer:

```
PUBLIC>select cast('123.456' as number(6,3)),
       cast(123.456 as integer);
+----------------------------+--------------------------+
| CAST('123.456' AS NUMBER(6,3)) | CAST(123.456 AS INTEGER) |
|----------------------------+--------------------------|
|                    123.456 |                      123 |
+----------------------------+--------------------------+
```

You can also choose to use the `::` operator instead of calling the `cast()` function:

```
PUBLIC>select '09/23/2023'::date date_val,
       '23-SEP-2023'::timestamp tmstmp_val,
       '123.456'::number(6,3) num_val;
+------------+-------------------------+---------+
| DATE_VAL   | TMSTMP_VAL              | NUM_VAL |
|------------+-------------------------+---------|
| 2023-09-23 | 2023-09-23 00:00:00.000 | 123.456 |
+------------+-------------------------+---------+
```

This is certainly the simplest way to convert values, and I will use it for any examples in later chapters that require conversions. The only downside to using `::` is that there is no "try" version similar to `try_cast()`, so if the conversion fails you will receive an error.

Wrap-Up

This chapter explored some of Snowflake's built-in functions for generating, converting, and manipulating data, covering character, numeric, and temporal data. For a complete up-to-date listing of available functions, please check out Snowflake's online documentation page (*https://oreil.ly/miCUa*).

Test Your Knowledge

The following exercises are designed to help you gain familiarity with some of Snowflake's built-in functions. Please see "Chapter 6" in Appendix B for solutions.

Exercise 6-1

Write a query that uses a function to alter the string 'cow it maked dende' by changing all occurrences of c to n, and all occurrences of d to s.

Exercise 6-2

Write a query that returns the numbers 1 through 10, one per row.

Exercise 6-3

Write a query that returns the number of days between the dates 01-JAN-2024 and 15-AUG-2025.

Exercise 6-4

Write a query that sums the numeric year, month, and day for the date 27-SEP-2025.

Grouping and Aggregates

Databases must store data at the lowest level of granularity needed for any particular operation. For example, the Snowflake sample database stores data about customer orders, which is needed for business operations such as billing and inventory management. However, you can opt to work with the data at higher levels, such as yearly sales per region, which would be helpful for other parts of the business such as marketing and sales. This chapter discusses the ways that data in a Snowflake database can be grouped together to meet various types of business needs.

Grouping Concepts

Let's say you were asked by the vice president of the marketing department to help with a special promotion to reward the best customers with 25% off their next order. This promotion will be for customers who have spent $1,800,000 or more or who have placed eight or more orders. Your job is to determine which customers will be eligible for the promotion.

The sample database has 115,269 orders, so you certainly don't want to read through all the data at that level of granularity. What you need to do is group the orders together by customer, then count the number of orders, and sum the total price of the orders. This can be achieved using the group by clause, which is used to group rows together using common values of one or more columns. Here's the first step in generating the data for the VP of marketing:

```
PUBLIC>select o_custkey
       from orders
       group by o_custkey;
+-----------+
| O_CUSTKEY |
|-----------|
|     51871 |
```

```
|     21319 |
|    149809 |
|     86845 |
|     78139 |
|     91106 |
|    123931 |
|     98794 |
|    122431 |
|     43975 |
... <66,066 rows omitted>
+-----------+
```

This query has returned 66,076 rows, which is the number of distinct custkey values on the Orders table. This is an improvement over looking through all 115,000 orders, but not by much. The next step is to count the number of orders and sum the total price of all orders for each customer. This can be accomplished by using the *aggregate functions* sum() and count(), which will be applied to all the rows within each group:

```
PUBLIC>select o_custkey,
         sum(o_totalprice) as total_sales,
         count(*) as number_of_orders
       from orders
       group by o_custkey;
+-----------+-------------+------------------+
| O_CUSTKEY | TOTAL_SALES | NUMBER_OF_ORDERS |
|-----------+-------------+------------------|
|    105646 |   282919.39 |                1 |
|     98555 |    47051.78 |                1 |
|     77194 |   693070.56 |                3 |
|     49132 |   257591.91 |                1 |
|    123553 |   215344.46 |                1 |
|    141986 |   248067.81 |                2 |
|    146348 |   104584.65 |                1 |
|    139328 |   481518.67 |                2 |
|     69016 |   220241.55 |                1 |
|     70753 |   124905.42 |                1 |
... <66,066 rows omitted>
+-----------+-------------+------------------+
```

The second column, total_sales, sums the totalprice column for all rows having the same custkey value, and the third column, number_of_orders, counts the number of rows having the same custkey value. Therefore, we know that the customer with the custkey value 77194 placed a total of three orders with a total price of over $693,070. This is the information we need, but the query is still returning far too many rows to be useful.

The last step needed to find the top customers is to filter out any rows with total sales of less than $1,800,000 or with a number of orders less than eight. Filtering is typically done in the where clause, as you learned in Chapter 2, but this type of filtering is done on values *after* the data has been grouped, which occurs after any conditions in the `where` clause have already been evaluated. Filtering on grouped data needs to be done in the `having` clause, which can only be used for queries including a `group by` clause. Here's the previous query with the addition of a `having` clause to help find the top customers:

```
PUBLIC>select o_custkey,
           sum(o_totalprice) as total_sales,
           count(*) as number_of_orders
        from orders
        group by o_custkey
        having sum(o_totalprice) >= 1800000
           or count(*) >= 8;
+------------+--------------+-------------------+
| O_CUSTKEY  | TOTAL_SALES  | NUMBER_OF_ORDERS  |
|------------+--------------+-------------------|
|      66103 |   1846159.58 |                 8 |
|      19942 |   1482217.71 |                 8 |
|     141352 |   1583313.81 |                 8 |
|      64804 |   1422490.86 |                 8 |
|      41581 |   1585564.71 |                 8 |
|      50542 |   1261984.14 |                 8 |
|      45088 |   1744140.58 |                 8 |
|       7033 |   1749076.08 |                 8 |
|       7597 |    957698.37 |                 8 |
|      37825 |   1696570.50 |                 9 |
|      97156 |   1406682.16 |                 8 |
|     120202 |   1870539.99 |                 8 |
|      36316 |   1826901.18 |                 8 |
|       7693 |   1300612.14 |                 8 |
|     119674 |   1391170.52 |                 8 |
|     121909 |   1610405.31 |                 8 |
+------------+--------------+-------------------+
```

You now have the data needed by the marketing department, and a total of 16 customers will be eligible for the promotion. Generating these results required a `group by` clause, the `sum()` and `count()` aggregate functions, and a `having` clause, all of which will be explored further in the following sections.

Aggregate Functions

Aggregate functions perform a specific operation across all rows within a group, such as counting the number of rows, summing numeric fields, or calculating averages. If your query does not include a `group by` clause, there is still a group, but it just happens to contain all of the rows in the result set. Here's an example with several aggregate functions operating on all rows in the `Orders` table:

```
PUBLIC>select count(*) as num_orders,
           min(o_totalprice) as min_price,
           max(o_totalprice) as max_price,
```

```
      avg(o_totalprice) as avg_price
    from orders;
+------------+-----------+-----------+-------------------+
| NUM_ORDERS | MIN_PRICE | MAX_PRICE |         AVG_PRICE |
|------------+-----------+-----------+-------------------|
|     115269 |    885.75 | 555285.16 | 187845.84979500 |
+------------+-----------+-----------+-------------------+
```

This query counts the number of orders and determines the minimum, maximum, and average `totalprice` value across all rows in the table. Let's say you want to extend this query to show the same calculations for each year rather than across the entire table:

```
PUBLIC>select date_part(year, o_orderdate) as order_year,
       count(*) as num_orders,
       min(o_totalprice) as min_price,
       max(o_totalprice) as max_price,
       avg(o_totalprice) as avg_price
    from orders;
000979 (42601): SQL compilation error:
[ORDERS.O_ORDERDATE] is not a valid group by expression
```

The problem here is that there is still only a single group (the entire table), and `date_part()` is not an aggregate function that can be applied to all rows in the group. The solution is to explicitly specify that the data should be grouped by year:

```
PUBLIC>select date_part(year, o_orderdate) as order_year,
       count(*) as num_orders,
       min(o_totalprice) as min_price,
       max(o_totalprice) as max_price,
       avg(o_totalprice) as avg_price
    from orders
    group by date_part(year, o_orderdate);
+------------+------------+-----------+-----------+---------------+
| ORDER_YEAR | NUM_ORDERS | MIN_PRICE | MAX_PRICE |     AVG_PRICE |
|------------+------------+-----------+-----------+---------------|
|       1997 |      17408 |    992.28 | 471220.08 | 186987.97800 |
|       1998 |      10190 |   1059.39 | 502742.76 | 188929.97532 |
|       1995 |      17637 |    885.75 | 499753.01 | 188100.11965 |
|       1994 |      17479 |   1021.55 | 489099.53 | 187566.44502 |
|       1992 |      17506 |   1087.90 | 555285.16 | 189062.87926 |
|       1993 |      17392 |    946.60 | 460118.47 | 188041.41387 |
|       1996 |      17657 |   1036.89 | 498599.91 | 186689.32167 |
+------------+------------+-----------+-----------+---------------+
```

The thing to keep in mind is that it is fine to use aggregate functions without a `group by` clause as long as you are applying the functions across every row in the result set. Otherwise, you will need a `group by` clause that includes all columns other than the aggregate functions from your `select` clause. The following sections describe many of the commonly used aggregate functions.

count() Function

Counting the number of rows belonging to each group is a very common operation, and you've already seen several examples in this chapter. However, there are a couple of variations that are worth discussing, the first being the combination of the count() function with the distinct operator:

```
PUBLIC>select count(*) as total_orders,
         count(distinct o_custkey) as num_customers,
         count(distinct date_part(year, o_orderdate)) as num_years
     from orders;
+--------------+---------------+-----------+
| TOTAL_ORDERS | NUM_CUSTOMERS | NUM_YEARS |
|--------------+---------------+-----------|
|       115269 |         66076 |         7 |
+--------------+---------------+-----------+
```

This query counts the total number of rows in the Orders table, just as before, but the next two columns count only the number of *distinct* values of custkey and the year portion of orderdate. The results tell us that 66,076 different customers placed a total of 115,269 orders over a period of seven years.

Another useful variation of the count() function is count_if(), which will count the number of rows for which a given condition evaluates as true. For example, let's say you want to count the number of orders placed in 1992 and 1995, with two columns in a single row rather than a row for each year:

```
PUBLIC>select
         count_if(1992 = date_part(year, o_orderdate)) num_1992,
         count_if(1995 = date_part(year, o_orderdate)) num_1995
     from orders;
+----------+----------+
| NUM_1992 | NUM_1995 |
|----------+----------|
|    17506 |    17637 |
+----------+----------+
```

Unfortunately, there aren't similar variations of the sum(), min(), and max() functions that allow for rows to be included or excluded, but as you'll see in Chapter 10, there are other ways to inject conditional logic into your aggregate functions.

min(), max(), avg(), and sum() Functions

When you are grouping data that includes numeric columns, you will often want to find the largest or smallest value within the group, compute the average value for the group, or sum the values across all rows in the group. The max(), min(), avg(), and sum() aggregate functions are used for these purposes, and max() and min() are also often used with date columns. Here's a query that finds the date of the first and last orders for each year, along with the average and total sales per year:

```
PUBLIC>select date_part(year, o_orderdate) as year,
        min(o_orderdate) as first_order,
        max(o_orderdate) as last_order,
        avg(o_totalprice) as avg_price,
        sum(o_totalprice) as tot_sales
    from orders
    group by date_part(year, o_orderdate);
+------+-------------+-------------+-------------+----------------+
| YEAR | FIRST_ORDER | LAST_ORDER  |  AVG_PRICE  |    TOT_SALES   |
|------+-------------+-------------+-------------+----------------|
| 1997 | 1997-01-01  | 1997-12-31  | 186987.9780 | 3255086721.08  |
| 1998 | 1998-01-01  | 1998-08-02  | 188929.9753 | 1925196448.52  |
| 1995 | 1995-01-01  | 1995-12-31  | 188100.1196 | 3317521810.43  |
| 1994 | 1994-01-01  | 1994-12-31  | 187566.4450 | 3278473892.67  |
| 1992 | 1992-01-01  | 1992-12-31  | 189062.8792 | 3309734764.39  |
| 1993 | 1993-01-01  | 1993-12-31  | 188041.4138 | 3270416270.14  |
| 1996 | 1996-01-01  | 1996-12-31  | 186689.3216 | 3296373352.79  |
+------+-------------+-------------+-------------+----------------+
```

As useful as these functions are when used with group by, Chapter 14 will show how to use these and other functions with custom-made groupings (using partition by) to perform the same types of calculations without the need to group rows.

listagg() Function

If you ever need to flatten data, which is common when generating XML or JSON documents, you will find the listagg() function to be extremely valuable. Listagg() generates a delimited list of values as a single column. Here's an example showing a list of all nations associated with each region:

```
PUBLIC>select r.r_name,
        listagg(n.n_name,',')
            within group (order by n.n_name) as nation_list
    from region r inner join nation n
        on r.r_regionkey = n.n_regionkey
    group by r.r_name;
+-------------+-----------------------------------------------+
| R_NAME      | NATION_LIST                                   |
|-------------+-----------------------------------------------|
| AFRICA      | ALGERIA,ETHIOPIA,KENYA,MOROCCO,MOZAMBIQUE     |
| AMERICA     | ARGENTINA,BRAZIL,CANADA,PERU,UNITED STATES    |
| MIDDLE EAST | EGYPT,IRAN,IRAQ,JORDAN,SAUDI ARABIA           |
| ASIA        | CHINA,INDIA,INDONESIA,JAPAN,VIETNAM           |
| EUROPE      | FRANCE,GERMANY,ROMANIA,RUSSIA,UNITED KINGDOM  |
+-------------+-----------------------------------------------+
```

In this example, I am asking listagg() to generate a comma-delimited list of Nation names for each Region (via the group by r.r_name clause), and I am asking that the list of names be in sorted order by name. Thus, the order by clause within the listagg() function is specific to the function output and has no bearing on the result set generated by the query. Therefore, you can add an order by clause to the end of the query as well and sort by any column you choose:

```
PUBLIC>select r.r_name,
         listagg(n.n_name,',')
           within group (order by n.n_name) nation_list
       from region r inner join nation n
         on r.r_regionkey = n.n_regionkey
       group by r.r_name
       order by r.r_name;
+--------------+----------------------------------------------+
| R_NAME       | NATION_LIST                                  |
|--------------+----------------------------------------------|
| AFRICA       | ALGERIA,ETHIOPIA,KENYA,MOROCCO,MOZAMBIQUE    |
| AMERICA      | ARGENTINA,BRAZIL,CANADA,PERU,UNITED STATES   |
| ASIA         | CHINA,INDIA,INDONESIA,JAPAN,VIETNAM          |
| EUROPE       | FRANCE,GERMANY,ROMANIA,RUSSIA,UNITED KINGDOM |
| MIDDLE EAST  | EGYPT,IRAN,IRAQ,JORDAN,SAUDI ARABIA          |
+--------------+----------------------------------------------+
```

Now the result set is sorted by Region name, whereas the lists of nations are sorted by Nation name. If there are duplicate values in the list generated by listagg(), you can specify distinct, in which case the list will contain only the unique values.

Generating Groups

As you have seen in previous examples, the group by clause is the mechanism for grouping rows of data. In this section, you will see how to group data by multiple columns, how to group data using expressions, and how to generate rollups within groups.

Multicolumn Grouping

All of the examples thus far have grouped data on a single column, but you can group on as many columns as you wish. The next example counts the number of customers in each country and market segment for customers in the America region:

```
PUBLIC>select n.n_name, c.c_mktsegment, count(*)
       from customer c inner join nation n
         on c.c_nationkey = n.n_nationkey
       where n.n_regionkey = 1
       group by n.n_name, c.c_mktsegment
       order by 1,2;
+---------------+---------------+----------+
| N_NAME        | C_MKTSEGMENT  | COUNT(*) |
|---------------+---------------+----------|
| ARGENTINA     | AUTOMOBILE    |      521 |
| ARGENTINA     | BUILDING      |      580 |
| ARGENTINA     | FURNITURE     |      488 |
| ARGENTINA     | HOUSEHOLD     |      516 |
```

```
| ARGENTINA      | MACHINERY  |    533 |
| BRAZIL         | AUTOMOBILE |    503 |
| BRAZIL         | BUILDING   |    551 |
| BRAZIL         | FURNITURE  |    492 |
| BRAZIL         | HOUSEHOLD  |    521 |
| BRAZIL         | MACHINERY  |    547 |
| CANADA         | AUTOMOBILE |    499 |
| CANADA         | BUILDING   |    555 |
| CANADA         | FURNITURE  |    511 |
| CANADA         | HOUSEHOLD  |    544 |
| CANADA         | MACHINERY  |    522 |
| PERU           | AUTOMOBILE |    560 |
| PERU           | BUILDING   |    541 |
| PERU           | FURNITURE  |    516 |
| PERU           | HOUSEHOLD  |    538 |
| PERU           | MACHINERY  |    470 |
| UNITED STATES  | AUTOMOBILE |    514 |
| UNITED STATES  | BUILDING   |    516 |
| UNITED STATES  | FURNITURE  |    522 |
| UNITED STATES  | HOUSEHOLD  |    532 |
| UNITED STATES  | MACHINERY  |    519 |
+----------------+------------+--------+
```

There are five different market segments, and five countries belonging to the America region, so the result set contains 25 rows. Later in this chapter, you will see how to generate additional rows with subtotals for each nation and market segment.

Grouping Using Expressions

The previous example showed how you can put multiple columns in your group by clause, but you aren't limited to just columns; you can also use multiple expressions to generate groupings. For example, let's say you have been asked to run a report for the last two years of operations (1997 and 1998) showing the number of months between when orders are placed and when the parts are shipped (using the line item.l_shipdate column). To do so, you will need to use the date_part() function to extract the year value from the order date, and the datediff() function to determine the number of months between the order and ship dates:

```
PUBLIC>select date_part(year, o.o_orderdate) as year,
         datediff(month, o.o_orderdate,
           l.l_shipdate) as months_to_ship,
         count(*)
       from orders o inner join lineitem l
         on o.o_orderkey = l.l_orderkey
       where o.o_orderdate >= '01-JAN-1997'::date
       group by date_part(year, o.o_orderdate),
         datediff(month, o.o_orderdate, l.l_shipdate)
       order by 1,2;
+------+----------------+----------+
| YEAR | MONTHS_TO_SHIP | COUNT(*) |
```

```
|------+----------------+---------|
| 1997 |              0 |    2195 |
| 1997 |              1 |    4601 |
| 1997 |              2 |    4644 |
| 1997 |              3 |    4429 |
| 1997 |              4 |    2245 |
| 1997 |              5 |       2 |
| 1998 |              0 |    1295 |
| 1998 |              1 |    2602 |
| 1998 |              2 |    2628 |
| 1998 |              3 |    2724 |
| 1998 |              4 |    1356 |
| 1998 |              5 |       1 |
+------+----------------+---------+
```

While this example uses all expressions, you can use any combination of columns and expressions in your group by clause.

Group By All

Snowflake is constantly evolving, with new features being added to many server functions, including the SQL implementation. Just before this book went to print, Snowflake added the group by all option, which is a nice shortcut when grouping data using expressions. Here's the previous example using group by all:

```
PUBLIC>select date_part(year, o.o_orderdate) as year,
        datediff(month, o.o_orderdate,
          l.l_shipdate) as months_to_ship,
        count(*)
      from orders o inner join lineitem l
            on o.o_orderkey = l.l_orderkey
      where o.o_orderdate >= '01-JAN-1997'::date
      group by all
      order by 1,2;
+------+----------------+---------+
| YEAR | MONTHS_TO_SHIP | COUNT(*) |
|------+----------------+---------|
| 1997 |              0 |    2195 |
| 1997 |              1 |    4601 |
| 1997 |              2 |    4644 |
| 1997 |              3 |    4429 |
| 1997 |              4 |    2245 |
| 1997 |              5 |       2 |
| 1998 |              0 |    1295 |
| 1998 |              1 |    2602 |
| 1998 |              2 |    2628 |
| 1998 |              3 |    2724 |
| 1998 |              4 |    1356 |
| 1998 |              5 |       1 |
+------+----------------+---------+
```

With this feature, the all keyword represents everything in the select statement that is *not* an aggregate function (e.g., sum() and count()), so if your query is grouping on complex expressions such as function calls or case expressions, using group by all will save you a lot of typing.

Generating Rollups

In "Multicolumn Grouping" on page 115, I showed an example of a multicolumn grouping that counted the number of customers in each country and market segment. Here it is again:

```
PUBLIC>select n.n_name, c.c_mktsegment, count(*)
       from customer c inner join nation n
        on c.c_nationkey = n.n_nationkey
       where n.n_regionkey = 1
       group by n.n_name, c.c_mktsegment
       order by 1,2;
```

N_NAME	C_MKTSEGMENT	COUNT(*)
ARGENTINA	AUTOMOBILE	521
ARGENTINA	BUILDING	580
ARGENTINA	FURNITURE	488
ARGENTINA	HOUSEHOLD	516
ARGENTINA	MACHINERY	533
BRAZIL	AUTOMOBILE	503
BRAZIL	BUILDING	551
BRAZIL	FURNITURE	492
BRAZIL	HOUSEHOLD	521
BRAZIL	MACHINERY	547
CANADA	AUTOMOBILE	499
CANADA	BUILDING	555
CANADA	FURNITURE	511
CANADA	HOUSEHOLD	544
CANADA	MACHINERY	522
PERU	AUTOMOBILE	560
PERU	BUILDING	541
PERU	FURNITURE	516
PERU	HOUSEHOLD	538
PERU	MACHINERY	470
UNITED STATES	AUTOMOBILE	514
UNITED STATES	BUILDING	516
UNITED STATES	FURNITURE	522
UNITED STATES	HOUSEHOLD	532
UNITED STATES	MACHINERY	519

Let's say that along with the counts for each country and market segment, you also want to know the total counts for each country across *all* market segments. This can be accomplished using the `rollup` option of the `group` by clause:

```
PUBLIC>select n.n_name, c.c_mktsegment, count(*)
       from customer c inner join nation n
         on c.c_nationkey = n.n_nationkey
       where n.n_regionkey = 1
       group by rollup(n.n_name, c.c_mktsegment)
       order by 1,2;
+----------------+--------------+----------+
| N_NAME         | C_MKTSEGMENT | COUNT(*) |
|----------------+--------------+----------|
| ARGENTINA      | AUTOMOBILE   |      521 |
| ARGENTINA      | BUILDING     |      580 |
| ARGENTINA      | FURNITURE    |      488 |
| ARGENTINA      | HOUSEHOLD    |      516 |
| ARGENTINA      | MACHINERY    |      533 |
| ARGENTINA      | NULL         |     2638 |
| BRAZIL         | AUTOMOBILE   |      503 |
| BRAZIL         | BUILDING     |      551 |
| BRAZIL         | FURNITURE    |      492 |
| BRAZIL         | HOUSEHOLD    |      521 |
| BRAZIL         | MACHINERY    |      547 |
| BRAZIL         | NULL         |     2614 |
| CANADA         | AUTOMOBILE   |      499 |
| CANADA         | BUILDING     |      555 |
| CANADA         | FURNITURE    |      511 |
| CANADA         | HOUSEHOLD    |      544 |
| CANADA         | MACHINERY    |      522 |
| CANADA         | NULL         |     2631 |
| PERU           | AUTOMOBILE   |      560 |
| PERU           | BUILDING     |      541 |
| PERU           | FURNITURE    |      516 |
| PERU           | HOUSEHOLD    |      538 |
| PERU           | MACHINERY    |      470 |
| PERU           | NULL         |     2625 |
| UNITED STATES  | AUTOMOBILE   |      514 |
| UNITED STATES  | BUILDING     |      516 |
| UNITED STATES  | FURNITURE    |      522 |
| UNITED STATES  | HOUSEHOLD    |      532 |
| UNITED STATES  | MACHINERY    |      519 |
| UNITED STATES  | NULL         |     2603 |
| NULL           | NULL         |    13111 |
+----------------+--------------+----------+
```

The `rollup` option generated six additional rows: one for each country, and a final row showing the total number of rows across the entire result set. The additional rows show `null` for the column that is being rolled up. For example, the sixth row has the value `Argentina` for the first column, a `null` value for the second column, and a value of 2,638 for the third column, meaning that there are a total of 2,638 customers in Argentina across all market segments. The last row has a null value for the first and second columns and a value of 13,111 for the third column, meaning that there are a total of 13,111 customers across all nations in the America region.

This feature is designed to save you some work if you need subtotals, but what would you do if you also want subtotals for each market segment? One answer would be to use rollup but switch the order of the columns:

```
PUBLIC>select n.n_name, c.c_mktsegment, count(*)
    from customer c inner join nation n
      on c.c_nationkey = n.n_nationkey
    where n.n_regionkey = 1
    group by rollup(c.c_mktsegment, n.n_name)
    order by 1,2;
+---------------+---------------+----------+
| N_NAME        | C_MKTSEGMENT  | COUNT(*) |
|---------------+---------------+----------|
| ARGENTINA     | AUTOMOBILE    |      521 |
| ARGENTINA     | BUILDING      |      580 |
| ARGENTINA     | FURNITURE     |      488 |
| ARGENTINA     | HOUSEHOLD     |      516 |
| ARGENTINA     | MACHINERY     |      533 |
| BRAZIL        | AUTOMOBILE    |      503 |
| BRAZIL        | BUILDING      |      551 |
| BRAZIL        | FURNITURE     |      492 |
| BRAZIL        | HOUSEHOLD     |      521 |
| BRAZIL        | MACHINERY     |      547 |
| CANADA        | AUTOMOBILE    |      499 |
| CANADA        | BUILDING      |      555 |
| CANADA        | FURNITURE     |      511 |
| CANADA        | HOUSEHOLD     |      544 |
| CANADA        | MACHINERY     |      522 |
| PERU          | AUTOMOBILE    |      560 |
| PERU          | BUILDING      |      541 |
| PERU          | FURNITURE     |      516 |
| PERU          | HOUSEHOLD     |      538 |
| PERU          | MACHINERY     |      470 |
| UNITED STATES | AUTOMOBILE    |      514 |
| UNITED STATES | BUILDING      |      516 |
| UNITED STATES | FURNITURE     |      522 |
| UNITED STATES | HOUSEHOLD     |      532 |
| UNITED STATES | MACHINERY     |      519 |
| NULL          | AUTOMOBILE    |     2597 |
| NULL          | BUILDING      |     2743 |
| NULL          | FURNITURE     |     2529 |
| NULL          | HOUSEHOLD     |     2651 |
| NULL          | MACHINERY     |     2591 |
| NULL          | NULL          |    13111 |
+---------------+---------------+----------+
```

Now there are subtotals for each market segment and a final total across all rows, but the subtotals for each country are gone. If you need subtotals created for *both* columns, you can use the cube option instead of rollup:

```
PUBLIC>select n.n_name, c.c_mktsegment, count(*)
       from customer c inner join nation n
         on c.c_nationkey = n.n_nationkey
       where n.n_regionkey = 1
       group by cube(c.c_mktsegment, n.n_name)
       order by 1,2;
+----------------+--------------+----------+
| N_NAME         | C_MKTSEGMENT | COUNT(*) |
|----------------+--------------+----------|
| ARGENTINA      | AUTOMOBILE   |      521 |
| ARGENTINA      | BUILDING     |      580 |
| ARGENTINA      | FURNITURE    |      488 |
| ARGENTINA      | HOUSEHOLD    |      516 |
| ARGENTINA      | MACHINERY    |      533 |
| ARGENTINA      | NULL         |     2638 |
| BRAZIL         | AUTOMOBILE   |      503 |
| BRAZIL         | BUILDING     |      551 |
| BRAZIL         | FURNITURE    |      492 |
| BRAZIL         | HOUSEHOLD    |      521 |
| BRAZIL         | MACHINERY    |      547 |
| BRAZIL         | NULL         |     2614 |
| CANADA         | AUTOMOBILE   |      499 |
| CANADA         | BUILDING     |      555 |
| CANADA         | FURNITURE    |      511 |
| CANADA         | HOUSEHOLD    |      544 |
| CANADA         | MACHINERY    |      522 |
| CANADA         | NULL         |     2631 |
| PERU           | AUTOMOBILE   |      560 |
| PERU           | BUILDING     |      541 |
| PERU           | FURNITURE    |      516 |
| PERU           | HOUSEHOLD    |      538 |
| PERU           | MACHINERY    |      470 |
| PERU           | NULL         |     2625 |
| UNITED STATES  | AUTOMOBILE   |      514 |
| UNITED STATES  | BUILDING     |      516 |
| UNITED STATES  | FURNITURE    |      522 |
| UNITED STATES  | HOUSEHOLD    |      532 |
| UNITED STATES  | MACHINERY    |      519 |
| UNITED STATES  | NULL         |     2603 |
| NULL           | AUTOMOBILE   |     2597 |
| NULL           | BUILDING     |     2743 |
| NULL           | FURNITURE    |     2529 |
| NULL           | HOUSEHOLD    |     2651 |
| NULL           | MACHINERY    |     2591 |
| NULL           | NULL         |    13111 |
+----------------+--------------+----------+
```

There are now 11 additional rows in the result set: one for each of the five country subtotals, one for each of the market segment subtotals, and one for the totals across all countries and market segments. You can look for the null values to determine which type of subtotal is shown (a null value for country name indicates the subtotal is for a market segment, while a null value for market segment indicates a subtotal for a country), but a better option is to use the grouping() function, which returns a 0 if the associated column is included in the subtotal, and 1 if the value is not included (which is also shown by a null value for that column). Here's the previous query, but with two additional grouping() columns for country and market segment:

```
PUBLIC>select n.n_name, c.c_mktsegment, count(*),
          grouping(n.n_name) name_sub,
          grouping(c.c_mktsegment) mktseg_sub
       from customer c inner join nation n
         on c.c_nationkey = n.n_nationkey
       where n.n_regionkey = 1
       group by cube(c.c_mktsegment, n.n_name)
       order by 1,2;
```

N_NAME	C_MKTSEGMENT	COUNT(*)	NAME_SUB	MKTSEG_SUB
ARGENTINA	AUTOMOBILE	521	0	0
ARGENTINA	BUILDING	580	0	0
ARGENTINA	FURNITURE	488	0	0
ARGENTINA	HOUSEHOLD	516	0	0
ARGENTINA	MACHINERY	533	0	0
ARGENTINA	NULL	2638	0	1
BRAZIL	AUTOMOBILE	503	0	0
BRAZIL	BUILDING	551	0	0
BRAZIL	FURNITURE	492	0	0
BRAZIL	HOUSEHOLD	521	0	0
BRAZIL	MACHINERY	547	0	0
BRAZIL	NULL	2614	0	1
CANADA	AUTOMOBILE	499	0	0
CANADA	BUILDING	555	0	0
CANADA	FURNITURE	511	0	0
CANADA	HOUSEHOLD	544	0	0
CANADA	MACHINERY	522	0	0
CANADA	NULL	2631	0	1
PERU	AUTOMOBILE	560	0	0
PERU	BUILDING	541	0	0
PERU	FURNITURE	516	0	0
PERU	HOUSEHOLD	538	0	0
PERU	MACHINERY	470	0	0
PERU	NULL	2625	0	1
UNITED STATES	AUTOMOBILE	514	0	0
UNITED STATES	BUILDING	516	0	0
UNITED STATES	FURNITURE	522	0	0
UNITED STATES	HOUSEHOLD	532	0	0
UNITED STATES	MACHINERY	519	0	0

```
| UNITED STATES | NULL        |     2603 |     0 |      1|
| NULL          | AUTOMOBILE  |     2597 |     1 |      0|
| NULL          | BUILDING    |     2743 |     1 |      0|
| NULL          | FURNITURE   |     2529 |     1 |      0|
| NULL          | HOUSEHOLD   |     2651 |     1 |      0|
| NULL          | MACHINERY   |     2591 |     1 |      0|
| NULL          | NULL        |    13111 |     1 |      1|
+---------------+-------------+----------+----------+-----------+
```

If you are generating a report using this data and need to include subtotals, you now know everything you need to determine whether a row is a total across both country and market segment, just country, just market segment, or a grand total across all countries and market segments.

Filtering on Grouped Data

In some cases, you may want to group on certain columns or expressions, but you want to exclude rows that aren't of interest. For example, let's say you want to find customers who generated more than $700,000 worth of orders in 1998. The first step is to generate a group for each customer and calculate the sum of the totalprice column for each customer:

```
PUBLIC>select o_custkey, sum(o_totalprice)
       from orders
       where 1998 = date_part(year, o_orderdate)
       group by o_custkey
       order by 1;
+-----------+-------------------+
| O_CUSTKEY | SUM(O_TOTALPRICE) |
|-----------+-------------------|
|        19 |         302071.17 |
|        56 |         275833.86 |
|        58 |         299919.14 |
|        61 |         205460.32 |
|        70 |         247555.65 |
|        71 |         103723.77 |
|        82 |         169060.30 |
|       124 |         268944.99 |
|       181 |         168293.04 |
|       194 |         210880.67 |
...<10,180 rows omitted>
+-----------+-------------------+
```

None of the customers in this abbreviated result set have orders totaling more than $300,000, and you certainly wouldn't want to scan through all 10,190 customers to find them. Instead, you can add a filter condition to return all rows where the second column is >= 700,000, but this condition cannot be put into the where clause:

```
PUBLIC>select o_custkey, sum(o_totalprice)
       from orders
```

```
      where 1998 = date_part(year, o_orderdate)
        and sum(o_totalprice) >= 700000
      group by o_custkey
      order by 1;
002035 (42601): SQL compilation error:
Invalid aggregate function in where clause [SUM(O_TOTALPRICE)]
```

All grouping operations are done *after* the where clause has been evaluated, so it is not possible to include filter conditions in your where clause that contain aggregate functions. Instead, there is a special having clause specifically for this purpose:

```
PUBLIC>select o_custkey, sum(o_totalprice)
      from orders
      where 1998 = date_part(year, o_orderdate)
      group by o_custkey
      having sum(o_totalprice) >= 700000
      order by 1;
+-----------+--------------------+
| O_CUSTKEY | SUM(O_TOTALPRICE)  |
|-----------+--------------------|
|      4309 |          719354.94 |
|      5059 |          734893.37 |
|     33487 |          727194.76 |
|     65434 |         1030712.34 |
|     90608 |          727770.25 |
|    138724 |          717744.86 |
+-----------+--------------------+
```

This query now contains two different filter conditions: one in the where clause to filter on rows in the Orders table, and another in the having clause to filter on values generated after rows have been grouped by customer.

Filtering with Snowsight

In Chapter 2, I showed how to use the built-in :daterange filter when executing queries using Snowsight. Figure 7-1 shows the query from Chapter 2, which retrieves rows from the Orders table using the :daterange filter in the where clause.

By using :daterange, you can choose a different set of dates using the filter menu in the top left corner, which for this example is set to the month of March 1997. You can then change the filter value to a different date range and re-execute without needing to modify the query.

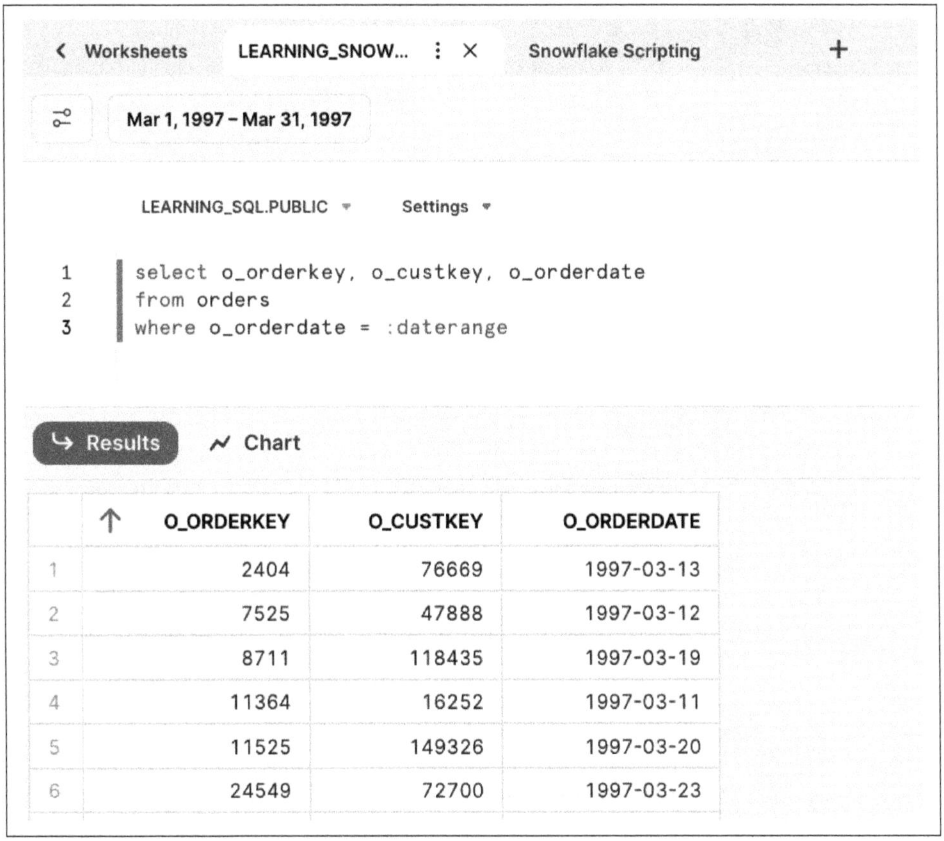

Figure 7-1. Snowsight query using :daterange filter

Snowsight also provides the :datebucket filter to use in your group by clause when grouping data. Figure 7-2 shows a query that counts the number of orders and sums the prices for data in the Orders table.

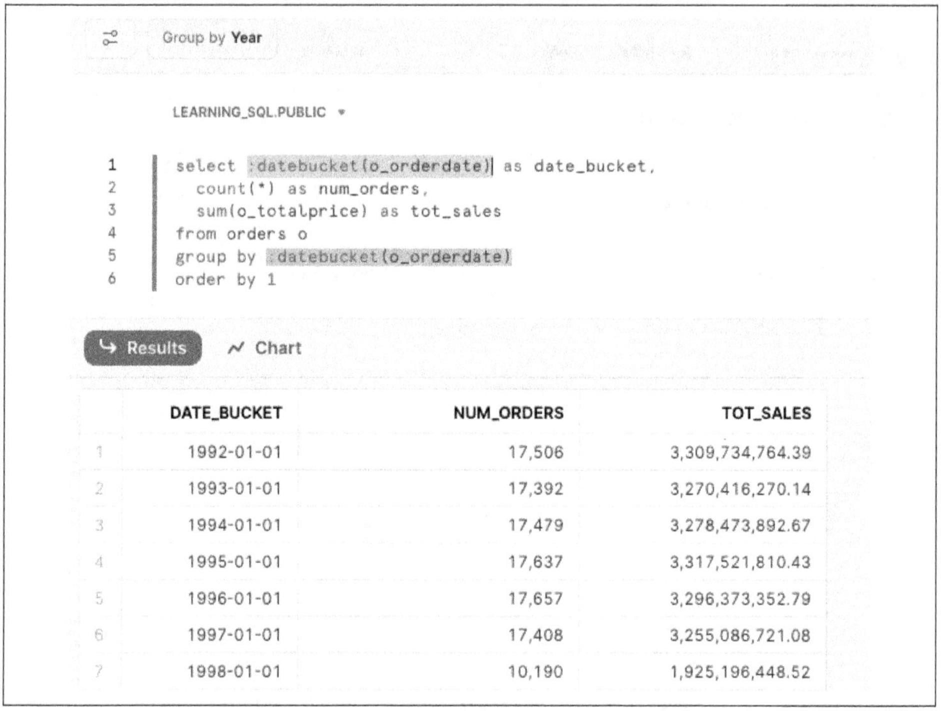

```
    Group by Year

    LEARNING_SQL.PUBLIC  ▾

1   select :datebucket(o_orderdate)| as date_bucket,
2     count(*) as num_orders,
3     sum(o_totalprice) as tot_sales
4   from orders o
5   group by :datebucket(o_orderdate)
6   order by 1
```

↳ Results   ∿ Chart

	DATE_BUCKET	NUM_ORDERS	TOT_SALES
1	1992-01-01	17,506	3,309,734,764.39
2	1993-01-01	17,392	3,270,416,270.14
3	1994-01-01	17,479	3,278,473,892.67
4	1995-01-01	17,637	3,317,521,810.43
5	1996-01-01	17,657	3,296,373,352.79
6	1997-01-01	17,408	3,255,086,721.08
7	1998-01-01	10,190	1,925,196,448.52

Figure 7-2. Snowsight query using :datebucket groupings

For this particular execution, the grouping is set to be yearly, so the result set contains seven rows: one for each year of Orders data. One difference between :datebucket and :daterange is that :datebucket will generally be included in both the select and group by clauses. If you want to change the grouping, click the "Group by" menu in the top left, as shown in Figure 7-3.

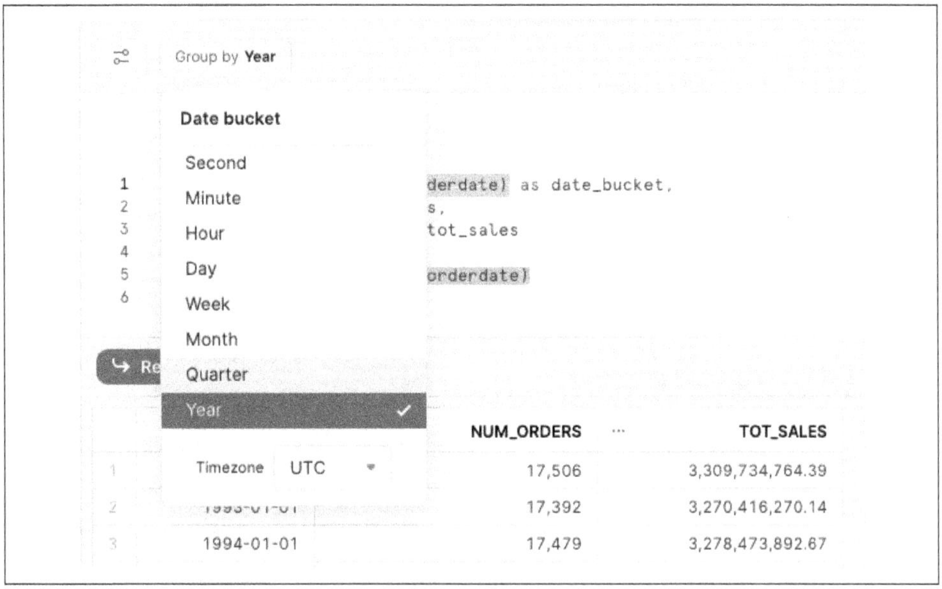

Figure 7-3. Snowsight "Group by" menu for `:datebucket` *queries*

As you can see, you can choose to group your data yearly, quarterly, and even all the way down to the second. Figure 7-4 shows how this query can be extended to include both `:daterange` and `:datebucket`.

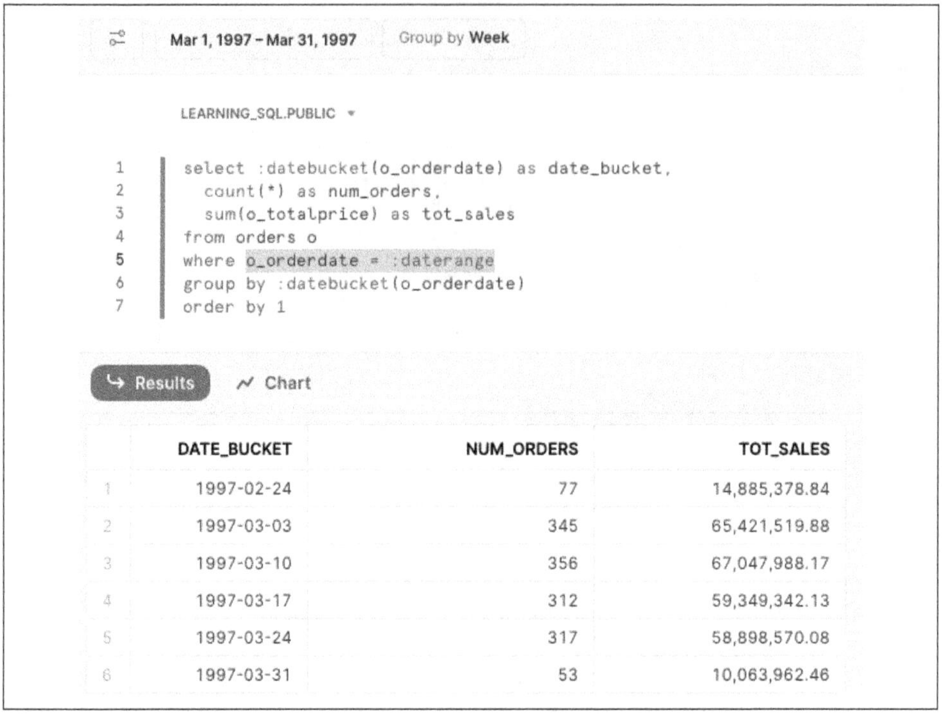

Figure 7-4. Snowsight query using both :daterange and :datebucket

There are now two menus at the top, one for :daterange (set to Mar, 1 1997–Mar 31, 1997) and the other for :datebucket (set to Week). The result set includes a row for every week including days in March of 1997. If you are doing data analysis, you will find these filters to be extremely helpful for slicing and dicing your data.

Wrap-Up

In this chapter, you learned how to group rows of data in order to compute sums, find highest/lowest values, and generate averages. You also learned how to apply filter conditions on grouped data using the having clause. Whether you are doing data analysis, generating rolled-up data for data warehouses, or writing reports, you will find the group by clause to be one of the most powerful tools in your SQL toolkit.

Test Your Knowledge

The following exercises are designed to test your understanding of grouping and aggregating. Please see "Chapter 7" in Appendix B for solutions.

Exercise 7-1

Write a query to count the number of rows in the Supplier table, along with determining the minimum and maximum values of the s_acctbal column.

Exercise 7-2

Modify the query from Exercise 7-1 to perform the same calculations, but for each value of s_nationkey rather than for the entire table.

Exercise 7-3

Modify the query from Exercise 7-2 to return only those rows with more than 300 suppliers per s_nationkey value.

Exercise 7-4

Using the query from Exercise 7-2, I can join to the Nation table using s_nationkey, and add Nation.n_regionkey to the group by clause, as in:

```
PUBLIC>select n.n_regionkey, s.s_nationkey,
       count(*), min(s.s_acctbal), max(s.s_acctbal)
    from supplier as s
    inner join nation n
      on s.s_nationkey = n.n_nationkey
    group by n.n_regionkey, s.s_nationkey;
```

Modify this query to generate rows for rollups for each n_regionkey value, rollups for each s_nationkey value, and a single rollup across all rows.

Subqueries

Subqueries are a powerful tool that can be used in `select`, `update`, `insert`, `delete`, and `merge` statements. This chapter will explore the different types of subqueries, and the different ways they can interact with your SQL statements.

Subqueries Defined

A subquery is a query that is contained within another SQL statement (referred to as the *containing statement* or *containing query* for the rest of this chapter). Subqueries are always surrounded by parentheses and generally run prior to the containing statement. Like any query, subqueries return a result set that can consist of a single row or multiple rows, and a single column or multiple columns. The type of result set returned by the subquery determines which operators the containing statement may use to interact with the data returned by the subquery.

Here's a simple example to get started:

```
PUBLIC>select n_nationkey, n_name from nation
      where n_regionkey =
        (select r_regionkey from region where r_name = 'ASIA');
+-------------+-----------+
| N_NATIONKEY | N_NAME    |
|-------------+-----------|
|           8 | INDIA     |
|           9 | INDONESIA |
|          12 | JAPAN     |
|          18 | CHINA     |
|          21 | VIETNAM   |
+-------------+-----------+
```

In this statement, the containing query is retrieving data from the `Nation` table, and the subquery returns the `regionkey` value for Asia from the `Region` table. The subquery runs first and returns the value 2, and the containing query then returns information about all nations with a `regionkey` value of 2. If you are thinking that the same result set could also be returned using a join rather than a subquery, you are correct:

```
PUBLIC>select n.n_nationkey, n.n_name
       from nation n inner join region r
       on n.n_regionkey = r.r_regionkey
       where r.r_name = 'ASIA';
+-------------+-----------+
| N_NATIONKEY | N_NAME    |
|-------------+-----------|
|           8 | INDIA     |
|           9 | INDONESIA |
|          12 | JAPAN     |
|          18 | CHINA     |
|          21 | VIETNAM   |
+-------------+-----------+
```

As you learn more and more about SQL, you will find that there are often multiple ways to generate the same results, some of which are more efficient or elegant than others.

Subquery Types

There are two types of subqueries, and the difference lies in whether the subquery can be executed separately from the containing query. The next several sections explore these two subquery types and show the different operators used to interact with them.

Uncorrelated Subqueries

The Asia table we have used so far is an *uncorrelated* subquery; it may be executed separately and does not reference anything from the containing query. Most subqueries that you encounter will be of this type unless you are writing `update` or `delete` statements which include subqueries. Along with being uncorrelated, the example table is known as a *scalar subquery*, meaning that it returns a single row having a single column. Scalar subqueries can appear on either side of a condition using the operators =, <>, <, >, <=, and >=. Here's the example again, but this time using an inequality condition:

```
PUBLIC>select n_nationkey, n_name from nation
       where n_regionkey <>
       (select r_regionkey from region where r_name = 'ASIA');
+-------------+----------------+
| N_NATIONKEY | N_NAME         |
|-------------+----------------|
|           0 | ALGERIA        |
```

```
|            1 | ARGENTINA      |
|            2 | BRAZIL         |
|            3 | CANADA         |
|            4 | EGYPT          |
|            5 | ETHIOPIA       |
|            6 | FRANCE         |
|            7 | GERMANY        |
|           10 | IRAN           |
|           11 | IRAQ           |
|           13 | JORDAN         |
|           14 | KENYA          |
|           15 | MOROCCO        |
|           16 | MOZAMBIQUE     |
|           17 | PERU           |
|           19 | ROMANIA        |
|           20 | SAUDI ARABIA   |
|           22 | RUSSIA         |
|           23 | UNITED KINGDOM |
|           24 | UNITED STATES  |
+--------------+----------------+
```

This version of the query returns all countries that are *not* in the Asia region. While the subquery in this example is quite simple, subqueries may be as complex as you need them to be, and they may be used in any of the available query clauses (select, from, where, group by, having, and order by).

If you use a subquery in an equality condition, but the subquery returns more than one row, you will receive an error. For example, if you modify the first query in this chapter such that the subquery returns all regionkey values *except* for Asia, you will receive the following error:

```
PUBLIC>select n_nationkey, n_name from nation
       where n_regionkey =
         (select r_regionkey from region where r_name <> 'ASIA');
090150 (22000): Single-row subquery returns more than one row.
```

Since the subquery is uncorrelated, you can run it by itself:

```
PUBLIC>select r_regionkey from region where r_name <> 'ASIA';
+-------------+
| R_REGIONKEY |
|-------------|
|           0 |
|           1 |
|           3 |
|           4 |
+-------------+
```

This query returns four rows, so when used as a subquery the containing query fails because the regionkey column cannot be *equal to* four values. The next two sections will demonstrate how you can handle subqueries that return either multiple rows or multiple columns.

Multiple-row, single-column subqueries

While you can't *equate* a single value to a set of values, you can determine if a single value can be found *within* a set of values. To do so, you can use the in operator:

```
PUBLIC>select n_nationkey, n_name from nation
       where n_regionkey in
         (select r_regionkey from region where r_name <> 'ASIA');
+--------------+-----------------+
| N_NATIONKEY | N_NAME          |
|--------------+-----------------|
|           0 | ALGERIA         |
|           1 | ARGENTINA       |
|           2 | BRAZIL          |
|           3 | CANADA          |
|           4 | EGYPT           |
|           5 | ETHIOPIA        |
|           6 | FRANCE          |
|           7 | GERMANY         |
|          10 | IRAN            |
|          11 | IRAQ            |
|          13 | JORDAN          |
|          14 | KENYA           |
|          15 | MOROCCO         |
|          16 | MOZAMBIQUE      |
|          17 | PERU            |
|          19 | ROMANIA         |
|          20 | SAUDI ARABIA    |
|          22 | RUSSIA          |
|          23 | UNITED KINGDOM |
|          24 | UNITED STATES  |
+--------------+-----------------+
```

You can also use not in to return rows where a value is *not* found within the set returned by the subquery:

```
PUBLIC>select n_nationkey, n_name from nation
       where n_regionkey not in
         (select r_regionkey from region
          where r_name = 'AMERICA' or r_name = 'EUROPE');
+--------------+---------------+
| N_NATIONKEY | N_NAME        |
|--------------+---------------|
|           0 | ALGERIA       |
|           4 | EGYPT         |
|           5 | ETHIOPIA      |
|           8 | INDIA         |
|           9 | INDONESIA     |
|          10 | IRAN          |
|          11 | IRAQ          |
|          12 | JAPAN         |
|          13 | JORDAN        |
|          14 | KENYA         |
```

```
|         15 | MOROCCO      |
|         16 | MOZAMBIQUE   |
|         18 | CHINA        |
|         20 | SAUDI ARABIA |
|         21 | VIETNAM      |
+------------+--------------+
```

The subquery in this example returns the two `regionkey` values for America and Europe, and the containing query returns all countries that are not in that set, which includes all countries from Africa, Asia, and Middle East.

Along with checking if a value can be found, or not found, in a set of values, it is also possible to perform comparisons on each value in a set. For example, let's say you want to find all customers whose total number of orders in 1996 exceeded any customer's total numbers in 1997. Here's one way to do it, using the `all` operator:

```
PUBLIC>select o_custkey, count(*) as num_orders
       from orders
       where 1996 = date_part(year, o_orderdate)
       group by o_custkey
       having count(*) > all
        (select count(*)
         from orders
         where 1997 = date_part(year, o_orderdate)
         group by o_custkey);
+------------+-------------+
| O_CUSTKEY  | NUM_ORDERS  |
|------------+-------------|
|      43645 |           5 |
+------------+-------------+
```

The subquery in this example returns the total number of orders for each customer in 1997, and the containing query returns all customers whose total orders in 1996 exceeds *all* of the values returned by the subquery.

Along with `all`, you can also use the `any` operator, which also compares a value to a set of values, but only needs to find a *single* instance where the comparison holds true. For example, let's say you want to find all orders in 1997 whose total price exceeded the maximum price for orders for any other year. The first step is to generate the list of maximum prices for each year other than 1997:

```
PUBLIC>select date_part(year, o_orderdate), max(o_totalprice)
       from orders
       where 1997 <> date_part(year, o_orderdate)
       group by date_part(year, o_orderdate)
       order by 1;
+------------------------------+-------------------+
| DATE_PART(YEAR, O_ORDERDATE) | MAX(O_TOTALPRICE) |
|------------------------------+-------------------|
|                         1992 |         555285.16 |
|                         1993 |         460118.47 |
```

```
|                         1994 |           489099.53 |
|                         1995 |           499753.01 |
|                         1996 |           498599.91 |
|                         1998 |           502742.76 |
+------------------------------+---------------------+
```

The next step is to construct a containing query that finds any order from 1997 whose total price exceeds any of these values:

```
PUBLIC>select o_custkey, o_orderdate, o_totalprice
      from orders
      where 1997 = date_part(year, o_orderdate)
        and o_totalprice > any
         (select max(o_totalprice)
          from orders
          where 1997 <> date_part(year, o_orderdate)
          group by date_part(year, o_orderdate));
+-----------+-------------+--------------+
| O_CUSTKEY | O_ORDERDATE | O_TOTALPRICE |
|-----------+-------------+--------------|
|    140506 | 1997-12-21  |    461118.75 |
|    148348 | 1997-01-31  |    465610.95 |
|     54602 | 1997-02-09  |    471220.08 |
+-----------+-------------+--------------+
```

As you can see, all of these orders have a total price greater than *at least one* of the values returned by the subquery (the smallest being 460,118.47 in 1993).

Multicolumn subqueries

So far, the subquery examples in this chapter have returned one or more rows having a single column. In certain situations, however, you can use subqueries that return two or more columns. Let's start with a query that finds the largest order for each year:

```
PUBLIC>select date_part(year, o_orderdate), max(o_totalprice)
      from orders
      group by date_part(year, o_orderdate)
      order by 1;
+------------------------------+---------------------+
| DATE_PART(YEAR, O_ORDERDATE) | MAX(O_TOTALPRICE)   |
|------------------------------+---------------------|
|                         1992 |           555285.16 |
|                         1993 |           460118.47 |
|                         1994 |           489099.53 |
|                         1995 |           499753.01 |
|                         1996 |           498599.91 |
|                         1997 |           471220.08 |
|                         1998 |           502742.76 |
+------------------------------+---------------------+
```

Next, let's say you want to find out additional details about each of these orders, such as the custkey and orderdate values. In order to find these rows, you will need to build a containing query that compares each order's year and total price to the two columns returned by the subquery:

```
PUBLIC>select o_custkey, o_orderdate, o_totalprice
       from orders
       where (date_part(year, o_orderdate), o_totalprice) in
        (select date_part(year, o_orderdate), max(o_totalprice)
         from orders
         group by date_part(year, o_orderdate))
       order by 2;
+-----------+-------------+--------------+
| O_CUSTKEY | O_ORDERDATE | O_TOTALPRICE |
|-----------+-------------+--------------|
|     21433 | 1992-11-30  |    555285.16 |
|     95069 | 1993-02-28  |    460118.47 |
|    121546 | 1994-10-20  |    489099.53 |
|     52516 | 1995-08-15  |    499753.01 |
|     56620 | 1996-05-22  |    498599.91 |
|     54602 | 1997-02-09  |    471220.08 |
|    100159 | 1998-07-28  |    502742.76 |
+-----------+-------------+--------------+
```

While there are two columns being compared in this example, there is no limit to the number of columns returned by the subquery, as long as the data types match between the containing query and the subquery.

Correlated Subqueries

So far in this chapter, all of the subqueries have been independent of the containing statement, meaning that the subqueries are run once, prior to the execution of the containing statement. A *correlated subquery*, on the other hand, references one or more columns from the containing statement, which means that both the subquery and containing query must run together. For example, the next query returns the set of customers who have placed at least $1,500,000 in orders:

```
PUBLIC>select c.c_name
       from customer c
       where 1500000 <=
        (select sum(o.o_totalprice)
         from orders o
         where o.o_custkey = c.c_custkey);
+--------------------+
| C_NAME             |
|--------------------|
| Customer#000007033 |
| Customer#000045088 |
| Customer#000051517 |
| Customer#000051847 |
```

```
| Customer#000052396 |
| Customer#000022924 |
| Customer#000029977 |
| Customer#000036316 |
| Customer#000037825 |
| Customer#000039604 |
| Customer#000041581 |
| Customer#000078727 |
| Customer#000080590 |
| Customer#000082315 |
| Customer#000089083 |
| Customer#000141352 |
| Customer#000147898 |
| Customer#000148394 |
| Customer#000148561 |
| Customer#000091462 |
| Customer#000102616 |
| Customer#000119671 |
| Customer#000066103 |
| Customer#000067051 |
| Customer#000120202 |
| Customer#000121909 |
| Customer#000132601 |
+--------------------+
```

Looking at the subquery, you can see that the condition in the where clause references a column from the Customer table in the containing query, which is what makes it a correlated subquery. For every row in the Customer table, the subquery is executed to determine the total price of all orders for that customer. Since there are 66,076 rows in the Customer table, the subquery is executed 66,076 times.

> Since the correlated subquery will be executed once for each row of the containing query, the use of correlated subqueries can cause performance issues if the containing query returns a large number of rows.

Exists operator

Correlated subqueries are often used with the exists operator, which is useful when you want to test for the existence of a particular relationship without regard for the quantity. For example, let's say you want to find all customers who have ever placed an order over $500,000, without regard for the number of orders or the exact amount of the order. The next query shows how the exists operator can be used for this purpose:

```
PUBLIC>select c.c_name
       from customer c
       where exists
         (select 1 from orders o
```

```
        where o.o_custkey = c.c_custkey
        and o.o_totalprice > 500000);
+---------------------+
| C_NAME              |
|---------------------|
| Customer#000100159  |
| Customer#000008936  |
| Customer#000021433  |
+---------------------+
```

Again, the subquery is executed once for each row in the Customer table, but this time the subquery either returns no rows (if the customer never placed an order above $500,000) or a single row if at least one order above $500,000 is found. When using exists, Snowflake is smart enough to stop execution of the subquery once the first matching row is found.

Correlated subqueries in update and delete statements

Along with select statements, you will find correlated subqueries to be useful in both update and delete statements. For example, your IT department may have a policy to remove rows from the Customer table for any customers who haven't placed an order in the past 5 years. This could be accomplished using the following statement:

```
delete from customer c
where not exists
(select 1 from orders o
 where o.o_custkey = c.c_custkey
   and o.o_orderdate > dateadd(year, -5, current_date))
```

This statement uses not exists, so it is finding rows in Customer where no rows exist in Orders with a date greater than current day minus 5 years.

If the policy is instead to mark the customer's record as inactive rather than deleting the record, you could modify the previous statement to use update instead:

```
update customer c
set inactive = 'Y'
where not exists
(select 1 from orders o
 where o.o_custkey = c.c_custkey
   and o.o_orderdate > dateadd(year, -5, current_date))
```

Here's an example that can be run against the Employee and Person tables:

```
PUBLIC>alter table employee add inactive varchar(1);

PUBLIC>update employee e set e.inactive = 'Y'
        where not exists
         (select 1 from person p
          where p.first_name || ' ' || p.last_name = e.emp_name);
```

```
+-----------------------+-------------------------------------+
| number of rows updated | number of multi-joined rows updated |
|-----------------------+-------------------------------------|
|                    5 |                                  0 |
+-----------------------+-------------------------------------+
```

For this example, I added a new column named `inactive` to the `Employee` table, and then ran an `update` statement to set the new column to `Y` if a matching row cannot be found in the `Person` table. Subqueries are commonly used in `update` and `delete` statements, since you will frequently need information from other tables when modifying or deleting rows.

Committing Database Changes

The previous `update` statement was executed while in *autocommit mode*, which is the default when using Snowflake. This means that the changes made were automatically committed as soon as the statement completed. This topic will be covered in detail in Chapter 11.

Subqueries as Data Sources

Since subqueries return result sets, they can be used in place of tables in `select` statements, as shown in the next two sections.

Subqueries in the from Clause

Tables consist of multiple rows and multiple columns, and the result set returned by a subquery also consists of multiple rows and columns. Therefore, tables and subqueries can both be used in the `from` clause of a query, and can even be joined to each other. Here's an example that shows how a subquery that groups data can be joined to another table to retrieve additional information:

```
PUBLIC>select c.c_name, o.total_dollars
       from
        (select o_custkey, sum(o_totalprice) as total_dollars
         from orders
         where 1998 = date_part(year, o_orderdate)
         group by o_custkey
         having sum(o_totalprice) >= 650000
        ) o
         inner join customer c
           on c.c_custkey = o.o_custkey
       order by 1;
+----------------------+----------------+
| C_NAME               | TOTAL_DOLLARS  |
|----------------------+----------------|
| Customer#000002948   |     663115.18  |
```

```
| Customer#000004309 |   719354.94 |
| Customer#000005059 |   734893.37 |
| Customer#000022924 |   686947.21 |
| Customer#000026729 |   654376.71 |
| Customer#000033487 |   727194.76 |
| Customer#000044116 |   699699.98 |
| Customer#000061120 |   656770.28 |
| Customer#000065434 |  1030712.34 |
| Customer#000074695 |   665357.12 |
| Customer#000074807 |   673802.06 |
| Customer#000090608 |   727770.25 |
| Customer#000097519 |   680678.45 |
| Customer#000098410 |   673907.68 |
| Customer#000102904 |   667912.44 |
| Customer#000138724 |   717744.86 |
+--------------------+---------------+
```

In this example, the subquery is given the alias o and is then joined to the Customer table using the custkey column. The subquery returns all customers having orders in 1998 of $650,000 or above, and the result set is then joined to the Customer table to allow the customer name to be returned instead of the custkey value.

Subqueries used as data sources must be uncorrelated; they are executed first, and the result set is held in memory until the containing query has completed. However, the next section shows how you can access the results of one subquery in another subquery by utilizing a with clause.

Common Table Expressions

Along with putting subqueries in the from clause, you also have the option to move your subqueries into a with clause, which must always appear at the top of your query above the select clause. Here's what the previous query would look like using a with clause:

```
PUBLIC>with big_orders as
       (select o_custkey, sum(o_totalprice) as total_dollars
        from orders
        where 1998 = date_part(year, o_orderdate)
        group by o_custkey
        having sum(o_totalprice) >= 650000
        )
       select c.c_name, big_orders.total_dollars
       from big_orders
         inner join customer c
         on c.c_custkey = big_orders.o_custkey
       order by 1;
+--------------------+---------------+
| C_NAME             | TOTAL_DOLLARS |
|--------------------+---------------|
| Customer#000002948 |     663115.18 |
```

```
| Customer#000004309 |    719354.94 |
| Customer#000005059 |    734893.37 |
| Customer#000022924 |    686947.21 |
| Customer#000026729 |    654376.71 |
| Customer#000033487 |    727194.76 |
| Customer#000044116 |    699699.98 |
| Customer#000061120 |    656770.28 |
| Customer#000065434 |   1030712.34 |
| Customer#000074695 |    665357.12 |
| Customer#000074807 |    673802.06 |
| Customer#000090608 |    727770.25 |
| Customer#000097519 |    680678.45 |
| Customer#000098410 |    673907.68 |
| Customer#000102904 |    667912.44 |
| Customer#000138724 |    717744.86 |
+--------------------+--------------+
```

In this version of the query, I have moved the subquery against the Orders table up into the with clause and given it the alias big_orders. The results are then joined to the Customer table using the custkey column, just as before. Subqueries in a with clause are known as *common table expressions*, or CTEs. Having a single CTE can make a query more readable, but if you have multiple CTEs in a with clause you can reference any subqueries defined above in the same with clause. Here's the previous query again, this time with both queries defined as CTEs:

```
PUBLIC>with big_orders as
        (select o_custkey, sum(o_totalprice) as total_dollars
         from orders
         where 1998 = date_part(year, o_orderdate)
         group by o_custkey
         having sum(o_totalprice) >= 650000
        ),
        big_orders_with_names as
        (select c.c_name, big_orders.total_dollars
         from big_orders
         inner join customer c
         on c.c_custkey = big_orders.o_custkey
        )
        select *
        from big_orders_with_names
        order by 1;
+--------------------+--------------+
| C_NAME             | TOTAL_DOLLARS |
|--------------------+--------------|
| Customer#000002948 |    663115.18 |
| Customer#000004309 |    719354.94 |
| Customer#000005059 |    734893.37 |
| Customer#000022924 |    686947.21 |
| Customer#000026729 |    654376.71 |
| Customer#000033487 |    727194.76 |
| Customer#000044116 |    699699.98 |
```

```
| Customer#000061120 |    656770.28 |
| Customer#000065434 |   1030712.34 |
| Customer#000074695 |    665357.12 |
| Customer#000074807 |    673802.06 |
| Customer#000090608 |    727770.25 |
| Customer#000097519 |    680678.45 |
| Customer#000098410 |    673907.68 |
| Customer#000102904 |    667912.44 |
| Customer#000138724 |    717744.86 |
+--------------------+--------------+
```

The with clause now has two subqueries; big_orders and big_orders_with_names. Additionally, the big_orders_with_names subquery retrieves data from the big_orders subquery, with is allowable because big_orders is defined first.

Using CTEs is a bit like creating a function in Java or Python: you can use the subqueries as many times as you want within a piece of code, the difference being that with SQL the results from the CTEs are discarded after the statement execution completes. You can also use CTEs to fabricate data sets that don't exist in your database, as shown in the next example:

```
PUBLIC>with dollar_ranges as
       (select *
        from (values (3, 'Bottom Tier', 650000, 700000),
                     (2, 'Middle Tier', 700001, 730000),
                     (1, 'Top Tier', 730001, 9999999))
               as dr (range_num, range_name, low_val, high_val)
       ),
       big_orders as
       (select o_custkey, sum(o_totalprice) as total_dollars
        from orders
        where 1998 = date_part(year, o_orderdate)
        group by o_custkey
        having sum(o_totalprice) >= 650000
       ),
       big_orders_with_names as
       (select c.c_name, big_orders.total_dollars
        from big_orders
        inner join customer c
        on c.c_custkey = big_orders.o_custkey
       )
       select dr.range_name,
         sum(round(bon.total_dollars,0)) rng_sum,
         listagg(bon.c_name,',')
           within group (order by bon.c_name) name_list
       from big_orders_with_names as bon
         inner join dollar_ranges as dr
         on bon.total_dollars between dr.low_val and dr.high_val
       group by dr.range_name;
+-------------+---------+-----------------------------------------+
| RANGE_NAME  | RNG_SUM | NAME_LIST                               |
|-------------+---------+-----------------------------------------|
```

```
| Top Tier    | 1765605 | Customer#000005059,Customer#000065434 |
| Middle Tier | 2892065 | Customer#000004309,Customer#000033487,
                          Customer#000090608,Customer#000138724 |
| Bottom Tier | 6722566 | Customer#000002948,Customer#000022924,
                          Customer#000026729,Customer#000044116,
                          Customer#000061120,Customer#000074695,
                          Customer#000074807,Customer#000097519,
                          Customer#000098410,Customer#000102904 |
+-------------+---------+---------------------------------------+
```

This query groups the results of the previous query into three ranges and sums the total prices for each range. The first CTE is named `dollar_ranges` and simply creates three rows of data for the ranges $650,000 to $700,000, $700,001 to $730,000, and $730,001 to $9,999,999. Here's what that result set looks like:

```
PUBLIC>with dollar_ranges as
         (select *
          from (values (3, 'Bottom Tier', 650000, 700000),
                       (2, 'Middle Tier', 700001, 730000),
                       (1, 'Top Tier', 730001, 9999999))
            as dr (range_num, range_name, low_val, high_val)
         )
         select * from dollar_ranges;
+-----------+-------------+---------+---------+
| RANGE_NUM | RANGE_NAME  | LOW_VAL | HIGH_VAL |
|-----------+-------------+---------+---------|
|         3 | Bottom Tier |  650000 |   700000 |
|         2 | Middle Tier |  700001 |   730000 |
|         1 | Top Tier    |  730001 |  9999999 |
+-----------+-------------+---------+---------+
```

This is used to group the results of the `big_orders_with_names` CTE, which is given the alias bon:

```
from big_orders_with_names as bon
  inner join dollar_ranges as dr
  on bon.total_dollars between dr.low_val and dr.high_val
```

Each row in `big_orders_with_names` falls into one of the 3 ranges, and then the total prices are summed and the customers in each range are listed (using the `listagg()` function, which was discussed in Chapter 7):

```
select dr.range_name,
  sum(bon.total_dollars) range_sum,
  listagg(bon.c_name,',')
    within group (order by bon.c_name) name_list
from big_orders_with_names as bon
  inner join dollar_ranges as dr
  on bon.total_dollars between dr.low_val and dr.high_val
group by dr.range_name
```

This is the most complex query thus far in the book, but I hope you will agree that using CTEs to modularize your code can make complex logic much easier to follow.

Wrap-Up

This chapter explored the many uses of subqueries, including both uncorrelated and correlated subqueries and the use of operators such as in and exists. You also saw how subqueries can be used as data sources, either in the from or with clauses. Subqueries are one of the most powerful and flexible tools in your SQL toolkit, so spend some time getting comfortable with the various ways in which they can be utilized.

Test Your Knowledge

The following exercises are designed to test your understanding of subqueries. Please see "Chapter 8" in Appendix B for solutions.

Exercise 8-1

Write a query against the Nation table that uses an uncorrelated subquery on the Region table to return the names of all nations except those in the America and Asia regions.

Exercise 8-2

Generate the same results as Exercise 8-1, but using a correlated subquery against the Region table.

Exercise 8-3

Write a query against the Customer table that returns the c_custkey and c_name columns for all customers who placed exactly four orders in 1997. Use an uncorrelated subquery against the Orders table.

Exercise 8-4

Modify the query from Exercise 8-3 to return the same results, but with a correlated subquery.

From Clause Revisited

While the different types of joins (inner, outer, cross) were discussed in Chapter 3, there is a lot more that can be done in the `from` clause in Snowflake. This chapter will explore some of these options.

This chapter makes use of the `Employee` table, which was created and populated back in Chapter 3. If you would like to run the example queries from this chapter but don't have this table in your schema, you can run the following statement:

```
create table employee
 (empid number, emp_name varchar(30), mgr_empid number)
as select *
   from (values
           (1001, 'Bob Smith', null),
           (1002, 'Susan Jackson', 1001),
           (1003, 'Greg Carpenter', 1001),
           (1004, 'Robert Butler', 1002),
           (1005, 'Kim Josephs', 1003),
           (1006, 'John Tyler', 1004));
```

Hierarchical Queries

Some data is hierarchical in nature, such as a family tree, where each data point has a relationship with other data points above and/or below. Another example is an employee table, where each employee's row contains a value to identify the employee's manager. There is already an `Employee` table in the `learning_sql` schema, so let's take another look at the data:

```
PUBLIC>select empid, emp_name, mgr_empid
       from employee;
```

```
+-------+----------------+-----------+
| EMPID | EMP_NAME       | MGR_EMPID |
|-------+----------------+-----------|
|  1001 | Bob Smith      |      NULL |
|  1002 | Susan Jackson  |      1001 |
|  1003 | Greg Carpenter |      1001 |
|  1004 | Robert Butler  |      1002 |
|  1005 | Kim Josephs    |      1003 |
|  1006 | John Tyler     |      1004 |
+-------+----------------+-----------+
```

Of the six rows in the table, five contain the empid value of the employee's manager; so, starting from the bottom row, John Tyler works for Robert Butler, who works for Susan Jackson, who works for Bob Smith. If you wanted to write a query to show these relationships, you could try to join the Employee table to itself multiple times:

```
PUBLIC>select e_1.emp_name, e_2.emp_name,
        e_3.emp_name, e_4.emp_name
     from employee e_1
       inner join employee e_2
       on e_1.mgr_empid = e_2.empid
       inner join employee e_3
       on e_2.mgr_empid = e_3.empid
       inner join employee e_4
       on e_3.mgr_empid = e_4.empid
      where e_1.emp_name = 'John Tyler';
+------------+---------------+---------------+-----------+
| EMP_NAME   | EMP_NAME      | EMP_NAME      | EMP_NAME  |
|------------+---------------+---------------+-----------|
| John Tyler | Robert Butler | Susan Jackson | Bob Smith |
+------------+---------------+---------------+-----------+
```

This query includes the Employee table four times, one for each level in the management hierarchy. While this approach does work for this example, it would not suffice if the company was very large with a deep and complex management structure. A more general approach is needed, and for these purposes Snowflake provides the connect by clause to traverse hierarchical relationships. Here's how it could be used to generate the management hierarchy, starting with John Tyler:

```
PUBLIC>select emp_name
     from employee
       start with emp_name = 'John Tyler'
       connect by prior mgr_empid = empid;
+---------------+
| EMP_NAME      |
|---------------|
| John Tyler    |
| Robert Butler |
| Susan Jackson |
| Bob Smith     |
+---------------+
```

The start by clause describes which row to start from, and the connect by clause describes how to traverse from one row to the next. The prior keyword is used to denote the current level, so when the query starts with John Tyler's row, the prior mgr_empid value is 1004, which is used to move to the row with empid of 1004 (Robert Butler's row). The nice thing about this approach is that it can handle any number of levels in the hierarchy, so the query stays the same no matter how many management levels there are.

Let's see what happens if the query is run in the opposite direction, starting with Bob Smith and moving down the hierarchy:

```
PUBLIC>select emp_name
       from employee
         start with emp_name = 'Bob Smith'
         connect by prior empid = mgr_empid;
+----------------+
| EMP_NAME       |
|----------------|
| Bob Smith      |
| Susan Jackson  |
| Greg Carpenter |
| Robert Butler  |
| Kim Josephs    |
| John Tyler     |
+----------------+
```

This time, Bob Smith's row is the starting point, and the connect by clause is reversed because we are traveling down the tree instead of up. Since every employee ultimately reports to Bob Smith (including himself), all six employees are listed. However, the results don't show any of the intermediate relationships, such as the fact that Robert Butler reports to Susan Jackson. If you want to see these relationships, you can use the built in function sys_connect_by_path() to see a description of the entire hierarchy up to that point:

```
PUBLIC>select emp_name,
          sys_connect_by_path(emp_name, ' : ') management_path
       from employee
         start with emp_name = 'Bob Smith'
         connect by prior empid = mgr_empid;
+----------------+-----------------------------------------------------------------+
| EMP_NAME       | MANAGEMENT_PATH                                                 |
|----------------+-----------------------------------------------------------------|
| Bob Smith      | : Bob Smith                                                     |
| Susan Jackson  | : Bob Smith : Susan Jackson                                     |
| Greg Carpenter | : Bob Smith : Greg Carpenter                                    |
| Robert Butler  | : Bob Smith : Susan Jackson : Robert Butler                     |
| Kim Josephs    | : Bob Smith : Greg Carpenter : Kim Josephs                      |
| John Tyler     | : Bob Smith : Susan Jackson : Robert Butler : John Tyler|       |
+----------------+-----------------------------------------------------------------+
```

As you can see, the combination of connect by with the sys_connect_by_path() function gives you a complete description of the hierarchies in your data.

Time Travel

Snowflake's Time Travel feature allows you to execute queries that will see your data as it was at a certain time in the past. To do so, you can use the at keyword to specify either a specific time or an offset from the current time, and Snowflake will retrieve the data as it was at that point in time. To demonstrate, I will start by adding a new row to the Employee table:

```
PUBLIC>insert into employee (empid, emp_name, mgr_empid)
       values (9999, 'Tim Traveler',1006);
+-------------------------+
| number of rows inserted |
|-------------------------|
|                       1 |
+-------------------------+
```

With the addition of Tim Traveler, there are now seven rows in Employee:

```
PUBLIC>select empid, emp_name, mgr_empid
       from employee;
+-------+-----------------+-----------+
| EMPID | EMP_NAME        | MGR_EMPID |
|-------+-----------------+-----------|
|  1001 | Bob Smith       |      NULL |
|  1002 | Susan Jackson   |      1001 |
|  1003 | Greg Carpenter  |      1001 |
|  1004 | Robert Butler   |      1002 |
|  1005 | Kim Josephs     |      1003 |
|  1006 | John Tyler      |      1004 |
|  9999 | Tim Traveler    |      1006 |
+-------+-----------------+-----------+
```

Using Time Travel, however, I can retrieve all of the rows as of one hour ago:

```
PUBLIC>select empid, emp_name, mgr_empid
       from employee
       at(offset => -3600);
+-------+-----------------+-----------+
| EMPID | EMP_NAME        | MGR_EMPID |
|-------+-----------------+-----------|
|  1001 | Bob Smith       |      NULL |
|  1002 | Susan Jackson   |      1001 |
|  1003 | Greg Carpenter  |      1001 |
|  1004 | Robert Butler   |      1002 |
|  1005 | Kim Josephs     |      1003 |
|  1006 | John Tyler      |      1004 |
+-------+-----------------+-----------+
```

This query specifies that the rows should be returned as the table existed one hour ago (−3,600 seconds). As you can see, Tim Traveler is not in the result set.

One of the uses of this feature would be to identify which rows were inserted over a particular time span. This next query uses the `minus` operator to compare the current state of the table with the state one hour ago:

```
PUBLIC>select empid, emp_name, mgr_empid
       from employee
       minus
       select empid, emp_name, mgr_empid
       from employee
       at(offset => -3600);
+-------+--------------+-----------+
| EMPID | EMP_NAME     | MGR_EMPID |
|-------+--------------+-----------|
|  9999 | Tim Traveler |      1006 |
+-------+--------------+-----------+
```

This query compares the seven rows currently in the table with the six rows in the table one hour ago and returns the difference, which is Tim Traveler's row. The default for Time Travel is one day in the past, but if you are using Snowflake's Enterprise edition you can run queries that see the state of the data up to 90 days in the past.

Pivot Queries

Pivoting is a common operation in data analysis, where rows of data need to be pivoted into columns. To illustrate, let's return to the `Orders` table and write a query that sums the total sales for each year after 1995:

```
PUBLIC>select date_part(year, o_orderdate) as year,
              round(sum(o_totalprice)) as total_sales
       from orders
       where 1995 <= date_part(year, o_orderdate)
       group by date_part(year, o_orderdate)
       order by 1;
+------+-------------+
| YEAR | TOTAL_SALES |
|------+-------------|
| 1995 |  3317521810 |
| 1996 |  3296373353 |
| 1997 |  3255086721 |
| 1998 |  1925196449 |
+------+-------------+
```

There are four rows in this result set, with each row consisting of the year and the total sales for that year. Next, let's say you are asked to format these results for a report that shows this data on a single row, with four columns showing the total sales for 1995, 1996, 1997, and 1998:

```
+------------+------------+------------+------------+
| 1995_SALES | 1996_SALES | 1997_SALES | 1998_SALES |
+------------+------------+------------+------------+
| 3317521810 | 3296373353 | 3255086721 | 1925196449 |
+------------+------------+------------+------------+
```

For these types of operations, Snowflake supplies a `pivot` clause to allow you to specify how you want the data to be presented. Here's a query that uses `pivot` to generate the desired results:

```
PUBLIC>select round(yr_1995) as "1995_sales",
         round(yr_1996) as "1996_sales",
         round(yr_1997) as "1997_sales",
         round(yr_1998) as "1998_sales"
       from (select date_part(year, o_orderdate) as year,
                    o_totalprice
             from orders
             where 1995 <= date_part(year, o_orderdate)
             )
       pivot (sum(o_totalprice)
       for year in (1995,1996,1997,1998))
       as pvt(yr_1995, yr_1996, yr_1997, yr_1998);
+------------+------------+------------+------------+
| 1995_sales | 1996_sales | 1997_sales | 1998_sales |
|------------+------------+------------+------------|
| 3317521810 | 3296373353 | 3255086721 | 1925196449 |
+------------+------------+------------+------------+
```

The subquery in the `from` clause retrieves the year and `totalprice` values for all orders in 1995 and later, and the `pivot` clause specifies that the `totalprice` values be summed into 4 columns, one each for the years 1995, 1996, 1997, and 1998. The third line in the `pivot` clause assigns column names to each of the columns (yr_1995, ..., yr_1998), which are then used in the `select` clause to round each value.

Snowflake also provides an `unpivot` clause that performs the opposite transformation (pivot data from columns into rows). To demonstrate, I'll take the previous `pivot` query, put it into a `with` clause, and then use a query with `unpivot` to return the result set to its original state:

```
PUBLIC>with year_pvt as
         (select round(yr_1995) as "1995",
            round(yr_1996) as "1996",
            round(yr_1997) as "1997",
            round(yr_1998) as "1998"
         from (select date_part(year, o_orderdate) as year,
                      o_totalprice
               from orders
               where 1995 <= date_part(year, o_orderdate)
               )
         pivot (sum(o_totalprice)
           for year in (1995,1996,1997,1998))
```

```
        as pvt(yr_1995, yr_1996, yr_1997, yr_1998)
      )
    select *
    from year_pvt
    unpivot (total_sales for year in
      ("1995", "1996", "1997", "1998"));
+------+-------------+
| YEAR | TOTAL_SALES |
|------+-------------|
| 1995 |  3317521810 |
| 1996 |  3296373353 |
| 1997 |  3255086721 |
| 1998 |  1925196449 |
+------+-------------+
```

In the `year_pvt` subquery, I used `pivot` to change the result set to have a single row with four columns, and in the outer query I used `unpivot` to change the result set back into four rows with two columns. In Chapter 10 I will show you another way to pivot data using `case` expressions.

Random Sampling

Sometimes it is useful to retrieve a subset of a table for tasks such as testing, and you want the subset to be different every time. For this purpose, Snowflake includes the `sample` clause to allow you to specify what percent of the rows you would like returned. For example, the `Supplier` table has 7,400 rows, but perhaps you'd like to return just 1/1,000 of the rows to run some tests. Here's what that could look like (your results will vary):

```
PUBLIC>select s_suppkey, s_name, s_nationkey
       from supplier
       sample (0.1);
+-----------+---------------------+-------------+
| S_SUPPKEY | S_NAME              | S_NATIONKEY |
|-----------+---------------------+-------------|
|      5572 | Supplier#000005572 |          21 |
|      3724 | Supplier#000003724 |          12 |
|      4243 | Supplier#000004243 |          15 |
|      2859 | Supplier#000002859 |           9 |
|      8112 | Supplier#000008112 |          22 |
|       129 | Supplier#000000129 |          15 |
|       791 | Supplier#000000791 |          22 |
|      8907 | Supplier#000008907 |           1 |
+-----------+---------------------+-------------+
```

In this example, 0.1 is specified as the probability, meaning that there should be a 0.1% chance that any particular row is included in the result set. If you run this query multiple times, you will get a different set of rows (and potentially a different number of rows) each time. When I ran this statement five times, the result sets included as few as four rows and as many as nine. If you need an exact number of rows, you can specify a row count:

```
PUBLIC>select s_suppkey, s_name, s_nationkey
       from supplier
       sample (10 rows);
+-----------+----------------------+-------------+
| S_SUPPKEY | S_NAME               | S_NATIONKEY |
|-----------+----------------------+-------------|
|      3785 | Supplier#000003785   |          14 |
|      7520 | Supplier#000007520   |          14 |
|      7593 | Supplier#000007593   |          13 |
|       436 | Supplier#000000436   |          20 |
|      2115 | Supplier#000002115   |          15 |
|      6447 | Supplier#000006447   |          24 |
|      9048 | Supplier#000009048   |          18 |
|      1475 | Supplier#000001475   |          17 |
|      4545 | Supplier#000004545   |          13 |
|      1017 | Supplier#000001017   |           2 |
+-----------+----------------------+-------------+
```

For this variation, your result set will always include 10 rows, but there will be a different set of rows returned each time the query is executed.

Full Outer Joins

In Chapter 3, you learned about outer joins, which are used to retrieve additional columns from a table without requiring a join condition to evaluate as true. Here's one of the examples from Chapter 3:

```
PUBLIC>select orders.ordernum, orders.custkey, customer.custname
       from
           (values (990, 101), (991, 102),
                   (992, 101), (993, 104))
              as orders (ordernum, custkey)
           left outer join
           (values (101, 'BOB'), (102, 'KIM'), (103, 'JIM'))
              as customer (custkey, custname)
           on orders.custkey = customer.custkey;
+----------+---------+----------+
| ORDERNUM | CUSTKEY | CUSTNAME |
|----------+---------+----------|
|      990 |     101 | BOB      |
|      991 |     102 | KIM      |
|      992 |     101 | BOB      |
|      993 |     104 | NULL     |
+----------+---------+----------+
```

The result set includes the fourth row from the orders data set (ordernum 993), but the custname column is null, since there is no row in the customer data set for cust key 104. This example includes an order with no matching customer, but there's also a customer (Jim) without any matching orders. If you want the result set to include *both* every order *and* every customer, you can specify a full outer join instead of a left outer join:

```
PUBLIC>select orders.ordernum, orders.custkey, customer.custname
       from
         (values (990, 101), (991, 102),
                 (992, 101), (993, 104))
           as orders (ordernum, custkey)
         full outer join
         (values (101, 'BOB'), (102, 'KIM'), (103, 'JIM'))
           as customer (custkey, custname)
         on orders.custkey = customer.custkey;
+----------+---------+----------+
| ORDERNUM | CUSTKEY | CUSTNAME |
|----------+---------+----------|
|      990 |     101 | BOB      |
|      991 |     102 | KIM      |
|      992 |     101 | BOB      |
|      993 |     104 | NULL     |
|     NULL |    NULL | JIM      |
+----------+---------+----------+
```

The result set now includes an additional row for Jim, so all four orders and all three customers are included. However, Jim's custkey value in the result set is null because orders.custkey is specified in the select clause. This can be fixed by using the nvl() function to return the custkey value from either the orders or customer data sets:

```
PUBLIC>select orders.ordernum,
         nvl(orders.custkey, customer.custkey) as custkey,
         customer.custname
       from
         (values (990, 101), (991, 102),
                 (992, 101), (993, 104))
           as orders (ordernum, custkey)
         full outer join
         (values (101, 'BOB'), (102, 'KIM'), (103, 'JIM'))
           as customer (custkey, custname)
         on orders.custkey = customer.custkey;
+----------+---------+----------+
| ORDERNUM | CUSTKEY | CUSTNAME |
|----------+---------+----------|
|      990 |     101 | BOB      |
|      991 |     102 | KIM      |
|      992 |     101 | BOB      |
|      993 |     104 | NULL     |
|     NULL |     103 | JIM      |
+----------+---------+----------+
```

When you specify full outer joins, you will generally want to use nvl() for any columns that can come from either of the tables.

Lateral Joins

Snowflake allows a subquery in the from clause to reference another table in the same from clause, which means that the subquery acts like a correlated subquery. This is done by specifying the lateral keyword, as shown in the following example:

```
PUBLIC>select ord.o_orderdate, ord.o_totalprice,
        cst.c_name, cst.c_address
      from orders ord
        inner join lateral
        (select c.c_name, c.c_address
         from customer c
         where c.c_custkey = ord.o_custkey
        ) cst
      where 1995 <= date_part(year, ord.o_orderdate)
        and ord.o_totalprice > 475000;
```

O_ORDERDATE	O_TOTALPRICE	C_NAME	C_ADDRESS
1995-08-15	499753.01	Customer#000052516	BUePeY1OPR...
1996-05-22	498599.91	Customer#000056620	QAnxRzFcVP...
1996-09-16	491096.90	Customer#000111926	yDC67043ir...
1998-07-28	502742.76	Customer#000100159	fcjfNCnKTf...

In this example, the cst subquery references the o_custkey column from the Orders table (alias ord), which is what makes it a correlated subquery. For the seven rows returned from the Orders table, the cst subquery is executed using the custkey value for that row. These same results can be generated using a standard inner join, so this is not a particularly compelling reason to use lateral, but the next example shows how the subquery can provide additional functionality:

```
PUBLIC>select ord.o_orderdate, ord.o_totalprice,
        li.num_line_items, li. last_shipdate
      from orders ord
        inner join lateral
        (select count(*) as num_line_items,
           max(l_shipdate) as last_shipdate
         from lineitem as l
         where l.l_orderkey = ord.o_orderkey
        ) li
      where 1995 <= date_part(year, ord.o_orderdate)
        and ord.o_totalprice > 475000;
```

O_ORDERDATE	O_TOTALPRICE	NUM_LINE_ITEMS	LAST_SHIPDATE
1996-05-22	498599.91	1	1996-08-28

```
| 1995-08-15 |      499753.01 |        1 | 1995-10-01 |
| 1996-09-16 |      491096.90 |        1 | 1996-10-23 |
| 1998-07-28 |      502742.76 |        1 | 1998-11-25 |
+------------+----------------+----------+------------+
```

In this case, the correlated subquery uses the aggregate functions `count()` and `max()` to retrieve the number of line items and maximum shipping date for each row returned from the `Orders` table.

Table Literals

Snowflake allows table names to be passed into a query as a string using the `table()` function. Here's a simple example:

```
PUBLIC>select * from table('region');
+-------------+-------------+-----------------------------+
| R_REGIONKEY | R_NAME      | R_COMMENT                   |
+-------------+-------------+-----------------------------+
|           0 | AFRICA      | lar deposits. blithely fin...|
|           1 | AMERICA     | hs use ironic, even reques...|
|           2 | ASIA        | ges. thinly even pinto bea...|
|           3 | EUROPE      | ly final courts cajole fur...|
|           4 | MIDDLE EAST | uickly special accounts ca...|
+-------------+-------------+-----------------------------+
```

In this example, the table name is passed in as a string (`'region'`), and the `table()` function then looks for a table of that name in the current schema. You can also pass in the database and schema names:

```
PUBLIC>select * from table('learning_sql.public.region');
+-------------+-------------+-----------------------------+
| R_REGIONKEY | R_NAME      | R_COMMENT                   |
+-------------+-------------+-----------------------------+
|           0 | AFRICA      | lar deposits. blithely fin...|
|           1 | AMERICA     | hs use ironic, even reques...|
|           2 | ASIA        | ges. thinly even pinto bea...|
|           3 | EUROPE      | ly final courts cajole fur...|
|           4 | MIDDLE EAST | uickly special accounts ca...|
+-------------+-------------+-----------------------------+
```

While this may not look terribly useful, since I already know the name of the table, things become more interesting when you are writing scripts. When you are working with a script or stored procedure (much more on this in Chapters 15 and 16), the table literals passed into the `table()` function will be evaluated at *runtime*, allowing for some very flexible code.

Here's a script written using the Snowflake Scripting language that will return the number of rows for all tables in the `Public` schema with names less than 10 characters in length:

```
PUBLIC>execute immediate $$
    declare
      v_tbl_nm varchar(50);
      v_tbl_cnt number(7);
      v_output varchar(99999) := 'Tables:';
      v_cur cursor for
        select table_name
        from learning_sql.information_schema.tables
        where table_schema = 'PUBLIC' and table_type <> 'VIEW'
          and length(table_name) < 10;
    begin
      for rec in v_cur do
        v_tbl_nm := rec.table_name;

        select count(*)
        into v_tbl_cnt
        from table(:v_tbl_nm);

        v_output := concat(v_output,' {',
          v_tbl_nm,' : ',v_tbl_cnt,'}');
      end for;
      return v_output;
    end;$$;
+-------------------------------------------------------------+
| anonymous block                                             |
|-------------------------------------------------------------|
| Tables: {CUSTOMER : 66076} {REGION : 5} {PART : 4000}       |
|         {SUPPLIER : 7400} {EMPLOYEE : 8}                    |
|         {LINEITEM : 119989} {NATION : 25}                   |
|         {PARTSUPP : 16000} {PERSON : 5} {ORDERS : 115269}   |
+-------------------------------------------------------------+
```

Obviously, this is a lot to throw at you, and you will learn all about Snowflake Scripting in later chapters, but here's the basic flow:

1. Iterate over the set of table names returned from a query against learn ing_sql.information_schema.

2. Set the value of the variable v_tbl_nm to the table name returned by the query.

3. Pass the v_tbl_nm variable into the table() function and count the number of rows in the table.

4. Add the table name and row count to a string.

5. Return the set of concatenated strings.

Whether you have a basic understanding of the script, the important point to remember is that you can use the table() function to generate a table name from a string literal, and that the string literals can be generated programmatically.

Wrap-Up

This chapter explored some of the interesting uses of the `from` clause. While some features such as hierarchical queries and pivots are available on several database platforms, other features, such as Time Travel, are unique to Snowflake.

Test Your Knowledge

The following exercises are designed to test your understanding of the `from` clause. Please see "Chapter 9" in Appendix B for solutions.

Exercise 9-1

The following query returns the number of customers in each market segment:

```
PUBLIC>select c_mktsegment as mktseg, count(*) tot_custs
        from customer
        group by c_mktsegment;
+------------+-----------+
| MKTSEG     | TOT_CUSTS |
|------------+-----------|
| AUTOMOBILE |     13192 |
| MACHINERY  |     13185 |
| BUILDING   |     13360 |
| FURNITURE  |     13125 |
| HOUSEHOLD  |     13214 |
+------------+-----------+
```

Use this query as the basis for a pivot query so that there is a single row with five columns, with each column having the name of a market segment.

Exercise 9-2

The following query counts the number of suppliers in each nation:

```
PUBLIC>select s_nationkey, count(*) as supplier_count
        from supplier
        group by s_nationkey;
+-------------+----------------+
| S_NATIONKEY | SUPPLIER_COUNT |
|-------------+----------------|
|          17 |            325 |
|          23 |            291 |
|          10 |            306 |
|          24 |            295 |
|          18 |            310 |
|           8 |            301 |
|           3 |            307 |
|          22 |            296 |
|          19 |            290 |
```

```
|            16 |            298 |
|             1 |            312 |
|             7 |            298 |
|            13 |            272 |
|            12 |            275 |
|             5 |            283 |
|            20 |            307 |
|            11 |            309 |
|             2 |            293 |
|             9 |            286 |
|            21 |            287 |
|             6 |            299 |
|            14 |            280 |
|            15 |            265 |
|             4 |            297 |
|             0 |            318 |
+---------------+----------------+
```

Modify this query to add the `Nation.n_name` column using a lateral join to the Nation table.

Exercise 9-3

The `Smith_History` table holds genealogy information for the Smith family:

```
Person_ID   Name        Father_Person_ID
---------   ---------   ----------------
    1       Thomas          (null)
    2       Clara           (null)
    3       Samuel          1
    4       Charles         1
    5       Beth            3
    6       Steven          4
    7       Sarah           6
    8       Robert          4
    9       Dorothy         8
   10       George          8
```

Thomas and Clara's parents are unknown at this point, so they have a null value for the father_person_id column. Write a query to walk the Smith family tree starting with Thomas, using the `sys_connect_by_path()` function to show the full ancestry. You can use the following with clause as a starter:

```
with smith_history as
 (select person_id, name, father_person_id
  from (values
          (1,'Thomas',null),
          (2,'Clara',null),
          (3,'Samuel',1),
          (4,'Charles',1),
          (5,'Beth',3),
          (6,'Steven',4),
          (7,'Sarah',6),
          (8,'Robert',4),
          (9,'Dorothy',8),
          (10,'George',8))
          as smith(person_id, name, father_person_id)
 )
```

Conditional Logic

In certain situations, you may want your SQL statement to behave differently depending on the values of certain columns or expressions, which is known as *conditional logic*. The mechanism used for conditional logic in SQL statements is the `case` expression, which can be utilized in `insert`, `update`, and `delete` statements, as well as in every clause of a `select` statement.

What Is Conditional Logic?

Conditional logic is the process by which one of several paths can be taken. For example, a company's order entry system may have logic specifying that a 10% discount be given if that customer's orders exceeded a certain value for the previous year. If you have written programs using a language like Python or Java, you are accustomed to using `if...then...else` statements, but the SQL language uses `case` expressions for conditional logic. The `case` expression works like a cascading if-then-else statement, evaluating a series of conditions in sequence. Here's a simple example:

```
PUBLIC>select c_custkey, c_name, c_acctbal,
    case
      when c_acctbal < 0 then 'generate refund'
      when c_acctbal = 0 then 'no action'
      else 'send bill'
    end as month_end_action
  from customer
  limit 15;
+-----------+--------------------+-----------+------------------+
| C_CUSTKEY | C_NAME             | C_ACCTBAL | MONTH_END_ACTION |
|-----------+--------------------+-----------+------------------|
|     60001 | Customer#000060001 |   9957.56 | send bill        |
|     60004 | Customer#000060004 |   7975.22 | send bill        |
|     60005 | Customer#000060005 |   2504.74 | send bill        |
```

```
|   60007 | Customer#000060007 |   6017.17 | send bill       |
|   60008 | Customer#000060008 |   5621.44 | send bill       |
|   60013 | Customer#000060013 |   -485.69 | generate refund |
|   60016 | Customer#000060016 |   4480.97 | send bill       |
|   60019 | Customer#000060019 |   3444.77 | send bill       |
|   60020 | Customer#000060020 |   1187.30 | send bill       |
|   60022 | Customer#000060022 |   -759.74 | generate refund |
|   60025 | Customer#000060025 |   7296.15 | send bill       |
|   60026 | Customer#000060026 |   7508.13 | send bill       |
|   60028 | Customer#000060028 |   3494.99 | send bill       |
|   60029 | Customer#000060029 |   9281.15 | send bill       |
|   60031 | Customer#000060031 |   6765.74 | send bill       |
+---------+--------------------+-----------+-----------------+
```

This query includes a `case` expression used to specify whether to send a bill or to generate a refund for each customer depending on whether the customer's account balance is negative or positive.

Case expressions can have multiple conditions (each starting with the when keyword), and the conditions are evaluated in order from top to bottom. Evaluation ends as soon as one condition evaluates as true. The next example includes a `case` expression with five conditions:

```
PUBLIC>select num.val,
         case
           when num.val > 90 then 'huge number'
           when num.val > 50 then 'really big number'
           when num.val > 20 then 'big number'
           when num.val > 10 then 'medium number'
           when num.val <= 10 then 'small number'
         end as num_size
        from (values (11), (12), (25), (99), (3)) as num (val);
+-----+---------------+
| VAL | NUM_SIZE      |
|-----+---------------|
|  11 | medium number |
|  12 | medium number |
|  25 | big number    |
|  99 | huge number   |
|   3 | small number  |
+-----+---------------+
```

In this example, the `case` expression completes at the first condition for one of the values (99), the third condition for another value (25), the fourth condition for two of the values (11 and 12), and the fifth condition for one value (3). The `case` expression evaluates to true for four different conditions for value 99, but since the conditions are evaluated in order the expression "huge number" is returned.

Types of Case Expressions

The next two sections explore the two different types of case expressions.

Searched Case Expressions

The `case` expressions demonstrated earlier in the chapter are examples of *searched case expressions*, which have the following syntax:

```
case
  when condition1 then expression1
  when condition2 then expression2
  ...
  when conditionN then expressionN
  [else expressionZ]
end
```

Searched `case` expressions can have multiple `when` clauses and an optional `else` clause to be returned if none of the `when` clauses evaluate as `true`. Case expressions can return any type of expression, including numbers, strings, dates, and even subqueries, as demonstrated in the following example:

```
PUBLIC>select p_partkey, p_retailprice,
       case
         when p_retailprice > 2000 then
         (select count(*)
          from lineitem li
          where li.l_partkey = p.p_partkey)
         else 0
       end as num_bigticket_orders
       from part p
       where p_retailprice between 1990 and 2010;
+-----------+---------------+---------------------+
| P_PARTKEY | P_RETAILPRICE | NUM_BIGTICKET_ORDERS |
|-----------+---------------+---------------------|
|    135958 |       1993.95 |                   0 |
|    147958 |       2005.95 |                  38 |
|    151958 |       2009.95 |                  36 |
|    148958 |       2006.95 |                  26 |
|    183908 |       1991.90 |                   0 |
|    136958 |       1994.95 |                   0 |
|    195908 |       2003.90 |                  24 |
|    196908 |       2004.90 |                  35 |
|    149958 |       2007.95 |                  36 |
|    191908 |       1999.90 |                   0 |
|    187908 |       1995.90 |                   0 |
|    185908 |       1993.90 |                   0 |
|    190908 |       1998.90 |                   0 |
|    138958 |       1996.95 |                   0 |
|    186908 |       1994.90 |                   0 |
|    140958 |       1998.95 |                   0 |
```

```
|  199908  |     2007.90 |                    25 |
|  133958  |     1991.95 |                     0 |
|  193908  |     2001.90 |                    28 |
|  198908  |     2006.90 |                    31 |
|  189908  |     1997.90 |                     0 |
|  150958  |     2008.95 |                    27 |
|  192908  |     2000.90 |                    36 |
|  182908  |     1990.90 |                     0 |
|  137958  |     1995.95 |                     0 |
|  134958  |     1992.95 |                     0 |
|  146958  |     2004.95 |                    30 |
|  142958  |     2000.95 |                    37 |
|  143958  |     2001.95 |                    34 |
|  144958  |     2002.95 |                    31 |
|  188908  |     1996.90 |                     0 |
|  139958  |     1997.95 |                     0 |
|  184908  |     1992.90 |                     0 |
|  132958  |     1990.95 |                     0 |
|  197908  |     2005.90 |                    31 |
|  141958  |     1999.95 |                     0 |
|  194908  |     2002.90 |                    26 |
|  145958  |     2003.95 |                    29 |
+-----------+--------------+----------------------+
```

This query looks at rows in the Part table and executes a subquery to count the number of times the part has been ordered only if the part's retail price is above $2,000.

Simple Case Expressions

The *simple case expression* is quite similar to the searched case expression but is a bit less flexible (and thus used less frequently). Here's the syntax:

```
case expression
  when value1 then expression1
  when value2 then expression2
  ...
  when valueN then expressionN
  [else expressionZ]
end
```

For this type of statement, an expression is evaluated and compared to a set of values. If a match is found, the corresponding expression is returned, and if no match is found, the expression in the optional else clause is returned. Here's an example using a simple case expression to decode the values stored in the orderstatus column:

```
PUBLIC>select o_orderkey,
        case o_orderstatus
          when 'P' then 'Partial'
          when 'F' then 'Filled'
          when 'O' then 'Open'
        end as status
      from orders
```

```
        limit 20;
+-------------+----------+
| O_ORDERKEY  | STATUS   |
|-------------+----------|
|     1200005 | Filled   |
|     1200128 | Partial  |
|     1200199 | Filled   |
|     1200257 | Open     |
|     1200418 | Filled   |
|     1200453 | Partial  |
|     1200582 | Open     |
|     1200611 | Open     |
|     1200614 | Filled   |
|     1200737 | Filled   |
|     1200738 | Filled   |
|     1200864 | Filled   |
|     1200868 | Open     |
|     1200870 | Open     |
|     1200899 | Open     |
|     1200928 | Open     |
|     1200932 | Open     |
|     1200995 | Open     |
|     1201057 | Filled   |
|     1201090 | Filled   |
+-------------+----------+
```

The case expression in this example represents a common use of simple case expressions, where a small number of values (in this case "P," "F," and "O") are translated into more meaningful strings.

Uses for Case Expressions

The following sections present a number of examples demonstrating the utility of conditional logic in SQL statements.

Pivot Operations

There are situations where you will want to pivot a result set from a number of rows into a single row with a number of columns. For example, here's a query that returns the total order prices for each year after 1994:

```
PUBLIC>select date_part(year, o_orderdate),
         round(sum(o_totalprice))
       from orders
       where date_part(year, o_orderdate) >= 1995
       group by date_part(year, o_orderdate)
       order by 1;
+------------------------------+---------------------------+
| DATE_PART(YEAR, O_ORDERDATE) | ROUND(SUM(O_TOTALPRICE))  |
|------------------------------+---------------------------|
```

```
|                1995 |                  3317521810 |
|                1996 |                  3296373353 |
|                1997 |                  3255086721 |
|                1998 |                  1925196449 |
+-----------------------------+-----------------------------+
```

Rather than presenting the data as one row per year, you may need to format the data for a report that shows all four years in single row:

```
+------------+------------+------------+------------+
| 1995       | 1996       | 1997       | 1998       |
|------------+------------+------------+------------|
| 3317521810 | 3296373353 | 3255086721 | 1925196449 |
+------------+------------+------------+------------+
```

This is known as a *pivot*, and it is a very common operation in data analysis and reporting. While Snowflake does include a `pivot` operation (see Chapter 9 for details), you can also pivot a result set using a set of `case` expressions. Here's what that would look like for this example:

```
PUBLIC>select
         round(sum(case when 1995 = date_part(year, o_orderdate)
                   then o_totalprice else 0 end)) as "1995",
         round(sum(case when 1996 = date_part(year, o_orderdate)
                   then o_totalprice else 0 end)) as "1996",
         round(sum(case when 1997 = date_part(year, o_orderdate)
                   then o_totalprice else 0 end)) as "1997",
         round(sum(case when 1998 = date_part(year, o_orderdate)
                   then o_totalprice else 0 end)) as "1998"
       from orders
       where date_part(year, o_orderdate) >= 1995;
+------------+------------+------------+------------+
|       1995 |       1996 |       1997 |       1998 |
|------------+------------+------------+------------|
| 3317521810 | 3296373353 | 3255086721 | 1925196449 |
+------------+------------+------------+------------+
```

Each of the four columns sums the values returned by a `case` expression, and each `case` expression returns a nonzero value only if the order was placed in the specified year (1995, 1996, 1997, or 1998). Since each column value is generated using an aggregate function (`sum()` in this example), there is no need for a `group by` clause.

Checking for Existence

You may run into a situation where you need to know if a certain relationship exists, without regard for the number of occurrences. For example, let's say you want to find out if a customer has ever placed an order over $400,000, but it doesn't matter how many such orders were placed. Here's how that could be accomplished using a `case` expression with a correlated subquery:

```
PUBLIC>select c_custkey, c_name,
        case
          when exists
          (select 1 from orders o
            where o.o_custkey = c.c_custkey
              and o.o_totalprice > 400000) then 'Big Spender'
          else 'Regular'
        end as cust_type
      from customer c
      where c_custkey between 74000 and 74020;
+-----------+--------------------+-------------+
| C_CUSTKEY | C_NAME             | CUST_TYPE   |
|-----------+--------------------+-------------|
|     74003 | Customer#000074003 | Big Spender |
|     74008 | Customer#000074008 | Regular     |
|     74011 | Customer#000074011 | Big Spender |
|     74014 | Customer#000074014 | Regular     |
|     74015 | Customer#000074015 | Regular     |
|     74000 | Customer#000074000 | Regular     |
|     74009 | Customer#000074009 | Regular     |
|     74020 | Customer#000074020 | Regular     |
|     74017 | Customer#000074017 | Regular     |
|     74012 | Customer#000074012 | Regular     |
|     74005 | Customer#000074005 | Regular     |
+-----------+--------------------+-------------+
```

Since the subquery is used with the `exists` operator, the first condition in the case expression evaluates as `true` as long as the subquery returns at least one row. For this particular sample of the `Customer` table, two customers were found to have at least one order over $400,000.

Conditional Updates

To continue with the previous example, let's say that you added the column `cust_type` to the `Customer` table (which I won't actually do to preserve the integrity of the test data) and wanted to populate the new column for all customers using the following logic:

```
"Big Spender" for any customer who placed an order over $400,000,
"Regular" for everyone else
```

This could be done simply by moving the `case` expression into the `set` clause of an `update` statement:

```
update customer as c
set cust_type =
case
  when exists
    (select 1 from orders as o
      where o.o_custkey = c.c_custkey
        and o.o_totalprice > 400000)
```

```
    then 'Big Spender'
  else 'Regular'
end;
```

If this statement were executed, the table would look similar to what was shown in the previous section:

```
PUBLIC>select c_custkey, c_name, cust_type
       from customer c
       where c_custkey between 74000 and 74020;
+-----------+---------------------+-------------+
| C_CUSTKEY | C_NAME              | CUST_TYPE   |
|-----------+---------------------+-------------|
|     74003 | Customer#000074003  | Big Spender |
|     74008 | Customer#000074008  | Regular     |
|     74011 | Customer#000074011  | Big Spender |
|     74014 | Customer#000074014  | Regular     |
|     74015 | Customer#000074015  | Regular     |
|     74000 | Customer#000074000  | Regular     |
|     74009 | Customer#000074009  | Regular     |
|     74020 | Customer#000074020  | Regular     |
|     74017 | Customer#000074017  | Regular     |
|     74012 | Customer#000074012  | Regular     |
|     74005 | Customer#000074005  | Regular     |
+-----------+---------------------+-------------+
```

Case expressions are also useful for **delete** statements, such as:

```
delete from customer c
where 1 =
case
  when not exists
   (select 1 from orders as o
    where o.o_custkey = c.c_custkey
      and o.o_totalprice > 1000)
    then 1
  when '31-DEC-1995' >
   (select max(o_orderdate) from orders as o
    where o.o_custkey = c.c_custkey)
    then 1
  else 0
end;
```

This statement would remove any customers who had never placed any orders over $1,000 or who hadn't placed any orders in 1996 or later. If you remove data and decide you'd like it back, you can always use Snowflake's Time Travel feature to retrieve it (see "Oops! Where's the Undo Button..." on page 84 in Chapter 5 for an example).

Modifying the Sample Data

If you do wish to experiment with modifying the data in any of the sample database tables (Customer, Orders, Lineitem, etc.), you can always reset a table to its original state by deleting all of the rows and reloading the data. Please see the Preface for information on how to create and load the sample database tables.

Functions for Conditional Logic

Along with case expressions, Snowflake also includes several built-in functions that are useful for conditional logic. The following sections will demonstrate a few of these functions, in some cases using examples from earlier in the chapter with matching case expressions to help illustrate.

iff() Function

If you only need a simple if-then-else expression having a single condition, you can use the iff() function:

```
PUBLIC>select c_custkey, c_name,
        case
          when exists
            (select 1 from orders o
             where o.o_custkey = c.c_custkey
               and o.o_totalprice > 400000) then 'Big Spender'
          else 'Regular'
        end as cust_type_case,
        iff(exists
            (select 1 from orders o
             where o.o_custkey = c.c_custkey
               and o.o_totalprice > 400000),
             'Big Spender','Regular') as cust_type_iff
        from customer c
        where c_custkey between 74000 and 74020;
+-----------+-------------------+----------------+---------------+
| C_CUSTKEY | C_NAME            | CUST_TYPE_CASE | CUST_TYPE_IFF |
|-----------+-------------------+----------------+---------------|
|     74011 | Customer#000074011 | Big Spender   | Big Spender   |
|     74003 | Customer#000074003 | Big Spender   | Big Spender   |
|     74005 | Customer#000074005 | Regular        | Regular       |
|     74015 | Customer#000074015 | Regular        | Regular       |
|     74017 | Customer#000074017 | Regular        | Regular       |
|     74008 | Customer#000074008 | Regular        | Regular       |
|     74020 | Customer#000074020 | Regular        | Regular       |
|     74000 | Customer#000074000 | Regular        | Regular       |
|     74012 | Customer#000074012 | Regular        | Regular       |
|     74009 | Customer#000074009 | Regular        | Regular       |
|     74014 | Customer#000074014 | Regular        | Regular       |
+-----------+-------------------+----------------+---------------+
```

For both the case expression and iff() function, a single condition is evaluated (the existence of a row in the orders table), resulting in either the string 'Big Spender' or 'Regular'. Keep in mind that the iff() function cannot be used if multiple conditions need to be evaluated.

ifnull() and nvl() Functions

You will likely run into situations, especially when writing reports, where you want to substitute a value such as 'unknown' or 'N/A' when a column is null. For these situations, you can use either the ifnull() or nvl() functions, as shown in the next example:

```
PUBLIC>select name,
         nvl(favorite_color,'Unknown') as favorite_color_nvl,
         ifnull(favorite_color,'Unknown') as favorite_color_isnull
     from (values ('Thomas','yellow'), ('Catherine','red'),
                  ('Richard','blue'), ('Rebecca',null))
     as person (name, favorite_color);
+-----------+--------------------+-----------------------+
| NAME      | FAVORITE_COLOR_NVL | FAVORITE_COLOR_ISNULL |
|-----------+--------------------+-----------------------|
| Thomas    | yellow             | yellow                |
| Catherine | red                | red                   |
| Richard   | blue               | blue                  |
| Rebecca   | Unknown            | Unknown               |
+-----------+--------------------+-----------------------+
```

In this simple example, one of the four people didn't specify a favorite color, so either the nvl() or ifnull() function can be used to substitute the value 'Unknown'.

These functions are also useful for cases where the value for a column can come from one of two different places. Here's a variation of an example from "Full Outer Joins" on page 154 using a full outer join:

```
PUBLIC>select orders.ordernum,
         case
           when orders.custkey is not null then orders.custkey
           when customer.custkey is not null then customer.custkey
         end as custkey_case,
         nvl(orders.custkey, customer.custkey) as custkey_nvl,
         ifnull(orders.custkey, customer.custkey)
           as custkey_ifnull,
         customer.custname as name
     from
      (values (990, 101), (991, 102),
              (992, 101), (993, 104))
        as orders (ordernum, custkey)
      full outer join
      (values (101, 'BOB'), (102, 'KIM'), (103, 'JIM'))
        as customer (custkey, custname)
```

```
       on orders.custkey = customer.custkey;
+-----------+--------------+--------------+-----------------+------+
| ORDERNUM  | CUSTKEY_CASE | CUSTKEY_NVL  | CUSTKEY_IFNULL  | NAME |
|-----------+--------------+--------------+-----------------+------|
|       990 |          101 |          101 |             101 | BOB  |
|       991 |          102 |          102 |             102 | KIM  |
|       992 |          101 |          101 |             101 | BOB  |
|       993 |          104 |          104 |             104 | NULL |
+-----------+--------------+--------------+-----------------+------+
```

In this example, the value for `custkey` can come from either the `customer` or `orders`
data sets, so conditional logic is needed to determine whether to use the `orders.cust`
`key` or `customer.custkey` value.

If you need to choose between more than two columns to find a nonnull value, you
can use the `coalesce()` function, which allows for an unlimited number of expressions to be evaluated.

decode() Function

The `decode()` function works just like a simple case expression; a single expression is
compared to a set of one or more values, and when a match is found the corresponding value is returned. Here's the example used earlier in the chapter, but with both a
simple case expression and a `decode()` function:

```
PUBLIC>select o_orderkey,
        case o_orderstatus
          when 'P' then 'Partial'
          when 'F' then 'Filled'
          when 'O' then 'Open'
        end as status_case,
        decode(o_orderstatus, 'P', 'Partial',
                              'F', 'Filled',
                              'O', 'Open') as status_decode
      from orders
      limit 20;
+------------+-------------+---------------+
| O_ORDERKEY | STATUS_CASE | STATUS_DECODE |
|------------+-------------+---------------|
|     600006 | Open        | Open          |
|     600037 | Filled      | Filled        |
|     600064 | Open        | Open          |
|     600065 | Filled      | Filled        |
|     600132 | Open        | Open          |
|     600165 | Filled      | Filled        |
|     600228 | Filled      | Filled        |
|     600262 | Open        | Open          |
|     600327 | Open        | Open          |
|     600484 | Open        | Open          |
|     600486 | Partial     | Partial       |
|     600519 | Open        | Open          |
```

```
|     600576 | Filled      | Filled        |
|     600612 | Filled      | Filled        |
|     600644 | Open        | Open          |
|     600707 | Open        | Open          |
|     600709 | Open        | Open          |
|     600806 | Filled      | Filled        |
|     600896 | Filled      | Filled        |
|     600961 | Open        | Open          |
+------------+-------------+---------------+
```

While some people prefer using decode( ) because it is less wordy, I prefer to use case because it is easier to understand and is portable between different database servers.

Wrap-Up

This chapter explored the use of conditional logic in SQL statements, including both searched and simple case expressions. Additionally, you were introduced to several of Snowflake's built-in functions used for conditional logic. Using conditional logic in your statements will make your code more flexible, allowing you to do more work with less coding.

Test Your Knowledge

The following exercises are designed to test your understanding of conditional logic. Please see "Chapter 10" in Appendix B for solutions.

Exercise 10-1

Add a column named order_status to the following query that will use a case expression to return the value 'order now' if the ps_availqty value is less than 100, 'order soon' if the ps_availqty value is between 101 and 1000, and 'plenty in stock' otherwise:

```
PUBLIC>select ps_partkey, ps_suppkey, ps_availqty
       from partsupp
       where ps_partkey between 148300 and 148450;
+-------------+-------------+--------------+
| PS_PARTKEY  | PS_SUPPKEY  | PS_AVAILQTY  |
|-------------+-------------+--------------|
|     148308  |       8309  |       9570   |
|     148308  |        823  |       7201   |
|     148308  |       3337  |       7917   |
|     148308  |       5851  |       8257   |
|     148358  |       8359  |       9839   |
|     148358  |        873  |       6917   |
|     148358  |       3387  |       1203   |
|     148358  |       5901  |          1   |
|     148408  |       8409  |         74   |
```

```
|      148408 |        923 |        341 |
|      148408 |       3437 |       4847 |
|      148408 |       5951 |       1985 |
+-------------+------------+------------+
```

Exercise 10-2

Rewrite the following query to use a searched case expression instead of a simple case expression:

```
PUBLIC>select o_orderdate, o_custkey,
        case o_orderstatus
          when 'P' then 'Partial'
          when 'F' then 'Filled'
          when 'O' then 'Open'
        end status
      from orders
      where o_orderkey > 5999500;
+-------------+------------+---------+
| O_ORDERDATE | O_CUSTKEY  | STATUS  |
|-------------+------------+---------|
| 1993-02-24  |      80807 | Filled  |
| 1995-05-06  |     124231 | Partial |
| 1995-06-03  |     141032 | Partial |
| 1994-07-20  |      30140 | Filled  |
| 1998-02-16  |      86125 | Open    |
| 1996-09-14  |     108310 | Open    |
| 1994-01-09  |      40673 | Filled  |
| 1995-11-19  |     124754 | Open    |
+-------------+------------+---------+
```

Exercise 10-3

The following query returns the number of suppliers in each region:

```
PUBLIC>select r_name, count(*)
      from nation n
      inner join region r on r.r_regionkey = n.n_regionkey
      inner join supplier s on s.s_nationkey = n.n_nationkey
      group by r_name;
+-------------+----------+
| R_NAME      | COUNT(*) |
|-------------+----------|
| AMERICA     |     1532 |
| AFRICA      |     1444 |
| EUROPE      |     1474 |
| MIDDLE EAST |     1491 |
| ASIA        |     1459 |
+-------------+----------+
```

Modify this query to use `case` expressions to pivot this data so that it looks as follows:

```
+---------+--------+--------+-------------+------+
| AMERICA | AFRICA | EUROPE | MIDDLE_EAST | ASIA |
|---------+--------+--------+-------------+------|
|    1532 |   1444 |   1474 |        1491 | 1459 |
+---------+--------+--------+-------------+------+
```

Transactions

This chapter explores *transactions*, which are the mechanism used to group a set of SQL statements together such that either all or none of the statements succeed.

What Is a Transaction?

A transaction is a series of SQL statements within a single database session, with the goal of having all of the changes either applied or undone as a unit. In other words, when using a transaction, you will never face a situation where some of your changes succeed and others fail. Consider the classic scenario of a bank transfer, where money is withdrawn from one account and deposited into another; if your money was withdrawn from your savings account but the deposit to your checking account fails, your money would disappear. Here's a pseudocode description of how a transaction would eliminate this possibility:

```
Begin Transaction
Update Savings_Account (remove $100 as long as balance >= $100)
Update Checking_Account (add $100)
If errors then
  Rollback Transaction
Else
  Commit Transaction
End If
```

The next section describes the ways that Snowflake handles transactions.

Explicit and Implicit Transactions

You can choose to start a transaction by issuing the `begin transaction` statement, after which all following SQL statements will be considered part of the transaction until you issue a `commit` or `rollback` statement. This is known as an *explicit transaction* because you are instructing Snowflake to start a transaction. Here's an example with two `insert` statements inside a single transaction:

```
PUBLIC>begin transaction;
+----------------------------------+
| status                           |
|----------------------------------|
| Statement executed successfully. |
+----------------------------------+
1 Row(s) produced. Time Elapsed: 0.142s

PUBLIC>insert into person (first_name, last_name, birth_date,
                           eye_color, occupation)
       values ('John','Sanford','2002-03-22'::date,
               'brown','analyst');
+------------------------+
| number of rows inserted |
|------------------------|
|                      1 |
+------------------------+
1 Row(s) produced. Time Elapsed: 1.307s

PUBLIC>insert into employee (empid, emp_name, mgr_empid)
       values (1007, 'John Sanford',1002);
+------------------------+
| number of rows inserted |
|------------------------|
|                      1 |
+------------------------+
1 Row(s) produced. Time Elapsed: 0.492s

PUBLIC>commit;
+----------------------------------+
| status                           |
|----------------------------------|
| Statement executed successfully. |
+----------------------------------+
1 Row(s) produced. Time Elapsed: 0.879s
```

The `commit` statement applied both changes to the database; if I had issued a `roll back` instead, both changes would have been undone.

If you execute an `insert`, `update`, `delete`, or `merge` statement without first starting a transaction, then a transaction is automatically started for you by Snowflake. This is known as an *implicit transaction* because you did not start the transaction yourself. What happens next depends on whether your session is in *autocommit mode*. When you are in autocommit mode, which is the default setting, every modification to the database will be committed individually if the statement succeeds, and rolled back otherwise. Therefore, if you execute four `update` statements and the first three succeed but the fourth one fails, it will be up to you to undo the changes made by the first three statements if the changes are related.

To check if autocommit is enabled for your session, you can use the show parameters command:

```
PUBLIC>show parameters like 'autocommit';
+-------------+-------+---------+---------+-------------+
| key         | value | default | level   | description |
|-------------+-------+---------+---------+-------------|
| AUTOCOMMIT  | true  | true    | SESSION | ...         |
+-------------+-------+---------+---------+-------------+
```

If your session is *not* in autocommit mode, and you modify the database without first issuing begin transaction, there are several ways in which your implicit transaction can end:

- You execute a data definition language (DDL) command, such as create table.
- You change the autocommit setting (using alter session set autocommit or alter session unset autocommit).
- You start a transaction explicitly with begin transaction.
- You end your database session.
- You issue a commit or rollback.

For the first three cases, Snowflake will issue a commit if there are any pending changes and then start a new transaction. If you end your session, however, any pending changes will be rolled back.

If you want to enable or disable autocommit in your session, you can use the alter session command; here's an example showing how to disable autocommit:

```
PUBLIC>alter session set autocommit = false;
+----------------------------------+
| status                           |
|----------------------------------|
| Statement executed successfully. |
+----------------------------------+
PUBLIC>show parameters like 'autocommit';
+-------------+-------+---------+---------+-------------+
| key         | value | default | level   | description |
|-------------+-------+---------+---------+-------------|
| AUTOCOMMIT  | false | true    | SESSION | ...         |
+-------------+-------+---------+---------+-------------+
```

If this all seems a bit confusing, then I suggest you adopt the following best practices:

- Explicitly start transactions using begin transaction.
- Resolve all transactions using commit or rollback prior to ending session.
- Explicitly end any open transactions prior to issuing DDL commands.

The next section discusses some considerations for modifying data in Snowflake.

Related Topics

The following sections discuss some Snowflake behaviors related to transactions.

Finding Open Transactions

Snowflake supplies the show transactions statement to list any open transactions. In the following example, a transaction is started, an update statement is executed, and then show transactions is called:

```
PUBLIC>begin transaction;
+---------------------------------+
| status                          |
|---------------------------------|
| Statement executed successfully. |
+---------------------------------+

PUBLIC>update employee set mgr_empid = 1004
       where empid = 1007;
+-----------------------+------------------------------------+
| number of rows updated | number of multi-joined rows updated |
|-----------------------+------------------------------------|
|                     1 |                                  0 |
+-----------------------+------------------------------------+

PUBLIC>show transactions;
+----------------------+----------+------------------+
|                   id | user     |          session |
|----------------------+----------+------------------|
| 1670360562906000000 | ALANBEAU | 738725785436166 |
+----------------------+----------+------------------+
        ---------------------------------------+
        name                                   |
        ---------------------------------------+
        45b9d0fe-eb58-459d-946a-570e8b948347   |
        ---------------------------------------+
            ----------------------------------+---------+-------+
            started_on                        | state   | scope |
            ----------------------------------+---------+-------|
            2022-12-06 13:02:42.906 -0800     | running |     0 |
            ----------------------------------+---------+-------+
```

If you should run into a problem that requires a transaction to be canceled, the output from `show transactions` should give you all the necessary information.

Isolation Levels

The concept of an *isolation level* is pertinent to a discussion of transactions because isolation deals with when changes are visible to other sessions. For example, let's say session A starts a transaction, modifies 10,000 rows in table XYZ, and then issues a `rollback`. If session B issues a query against table XYZ after session A's transaction has started but before the changes were rolled back, what should session B's query return? Some database servers provide multiple options, including a *dirty read* option, which allows one session to see uncommitted changes from other sessions. Snowflake, however, only allows a statement to see *committed* changes, so Snowflake is said to have an isolation level of *read committed*. This extends throughout the execution of the statement, so even if a query takes an hour to complete, the server must guarantee that no changes made after the statement began executing will be visible to the query.

There are a couple of caveats worth discussing regarding the isolation level. If you start a transaction and then execute two `update` statements (let's call them Update A and Update B), you need to keep in mind the following:

- Update B will see the uncommitted changes from Update A.
- Update B will see any changes committed by other sessions, even if the commit happened while Update A was executing.

Therefore, SQL statements will see uncommitted changes made within the same transaction, but only committed changes made by other transactions. Also, multiple statements in the same transaction may see different views of the data as other transactions commit their changes.

Locking

All database servers use locks to prevent multiple sessions from modifying the same data. If one user updates a row in a table, a lock is held until the transaction ends, which protects against another transaction modifying the same row. However, there are different levels, or *granularities*, of locking:

- Table locks, where an entire table is locked when any row is modified
- Page locks, where a subset of a table's rows are locked (rows in the same physical page or block)
- Row locks, where only the modified rows are locked

As you might imagine, table locks are easy to administer but are problematic when multiple users are modifying data in the same table. Row-level locks, on the other hand, provide the highest level of concurrent access, but also take the most overhead to administer.

Snowflake's locking scheme is a bit harder to nail down but lies somewhere between table-level and page-level locking. Snowflake automatically breaks tables into pieces, called *micropartitions*, which hold between 50MB and 500MB of uncompressed data. If multiple transactions attempt to modify or delete data in the same micropartition, one session will be *blocked* and must wait until the other session's transaction completes. The following sections explore some of the related issues.

Lock wait time

When a session is blocked waiting for a lock to be released, it will wait for a configurable amount of time and then fail if the lock has not been released. The maximum number of seconds can be set using the lock_timeout parameter, which can be set at the session level:

```
PUBLIC>alter session set lock_timeout=600;
+----------------------------------+
| status                           |
|----------------------------------|
| Statement executed successfully. |
+----------------------------------+
```

This statement sets the maximum lock wait to 10 minutes. While it is possible to set this value to 0, it is not recommended since it will cause an error to be thrown every time a lock is encountered. The default timeout is 12 hours, which is a very long time, so you may want to consider setting the value to something smaller.

Deadlocks

A deadlock is a scenario where session A is waiting for a lock held by session B, and session B is waiting for a lock held by session A. While this is generally a rare occurrence, it does happen, and database servers need to have a strategy to resolve deadlocks. When Snowflake identifies a deadlock, it chooses the session having the most recent statement to be the victim, allowing the other transaction to progress. It can take Snowflake a while to detect a deadlock, however, so setting the lock_timeout parameter to a lower value might help resolve these situations faster. If you encounter a deadlock situation and identify a transaction that you would like to abort, you can use the system function system$abort_transaction() to do so.

Transactions and Stored Procedures

Stored procedures will be covered in Chapter 16, but here are some considerations concerning how stored procedures can participate in transactions. A stored procedure is a compiled program written using Snowflake's Scripting language (see Chapter 15). Even if you don't write your own stored procedures, you may need to call existing stored procedures within your transactions, so here are a few rules to consider:

- A stored procedure cannot end a transaction started outside of the stored procedure.

- If a stored procedure starts a transaction, it must also complete it by issuing either a commit or rollback. No transaction started within a stored procedure can be unresolved when the stored procedure completes.

- A stored procedure can contain 0, 1, or several transactions, and not all statements within the stored procedure must be within a transaction.

If you are working on a team that uses stored procedures, it is always a good idea to discuss *transactional flow*, which helps define who should ultimately have control of transaction scope. Otherwise, you could end up with partially committed work.

Wrap-Up

In this chapter, you learned about transactions and how they can be either implicit (via autocommit) or explicit (via begin transaction). You also learned about related concepts such as locking and isolation levels. When writing code that modifies data, it is always a good idea to understand what happens if an error is encountered, and whether your code will always be executed independently or as part of another process.

Test Your Knowledge

The following exercise is designed to test your understanding of transactions. Please see "Chapter 11" in Appendix B for solutions.

Exercise 11-1

Generate a unit of work to transfer $50 from account 123 to account 789. You will need to insert two rows into the transactions table and update two rows in the account table. Use the following table definitions/data:

```
                Account:
account_id avail_balance last_activity_date
---------- ------------- -------------------
123        500           2023-07-10 20:53:27
789        75            2023-06-22 15:18:35

                Transactions:
txn_id txn_date    account_id  txn_type_cd amount
------ ----------- ----------- ----------- --------
1001   2023-05-15  123         C           500
1002   2023-06-01  789         C           75
```

Use `txn_type_cd = 'C'` to indicate a credit (addition), and `txn_type_cd = 'D'` to indicate a debit (subtraction).

Views

Well-designed applications generally expose a public interface while keeping implementation details private, which insulates end users from complexity and future changes. With Snowflake, you can store data in tables but provide access to that data through a set of views (and/or *table functions*, which are covered in Chapter 17). This chapter discusses what views are, how they are created, and when and how you might want to use them.

What Is a View?

A view is a database object similar to a table, but views can only be queried. Views do not involve any data storage (with the exception of *materialized views*, which are discussed later). One way to think of a view is as a named query, stored in the database for easy use. If you run a report on the last business day of each month, you could create a view containing the query used to generate the report, and then query the view each month. This is just one of several uses of views, some of which will be discussed later in the chapter.

Creating Views

Views are created using the `create view` statement, which is essentially a name followed by a query. Here's a simple example of a view that includes four columns from the Employee table:

```
PUBLIC>create view employee_vw
       as
       select empid, emp_name, mgr_empid, inactive
       from employee;
```

```
+-------------------------------------+
| status                              |
|-------------------------------------|
| View EMPLOYEE_VW successfully created. |
+-------------------------------------+
```

The output of employee_vw looks just like the output of a table:

```
PUBLIC>describe employee_vw;
+-----------+-------------+--------+-------+---------+...
| name      | type        | kind   | null? | default |...
|-----------+-------------+--------+-------+---------+...
| EMPID     | NUMBER(4,0) | COLUMN | Y     | NULL    |...
| EMP_NAME  | VARCHAR(14) | COLUMN | Y     | NULL    |...
| MGR_EMPID | NUMBER(4,0) | COLUMN | Y     | NULL    |...
| INACTIVE  | VARCHAR(1)  | COLUMN | Y     | NULL    |...
+-----------+-------------+--------+-------+---------+...
```

The view definition shows the column names and data types (such as NUMBER(4,0) for the empid column), which are derived from the underlying table (Employee in this case). While the Employee table has six columns, only the four specified in the create view statement are accessible through this view.

The view can also be queried just like a table:

```
PUBLIC>select * from employee_vw;
+-------+----------------+-----------+----------+
| EMPID | EMP_NAME       | MGR_EMPID | INACTIVE |
|-------+----------------+-----------+----------|
|  1001 | Bob Smith      |      NULL | NULL     |
|  1002 | Susan Jackson  |      1001 | Y        |
|  1003 | Greg Carpenter |      1001 | Y        |
|  1004 | Robert Butler  |      1002 | Y        |
|  1005 | Kim Josephs    |      1003 | Y        |
|  1006 | John Tyler     |      1004 | Y        |
|  9999 | Tim Traveler   |      1006 | NULL     |
|  1007 | John Sanford   |      1002 | NULL     |
+-------+----------------+-----------+----------+
```

When defining a view, you have the option of providing your own names for the view columns, rather than having them derived from the underlying tables. Here's another create view statement that creates a view on top of the Person table, but provides alternate names for each column:

```
PUBLIC>create view person_vw (fname, lname, dob, eyes)
       as
       select first_name, last_name, birth_date, eye_color
       from person;
+-------------------------------------+
| status                              |
|-------------------------------------|
| View PERSON_VW successfully created. |
+-------------------------------------+
```

The view definition shows the column names specified in the `create view` statement, rather than the associated column names from the `Person` table:

```
PUBLIC>describe person_vw;
+-------+------------+--------+-------+---------+...
| name  | type       | kind   | null? | default |...
|-------+------------+--------+-------+---------+...
| FNAME | VARCHAR(50)| COLUMN | Y     | NULL    |...
| LNAME | VARCHAR(50)| COLUMN | Y     | NULL    |...
| DOB   | DATE       | COLUMN | Y     | NULL    |...
| EYES  | VARCHAR(10)| COLUMN | Y     | NULL    |...
+-------+------------+--------+-------+---------+...
```

Both of the views created thus far utilize very simple queries, but you can create views with far more interesting `select` statements. Here's a view definition that joins several tables from the sample database and includes `where`, `group by`, and `having` clauses:

```
PUBLIC>create view big_spenders_1998_vw
         (custkey, cust_name, total_order_dollars)
       as
       select o_custkey, c.c_name, sum(o_totalprice)
       from orders as o
       inner join customer as c
         on o.o_custkey = c.c_custkey
       where 1998 = date_part(year, o.o_orderdate)
       group by o.o_custkey, c.c_name
       having sum(o.o_totalprice) >= 500000;
+------------------------------------------------+
| status                                         |
|------------------------------------------------|
| View BIG_SPENDERS_1998_VW successfully created. |
+------------------------------------------------+
```

A view such as this one might be useful for members of the marketing and sales departments to help identify customers for sales promotions. Here are the results of a query against this view:

```
PUBLIC>select * from big_spenders_1998_vw;
+---------+--------------------+---------------------+
| CUSTKEY | CUST_NAME          | TOTAL_ORDER_DOLLARS |
|---------+--------------------+---------------------|
|   24877 | Customer#000024877 |         1578899.25  |
|   99025 | Customer#000099025 |         1508688.47  |
|   26518 | Customer#000026518 |         1684033.20  |
|      19 | Customer#000000019 |         1583979.98  |
|   27970 | Customer#000027970 |         1533905.90  |
|  119539 | Customer#000119539 |         1786908.24  |
|  106000 | Customer#000106000 |         1524573.97  |
+---------+--------------------+---------------------+
```

The next section will explore some of the ways views can be utilized.

Using Views

Views can be used in queries anywhere that tables can be used, meaning that you can join views, execute subqueries against views, use them in common table expressions, etc. Here's a query that joins the person_vw and employee_vw views together:

```
PUBLIC>select p.fname, p.lname, e.empid
    from person_vw as p
    inner join employee_vw as e
    on e.emp_name = concat(p.fname,' ',p.lname);
+-------+----------+-------+
| FNAME | LNAME    | EMPID |
|-------+----------+-------|
| Bob   | Smith    |  1001 |
| John  | Sanford  |  1007 |
+-------+----------+-------+
```

You can also use views and tables in the same query. The next example queries the person_vw view in the with clause (a.k.a. common table expression) and then joins to the Employee table:

```
PUBLIC>with p as
        (select concat(fname,' ',lname) as full_name, dob
         from person_vw
        )
        select p.full_name, p.dob, e.empid
        from p
        inner join employee as e
          on p.full_name = e.emp_name;
+--------------+------------+-------+
| FULL_NAME    | DOB        | EMPID |
|--------------+------------+-------|
| Bob Smith    | 2000-01-22 |  1001 |
| John Sanford | 2002-03-22 |  1007 |
+--------------+------------+-------+
```

While Snowflake doesn't allow data to be modified using a view, you can use views interchangeably with tables in your select statements.

Why Use Views?

At this point you might be wondering: if views can be used just like tables, what exactly is the benefit of using views? The following sections will illustrate some situations where views can be beneficial.

Data Security

This section illustrates the use of views to restrict access to columns and rows.

Restricting column access

Before discussing the topic of data security, let's create some data that would generally be considered to be sensitive. The next statement adds a `salary` column to the `Employee` table:

```
PUBLIC>alter table employee add salary number(7,0);
+----------------------------------+
| status                           |
|----------------------------------|
| Statement executed successfully. |
+----------------------------------+
```

Next, let's assign a salary to each employee, using the built-in `uniform()` function to generate a random number between 50,000 and 200,000:

```
PUBLIC>update employee
       set salary = uniform(50000, 200000, random());
+----------------------+------------------------------------+
| number of rows updated | number of multi-joined rows updated |
|----------------------+------------------------------------|
|                    8 |                                  0 |
+----------------------+------------------------------------+
```

Here are the results:

```
PUBLIC>select empid, emp_name, salary
       from employee;
+-------+----------------+--------+
| EMPID | EMP_NAME       | SALARY |
|-------+----------------+--------|
|  1001 | Bob Smith      |  64176 |
|  1002 | Susan Jackson  |  97197 |
|  1003 | Greg Carpenter |  93561 |
|  1004 | Robert Butler  |  72472 |
|  1005 | Kim Josephs    | 164615 |
|  1006 | John Tyler     | 169274 |
|  9999 | Tim Traveler   |  61748 |
|  1007 | John Sanford   |  67637 |
+-------+----------------+--------+
```

Now that we have each employee's salary in the `Employee` table, it's a good time to discuss who should have access to this sensitive information. While the members of the human resources department will need to have access to salary information, let's say that the VP of human resources has decreed that managers can see what range each employee's salary falls in (without seeing the actual salary), while nonmanagers won't have any access to salary information.

To implement this strategy, managers will no longer have permissions on the `Employee` table but will instead access employee information using the new `employee_manager_vw` view, which is defined as follows:

```
PUBLIC>create view employee_manager_vw
     (empid, emp_name, mgr_empid, salary_range)
     as
     select empid, emp_name, mgr_empid,
       case
         when salary <= 75000 then 'Low'
         when salary <= 125000 then 'Medium'
         else 'High'
       end as salary_range
     from employee;
+---------------------------------------------------+
| status                                            |
|---------------------------------------------------|
| View EMPLOYEE_MANAGER_VW successfully created.     |
+---------------------------------------------------+
```

Here's what the data looks like using this view:

```
PUBLIC>select * from employee_manager_vw;
+--------+-----------------+------------+--------------+
| EMPID  | EMP_NAME        | MGR_EMPID  | SALARY_RANGE |
|--------+-----------------+------------+--------------|
|  1001  | Bob Smith       |     NULL   | Low          |
|  1002  | Susan Jackson   |     1001   | Medium       |
|  1003  | Greg Carpenter  |     1001   | Medium       |
|  1004  | Robert Butler   |     1002   | Low          |
|  1005  | Kim Josephs     |     1003   | High         |
|  1006  | John Tyler      |     1004   | High         |
|  9999  | Tim Traveler    |     1006   | Low          |
|  1007  | John Sanford    |     1002   | Low          |
+--------+-----------------+------------+--------------+
```

For nonmanagers, access to the Employee table can be revoked and replaced with the employee_vw view (created in "Creating Views" on page 185), which does not include any salary information:

```
PUBLIC>select * from employee_vw;
+--------+-----------------+------------+----------+
| EMPID  | EMP_NAME        | MGR_EMPID  | INACTIVE |
|--------+-----------------+------------+----------|
|  1001  | Bob Smith       |     NULL   | NULL     |
|  1002  | Susan Jackson   |     1001   | Y        |
|  1003  | Greg Carpenter  |     1001   | Y        |
|  1004  | Robert Butler   |     1002   | Y        |
|  1005  | Kim Josephs     |     1003   | Y        |
|  1006  | John Tyler      |     1004   | Y        |
|  9999  | Tim Traveler    |     1006   | NULL     |
|  1007  | John Sanford    |     1002   | NULL     |
+--------+-----------------+------------+----------+
```

Using these two views, nobody outside of the human resources department will be able to see actual salary data, while managers will see only predefined salary ranges.

Restricting row access

While views can be used in this way to restrict access to certain columns, what if you want to restrict which *rows* can be accessed by certain users? For example, let's say that we only want a department manager to be able to access information about the employees in the same department. For this purpose, Snowflake provides *secure views*, which allow you to restrict access to rows based on either the database username (via the `current_user()` function) or the database roles assigned to a user (via the `current_role()` function). The following query shows the results from these two functions in my session:

```
PUBLIC>select current_user(), current_role();
+----------------+----------------+
| CURRENT_USER() | CURRENT_ROLE() |
|----------------+----------------|
| ALANBEAU       | ACCOUNTADMIN   |
+----------------+----------------+
```

To demonstrate how secure views work, I will create two new tables, `department` and `empl_dept`, to create a set of departments and assign employees to the different departments:

```
PUBLIC>create table department as
        select dept_id, dept_name, auth_username
        from (values (1, 'ACCOUNTING', 'JOHNSMITH'),
          (2, 'FINANCE', 'ALANBEAU'),
          (3, 'SHIPPING', 'JANEDOE'))
          as dept(dept_id, dept_name, auth_username);
+---------------------------------------+
| status                                |
|---------------------------------------|
| Table DEPARTMENT successfully created.|
+---------------------------------------+

PUBLIC>create table empl_dept as
        select empid, dept_id
        from (values (1001, 1), (1002, 2), (1003, 1),
          (1004, 3), (1005, 2), (1006, 3))
          as empdpt(empid, dept_id);
+--------------------------------------+
| status                               |
|--------------------------------------|
| Table EMPL_DEPT successfully created.|
+--------------------------------------+
```

Here's a look at the data in these new tables:

```
PUBLIC>select d.dept_id, d.dept_name, d.auth_username,
          e.empid, e.emp_name
        from department d
        inner join empl_dept ed on d.dept_id = ed.dept_id
        inner join employee e on e.empid = ed.empid;
```

```
+---------+-----------+---------------+-------+----------------+
| DEPT_ID | DEPT_NAME | AUTH_USERNAME | EMPID | EMP_NAME       |
|---------+-----------+---------------+-------+----------------|
|       1 | ACCOUNTING | JOHNSMITH    |  1001 | Bob Smith      |
|       2 | FINANCE    | ALANBEAU     |  1002 | Susan Jackson  |
|       1 | ACCOUNTING | JOHNSMITH    |  1003 | Greg Carpenter |
|       3 | SHIPPING   | JANEDOE      |  1004 | Robert Butler  |
|       2 | FINANCE    | ALANBEAU     |  1005 | Kim Josephs    |
|       3 | SHIPPING   | JANEDOE      |  1006 | John Tyler     |
+---------+-----------+---------------+-------+----------------+
```

Looking at the data, I have made myself the manager of the finance department and assigned Susan Jackson and Kim Josephs to my department. Here's a query that joins these two new tables to Employee to show all of the employees I am authorized to see:

```
PUBLIC>select e.empid, e.emp_name, d.dept_name
       from employee e
       inner join empl_dept ed on e.empid = ed.empid
       inner join department d on ed.dept_id = d.dept_id
       where d.auth_username = current_user();
+-------+---------------+-----------+
| EMPID | EMP_NAME      | DEPT_NAME |
|-------+---------------+-----------|
|  1002 | Susan Jackson | FINANCE   |
|  1005 | Kim Josephs   | FINANCE   |
+-------+---------------+-----------+
```

I can use this query to build a secure view called my_employees:

```
PUBLIC>create secure view my_employees as
       select e.empid, e.emp_name, d.dept_name
       from employee e
       inner join empl_dept ed on e.empid = ed.empid
       inner join department d on ed.dept_id = d.dept_id
       where d.auth_username = current_user();
+-----------------------------------------+
| status                                  |
|-----------------------------------------|
| View MY_EMPLOYEES successfully created. |
+-----------------------------------------+
```

When I query the view, I see only data for Susan Jackson and Kim Josephs:

```
PUBLIC>select * from my_employees;
+-------+---------------+-----------+
| EMPID | EMP_NAME      | DEPT_NAME |
|-------+---------------+-----------|
|  1002 | Susan Jackson | FINANCE   |
|  1005 | Kim Josephs   | FINANCE   |
+-------+---------------+-----------+
```

Any other user executing this query would see only members of the accounting department (for username JOHNSMITH) or the shipping department (for username JANEDOE), and for any other users the my_employees view would return no rows.[1]

Using secure views also limits who can see the view definition; only users having the same role as the one with which the view was built will be able to retrieve the view definition from Snowflake. Here's one way to retrieve the view definition:

```
PUBLIC>select get_ddl('view','my_employees');
+----------------------------------------------------------+
| GET_DDL('VIEW','MY_EMPLOYEES')                           |
|----------------------------------------------------------|
| create or replace secure view MY_EMPLOYEES(              |
|     EMPID,                                                |
|     EMP_NAME,                                             |
|     DEPT_NAME                                             |
| ) as                                                     |
| select e.empid, e.emp_name, d.dept_name                  |
|         from employee e                                  |
|         inner join empl_dept ed on e.empid = ed.empid    |
|         inner join department d on ed.dept_id = d.dept_id |
|         where d.auth_username = current_user();          |
+----------------------------------------------------------+
```

I can retrieve the view definition because I created the view, but another user without the same role would not be successful. Hiding the view definition makes sense in that if you are creating a mechanism to restrict access to data, you should probably also limit access to the mechanism used to do so.

Data Aggregation

Data analysis and reporting are generally done with aggregated data, which, depending on the design of the database, can lead to some very complex queries. Rather than providing the users access to the tables, you can create views to make it seem as if data has been preaggregated. For example, if the manager of the parts department needs to run reports showing the aggregate sales and available quantities for all parts sold by the company, you could create the following view:

```
PUBLIC>create view yearly_part_sales_vw
       as
       with part_supply as
        (select p.p_partkey as partkey,
           p.p_name as part_name,
           sum(ps.ps_availqty) as avail_qty
         from part p
```

---

1 In practice, secure views will generally be built using roles and not usernames, but for the sake of simplicity I have used usernames.

```
      inner join partsupp ps
        on p.p_partkey = ps.ps_partkey
      group by p.p_partkey, p.p_name
    ),
    part_sales as
    (select date_part(year, o.o_orderdate) as order_year,
       li.l_partkey as partkey,
       count(*) as sales_qty,
       max(li.l_shipdate - o.o_orderdate) max_backlog_days
     from orders o
     inner join lineitem li
       on o.o_orderkey = li.l_orderkey
     group by date_part(year, o_orderdate),
       li.l_partkey
    )
  select p_sply.partkey,
    p_sply.part_name,
    p_sply.avail_qty,
    p_sale.order_year,
    p_sale.sales_qty,
    p_sale.max_backlog_days
  from part_supply p_sply
  inner join part_sales p_sale
    on p_sply.partkey = p_sale.partkey;
+----------------------------------------------+
| status                                       |
|----------------------------------------------|
| View YEARLY_PART_SALES successfully created. |
+----------------------------------------------+
```

Using this view, the manager could write a simple query to find the top 10 best-selling parts in 1998 along with the available quantities:

```
PUBLIC>select partkey, sales_qty, avail_qty
       from yearly_part_sales_vw
       where order_year = 1998
       order by sales_qty desc
       limit 10;
+---------+-----------+-----------+
| PARTKEY | SALES_QTY | AVAIL_QTY |
|---------+-----------+-----------|
|  100458 |        11 |     17092 |
|    4558 |        10 |     19220 |
|   10658 |         9 |     27821 |
|    4308 |         9 |     17706 |
|  143508 |         9 |     10898 |
|    2308 |         8 |     20263 |
|  163858 |         8 |     18021 |
|   92508 |         8 |     27903 |
|   36058 |         8 |     23578 |
|   42208 |         8 |     21672 |
+---------+-----------+-----------+
```

If the manager uses this view frequently enough, you might create a table to store the preaggregated data rather than incur the cost of grouping the rows each time.

Materialized Views

Snowflake customers using the Enterprise edition have the ability to create *materialized views*, which are essentially tables built using a view definition and then automatically refreshed via background processes. Using materialized views will generally reduce computation time for queries but will incur additional storage space/fees and computation fees for the upkeep of the materialized view, so it is important to consider the number of times the materialized data will be queried versus the amount of data being stored and the frequency with which the data changes.

Creating a materialized view is a simple matter of using `create materialized view` instead of `create view`. Once created, Snowflake will update the stored data as changes are made to the underlying tables from the view definition. For example, if the `yearly_part_sales_vw` view was dropped and recreated as a materialized view, any future changes made to the `Orders`, `Lineitem`, `Part`, and `Partsupp` tables would need to be reflected in the materialized view data. Snowflake does these updates for you so that any queries against materialized views will return current data.

Hiding Complexity

Another common use of views is to shield your user community from complex calculations or data relationships. For example, the process of calculating the cost of a customer's order can include list prices, discounts, sale prices, state tax calculations, etc. Because it is critical to the company to charge the correct amount, it might be beneficial to create a view for the sales department that includes columns that contain various calculations, such as:

```
PUBLIC>create view order_calculation_vw
     as
     select o.o_orderkey,
       sum((li.l_extendedprice * (1 - li.l_discount))
         * li.l_quantity) order_total,
       sum((li.l_extendedprice * (1 - li.l_discount))
         * li.l_quantity * li.l_tax) state_sales_tax
     from orders o
     inner join lineitem li
       on o.o_orderkey = li.l_orderkey
     group by o.o_orderkey;
+------------------------------------------------+
| status                                         |
|------------------------------------------------|
| View ORDER_CALCULATION_VW successfully created. |
+------------------------------------------------+
```

Once the sales department starts using this view, you could add additional calculations for seasonal sales, customer loyalty programs, and other discounts and promotions, and you could be sure that all of the sales associates will generate correct customer invoices.

Considerations When Using Views

While views can be an important part of your data-access strategy, there are a few potential drawbacks to consider. First, you need to understand that when a view is created, Snowflake gathers information about the view (also known as *metadata*, which is covered in Chapter 13) using the state of the database at that point. If you later add, modify, or drop columns in one of the tables used by the view's query, the view definition will not be automatically changed. Furthermore, if you drop a column that is used by a view, the view will be internally marked as invalid, and you will need to modify the view definition and re-create the view before it can be used again.

A second consideration involves naming your views, and even though views and tables are not the same thing, they share a namespace, so you can't have a table and a view with the same name. If I want to build a view to be used instead of a table, I generally add the suffix _vw to all of my view names, which allows me to have a table named abc and a view named abc_vw, which generally makes it clear to my user community what is going on.

The third, and more subtle, consideration when using views is that while the views are great at hiding complexity, the people using the views are generally unaware of this complexity. This is both a good thing and potentially a bad thing. If a user writes a query using a single view, there will generally be no issues, but some of the more adventurous users may start joining multiple views together, using views in subqueries, and doing other things that you never considered when you created the view. Joining two or three views with complex underlying queries can result in poor performance, which results in increased computation costs and unhappy users.[2]

While database performance is a broad and important topic, it is generally not covered in this book. Since I mentioned performance as an issue for views, however, let me show you one method to look for long-running queries in Snowflake:

```
PUBLIC>select query_id, total_elapsed_time as runtime,
       substr(query_text,1,40)
    from table(learning_sql.information_schema.query_history())
    where total_elapsed_time > 5000
    order by start_time;
```

---

2 If you do have views that are aggregating a great deal of data, they are good candidates for being changed to materialized views, which can alleviate the performance issues.

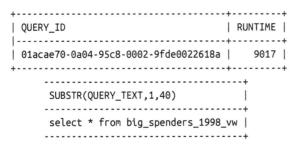

```
+----------------------------------------+---------+
| QUERY_ID                               | RUNTIME |
|----------------------------------------+---------|
| 01acae70-0a04-95c8-0002-9fde0022618a   |    9017 |
+----------------------------------------+---------+
      ------------------------------------+
          SUBSTR(QUERY_TEXT,1,40)         |
      ------------------------------------+
          select * from big_spenders_1998_vw |
      ------------------------------------+
```

This query uses *information_schema*, which is covered in Chapter 13, to look for any queries that took more than 5,000 milliseconds to complete. The query returned a single result, showing that my query from earlier in the chapter against the `big_spenders_1998_vw` view took over 9 seconds to complete. You can use queries such as this one to monitor for long-running queries, regardless of whether they use views.

Wrap-Up

In this chapter, you learned about views and how they can be used for data security and hiding complexity from your user community. You also saw how secure views can be employed to provide row-level security.

Test Your Knowledge

The following exercises are designed to test your understanding of views. Please see "Chapter 12" in Appendix B for solutions.

Exercise 12-1

Consider the following query and result set against a view:

```
PUBLIC>select * from region_totalsales_vw;
+-------------+----------------+
| REGION_NAME | SUM_TOTALPRICE |
|-------------+----------------|
| ASIA        |   4378591175.90 |
| AMERICA     |   4321075685.27 |
| EUROPE      |   4391712838.03 |
| AFRICA      |   4239225325.42 |
| MIDDLE EAST |   4322198235.40 |
+-------------+----------------+
```

Write the view definition for `region_totalsales_vw`. You will need to join the `Region`, `Nation`, `Customer`, and `Orders` tables. Your column names should match what is shown in the result set.

Exercise 12-2

The `Supplier` table looks as follows:

```
PUBLIC>desc supplier;
```

```
+--------------+---------------+--------+-------+
| name         | type          | kind   | null? |
|--------------+---------------+--------+-------|
| S_SUPPKEY    | NUMBER(38,0)  | COLUMN | Y     |
| S_NAME       | VARCHAR(25)   | COLUMN | Y     |
| S_ADDRESS    | VARCHAR(40)   | COLUMN | Y     |
| S_NATIONKEY  | NUMBER(38,0)  | COLUMN | Y     |
| S_PHONE      | VARCHAR(15)   | COLUMN | Y     |
| S_ACCTBAL    | NUMBER(12,2)  | COLUMN | Y     |
| S_COMMENT    | VARCHAR(101)  | COLUMN | Y     |
+--------------+---------------+--------+-------+
```

Create a view called `supplier_vw` that includes the following fields:

- `s_suppkey` as `keyval`
- `s_name` as `supplier_name`
- `partial_phone` (obscure all but last 4 digits of `s_phone`)
- `acct_status` (negative if `s_acctbal` < 0, `positive` otherwise)

For testing, you can work with `s_suppkey` between 1 and 50. To obscure the phone number, replace any digit (except the last four) with a *. There are many possible Snowflake functions that could be used to obscure part of the phone number, including `substr()`, `right()`, `length()`, `translate()`, `regexp_replace()`, etc. Results should look like:

```
PUBLIC>select * from supplier_vw
       where keyval between 1 and 50;
+--------+--------------------+-------------------+-------------+
| KEYVAL | SUPPLIER_NAME      | PARTIAL_PHONE     | ACCT_STATUS |
|--------+--------------------+-------------------+-------------|
|      1 | Supplier#000000001 | **-***-***-1736   | positive    |
|      4 | Supplier#000000004 | **-***-***-7479   | positive    |
|      7 | Supplier#000000007 | **-***-***-2201   | positive    |
|      9 | Supplier#000000009 | **-***-***-8662   | positive    |
|     10 | Supplier#000000010 | **-***-***-8585   | positive    |
|     11 | Supplier#000000011 | **-***-***-1505   | positive    |
|     12 | Supplier#000000012 | **-***-***-7181   | positive    |
|     13 | Supplier#000000013 | **-***-***-7813   | positive    |
|     14 | Supplier#000000014 | **-***-***-5058   | positive    |
|     15 | Supplier#000000015 | **-***-***-6394   | positive    |
|     16 | Supplier#000000016 | **-***-***-4215   | positive    |
|     17 | Supplier#000000017 | **-***-***-9219   | positive    |
|     18 | Supplier#000000018 | **-***-***-1115   | positive    |
```

```
|    19 | Supplier#000000019 | **-***-***-2731 | positive |
|    20 | Supplier#000000020 | **-***-***-6730 | positive |
|    21 | Supplier#000000021 | **-***-***-5816 | positive |
|    22 | Supplier#000000022 | **-***-***-2814 | negative |
|    23 | Supplier#000000023 | **-***-***-5776 | positive |
|    24 | Supplier#000000024 | **-***-***-2254 | positive |
|    25 | Supplier#000000025 | **-***-***-3541 | positive |
|    26 | Supplier#000000026 | **-***-***-4436 | positive |
|    27 | Supplier#000000027 | **-***-***-2028 | positive |
|    28 | Supplier#000000028 | **-***-***-8460 | negative |
|    29 | Supplier#000000029 | **-***-***-5922 | negative |
|    30 | Supplier#000000030 | **-***-***-4852 | positive |
|    31 | Supplier#000000031 | **-***-***-4159 | positive |
|    33 | Supplier#000000033 | **-***-***-9374 | positive |
|    35 | Supplier#000000035 | **-***-***-5245 | positive |
|    36 | Supplier#000000036 | **-***-***-3679 | positive |
|    37 | Supplier#000000037 | **-***-***-1330 | positive |
|    39 | Supplier#000000039 | **-***-***-5633 | positive |
|    41 | Supplier#000000041 | **-***-***-2525 | positive |
|    42 | Supplier#000000042 | **-***-***-6317 | positive |
|    43 | Supplier#000000043 | **-***-***-4862 | positive |
|    45 | Supplier#000000045 | **-***-***-8862 | positive |
|    47 | Supplier#000000047 | **-***-***-4471 | positive |
|    48 | Supplier#000000048 | **-***-***-9498 | positive |
+--------+--------------------+------------------+------------+
```

Metadata

When you create schema items to store information about your customers, products, experiment results, health records, or whatever is of importance to your organization, Snowflake needs to keep track of all of your tables, columns, clusters, views, and other database objects. Not surprisingly, Snowflake stores this information in a database for internal use, but also makes this information, known as *metadata*, available for database users. This chapter explores the different types of available metadata, along with some examples of how it can be used.

information_schema

Snowflake makes its metadata available via a set of views in the information_schema schema. If you are using Snowsight, you can see *information_schema* listed under every database, including Snowflake's sample databases, as shown in Figure 13-1.

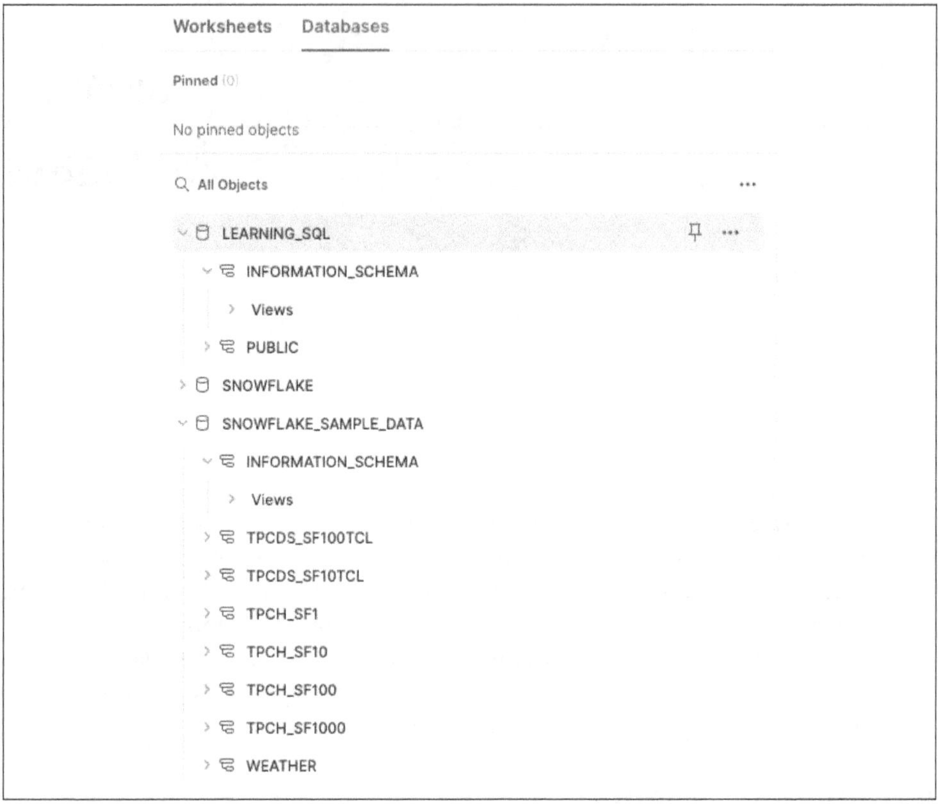

Figure 13-1. Snowflake's database listing

If you expand Views under *information_schema*, you will see a listing of 25 different views covering schema items as shown in Figure 13-2 (*Databases, Tables, Views, Columns*), security (*Applicable_Roles, Enabled_Roles, Object_Privileges, Usage_Privileges*), data movement (*External_Tables, File_Formats, Load_History, Pipes, Replication_Databases*), and programs (*Functions, Stored Procedures*).

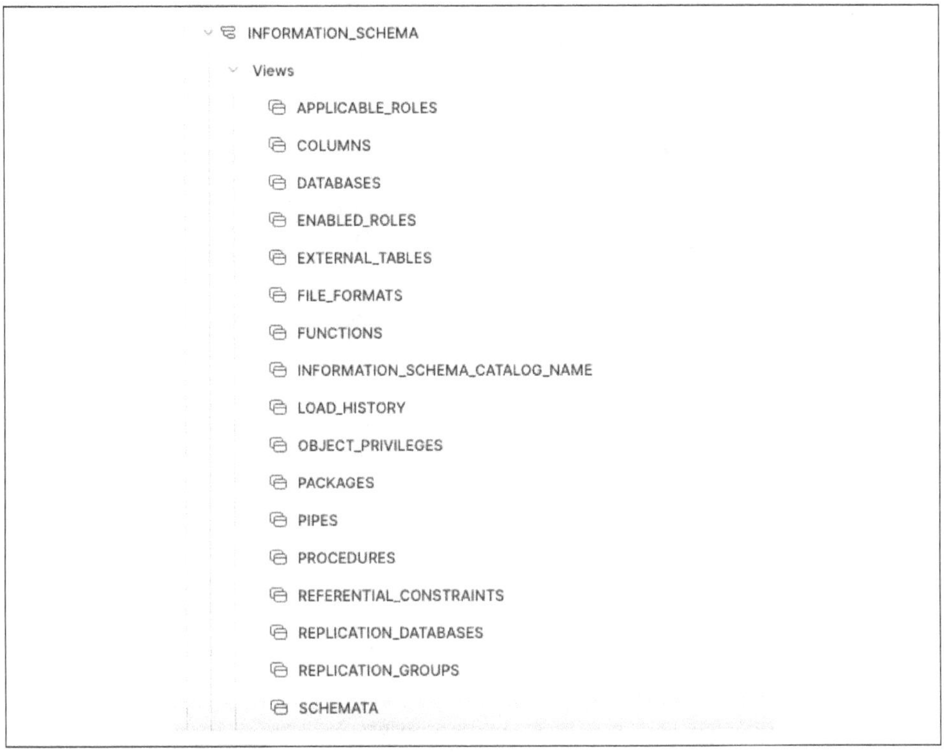

Views
- APPLICABLE_ROLES
- COLUMNS
- DATABASES
- ENABLED_ROLES
- EXTERNAL_TABLES
- FILE_FORMATS
- FUNCTIONS
- INFORMATION_SCHEMA_CATALOG_NAME
- LOAD_HISTORY
- OBJECT_PRIVILEGES
- PACKAGES
- PIPES
- PROCEDURES
- REFERENTIAL_CONSTRAINTS
- REPLICATION_DATABASES
- REPLICATION_GROUPS
- SCHEMATA

Figure 13-2. Information_Schema views

When using SnowSQL, you can set your schema to information_schema and query these views directly. Here's a query that shows all of the tables and views that I have created in my learning_sql.public schema:

```
PUBLIC>use schema learning_sql.information_schema;
+--------------------------------+
| status                         |
|--------------------------------|
| Statement executed successfully. |
+--------------------------------+
INFORMATION_SCHEMA>select table_name, table_type, row_count
                from tables
                where table_schema = 'PUBLIC';
+----------------------------+------------+-----------+
| TABLE_NAME                 | TABLE_TYPE | ROW_COUNT |
|----------------------------+------------+-----------|
| DATE_EXAMPLE               | BASE TABLE |         3 |
| EMPLOYEE                   | BASE TABLE |         8 |
| NATION                     | BASE TABLE |        25 |
| ORDER_CALCULATION_VW       | VIEW       |      NULL |
| PARTSUPP                   | BASE TABLE |     16000 |
| WH_COUNTRY_MONTHLY_SALES   | BASE TABLE |        60 |
```

```
| EMPLOYEE_VW             | VIEW       |    NULL |
| LINEITEM                | BASE TABLE |  119989 |
| ORDERS                  | BASE TABLE |  115269 |
| PERSON                  | BASE TABLE |       5 |
| YEARLY_PART_SALES_VW     | VIEW       |    NULL |
| BIG_SPENDERS_1998_VW     | VIEW       |    NULL |
| PERSON_VW               | VIEW       |    NULL |
| CUSTOMER                | BASE TABLE |   66076 |
| EMPLOYEE_MANAGER_VW      | VIEW       |    NULL |
| PERSON_REFRESH          | BASE TABLE |       6 |
| REGION                  | BASE TABLE |       5 |
| SUPPLIER                | BASE TABLE |    7400 |
| PART                    | BASE TABLE |    4000 |
+-------------------------+------------+---------+
```

As you can see, querying `information_schema.tables` returns information about both tables and views, but if you only want information about views you can query `information_schema.views`:

```
INFORMATION_SCHEMA>select table_name,
                      substr(view_definition, 1, 100) view_def
                   from views
                   where table_schema = 'PUBLIC';
+----------------------+------------------------------------------+
| TABLE_NAME           | VIEW_DEF                                 |
|----------------------+------------------------------------------|
| BIG_SPENDERS_1998_VW | create view big_spenders_1998_vw         |
|                      |   (custkey, cust_name,                   |
|                      |    total_order_dollars) as               |
|                      | select o_custkey, c.                     |
| EMPLOYEE_MANAGER_VW  | create view employee_manager_vw          |
|                      |   (empid, emp_name, mgr_empid,           |
|                      |    salary_range) as                      |
|                      | select empid, emp_nam                    |
| EMPLOYEE_VW          | create view employee_vw                  |
|                      |   as                                     |
|                      | select empid, emp_name, mgr_empid,       |
|                      |    inactive from employee;               |
| ORDER_CALCULATION_VW | create view order_calculation_vw         |
|                      |   as                                     |
|                      | select o.o_orderkey,                     |
|                      |   sum((li.l_extendedprice * (1 - li.l_d  |
| PERSON_VW            | create view person_vw (fname, lname,     |
|                      |   dob, eyes) as                          |
|                      | select first_name, last_name, birth_dat  |
| YEARLY_PART_SALES_VW | create view yearly_part_sales_vw         |
|                      |   as                                     |
|                      | with part_supply as                      |
|                      |   (select p.p_partkey as partkey,        |
|                      |     p.p_nam                              |
+----------------------+------------------------------------------+
```

This query returns the name of each view, along with the first 100 characters of the view definition.

The next query returns information about all columns in the learning_sql.public schema:

```
INFORMATION_SCHEMA>select table_name, column_name,
                     concat(data_type,
                       case
                         when data_type = 'TEXT' then
                           concat('(',character_maximum_length,
                             ')')
                         when data_type = 'NUMBER' then
                           concat('(',numeric_precision, ',',
                             numeric_scale,')')
                         else ''
                       end) column_def
                     from columns
                     where table_schema = 'PUBLIC'
                     order by table_name, ordinal_position;
+-----------------------------+-------------------------+----------------+
| TABLE_NAME                  | COLUMN_NAME             | COLUMN_DEF     |
|-----------------------------+-------------------------+----------------|
| BIG_SPENDERS_1998_VW        | CUSTKEY                 | NUMBER(38,0)   |
| BIG_SPENDERS_1998_VW        | CUST_NAME               | TEXT(25)       |
| BIG_SPENDERS_1998_VW        | TOTAL_ORDER_DOLLARS     | NUMBER(24,2)   |
| CUSTOMER                    | C_CUSTKEY               | NUMBER(38,0)   |
| CUSTOMER                    | C_NAME                  | TEXT(25)       |
| CUSTOMER                    | C_ADDRESS               | TEXT(40)       |
| CUSTOMER                    | C_NATIONKEY             | NUMBER(38,0)   |
| CUSTOMER                    | C_PHONE                 | TEXT(15)       |
| CUSTOMER                    | C_ACCTBAL               | NUMBER(12,2)   |
| CUSTOMER                    | C_MKTSEGMENT            | TEXT(10)       |
| CUSTOMER                    | C_COMMENT               | TEXT(117)      |
| DATE_EXAMPLE                | DT                      | DATE           |
| EMPLOYEE                    | EMPID                   | NUMBER(4,0)    |
| EMPLOYEE                    | EMP_NAME                | TEXT(30)       |
| EMPLOYEE                    | MGR_EMPID               | NUMBER(4,0)    |
| EMPLOYEE                    | BIRTH_NATIONKEY         | NUMBER(38,0)   |
| EMPLOYEE                    | CURRENT_NATIONKEY       | NUMBER(38,0)   |
| EMPLOYEE                    | INACTIVE                | TEXT(1)        |
| EMPLOYEE                    | SALARY                  | NUMBER(7,0)    |
| EMPLOYEE_MANAGER_VW         | EMPID                   | NUMBER(4,0)    |
| EMPLOYEE_MANAGER_VW         | EMP_NAME                | TEXT(14)       |
| EMPLOYEE_MANAGER_VW         | MGR_EMPID               | NUMBER(4,0)    |
| EMPLOYEE_MANAGER_VW         | SALARY_RANGE            | TEXT(6)        |
| EMPLOYEE_VW                 | EMPID                   | NUMBER(4,0)    |
| EMPLOYEE_VW                 | EMP_NAME                | TEXT(14)       |
| EMPLOYEE_VW                 | MGR_EMPID               | NUMBER(4,0)    |
| EMPLOYEE_VW                 | INACTIVE                | TEXT(1)        |
| LINEITEM                    | L_ORDERKEY              | NUMBER(38,0)   |
| LINEITEM                    | L_PARTKEY               | NUMBER(38,0)   |
```

```
...< 64 rows omitted>
| SUPPLIER                 | S_SUPPKEY        | NUMBER(38,0) |
| SUPPLIER                 | S_NAME           | TEXT(25)     |
| SUPPLIER                 | S_ADDRESS        | TEXT(40)     |
| SUPPLIER                 | S_NATIONKEY      | NUMBER(38,0) |
| SUPPLIER                 | S_PHONE          | TEXT(15)     |
| SUPPLIER                 | S_ACCTBAL        | NUMBER(12,2) |
| SUPPLIER                 | S_COMMENT        | TEXT(101)    |
| WH_COUNTRY_MONTHLY_SALES | SALES_YEAR       | NUMBER(38,0) |
| WH_COUNTRY_MONTHLY_SALES | SALES_MONTH      | NUMBER(38,0) |
| WH_COUNTRY_MONTHLY_SALES | REGION_NAME      | TEXT(20)     |
| WH_COUNTRY_MONTHLY_SALES | COUNTRY_NAME     | TEXT(30)     |
| WH_COUNTRY_MONTHLY_SALES | TOTAL_SALES      | NUMBER(38,0) |
| YEARLY_PART_SALES_VW     | PARTKEY          | NUMBER(38,0) |
| YEARLY_PART_SALES_VW     | PART_NAME        | TEXT(55)     |
| YEARLY_PART_SALES_VW     | AVAIL_QTY        | NUMBER(38,0) |
| YEARLY_PART_SALES_VW     | ORDER_YEAR       | NUMBER(4,0)  |
| YEARLY_PART_SALES_VW     | SALES_QTY        | NUMBER(18,0) |
| YEARLY_PART_SALES_VW     | MAX_BACKLOG_DAYS | NUMBER(9,0)  |
+--------------------------+------------------+--------------+
```

The values for `column_def` are built using an expression that uses the `data_type`, `character_maximum_length`, `numeric_precision`, and `numeric_scale` columns to construct a definition string.

Working with Metadata

Having the ability to retrieve information about your schema objects via SQL queries opens up some interesting possibilities. This section shows several ways in which you can make use of the metadata information in `information_schema`.

Schema Discovery

If you know what you're looking for, there isn't any particular advantage to writing a query using `information_schema` when you can simply use the `describe` command. For example, if you simply want to see the definition of the `employee` table, you can just do the following:

```
INFORMATION_SCHEMA>describe employee;
+-------------------+--------------+--------+-------+...
| name              | type         | kind   | null? |...
|-------------------+--------------+--------+-------+...
| EMPID             | NUMBER(4,0)  | COLUMN | Y     |...
| EMP_NAME          | VARCHAR(14)  | COLUMN | Y     |...
| MGR_EMPID         | NUMBER(4,0)  | COLUMN | Y     |...
| BIRTH_NATIONKEY   | NUMBER(38,0) | COLUMN | Y     |...
| CURRENT_NATIONKEY | NUMBER(38,0) | COLUMN | Y     |...
| INACTIVE          | VARCHAR(1)   | COLUMN | Y     |...
| SALARY            | NUMBER(7,0)  | COLUMN | Y     |...
+-------------------+--------------+--------+-------+
```

Let's say, however, that you have been asked to ensure that all columns holding a person's last name can handle up to 50 characters, and you want to find all tables that include either the lname or last_name column. While you could describe every table in your schema looking for the columns, a query using information_schema.column should be faster and more accurate:

```
INFORMATION_SCHEMA>select table_name, data_type,
                          character_maximum_length
                   from columns
                   where table_schema = 'PUBLIC'
                   and column_name in ('LNAME','LAST_NAME');
+----------------+-----------+--------------------------+
| TABLE_NAME     | DATA_TYPE | CHARACTER_MAXIMUM_LENGTH |
|----------------+-----------+--------------------------|
| PERSON_REFRESH | TEXT      |                        9 |
| PERSON         | TEXT      |                       50 |
| PERSON_VW      | TEXT      |                       50 |
+----------------+-----------+--------------------------+
```

You can also write queries to find out when schema objects were last modified, which might be useful if you were to come back from vacation and want to find out what your teammates were up to while you were away:

```
INFORMATION_SCHEMA>select table_name, last_altered
                   from tables
                   where table_schema = 'PUBLIC'
                   order by 2 desc;
+---------------------------+-----------------------------+
| TABLE_NAME                | LAST_ALTERED                |
|---------------------------+-----------------------------|
| ORDER_CALCULATION_VW      | 2023-02-28 10:11:36.080 -0800 |
| YEARLY_PART_SALES_VW      | 2023-02-28 10:06:26.598 -0800 |
| CUSTOMER                  | 2023-02-28 06:55:22.643 -0800 |
| ORDERS                    | 2023-02-28 06:53:20.333 -0800 |
| LINEITEM                  | 2023-02-28 06:51:43.050 -0800 |
| SUPPLIER                  | 2023-02-28 06:49:40.113 -0800 |
| PARTSUPP                  | 2023-02-28 06:45:21.465 -0800 |
| PART                      | 2023-02-28 06:44:36.345 -0800 |
| NATION                    | 2023-02-28 06:43:47.480 -0800 |
| REGION                    | 2023-02-28 06:42:34.603 -0800 |
| WH_COUNTRY_MONTHLY_SALES  | 2023-02-14 10:21:01.555 -0800 |
| EMPLOYEE                  | 2023-01-17 07:11:12.266 -0800 |
| EMPLOYEE_MANAGER_VW       | 2022-12-09 16:45:01.437 -0800 |
| BIG_SPENDERS_1998_VW      | 2022-12-09 11:07:35.887 -0800 |
| PERSON_VW                 | 2022-12-09 10:37:25.706 -0800 |
| EMPLOYEE_VW               | 2022-12-09 10:07:49.054 -0800 |
| PERSON                    | 2022-12-06 06:51:15.246 -0800 |
| DATE_EXAMPLE              | 2022-10-24 12:40:51.040 -0700 |
| PERSON_REFRESH            | 2022-10-24 12:14:15.100 -0700 |
+---------------------------+-----------------------------+
```

Unfortunately, Snowflake's Time Travel feature does not work with views, so you can't write queries using the at clause to compare the current metadata with what it looked like an hour ago.

Deployment Verification

Many companies make database modifications once a month, usually in the evening or on a weekend when few users would be active. After deploying a set of database changes, it's a good idea to verify that all changes have been successfully made before allowing users back on the system. For example, let's say that part of a monthly deployment includes a change in the size of the emp_name column in the public .employee table:

```
INFORMATION_SCHEMA>alter table public.employee
                   modify emp_name varchar(30);
+----------------------------------+
| status                           |
|----------------------------------|
| Statement executed successfully. |
+----------------------------------+
```

After the deployment is completed, the following query can be run to find all changes made to tables in the past hour:

```
INFORMATION_SCHEMA>select table_schema, table_name
                   from tables
                   where last_altered >
                     dateadd(hour, -1, current_date);
+--------------+------------+
| TABLE_SCHEMA | TABLE_NAME |
|--------------+------------|
| PUBLIC       | EMPLOYEE   |
+--------------+------------+
```

If the deployment also included dropping or adding columns to tables or views, you could run a query to count the number of columns in each table:

```
INFORMATION_SCHEMA>select table_name, count(*) num_columns
                   from columns
                   where table_schema = 'PUBLIC'
                   group by table_name
                   order by 1;
+----------------------------+-------------+
| TABLE_NAME                 | NUM_COLUMNS |
|----------------------------+-------------|
| BIG_SPENDERS_1998_VW       |           3 |
| CUSTOMER                   |           8 |
| DATE_EXAMPLE               |           1 |
| EMPLOYEE                   |           7 |
| EMPLOYEE_MANAGER_VW        |           4 |
| EMPLOYEE_VW                |           4 |
```

```
| LINEITEM                     |       16 |
| NATION                       |        4 |
| ORDERS                       |        9 |
| ORDER_CALCULATION_VW         |        3 |
| PART                         |        9 |
| PARTSUPP                     |        5 |
| PERSON                       |        7 |
| PERSON_REFRESH               |        6 |
| PERSON_VW                    |        4 |
| REGION                       |        3 |
| SUPPLIER                     |        7 |
| WH_COUNTRY_MONTHLY_SALES     |        5 |
| YEARLY_PART_SALES_VW         |        6 |
+------------------------------+----------+
```

If you run this query before and after the deployment, you can verify that the appropriate number of column changes were made.

Generating Administration Scripts

You can also query `information_schema` tables to generate SQL statements that can then be executed. For example, let's say your team has a database used by the QA team that needs to be refreshed periodically with a set of test data. You could run the following query to generate a set of `delete` statements for every table in a given schema:

```
INFORMATION_SCHEMA>select
                   concat('DELETE FROM ',table_name,';') cmnd_str
                   from tables
                   where table_schema = 'PUBLIC'
                     and table_type = 'BASE TABLE';
+----------------------------------------+
| CMND_STR                               |
|----------------------------------------|
| DELETE FROM CUSTOMER;                  |
| DELETE FROM DATE_EXAMPLE;              |
| DELETE FROM EMPLOYEE;                  |
| DELETE FROM LINEITEM;                  |
| DELETE FROM NATION;                    |
| DELETE FROM ORDERS;                    |
| DELETE FROM PART;                      |
| DELETE FROM PARTSUPP;                  |
| DELETE FROM PERSON;                    |
| DELETE FROM PERSON_REFRESH;            |
| DELETE FROM REGION;                    |
| DELETE FROM SUPPLIER;                  |
| DELETE FROM WH_COUNTRY_MONTHLY_SALES;  |
+----------------------------------------+
```

While the query has returned the statements that need to be executed, it would be helpful to remove the formatting around the result set to facilitate copy/paste of the query results. This can be done by setting the output_format option in SnowSQL before running the query:

```
INFORMATION_SCHEMA>!set output_format=plain;
INFORMATION_SCHEMA>select
                   concat('DELETE FROM ',table_name,';') cmnd_str
                   from tables
                   where table_schema = 'PUBLIC'
                     and table_type = 'BASE TABLE';
CMND_STR
DELETE FROM CUSTOMER;
DELETE FROM DATE_EXAMPLE;
DELETE FROM EMPLOYEE;
DELETE FROM LINEITEM;
DELETE FROM NATION;
DELETE FROM ORDERS;
DELETE FROM PART;
DELETE FROM PARTSUPP;
DELETE FROM PERSON;
DELETE FROM PERSON_REFRESH;
DELETE FROM REGION;
DELETE FROM SUPPLIER;
DELETE FROM WH_COUNTRY_MONTHLY_SALES;
```

Setting the formatting to plain removes the '+', '-', and '|' characters surrounding the results, allowing the delete statements to be copied and pasted cleanly. When finished, you can opt to set the formatting back to the default, which is psql, or to any other available option, such as grid, html, json, or csv.

get_ddl() Function

Along with the information_schema views, which are implemented by most other relational databases (and are thus reasonably portable), Snowflake also provides the built-in get_ddl() function to help with databases administration tasks. This function can be used to generate statements useful for creating tables, views, or entire schemas. Additionally, the function can generate statements used to construct stored procedures, pipes, sequences, and other types of Snowflake objects.

For example, the following query generates a statement that could be used to create the public.employee table (with output formatting still set to plain):

```
INFORMATION_SCHEMA>select get_ddl('table','public.employee');
GET_DDL('TABLE','PUBLIC.EMPLOYEE')
create or replace TABLE EMPLOYEE (
    EMPID NUMBER(4,0),
    EMP_NAME VARCHAR(30),
    MGR_EMPID NUMBER(4,0),
```

```
      BIRTH_NATIONKEY NUMBER(38,0),
      CURRENT_NATIONKEY NUMBER(38,0),
      INACTIVE VARCHAR(1),
      SALARY NUMBER(7,0)
);
```

The resulting statement could be used to create an Employee table in another schema or database, such as a separate database used for testing. View definitions can also be generated by get_ddl():

```
INFORMATION_SCHEMA>select get_ddl('view','public.employee_vw');
GET_DDL('VIEW','PUBLIC.EMPLOYEE_VW')
create or replace view EMPLOYEE_VW(
    EMPID,
    EMP_NAME,
    MGR_EMPID,
    INACTIVE
) as
select empid, emp_name, mgr_empid, inactive
from employee;
```

You can also generate a set of scripts for an entire schema:

```
INFORMATION_SCHEMA>select get_ddl('schema','public');
GET_DDL('SCHEMA','PUBLIC')
create or replace schema PUBLIC;
create or replace TABLE EMPLOYEE (
    EMPID NUMBER(4,0),
    EMP_NAME VARCHAR(30),
    MGR_EMPID NUMBER(4,0),
    BIRTH_NATIONKEY NUMBER(38,0),
    CURRENT_NATIONKEY NUMBER(38,0),
    INACTIVE VARCHAR(1),
    SALARY NUMBER(7,0)
); ,
create or replace TABLE PERSON (
    FIRST_NAME VARCHAR(50),
    LAST_NAME VARCHAR(50),
    BIRTH_DATE DATE,
    EYE_COLOR VARCHAR(10),
    OCCUPATION VARCHAR(50),
    CHILDREN ARRAY,
    YEARS_OF_EDUCATION NUMBER(2,0)
);
<... rows omitted...>
create or replace view YEARLY_PART_SALES_VW(
        PARTKEY,
        PART_NAME,
        AVAIL_QTY,
        ORDER_YEAR,
        SALES_QTY,
        MAX_BACKLOG_DAYS
) as
```

```
with part_supply as
  (select p.p_partkey as partkey,
      p.p_name as part_name,
      sum(ps.ps_availqty) as avail_qty
    from snowflake_sample_data.tpch_sf1.part p
    inner join snowflake_sample_data.tpch_sf1.partsupp ps
      on p.p_partkey = ps.ps_partkey
    group by p.p_partkey, p.p_name
  ),
  part_sales as
  (select date_part(year, o.o_orderdate) as order_year,
      li.l_partkey as partkey,
      count(*) as sales_qty,
      max(li.l_shipdate - o.o_orderdate) max_backlog_days
    from snowflake_sample_data.tpch_sf1.orders o
    inner join snowflake_sample_data.tpch_sf1.lineitem li
      on o.o_orderkey = li.l_orderkey
    group by date_part(year, o_orderdate),
      li.l_partkey
  )
select p_sply.partkey,
  p_sply.part_name,
  p_sply.avail_qty,
  p_sale.order_year,
  p_sale.sales_qty,
  p_sale.max_backlog_days
from part_supply p_sply
inner join part_sales p_sale
  on p_sply.partkey = p_sale.partkey;
```

Using a combination of the get_ddl() function and queries against information_
schema views, you should be able to generate scripts for just about any administrative
task.

account_usage

Along with the information_schema views that are created within each schema,
Snowflake also makes a set of views available at the account level, under the Snowflake database. Figure 13-3 shows some of the views available in the snow
flake.account_usage schema.

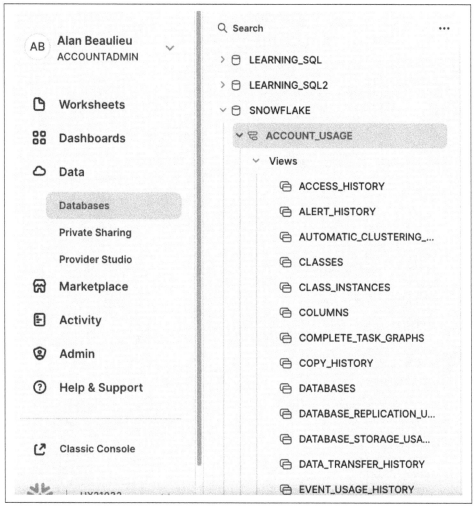

Figure 13-3. account_usage views

The set of `account_usage` views overlaps with `information_schema` but includes a number of other views as well. Here's a query to show how they line up:

```
PUBLIC>with infor_schema as
        (select table_name
         from learning_sql.information_schema.views
         where table_schema = 'INFORMATION_SCHEMA')
       ,acct_usage as
        (select table_name
         from snowflake.information_schema.views
         where table_schema = 'ACCOUNT_USAGE')
       select all_views.table_name,
          case when infor_schema.table_name is not null then 'X'
```

```
          else ' ' end as info_sch,
       case when acct_usage.table_name is not null then 'X'
          else ' ' end as acct_usg
     from
      (select table_name from infor_schema
       union
       select table_name from acct_usage
      ) all_views
      left outer join infor_schema
        on infor_schema.table_name = all_views.table_name
      left outer join acct_usage
        on acct_usage.table_name = all_views.table_name
     order by 1;
```

TABLE_NAME	INFO_SCH	ACCT_USG
ACCESS_HISTORY		X
ALERT_HISTORY		X
APPLICABLE_ROLES	X	
AUTOMATIC_CLUSTERING_HISTORY		X
COLUMNS	X	X
COMPLETE_TASK_GRAPHS		X
COPY_HISTORY		X
DATABASES	X	X
DATABASE_REPLICATION_USAGE_HISTORY		X
DATABASE_STORAGE_USAGE_HISTORY		X
DATA_TRANSFER_HISTORY		X
ENABLED_ROLES	X	
EVENT_TABLES	X	
EVENT_USAGE_HISTORY		X
EXTERNAL_TABLES	X	
FILE_FORMATS	X	X
FUNCTIONS	X	X
GRANTS_TO_ROLES		X
GRANTS_TO_USERS		X
INFORMATION_SCHEMA_CATALOG_NAME	X	
LOAD_HISTORY	X	X
LOCK_WAIT_HISTORY		X
LOGIN_HISTORY		X
MASKING_POLICIES		X
MATERIALIZED_VIEW_REFRESH_HISTORY		X
METERING_DAILY_HISTORY		X
METERING_HISTORY		X
OBJECT_DEPENDENCIES		X
OBJECT_PRIVILEGES	X	
PACKAGES	X	
PASSWORD_POLICIES		X
PIPES	X	X
PIPE_USAGE_HISTORY		X
POLICY_REFERENCES		X
PROCEDURES	X	X
QUERY_ACCELERATION_ELIGIBLE		X

```
| QUERY_HISTORY                              |          | X        |          |
| REFERENTIAL_CONSTRAINTS                    | X        | X        |          |
| REPLICATION_DATABASES                      | X        |          |          |
| REPLICATION_GROUPS                         | X        |          |          |
| REPLICATION_GROUP_REFRESH_HISTORY          |          | X        |          |
| REPLICATION_GROUP_USAGE_HISTORY            |          | X        |          |
| REPLICATION_USAGE_HISTORY                  |          | X        |          |
| ROLES                                      |          | X        |          |
| ROW_ACCESS_POLICIES                        |          | X        |          |
| SCHEMATA                                   | X        | X        |          |
| SEARCH_OPTIMIZATION_HISTORY                |          | X        |          |
| SEQUENCES                                  | X        | X        |          |
| SERVERLESS_TASK_HISTORY                    |          | X        |          |
| SESSIONS                                   |          | X        |          |
| SESSION_POLICIES                           |          | X        |          |
| SNOWPIPE_STREAMING_CLIENT_HISTORY          |          | X        |          |
| SNOWPIPE_STREAMING_FILE_MIGRATION_HISTORY  |          | X        |          |
| STAGES                                     | X        | X        |          |
| STAGE_STORAGE_USAGE_HISTORY                |          | X        |          |
| STORAGE_USAGE                              |          | X        |          |
| TABLES                                     | X        | X        |          |
| TABLE_CONSTRAINTS                          | X        | X        |          |
| TABLE_PRIVILEGES                           | X        |          |          |
| TABLE_STORAGE_METRICS                      | X        | X        |          |
| TAGS                                       |          | X        |          |
| TAG_REFERENCES                             |          | X        |          |
| TASK_HISTORY                               |          | X        |          |
| TASK_VERSIONS                              |          | X        |          |
| USAGE_PRIVILEGES                           | X        |          |          |
| USERS                                      |          | X        |          |
| VIEWS                                      | X        | X        |          |
| WAREHOUSE_EVENTS_HISTORY                   |          | X        |          |
| WAREHOUSE_LOAD_HISTORY                     |          | X        |          |
| WAREHOUSE_METERING_HISTORY                 |          | X        |          |
+--------------------------------------------+----------+----------+
```

If you want to find out information about tables, columns, databases, or views, you can use either information_schema or account_usage. If you want information about things at the account level, such as login history, storage usage, or grants, you will need to use account_usage.

Advantages to using the views in account_usage over information_schema include:

Data retention

    Historic data is available for a year in account_usage, whereas history may only be kept for a few days in information_schema.

Dropped objects

    If you drop a table or view, it will no longer be visible using information_schema, whereas you can still find it in account_usage.

One disadvantage to using account_usage, however, is a latency of between 45 minutes and 3 hours before schema changes are visible in account_usage. Here's a query against account_usage.views which shows all of the views I have created over the past six months or so:

```
PUBLIC>select table_name, table_owner, deleted
       from snowflake.account_usage.views
       order by 1, 4;
+----------------------+--------------+-------------------------+
| TABLE_NAME           | TABLE_OWNER  | DELETED                 |
|----------------------+--------------+-------------------------|
| BIG_SPENDERS_1998_VW | ACCOUNTADMIN | NULL                    |
| EMPLOYEE_MANAGER_VW  | ACCOUNTADMIN | NULL                    |
| EMPLOYEE_VW          | ACCOUNTADMIN | NULL                    |
| MY_EMPLOYEES         | ACCOUNTADMIN | NULL                    |
| ORDER_CALCULATION_VW | NULL         | 2023-02-28 10:11:36.069 |
| ORDER_CALCULATION_VW | ACCOUNTADMIN | NULL                    |
| PERSON_VW            | ACCOUNTADMIN | NULL                    |
| REGION_TOTALSALES_VW | ACCOUNTADMIN | NULL                    |
| SUPPLIER_VW          | ACCOUNTADMIN | 2023-06-02 10:53:32.715 |
| SUPPLIER_VW          | ACCOUNTADMIN | NULL                    |
| YEARLY_PART_SALES    | NULL         | 2022-12-20 12:03:23.913 |
| YEARLY_PART_SALES_VW | NULL         | 2023-02-28 10:06:26.584 |
| YEARLY_PART_SALES_VW | ACCOUNTADMIN | NULL                    |
+----------------------+--------------+-------------------------+
```

The results show a history of when views were dropped and re-created. For example, the order_calculation_vw view was dropped on February 28, 2023, and then re-created, possibly to add a new column or to modify the view's underlying query.

I can also use account_usage to see what I've been up to for the past 24 hours:

```
PUBLIC>select substr(query_text, 1, 40) partial_query,
       total_elapsed_time as runtime, rows_produced as num_rows
       from snowflake.account_usage.query_history
       where start_time > current_date - 1
       and query_text not like 'SHOW%'
       and rows_produced > 0;
+------------------------------------------+---------+----------+
| PARTIAL_QUERY                            | RUNTIME | NUM_ROWS |
|------------------------------------------+---------+----------|
| with active_contracts as (              |    2201 |        1 |
|   select dist                           |         |          |
| select  usage_date,   account_name as ac|    2318 |        7 |
| select substr(query_text, 1, 40) partial|    1017 |        3 |
| select * from snowflake.account_usage.lo|    4319 |        8 |
| select * from snowflake.account_usage.qu|    1747 |      311 |
| select substr(query_text, 1, 40) partial|    1227 |      187 |
| select query_text,                      |     879 |       14 |
|   total_elapsed_time                     |         |          |
| select substr(query_text, 1, 40) partial|    1189 |      139 |
+------------------------------------------+---------+----------+
```

This query retrieves all of the SQL statements executed from my account over the past day, showing the first 40 characters of the statement along with the elapsed time in milliseconds and the number of rows returned. Querying the account_history.query_history view can be a great way to keep tabs on what your user community is doing, check for performance issues, and see which database objects are being utilized.

Wrap-Up

In this chapter, you learned about what metadata is, how it is made available, and how it can be useful to you for various tasks. You also learned about both schema-level and account-level views.

Test Your Knowledge

The following exercises are designed to test your understanding of metadata. Please see "Chapter 13" in Appendix B for solutions.

Exercise 13-1

Retrieve the names of all tables along with their row counts using the `information_schema.tables` view. Retrieve only tables having more than 1000 rows.

Exercise 13-2

Write a query against `account_usage.views` that returns the name of any view that has been created more than once.

Window Functions

The SQL language has been around for a long time, and for many years the result sets from queries had to be fed into spreadsheets or reporting engines where additional logic was performed to generate the desired final results. For example, subtotals, rankings, and row-to-row comparisons could not be generated within a query and required external processing. Thankfully, modern SQL implementations, including Snowflake's, offer a host of built-in functions used to generate additional column values after the from, where, group by, and having clauses of a query have been evaluated. These functions, known as *window functions*, are examined in detail in this chapter.

Windowing Concepts

Before diving into the various window functions, it will be helpful to understand what windows are, how they are defined, and how they are utilized.

Data Windows

Data windows are subsets of rows in a result set. You are already familiar with this concept if you have utilized the group by clause, which groups rows into subsets based on data values. When using group by, you can apply functions such as max(), min(), count(), and sum() across the rows in each group. A *data window* is similar to a group, except that windows are created when the select clause is being evaluated. Once data windows have been defined, you can apply *windowing functions*, such as max() and rank(), to the data in each data window.

A data window can span a single row or all of the rows in the result set, or anything in between, and you can define multiple data windows within the same query. To illustrate, let's say you are writing a report that sums total orders by year and quarter for the years 1995 through 1997. Here's the query to generate the results:

```
PUBLIC>select date_part(year, o_orderdate) year,
        date_part(quarter, o_orderdate) quarter,
        sum(o_totalprice) tot_sales
    from orders
    where date_part(year, o_orderdate) between 1995 and 1997
    group by date_part(year, o_orderdate),
        date_part(quarter, o_orderdate)
    order by 1,2;
```

YEAR	QUARTER	TOT_SALES
1995	1	828280426.28
1995	2	818992304.21
1995	3	845652776.68
1995	4	824596303.26
1996	1	805551195.59
1996	2	809903462.32
1996	3	841091513.43
1996	4	839827181.45
1997	1	793402839.95
1997	2	824211569.74
1997	3	824176170.61
1997	4	813296140.78

Along with the quarterly sales totals, the report should also show the quarter's percentage of yearly sales (all four quarters of the same year). Before reading this chapter, you may have been tempted to load the previous results into Excel or write a Python script to generate the additional column, but you can easily generate these results by defining multiple data windows, each window containing rows in the same year. Here's what it looks like:

```
PUBLIC>select date_part(year, o_orderdate) year,
        date_part(quarter, o_orderdate) qrter,
        sum(o_totalprice) tot_sales,
        sum(sum(o_totalprice))
          over (partition by
            date_part(year, o_orderdate)) tot_yrly_sales
    from orders
    where date_part(year, o_orderdate) between 1995 and 1997
    group by date_part(year, o_orderdate),
        date_part(quarter, o_orderdate)
    order by 1,2;
```

YEAR	QRTER	TOT_SALES	TOT_YRLY_SALES
1995	1	828280426.28	3317521810.43
1995	2	818992304.21	3317521810.43
1995	3	845652776.68	3317521810.43

```
| 1995 |   4 | 824596303.26 |  3317521810.43 |
| 1996 |   1 | 805551195.59 |  3296373352.79 |
| 1996 |   2 | 809903462.32 |  3296373352.79 |
| 1996 |   3 | 841091513.43 |  3296373352.79 |
| 1996 |   4 | 839827181.45 |  3296373352.79 |
| 1997 |   1 | 793402839.95 |  3255086721.08 |
| 1997 |   2 | 824211569.74 |  3255086721.08 |
| 1997 |   3 | 824176170.61 |  3255086721.08 |
| 1997 |   4 | 813296140.78 |  3255086721.08 |
+------+------+--------------+----------------+
```

The `tot_yrly_sales` column uses a `partition` by clause to define a data window for all rows in the same year. Thus, there are 3 data windows defined, one each for the years 1995, 1996, and 1997. The total values for each year are generated by "summing the sums," which is why you see the `sum()` function used twice:

```
sum(sum(o_totalprice))
```

The first summation generates the total sales for each quarter, and the outer summation generates the total sales for all quarters in the same data window (year). Now that you have the yearly totals, you can complete the query by using the window function as a denominator to calculate the percentage:

```
PUBLIC>select date_part(year, o_orderdate) year,
       date_part(quarter, o_orderdate) qrter,
       sum(o_totalprice) tot_sales,
       round(sum(o_totalprice) /
         sum(sum(o_totalprice))
           over (partition by date_part(year, o_orderdate))
         * 100, 1) pct_of_yrly_sales
     from orders
     where date_part(year, o_orderdate) between 1995 and 1997
     group by date_part(year, o_orderdate),
       date_part(quarter, o_orderdate)
     order by 1,2;
+------+-------+--------------+-------------------+
| YEAR | QRTER |    TOT_SALES | PCT_OF_YRLY_SALES |
|------+-------+--------------+-------------------|
| 1995 |     1 | 828280426.28 |              25.0 |
| 1995 |     2 | 818992304.21 |              24.7 |
| 1995 |     3 | 845652776.68 |              25.5 |
| 1995 |     4 | 824596303.26 |              24.9 |
| 1996 |     1 | 805551195.59 |              24.4 |
| 1996 |     2 | 809903462.32 |              24.6 |
| 1996 |     3 | 841091513.43 |              25.5 |
| 1996 |     4 | 839827181.45 |              25.5 |
| 1997 |     1 | 793402839.95 |              24.4 |
| 1997 |     2 | 824211569.74 |              25.3 |
| 1997 |     3 | 824176170.61 |              25.3 |
| 1997 |     4 | 813296140.78 |              25.0 |
+------+-------+--------------+-------------------+
```

No need for Excel or Python. All you need is SQL, and the rest of this chapter will demonstrate a number of powerful window functions that should meet most of your reporting and data science needs.

Partitioning and Sorting

In the previous section, you saw an example of how data windows are defined using the partition by clause. For some windowing functions, such as sum() and avg(), defining the data window is all that is needed. For other types of window functions, however, it is necessary to *sort* the rows within each window, which necessitates the use of an order by clause. For example, let's say you are asked to assign a ranking to each quarter in a year to show which quarter had the highest total sales (rank = 1), the next highest sales (rank = 2), and so on. In order to assign rankings within a data window, you will need to describe how to order the rows, as shown in the next query:

```
PUBIC>select date_part(year, o_orderdate) year,
         date_part(quarter, o_orderdate) qrter,
         sum(o_totalprice) tot_sales,
         rank()
           over (partition by date_part(year, o_orderdate)
             order by sum(o_totalprice) desc) qtr_rank_per_year
       from orders
       where date_part(year, o_orderdate) between 1995 and 1997
       group by date_part(year, o_orderdate),
         date_part(quarter, o_orderdate)
       order by 1,2;
```

YEAR	QRTER	TOT_SALES	QTR_RANK_PER_YEAR
1995	1	828280426.28	2
1995	2	818992304.21	4
1995	3	845652776.68	1
1995	4	824596303.26	3
1996	1	805551195.59	4
1996	2	809903462.32	3
1996	3	841091513.43	1
1996	4	839827181.45	2
1997	1	793402839.95	4
1997	2	824211569.74	1
1997	3	824176170.61	2
1997	4	813296140.78	3

This example uses both the partition by and order by clauses to define the data window and describe the sort order within each window. However, if you want to generate a ranking across an entire result set, you can omit the partition by clause:

```
PUBLIC>select date_part(year, o_orderdate) year,
         date_part(quarter, o_orderdate) qrter,
         sum(o_totalprice) tot_sales,
```

```
      rank()
        over (order by sum(o_totalprice) desc) qtr_ranking
    from orders
    where date_part(year, o_orderdate) between 1995 and 1997
    group by date_part(year, o_orderdate),
      date_part(quarter, o_orderdate)
    order by 1,2;
```

YEAR	QRTER	TOT_SALES	QTR_RANKING
1995	1	828280426.28	4
1995	2	818992304.21	8
1995	3	845652776.68	1
1995	4	824596303.26	5
1996	1	805551195.59	11
1996	2	809903462.32	10
1996	3	841091513.43	2
1996	4	839827181.45	3
1997	1	793402839.95	12
1997	2	824211569.74	6
1997	3	824176170.61	7
1997	4	813296140.78	9

Rather than assigning the ranking values 1 through 4 within each year, this version of the query assigns the ranks 1 through 12 across the 12 rows of the result set. Since the rankings are assigned across the entire result set, there is no need for a partition by clause, because there is only a single data window covering all 12 rows.

order by Overload

Unfortunately, the clause used to sort rows within data windows has the same name as the clause used to sort result sets: order by. Keep in mind that using order by within a windowing function (generally within the over(...) clause) does *not* influence the order of the final result set; if you want your query results to be sorted, you will need another order by clause at the end of your query.

Ranking

People love to rank things. An article about travel might define the "Top 10 Vacation Destinations," and you will find plenty of song lists proclaiming the "Top 100 Songs of All Time!" Companies also like to generate rankings, but for more practical purposes. For example, identifying the best products or market regions helps organizations make strategic decisions about future investments. Snowflake provides several different flavors of ranking functions, as will be shown in the following sections.

Ranking Functions

There are three main ranking functions, and they differ largely in how ties are handled. For example, if you are generating a top 10 ranking of salespeople, and two of the salespersons tie for first place, do you assign them both a ranking of 1? If so, does the next person on the list get a ranking of 2 or 3? Table 14-1 defines how the ranking functions differ.

Table 14-1. Snowflake ranking functions

Ranking function	Description
row_number()	Assigns unique ranking to each row, ties handled arbitrarily, no gaps in ranking
rank()	Assigns same ranking in case of a tie, leaves gaps in ranking
dense_rank()	Assigns same ranking in case of a tie, no gaps in ranking

The row_number() function pays no attention to ties, whereas the rank() and dense_rank() functions will assign the same ranking when there is a tie. Additionally, rank() will leave a gap in the rankings when a tie occurs, whereas dense_rank() does not. To illustrate, the next query counts the number of orders for each customer in 1996, in descending order (only first 10 rows retrieved):

```
PUBLIC>select o_custkey, count(*) num_orders
       from orders o
       where 1996 = date_part(year, o.o_orderdate)
       group by o_custkey
       order by 2 desc
       limit 10;
+-----------+------------+
| O_CUSTKEY | NUM_ORDERS |
|-----------+------------|
|     43645 |          5 |
|     55120 |          4 |
|     71731 |          4 |
|     60250 |          4 |
|     55849 |          4 |
|    104692 |          4 |
|     20743 |          3 |
|    118636 |          3 |
|      4618 |          3 |
|     63620 |          3 |
+-----------+------------+
```

Looking at the top of the result set, there is a single customer with five orders, another five customers with four orders, and then four customers having three orders. Next, let's use all three of the ranking functions to see how the resulting rankings differ for these same 10 customers:

```
PUBLIC>select o_custkey, count(*) num_orders,
              row_number() over (order by count(*) desc) row_num_rnk,
```

```
        rank() over (order by count(*) desc) rank_rnk,
        dense_rank() over (order by count(*) desc) dns_rank_rnk
      from orders o
      where 1996 = date_part(year, o.o_orderdate)
      group by o_custkey
      having o_custkey in (43645,55120,71731,60250,55849,
                           104692,20743,118636,4618,63620)
      order by 2 desc;
```

```
+-----------+-------------+-------------+-----------+---------------+
| O_CUSTKEY | NUM_ORDERS  | ROW_NUM_RNK | RANK_RNK  | DNS_RANK_RNK  |
|-----------+-------------+-------------+-----------+---------------|
|     43645 |           5 |           1 |         1 |             1 |
|     55120 |           4 |           2 |         2 |             2 |
|    104692 |           4 |           3 |         2 |             2 |
|     60250 |           4 |           4 |         2 |             2 |
|     55849 |           4 |           5 |         2 |             2 |
|     71731 |           4 |           6 |         2 |             2 |
|     20743 |           3 |           7 |         7 |             3 |
|    118636 |           3 |          10 |         7 |             3 |
|      4618 |           3 |           8 |         7 |             3 |
|     63620 |           3 |           9 |         7 |             3 |
+-----------+-------------+-------------+-----------+---------------+
```

All three ranking functions specify order by count(*) desc as the ranking criteria, which will result in a ranking of 1 for the customer with the highest number of orders. While all three functions return the same rankings for the first two rows, differences start to appear on line three, which corresponds to the second customer with four orders. Moving to the bottom of the result set, you can see that the dense_rank() function only assigns the rankings 1 through 3, whereas rank() assigns the rankings 1, 2, and 7. Therefore, deciding whether to leave gaps in the rankings can make a big difference, especially when there are many rows having the same value for the ranking criteria.

Top/Bottom/Nth Ranking

While there are numerous situations where you might want to assign rankings across an entire result set, sometimes you are really interested only in the top- or bottom-ranked row. Additionally, you may want to know something about the top- or bottom-ranked row, such as the value of one of the columns in the result set. For this type of functionality, you can use the first_value() and last_value() functions. To illustrate, let's return to a query from earlier in the chapter, which sums the total sales for each quarter in years 1995 through 1997:

```
PUBLIC>select date_part(year, o_orderdate) year,
       date_part(quarter, o_orderdate) qrter,
       sum(o_totalprice) tot_sales
      from orders
      where date_part(year, o_orderdate) between 1995 and 1997
      group by date_part(year, o_orderdate),
```

```
        date_part(quarter, o_orderdate)
      order by 1,2;
+------+-------+---------------+
| YEAR | QRTER |     TOT_SALES |
|------+-------+---------------|
| 1995 |     1 | 828280426.28  |
| 1995 |     2 | 818992304.21  |
| 1995 |     3 | 845652776.68  |
| 1995 |     4 | 824596303.26  |
| 1996 |     1 | 805551195.59  |
| 1996 |     2 | 809903462.32  |
| 1996 |     3 | 841091513.43  |
| 1996 |     4 | 839827181.45  |
| 1997 |     1 | 793402839.95  |
| 1997 |     2 | 824211569.74  |
| 1997 |     3 | 824176170.61  |
| 1997 |     4 | 813296140.78  |
+------+-------+---------------+
```

Imagine you've been asked to calculate the percentage difference between each quarter's sales and the best and worst quarter's sales (two separate columns). For this type of analysis, you don't care about intermediate rankings; you just need the top and bottom rankings, and the total sales value from each. Here's how you can identify the best and worst sales across all 12 quarters using `first_value()` and `last_value()`:

```
PUBLIC>select date_part(year, o_orderdate) year,
          date_part(quarter, o_orderdate) qrter,
          sum(o_totalprice) tot_sales,
          first_value(sum(o_totalprice))
            over (order by sum(o_totalprice) desc) top_sales,
          last_value(sum(o_totalprice))
            over (order by sum(o_totalprice) desc) btm_sales
       from orders
       where date_part(year, o_orderdate) between 1995 and 1997
       group by date_part(year, o_orderdate),
          date_part(quarter, o_orderdate)
       order by 1,2;
+------+-------+---------------+---------------+---------------+
| YEAR | QRTER |     TOT_SALES |     TOP_SALES |     BTM_SALES |
|------+-------+---------------+---------------+---------------|
| 1995 |     1 | 828280426.28  | 845652776.68  | 793402839.95  |
| 1995 |     2 | 818992304.21  | 845652776.68  | 793402839.95  |
| 1995 |     3 | 845652776.68  | 845652776.68  | 793402839.95  |
| 1995 |     4 | 824596303.26  | 845652776.68  | 793402839.95  |
| 1996 |     1 | 805551195.59  | 845652776.68  | 793402839.95  |
| 1996 |     2 | 809903462.32  | 845652776.68  | 793402839.95  |
| 1996 |     3 | 841091513.43  | 845652776.68  | 793402839.95  |
| 1996 |     4 | 839827181.45  | 845652776.68  | 793402839.95  |
| 1997 |     1 | 793402839.95  | 845652776.68  | 793402839.95  |
| 1997 |     2 | 824211569.74  | 845652776.68  | 793402839.95  |
| 1997 |     3 | 824176170.61  | 845652776.68  | 793402839.95  |
```

```
| 1997 |      4 | 813296140.78 | 845652776.68 | 793402839.95 |
+------+-------+--------------+--------------+--------------+
```

Now that each row contains the best and worst sales across all 12 quarters, it is a simple matter of using the values as a denominator in a percentage calculation:

```
PUBLIC>select date_part(year, o_orderdate) year,
         date_part(quarter, o_orderdate) qrter,
         sum(o_totalprice) tot_sales,
         round(sum(o_totalprice) /
           first_value(sum(o_totalprice))
             over (order by sum(o_totalprice) desc)
           * 100, 1) pct_top_sales,
         round(sum(o_totalprice) /
           last_value(sum(o_totalprice))
             over (order by sum(o_totalprice) desc)
           * 100, 1) pct_btm_sales
       from orders
       where date_part(year, o_orderdate) between 1995 and 1997
       group by date_part(year, o_orderdate),
         date_part(quarter, o_orderdate)
       order by 1,2;
+------+-------+--------------+---------------+---------------+
| YEAR | QRTER |    TOT_SALES | PCT_TOP_SALES | PCT_BTM_SALES |
|------+-------+--------------+---------------+---------------|
| 1995 |     1 | 828280426.28 |          97.9 |         104.4 |
| 1995 |     2 | 818992304.21 |          96.8 |         103.2 |
| 1995 |     3 | 845652776.68 |         100.0 |         106.6 |
| 1995 |     4 | 824596303.26 |          97.5 |         103.9 |
| 1996 |     1 | 805551195.59 |          95.3 |         101.5 |
| 1996 |     2 | 809903462.32 |          95.8 |         102.1 |
| 1996 |     3 | 841091513.43 |          99.5 |         106.0 |
| 1996 |     4 | 839827181.45 |          99.3 |         105.9 |
| 1997 |     1 | 793402839.95 |          93.8 |         100.0 |
| 1997 |     2 | 824211569.74 |          97.5 |         103.9 |
| 1997 |     3 | 824176170.61 |          97.5 |         103.9 |
| 1997 |     4 | 813296140.78 |          96.2 |         102.5 |
+------+-------+--------------+---------------+---------------+
```

Next, let's say that the comparison should be made within each year, rather than across all three. In other words, show the percentage comparison of each quarter's sales to the best and worst quarters *within the same year*. To do so, you just need to add a partition by clause within the first_value() and last_value() functions:

```
PUBLIC>select date_part(year, o_orderdate) year,
         date_part(quarter, o_orderdate) qrter,
         sum(o_totalprice) tot_sales,
         round(sum(o_totalprice) /
           first_value(sum(o_totalprice))
             over (partition by date_part(year, o_orderdate)
               order by sum(o_totalprice) desc)
           * 100, 1) pct_top_sales,
         round(sum(o_totalprice) /
```

```
        last_value(sum(o_totalprice))
          over (partition by date_part(year, o_orderdate)
            order by sum(o_totalprice) desc)
        * 100, 1) pct_btm_sales
    from orders
    where date_part(year, o_orderdate) between 1995 and 1997
    group by date_part(year, o_orderdate),
      date_part(quarter, o_orderdate)
    order by 1,2;
```

```
+------+-------+---------------+----------------+----------------+
| YEAR | QRTER |     TOT_SALES | PCT_TOP_SALES | PCT_BTM_SALES |
|------+-------+---------------+----------------+----------------|
| 1995 |     1 | 828280426.28 |           97.9 |          101.1 |
| 1995 |     2 | 818992304.21 |           96.8 |          100.0 |
| 1995 |     3 | 845652776.68 |          100.0 |          103.3 |
| 1995 |     4 | 824596303.26 |           97.5 |          100.7 |
| 1996 |     1 | 805551195.59 |           95.8 |          100.0 |
| 1996 |     2 | 809903462.32 |           96.3 |          100.5 |
| 1996 |     3 | 841091513.43 |          100.0 |          104.4 |
| 1996 |     4 | 839827181.45 |           99.8 |          104.3 |
| 1997 |     1 | 793402839.95 |           96.3 |          100.0 |
| 1997 |     2 | 824211569.74 |          100.0 |          103.9 |
| 1997 |     3 | 824176170.61 |          100.0 |          103.9 |
| 1997 |     4 | 813296140.78 |           98.7 |          102.5 |
+------+-------+---------------+----------------+----------------+
```

Along with first_value() and last_value(), you can also use the nth_value() function if you want values from the row with the Nth ranking (2nd, 3rd, etc.) rather than the top of bottom row. The next query uses first_value() and nth_value() to determine the best and second-best quarter number for each year:

```
PUBLIC>select date_part(year, o_orderdate) year,
        date_part(quarter, o_orderdate) qrter,
        sum(o_totalprice),
        first_value(date_part(quarter, o_orderdate))
          over (partition by date_part(year, o_orderdate)
            order by sum(o_totalprice) desc) best_qtr,
        nth_value(date_part(quarter, o_orderdate),2)
          over (partition by date_part(year, o_orderdate)
            order by sum(o_totalprice) desc) next_best_qtr
    from orders
    where date_part(year, o_orderdate) between 1995 and 1997
    group by date_part(year, o_orderdate),
      date_part(quarter, o_orderdate)
    order by 1,2;
```

```
+------+-------+-------------------+----------+----------------+
| YEAR | QRTER | SUM(O_TOTALPRICE) | BEST_QTR | NEXT_BEST_QTR |
|------+-------+-------------------+----------+----------------|
| 1995 |     1 |      828280426.28 |        3 |              1 |
| 1995 |     2 |      818992304.21 |        3 |              1 |
| 1995 |     3 |      845652776.68 |        3 |              1 |
| 1995 |     4 |      824596303.26 |        3 |              1 |
```

```
| 1996 |   1 |     805551195.59 |    3 |    4 |
| 1996 |   2 |     809903462.32 |    3 |    4 |
| 1996 |   3 |     841091513.43 |    3 |    4 |
| 1996 |   4 |     839827181.45 |    3 |    4 |
| 1997 |   1 |     793402839.95 |    2 |    3 |
| 1997 |   2 |     824211569.74 |    2 |    3 |
| 1997 |   3 |     824176170.61 |   .2 |    3 |
| 1997 |   4 |     813296140.78 |    2 |    3 |
+------+------+--------------------+----------+---------------+
```

The nth_value() function has an additional parameter to let you specify the number of value of "N," which in this case is 2. There is also an option to specify whether you want N rows from the top or bottom of the ranking, so here's another variation that shows the best quarter and the second-worst quarter per year:

```
PUBLIC>select date_part(year, o_orderdate) year,
        date_part(quarter, o_orderdate) qrter,
        sum(o_totalprice),
        first_value(date_part(quarter, o_orderdate))
          over (partition by date_part(year, o_orderdate)
            order by sum(o_totalprice) desc) best_qtr,
        nth_value(date_part(quarter, o_orderdate),2)
          from last
          over (partition by date_part(year, o_orderdate)
            order by sum(o_totalprice) desc) next_worst_qtr
      from orders
      where date_part(year, o_orderdate) between 1995 and 1997
      group by date_part(year, o_orderdate),
        date_part(quarter, o_orderdate)
      order by 1,2;
```

YEAR	QRTER	SUM(O_TOTALPRICE)	BEST_QTR	NEXT_WORST_QTR
1995	1	828280426.28	3	4
1995	2	818992304.21	3	4
1995	3	845652776.68	3	4
1995	4	824596303.26	3	4
1996	1	805551195.59	3	2
1996	2	809903462.32	3	2
1996	3	841091513.43	3	2
1996	4	839827181.45	3	2
1997	1	793402839.95	2	4
1997	2	824211569.74	2	4
1997	3	824176170.61	2	4
1997	4	813296140.78	2	4

I think you will agree that these functions offer quite a bit of flexibility when comparing values between different rows in your result set.

Qualify Clause

At the top of this chapter, I mentioned that window functions are executed *after* the where, group by, and having clauses have been evaluated. This means that you can't add a filter condition in your where clause based on the results of a window function such as rank(). This would generally force you to do something like the following if you wanted to retrieve the five nations having the most suppliers:

```
PUBLIC>select name, num_suppliers
       from
        (select n.n_name as name, count(*) as num_suppliers,
          rank() over (order by count(*) desc) as rnk
        from supplier s
          inner join nation n on n.n_nationkey = s.s_nationkey
        group by n.n_name
        ) top_suppliers
        where rnk <= 5;
+-----------+----------------+
| NAME      | NUM_SUPPLIERS  |
|-----------+----------------|
| PERU      |            325 |
| ALGERIA   |            318 |
| ARGENTINA |            312 |
| CHINA     |            310 |
| IRAQ      |            309 |
+-----------+----------------+
```

While this approach works, it is a bit clumsy to have to use subqueries every time you want to filter on the results of a ranking function. For this purpose, Snowflake has added a new clause named qualify, which is specifically designed for filtering based on the results of window functions. Here's the previous query again, but this time using a qualify clause:

```
PUBLIC>select n.n_name as name, count(*) as num_suppliers,
        rank() over (order by count(*) desc) as rnk
        from supplier s
          inner join nation n on n.n_nationkey = s.s_nationkey
        group by n.n_name
        qualify rnk <= 5;
+-----------+----------------+-----+
| NAME      | NUM_SUPPLIERS  | RNK |
|-----------+----------------+-----|
| PERU      |            325 |   1 |
| ALGERIA   |            318 |   2 |
| ARGENTINA |            312 |   3 |
| CHINA     |            310 |   4 |
| IRAQ      |            309 |   5 |
+-----------+----------------+-----+
```

With qualify, you can put your filter conditions in the same query that calls the window functions, and you can use the column alias (rnk in this case) from the window function in the select clause. You can also put the window functions *within* the qualify clause, which is useful if you want the top N rows but don't need to know the actual rankings. Here's the previous query, but with the rank() function moved from select to qualify:

```
PUBLIC>select n.n_name as name, count(*) as num_suppliers
      from supplier s
         inner join nation n on n.n_nationkey = s.s_nationkey
      group by n.n_name
      qualify rank() over (order by count(*) desc) <= 5;
+-----------+----------------+
| NAME      | NUM_SUPPLIERS  |
|-----------+----------------|
| PERU      |            325 |
| ALGERIA   |            318 |
| ARGENTINA |            312 |
| CHINA     |            310 |
| IRAQ      |            309 |
+-----------+----------------+
```

Therefore, the qualify clause can contain filter conditions that reference window functions in the select clause, or it can contain filter conditions that include calls to window functions.

Another way to find the top N rows based on a ranking is to use the top subclause of the select clause. Here's what that looks like for the top five nation query:

```
PUBLIC>select top 5
         n.n_name as name, count(*) as num_suppliers,
         rank() over (order by count(*) desc) as rnk
      from supplier s
         inner join nation n on n.n_nationkey = s.s_nationkey
      group by n.n_name
      order by 3;
+-----------+----------------+-----+
| NAME      | NUM_SUPPLIERS  | RNK |
|-----------+----------------+-----|
| PERU      |            325 |   1 |
| ALGERIA   |            318 |   2 |
| ARGENTINA |            312 |   3 |
| CHINA     |            310 |   4 |
| IRAQ      |            309 |   5 |
+-----------+----------------+-----+
```

This query only makes sense if an order by clause is included, as otherwise the five rows returned would be arbitrary. While using top makes your intent clear, I find that the qualify clause is much more flexible because you can specify complete filter conditions.

Reporting Functions

Along with generating rankings, another common use for window functions is to find outliers (e.g., min or max values) or to generate sums or averages across an entire data set. For these types of uses, you will be using aggregate functions like min(), max(), and sum(), but instead of using them with a group by clause, you will pair them with partition by and/or order by clauses.

Let's start with a query that sums total sales per year for all countries in the Asia region:

```
PUBLIC>select n.n_name, date_part(year, o_orderdate) as year,
        sum(o.o_totalprice) as total_sales
     from region r
     inner join nation n
       on r.r_regionkey = n.n_regionkey
     inner join customer c
       on n.n_nationkey = c.c_nationkey
     inner join orders o
       on o.o_custkey = c.c_custkey
     where r.r_name = 'ASIA'
     group by n.n_name, date_part(year, o_orderdate)
     order by 1,2;
+-----------+------+--------------+
| N_NAME    | YEAR | TOTAL_SALES  |
|-----------+------+--------------|
| CHINA     | 1992 | 139188741.34 |
| CHINA     | 1993 | 128182471.75 |
| CHINA     | 1994 | 147758796.10 |
| CHINA     | 1995 | 136166806.51 |
| CHINA     | 1996 | 140645511.48 |
| CHINA     | 1997 | 129644871.64 |
| CHINA     | 1998 |  80074704.96 |
| INDIA     | 1992 | 136980167.32 |
| INDIA     | 1993 | 129244478.73 |
| INDIA     | 1994 | 127425713.08 |
| INDIA     | 1995 | 129235566.26 |
| INDIA     | 1996 | 132290605.57 |
| INDIA     | 1997 | 128123889.04 |
| INDIA     | 1998 |  83999645.32 |
| INDONESIA | 1992 | 140013458.45 |
| INDONESIA | 1993 | 126743272.52 |
| INDONESIA | 1994 | 127142722.42 |
| INDONESIA | 1995 | 135375411.46 |
| INDONESIA | 1996 | 123524947.21 |
| INDONESIA | 1997 | 133559192.95 |
| INDONESIA | 1998 |  79817061.71 |
| JAPAN     | 1992 | 137784961.23 |
| JAPAN     | 1993 | 131607347.47 |
| JAPAN     | 1994 | 126846662.01 |
| JAPAN     | 1995 | 130370308.88 |
```

```
| JAPAN     | 1996 | 128591246.23 |
| JAPAN     | 1997 | 133507984.20 |
| JAPAN     | 1998 |  78711228.07 |
| VIETNAM   | 1992 | 132148606.67 |
| VIETNAM   | 1993 | 141297287.92 |
| VIETNAM   | 1994 | 125154253.89 |
| VIETNAM   | 1995 | 132090365.47 |
| VIETNAM   | 1996 | 139046819.16 |
| VIETNAM   | 1997 | 128811392.94 |
| VIETNAM   | 1998 |  77484675.94 |
+-----------+------+--------------+
```

Next, let's add two additional columns: one to show the total sales *per* country across *all* years, and another to show total sales across *all* countries in *each* year. To do so, we will use two sum() functions along with partition by clauses to generate the appropriate data windows:

```
PUBLIC>select n.n_name, date_part(year, o_orderdate) as year,
        sum(o.o_totalprice) as total_sales,
        sum(sum(o.o_totalprice))
          over (partition by n.n_name) as tot_cntry_sls,
        sum(sum(o.o_totalprice))
          over (partition by date_part(year, o_orderdate))
            as tot_yrly_sls
      from region r
      inner join nation n
        on r.r_regionkey = n.n_regionkey
      inner join customer c
        on n.n_nationkey = c.c_nationkey
      inner join orders o
        on o.o_custkey = c.c_custkey
      where r.r_name = 'ASIA'
      group by n.n_name, date_part(year, o_orderdate)
      order by 1,2;
+-----------+------+--------------+---------------+--------------+
| N_NAME    | YEAR |  TOTAL_SALES | TOT_CNTRY_SLS | TOT_YRLY_SLS |
|-----------+------+--------------+---------------+--------------|
| CHINA     | 1992 | 139188741.34 |  901661903.78 | 686115935.01 |
| CHINA     | 1993 | 128182471.75 |  901661903.78 | 657074858.39 |
| CHINA     | 1994 | 147758796.10 |  901661903.78 | 654328147.50 |
| CHINA     | 1995 | 136166806.51 |  901661903.78 | 663238458.58 |
| CHINA     | 1996 | 140645511.48 |  901661903.78 | 664099129.65 |
| CHINA     | 1997 | 129644871.64 |  901661903.78 | 653647330.77 |
| CHINA     | 1998 |  80074704.96 |  901661903.78 | 400087316.00 |
| INDIA     | 1992 | 136980167.32 |  867300065.32 | 686115935.01 |
| INDIA     | 1993 | 129244478.73 |  867300065.32 | 657074858.39 |
| INDIA     | 1994 | 127425713.08 |  867300065.32 | 654328147.50 |
| INDIA     | 1995 | 129235566.26 |  867300065.32 | 663238458.58 |
| INDIA     | 1996 | 132290605.57 |  867300065.32 | 664099129.65 |
| INDIA     | 1997 | 128123889.04 |  867300065.32 | 653647330.77 |
| INDIA     | 1998 |  83999645.32 |  867300065.32 | 400087316.00 |
| INDONESIA | 1992 | 140013458.45 |  866176066.72 | 686115935.01 |
```

```
| INDONESIA | 1993 | 126743272.52 |   866176066.72 | 657074858.39 |
| INDONESIA | 1994 | 127142722.42 |   866176066.72 | 654328147.50 |
| INDONESIA | 1995 | 135375411.46 |   866176066.72 | 663238458.58 |
| INDONESIA | 1996 | 123524947.21 |   866176066.72 | 664099129.65 |
| INDONESIA | 1997 | 133559192.95 |   866176066.72 | 653647330.77 |
| INDONESIA | 1998 |  79817061.71 |   866176066.72 | 400087316.00 |
| JAPAN     | 1992 | 137784961.23 |   867419738.09 | 686115935.01 |
| JAPAN     | 1993 | 131607347.47 |   867419738.09 | 657074858.39 |
| JAPAN     | 1994 | 126846662.01 |   867419738.09 | 654328147.50 |
| JAPAN     | 1995 | 130370308.88 |   867419738.09 | 663238458.58 |
| JAPAN     | 1996 | 128591246.23 |   867419738.09 | 664099129.65 |
| JAPAN     | 1997 | 133507984.20 |   867419738.09 | 653647330.77 |
| JAPAN     | 1998 |  78711228.07 |   867419738.09 | 400087316.00 |
| VIETNAM   | 1992 | 132148606.67 |   876033401.99 | 686115935.01 |
| VIETNAM   | 1993 | 141297287.92 |   876033401.99 | 657074858.39 |
| VIETNAM   | 1994 | 125154253.89 |   876033401.99 | 654328147.50 |
| VIETNAM   | 1995 | 132090365.47 |   876033401.99 | 663238458.58 |
| VIETNAM   | 1996 | 139046819.16 |   876033401.99 | 664099129.65 |
| VIETNAM   | 1997 | 128811392.94 |   876033401.99 | 653647330.77 |
| VIETNAM   | 1998 |  77484675.94 |   876033401.99 | 400087316.00 |
+-----------+------+--------------+----------------+--------------+
```

You could use these additional columns to calculate percentages per country or per year. You may also be interested in comparing to the average or maximum values within a window:

```
PUBLIC>select n.n_name, date_part(year, o_orderdate) as year,
        sum(o.o_totalprice) as total_sales,
        max(sum(o.o_totalprice))
          over (partition by n.n_name) as max_cntry_sls,
        avg(round(sum(o.o_totalprice)))
          over (partition by date_part(year, o_orderdate))
            as avg_yrly_sls
      from region r
      inner join nation n
        on r.r_regionkey = n.n_regionkey
      inner join customer c
        on n.n_nationkey = c.c_nationkey
      inner join orders o
        on o.o_custkey = c.c_custkey
      where r.r_name = 'ASIA'
      group by n.n_name, date_part(year, o_orderdate)
      order by 1,2;
+-----------+------+--------------+---------------+--------------+
| N_NAME    | YEAR | TOTAL_SALES  | MAX_CNTRY_SLS | AVG_YRLY_SLS |
|-----------+------+--------------+---------------+--------------|
| CHINA     | 1992 | 139188741.34 |  147758796.10 | 137223186.80 |
| CHINA     | 1993 | 128182471.75 |  147758796.10 | 131414971.80 |
| CHINA     | 1994 | 147758796.10 |  147758796.10 | 130865629.40 |
| CHINA     | 1995 | 136166806.51 |  147758796.10 | 132647691.60 |
| CHINA     | 1996 | 140645511.48 |  147758796.10 | 132819825.80 |
| CHINA     | 1997 | 129644871.64 |  147758796.10 | 130729466.20 |
```

```
| CHINA     | 1998 |  80074704.96 | 147758796.10 |  80017463.20 |
| INDIA     | 1992 | 136980167.32 | 136980167.32 | 137223186.80 |
| INDIA     | 1993 | 129244478.73 | 136980167.32 | 131414971.80 |
| INDIA     | 1994 | 127425713.08 | 136980167.32 | 130865629.40 |
| INDIA     | 1995 | 129235566.26 | 136980167.32 | 132647691.60 |
| INDIA     | 1996 | 132290605.57 | 136980167.32 | 132819825.80 |
| INDIA     | 1997 | 128123889.04 | 136980167.32 | 130729466.20 |
| INDIA     | 1998 |  83999645.32 | 136980167.32 |  80017463.20 |
| INDONESIA | 1992 | 140013458.45 | 140013458.45 | 137223186.80 |
| INDONESIA | 1993 | 126743272.52 | 140013458.45 | 131414971.80 |
| INDONESIA | 1994 | 127142722.42 | 140013458.45 | 130865629.40 |
| INDONESIA | 1995 | 135375411.46 | 140013458.45 | 132647691.60 |
| INDONESIA | 1996 | 123524947.21 | 140013458.45 | 132819825.80 |
| INDONESIA | 1997 | 133559192.95 | 140013458.45 | 130729466.20 |
| INDONESIA | 1998 |  79817061.71 | 140013458.45 |  80017463.20 |
| JAPAN     | 1992 | 137784961.23 | 137784961.23 | 137223186.80 |
| JAPAN     | 1993 | 131607347.47 | 137784961.23 | 131414971.80 |
| JAPAN     | 1994 | 126846662.01 | 137784961.23 | 130865629.40 |
| JAPAN     | 1995 | 130370308.88 | 137784961.23 | 132647691.60 |
| JAPAN     | 1996 | 128591246.23 | 137784961.23 | 132819825.80 |
| JAPAN     | 1997 | 133507984.20 | 137784961.23 | 130729466.20 |
| JAPAN     | 1998 |  78711228.07 | 137784961.23 |  80017463.20 |
| VIETNAM   | 1992 | 132148606.67 | 141297287.92 | 137223186.80 |
| VIETNAM   | 1993 | 141297287.92 | 141297287.92 | 131414971.80 |
| VIETNAM   | 1994 | 125154253.89 | 141297287.92 | 130865629.40 |
| VIETNAM   | 1995 | 132090365.47 | 141297287.92 | 132647691.60 |
| VIETNAM   | 1996 | 139046819.16 | 141297287.92 | 132819825.80 |
| VIETNAM   | 1997 | 128811392.94 | 141297287.92 | 130729466.20 |
| VIETNAM   | 1998 |  77484675.94 | 141297287.92 |  80017463.20 |
+-----------+------+--------------+--------------+--------------+
```

This query calculates the maximum sales per country across all years, and the average sales per year across all countries.

Positional Windows

So far in this chapter, all data windows have been created using the `partition by` clause, which places rows into data windows based on common values. There are cases, however, when you will want to define data windows based on *proximity* rather than on values. For example, you may want to calculate rolling averages, which might require a data window to be built for each row including the prior, current, and next row. Another example is a running total, where data windows are built from the first row up to the current row. For these types of calculations, you will need to use an `order by` clause to define how the rows should be ordered, and a `rows` clause to specify which rows should be included in the data window.

To illustrate, let's return to the example earlier in the chapter that sums sales by year and quarter:

```
PUBLIC>select date_part(year, o_orderdate) year,
       date_part(quarter, o_orderdate) qrter,
       sum(o_totalprice) as total_sales
     from orders
     where date_part(year, o_orderdate) between 1995 and 1997
     group by date_part(year, o_orderdate),
       date_part(quarter, o_orderdate)
     order by 1,2;
+------+-------+---------------+
| YEAR | QRTER |   TOTAL_SALES |
|------+-------+---------------|
| 1995 |     1 | 828280426.28  |
| 1995 |     2 | 818992304.21  |
| 1995 |     3 | 845652776.68  |
| 1995 |     4 | 824596303.26  |
| 1996 |     1 | 805551195.59  |
| 1996 |     2 | 809903462.32  |
| 1996 |     3 | 841091513.43  |
| 1996 |     4 | 839827181.45  |
| 1997 |     1 | 793402839.95  |
| 1997 |     2 | 824211569.74  |
| 1997 |     3 | 824176170.61  |
| 1997 |     4 | 813296140.78  |
+------+-------+---------------+
```

Let's say you've been asked to calculate a three-month running average for each quarter, which requires each row to have a data window that includes the prior, current, and next quarters. For example, the three-month rolling average for quarter 1 of 1996 would include the values from quarter 4 of 1995, quarter 1 of 1996, and quarter 2 of 1996. Here's how you define the data windows using the rows clause:

```
PUBLIC>select date_part(year, o_orderdate) year,
       date_part(quarter, o_orderdate) qrter,
       sum(o_totalprice) as total_sales,
       avg(sum(o_totalprice))
         over (order by date_part(year, o_orderdate),
           date_part(quarter, o_orderdate)
         rows between 1 preceding and 1 following)
         as rolling_avg
     from orders
     where date_part(year, o_orderdate) between 1995 and 1997
     group by date_part(year, o_orderdate),
       date_part(quarter, o_orderdate)
     order by 1,2;
+------+-------+---------------+------------------+
| YEAR | QRTER |   TOTAL_SALES |      ROLLING_AVG |
|------+-------+---------------+------------------|
| 1995 |     1 | 828280426.28  | 823636365.24500  |
| 1995 |     2 | 818992304.21  | 830975169.05666  |
| 1995 |     3 | 845652776.68  | 829747128.05000  |
| 1995 |     4 | 824596303.26  | 825266758.51000  |
| 1996 |     1 | 805551195.59  | 813350320.39000  |
```

```
| 1996 |    2 | 809903462.32 | 818848723.78000 |
| 1996 |    3 | 841091513.43 | 830274052.40000 |
| 1996 |    4 | 839827181.45 | 824773844.94333 |
| 1997 |    1 | 793402839.95 | 819147197.04666 |
| 1997 |    2 | 824211569.74 | 813930193.43333 |
| 1997 |    3 | 824176170.61 | 820561293.71000 |
| 1997 |    4 | 813296140.78 | 818736155.69500 |
+------+------+--------------+-----------------+
```

Defining windows positionally depends on an order by clause to determine the ordering of the rows. In this example, the rows clause specifies that the window should include all rows between the prior (one preceding) and next (one following) rows. You might be wondering how this calculation works for the first row (which has no preceding row) or the last row (which has no following row). In both cases, the averages are calculated with just two rows, since that is all that's available.

For running totals, you will want to define a data window that starts with the first row and ends with the current row. Here's how you could use rows unbounded preceding to generate a running total of quarterly sales:

```
PUBLIC>select date_part(year, o_orderdate) year,
         date_part(quarter, o_orderdate) qrter,
         sum(o_totalprice) as total_sales,
         sum(sum(o_totalprice))
           over (order by date_part(year, o_orderdate),
             date_part(quarter, o_orderdate)
           rows unbounded preceding) as running_total
       from orders
       where date_part(year, o_orderdate) between 1995 and 1997
       group by date_part(year, o_orderdate),
         date_part(quarter, o_orderdate)
       order by 1,2;
+------+-------+--------------+----------------+
| YEAR | QRTER | TOTAL_SALES  | RUNNING_TOTAL  |
|------+-------+--------------+----------------|
| 1995 |     1 | 828280426.28 |    828280426.28 |
| 1995 |     2 | 818992304.21 |   1647272730.49 |
| 1995 |     3 | 845652776.68 |   2492925507.17 |
| 1995 |     4 | 824596303.26 |   3317521810.43 |
| 1996 |     1 | 805551195.59 |   4123073006.02 |
| 1996 |     2 | 809903462.32 |   4932976468.34 |
| 1996 |     3 | 841091513.43 |   5774067981.77 |
| 1996 |     4 | 839827181.45 |   6613895163.22 |
| 1997 |     1 | 793402839.95 |   7407298003.17 |
| 1997 |     2 | 824211569.74 |   8231509572.91 |
| 1997 |     3 | 824176170.61 |   9055685743.52 |
| 1997 |     4 | 813296140.78 |   9868981884.30 |
+------+-------+--------------+----------------+
```

The data window for the first row contains just itself; the data window for the second row contains the first two rows; and the data window for the last row contains all 12 of the rows.

If you only need to get a value from a single row based on its position in the result set, you can use the lag() and lead() functions, which allow you to retrieve a column from a nearby row. This would be useful if you wanted to calculate the percentage change from the previous quarter, for example. Here's how you could use the lag() function to find the prior quarter's total sales:

```
PUBLIC>select date_part(year, o_orderdate) year,
        date_part(quarter, o_orderdate) qrter,
        sum(o_totalprice) as total_sales,
        lag(sum(o_totalprice),1)
          over (order by date_part(year, o_orderdate),
            date_part(quarter, o_orderdate)) as prior_qtr
      from orders
      where date_part(year, o_orderdate) between 1995 and 1997
      group by date_part(year, o_orderdate),
        date_part(quarter, o_orderdate)
      order by 1,2;
+------+-------+---------------+---------------+
| YEAR | QRTER |  TOTAL_SALES  |   PRIOR_QTR   |
|------+-------+---------------+---------------|
| 1995 |     1 | 828280426.28  |          NULL |
| 1995 |     2 | 818992304.21  |  828280426.28 |
| 1995 |     3 | 845652776.68  |  818992304.21 |
| 1995 |     4 | 824596303.26  |  845652776.68 |
| 1996 |     1 | 805551195.59  |  824596303.26 |
| 1996 |     2 | 809903462.32  |  805551195.59 |
| 1996 |     3 | 841091513.43  |  809903462.32 |
| 1996 |     4 | 839827181.45  |  841091513.43 |
| 1997 |     1 | 793402839.95  |  839827181.45 |
| 1997 |     2 | 824211569.74  |  793402839.95 |
| 1997 |     3 | 824176170.61  |  824211569.74 |
| 1997 |     4 | 813296140.78  |  824176170.61 |
+------+-------+---------------+---------------+
```

In this example, I am specifying lag(sum(o_totalprice),1) to instruct Snowflake to go back one row in the sort order and retrieve the sum(o_totalprice) value. As you can see, the value is null for the first row since there is no prior row. Now that you have values for the current and prior quarters on the same row, you would just need to do the calculation to determine the percentage change ((current value - prior value) / prior_value * 100).

If you want to pull a value from the next row in the sort order, rather than the previous row, you can use the lead() function:

```
PUBLIC>select date_part(year, o_orderdate) year,
        date_part(quarter, o_orderdate) qrter,
```

```
          sum(o_totalprice) as total_sales,
          lead(sum(o_totalprice),1)
            over (order by date_part(year, o_orderdate),
              date_part(quarter, o_orderdate)) as next_qtr
      from orders
      where date_part(year, o_orderdate) between 1995 and 1997
      group by date_part(year, o_orderdate),
        date_part(quarter, o_orderdate)
      order by 1,2;
+------+-------+--------------+--------------+
| YEAR | QRTER |  TOTAL_SALES |    NEXT_QTR  |
|------+-------+--------------+--------------|
| 1995 |     1 | 828280426.28 | 818992304.21 |
| 1995 |     2 | 818992304.21 | 845652776.68 |
| 1995 |     3 | 845652776.68 | 824596303.26 |
| 1995 |     4 | 824596303.26 | 805551195.59 |
| 1996 |     1 | 805551195.59 | 809903462.32 |
| 1996 |     2 | 809903462.32 | 841091513.43 |
| 1996 |     3 | 841091513.43 | 839827181.45 |
| 1996 |     4 | 839827181.45 | 793402839.95 |
| 1997 |     1 | 793402839.95 | 824211569.74 |
| 1997 |     2 | 824211569.74 | 824176170.61 |
| 1997 |     3 | 824176170.61 | 813296140.78 |
| 1997 |     4 | 813296140.78 |         NULL |
+------+-------+--------------+--------------+
```

In this example, the next_qtr column is picking up the total_sales value from the next quarter. As you might expect, the last row has a null value for next_qtr, since there are no further rows in the result set.

Other Window Functions

There are a number of additional window functions available in Snowflake, many of which would be useful for statistical analysis. For example, there are functions useful for computing standard deviations and variances, percentiles, and linear regressions. I will not be covering these functions, but I would like to demonstrate one last function named listagg(), which I find useful for both analysis and development. The listagg() function pivots data into a single delimited string, as demonstrated by the following query, which returns each region along with a comma-delimited list of associated nations:

```
PUBLIC>select r.r_name as region,
         listagg(n.n_name, ',') within group (order by n.n_name)
           as nation_list
     from region r
     inner join nation n
     on r.r_regionkey = n.n_regionkey
     group by r.r_name
     order by 1;
+-------------+---------------------------------------------------+
```

```
| REGION       | NATION_LIST                                      |
|--------------+--------------------------------------------------|
| AFRICA       | ALGERIA,ETHIOPIA,KENYA,MOROCCO,MOZAMBIQUE        |
| AMERICA      | ARGENTINA,BRAZIL,CANADA,PERU,UNITED STATES       |
| ASIA         | CHINA,INDIA,INDONESIA,JAPAN,VIETNAM              |
| EUROPE       | FRANCE,GERMANY,ROMANIA,RUSSIA,UNITED KINGDOM     |
| MIDDLE EAST  | EGYPT,IRAN,IRAQ,JORDAN,SAUDI ARABIA              |
+--------------+--------------------------------------------------+
```

In this example, `listagg()` generates a list of nations in alphabetical order for each region. Unfortunately, `listagg()` has a different syntax than the other window functions and uses a `within group` clause to specify ordering rather than an `over` clause. Also, if you want to further split your result set into data windows, you can add an `over (partition by ...)` clause as well. In some cases, you can use the `partition by` clause instead of using a `group by` clause, although you will likely need to add `distinct` to remove duplicates. Here's the previous query without a `group by` clause but instead using `partition by`:

```
PUBLIC>select distinct r.r_name as region,
          listagg(n.n_name, ',')
            within group (order by n.n_name)
            over (partition by r.r_name)
            as nation_list
        from region r
        inner join nation n
          on r.r_regionkey = n.n_regionkey
        order by 1;
+--------------+--------------------------------------------------+
| REGION       | NATION_LIST                                      |
|--------------+--------------------------------------------------|
| AFRICA       | ALGERIA,ETHIOPIA,KENYA,MOROCCO,MOZAMBIQUE        |
| AMERICA      | ARGENTINA,BRAZIL,CANADA,PERU,UNITED STATES       |
| ASIA         | CHINA,INDIA,INDONESIA,JAPAN,VIETNAM              |
| EUROPE       | FRANCE,GERMANY,ROMANIA,RUSSIA,UNITED KINGDOM     |
| MIDDLE EAST  | EGYPT,IRAN,IRAQ,JORDAN,SAUDI ARABIA              |
+--------------+--------------------------------------------------+
```

Whichever way you use it, I think you will find `listagg()` to be a handy function any time you need to flatten or pivot a set of values.

Wrap-Up

This chapter covered several different flavors of window functions, including ranking and reporting functions. The functions covered in this chapter will allow you to augment your result set with additional columns to perform subtotals and rankings, compute rolling sums and averages, and retrieve column values from surrounding rows. This chapter also introduced a new clause named `qualify`, which is specifically designed for filtering based on the results from window functions. If you were to ask me which chapter in this book would help you to really shine compared to your peers, this would be it.

Test Your Knowledge

The following exercises are designed to test your understanding of window functions. Please see "Chapter 14" in Appendix B for solutions.

All of the exercises add window functions to the following query:

```
PUBLIC>select date_part(year, o_orderdate) as order_year,
        count(*) as num_orders, sum(o_totalprice) as tot_sales
    from orders
    group by date_part(year, o_orderdate);
+------------+------------+----------------+
| ORDER_YEAR | NUM_ORDERS |     TOT_SALES  |
|------------+------------+----------------|
|       1997 |      17408 | 3255086721.08 |
|       1998 |      10190 | 1925196448.52 |
|       1995 |      17637 | 3317521810.43 |
|       1994 |      17479 | 3278473892.67 |
|       1992 |      17506 | 3309734764.39 |
|       1993 |      17392 | 3270416270.14 |
|       1996 |      17657 | 3296373352.79 |
+------------+------------+----------------+
```

Exercise 14-1

Add two columns to generate rankings for num_orders and tot_sales. The highest value should receive a ranking of 1.

Exercise 14-2

Add a qualify clause to the query in Exercise 14-1 to return only rows where either ranking is 2 or 6.

Exercise 14-3

Starting again with the original query, add a column to compute the total sales across all years (grand total). The value will be the same for each row.

Exercise 14-4

Modify the window function from Exercise 14-3 to generate a running sum instead of a grand total. Each row's value should be the sum of itself and all prior years.

Snowflake Scripting Language

As mentioned in the Preface, SQL is a *nonprocedural language*, meaning that you define the desired results but not the steps needed to generate the results. This means that it's up to Snowflake to determine the best (and hopefully fastest) method to retrieve the data, using the information it has gathered about your tables. Now it's time to switch gears and discuss Snowflake's *procedural* language, known as Snowflake Scripting language. This chapter will demonstrate the different language components, and the following two chapters will show how to use the Snowflake Scripting to build stored procedures and table functions.

A Little Background

If you've worked with databases other than Snowflake, you may already be familiar with using an embedded (executed from inside the database) procedural language. Some examples are Oracle's PL/SQL or Microsoft's Transact-SQL. If you aren't familiar with these types of languages, just think of them as a language that includes the ability to execute `select`, `delete`, `update`, `insert`, and `merge` statements, along with constructs for variable definition, conditional logic (e.g., if-then-else), looping (e.g., `for` and `while`), and exception handling. You can build and execute scripts using Snowflake Scripting, and you can also compile and store your programs in the database (known as *stored procedures*).

There are multiple ways to interface with Snowflake. For example, if you write programs in Java, you can use Snowflake's JDBC driver to issue SQL commands from programs running outside of the database (from an application server, for example). Also, Snowflake provides the Snowpark API's for Java, Scala, and Python, which allow programmers to write programs using their choice of language and run them from inside Snowflake. If you are already familiar with JavaScript, you can use that language to build user-defined functions and procedures in Snowflake. If you are looking for a simple language to write database scripts and stored procedures, however, Snowflake Scripting, which was released in the Spring of 2022, will do the job nicely.

Coding Environment for Snowflake Scripting

Most of the examples in earlier chapters of this book (the SQL chapters) were executed using SnowSQL, which is Snowflake's command-line interface. SnowSQL was used because it is a simple interface without any distracting clutter, and because the example queries can be copied directly from the book (for those readers using an online version).

For the Snowflake Scripting examples, I will be using Snowsight, which is Snowflake's browser-based graphical interface. I have made this switch in order to help readers become comfortable with Snowsight, and because it's more likely that you'll be building your own procedures rather than copying/pasting from this text. To access Snowsight, use the URL sent to you when you created your Snowflake account, which should include your account name, cloud location, and cloud provider (`https://<account>.<location>.<provider>.snowflakecomputing.com`).

Scripting Blocks

The basic construct for writing scripts using Snowflake Scripting is known as a *block* and has the sections shown in Table 15-1:

Table 15-1. Scripting block sections

Section	Functionality
Declare	Optional start of block, used for declaring variables
Begin	Contains SQL and Scripting commands
Exception	Optional error-handling logic
End	End of block

Only the `begin` and `end` sections are mandatory; the `declare` section is only required if you need to declare variables used in the script, and the `exception` section is only needed if you want to explicitly handle any errors thrown during the execution of the script. A block with no name is called an *anonymous block*, whereas a named block is called a *stored procedure* (covered in the next chapter).

Figure 15-1 shows a very simple script using only `begin` and `end`.

Figure 15-1. Simple anonymous block

This script issues a simple query and then ends. Nothing is returned, no work is done, and no errors are thrown. Snowflake labels the script as an anonymous block and shows null as the return value. To execute the script, I clicked the Run button in the top right corner; Figure 15-2 shows the blue rectangle with a white arrow used to execute SQL statements and scripts.

Figure 15-2. Snowsight Run button

To make things a bit more interesting, Figure 15-3 shows a script with a `declare` section used to create a variable to hold the value returned by the `select` statement, along with a `return` statement to display the contents of the variable.

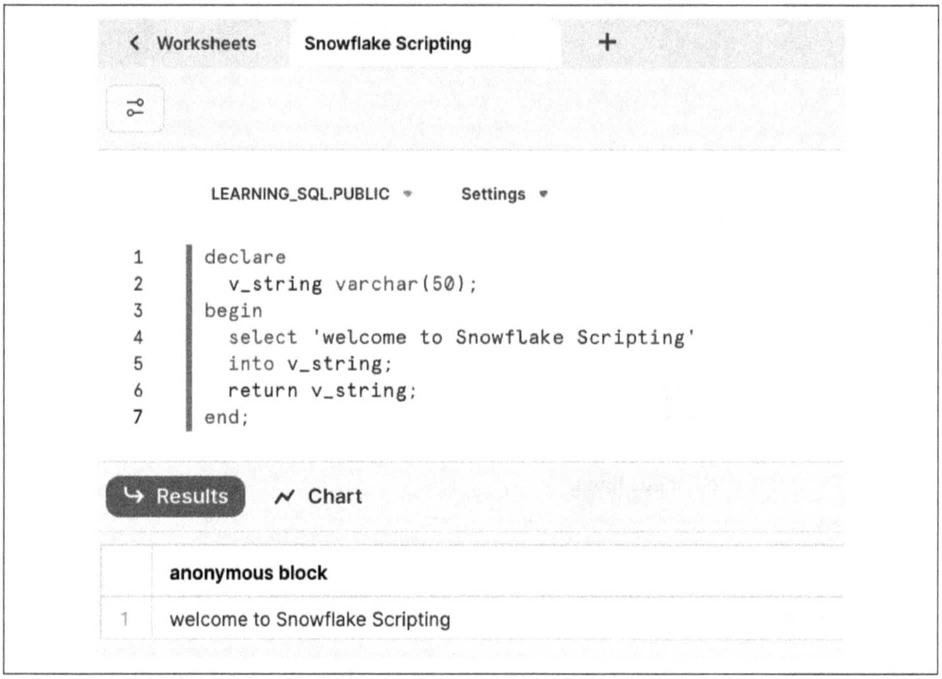

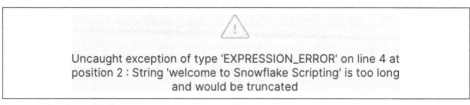

```
declare
  v_string varchar(50);
begin
  select 'welcome to Snowflake Scripting'
  into v_string;
  return v_string;
end;
```

Figure 15-3. Anonymous block with return value

Unlike the previous script, this one does something; it stores the result of the query in the `v_string` variable, and then returns the value contained by `v_string`. You can see the result on line 1 in the result window (with header "anonymous block").

The `v_string` variable is defined as `varchar(50)`, which is more than sufficient to hold the 30-character string `welcome to Snowflake Scripting`. If I define the variable as `varchar(10)`, however, the exception shown in Figure 15-4 will be raised.

Uncaught exception of type 'EXPRESSION_ERROR' on line 4 at position 2 : String 'welcome to Snowflake Scripting' is too long and would be truncated

Figure 15-4. Uncaught exception

This exception belongs to the *expression_error* category (more on this later); Figure 15-5 adds an `exception` section to the script in order to catch this exception.

```
                      Snowflake Scripting ▾

       ≗

                      LEARNING_SQL.PUBLIC ▾

            1      declare
            2        v_string varchar(10);
            3      begin
            4        select 'welcome to Snowflake Scripting'
            5        into v_string;
            6        return v_string;
            7      exception
            8        when expression_error then
            9          return 'Sorry, my bad';
           10      end;


         🗄 Objects      ☰ Editor      ↳ Results      〃 Chart

            anonymous block

          1   Sorry, my bad
```

Figure 15-5. Caught exception

This script *catches* the exception via when expression_error, and *handles* it by
returning the string 'Sorry, my bad'. Now we have a complete, although still very
simple, script that uses all four block sections. The only other thing to know about
scripting blocks is that they can be nested, so you can have blocks that contain other
blocks. This is especially helpful for lengthy scripts, since you can define variables and
catch exceptions locally, rather than having all your variable declarations at the very
top of the block and all the exception handling at the very bottom.

Scripting Statements

The following sections explore the different statements that can be used within your
scripts.

Value Assignment

If you have defined a variable in the declare section and wish to assign it a value, you
can use the variable := value format:

```
declare
  v_area number;
begin
```

```
    v_area := 5;
end;
```

You also have the option of defining variables on the fly and assigning values to them using the let statement:

```
declare
  v_area number;
begin
  let v_length number := 6;
  let v_width number := 3;
  v_area := v_length * v_width;
end;
```

In this example, the let statements are used to provide a variable name, type, and value to 2 different variables. You can also use let to define a *cursor*, which is essentially a pointer to a result set. After defining a cursor variable and assigning it to a query, you will open the cursor, fetch the results, and then close the cursor. Figure 15-6 shows a different version of the 'welcome to Snowflake Scripting' example again, but this time using a cursor.

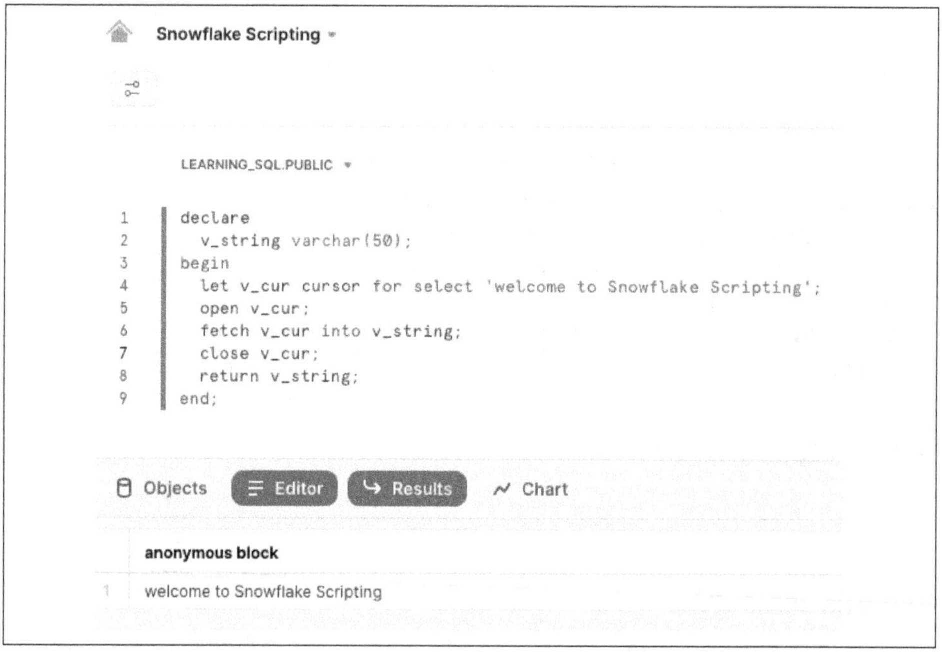

Figure 15-6. Creating a cursor using let

In this example, I only need to fetch a single row because I know that the query returns a single string. To retrieve more than one row, you need to use loops, which are covered later in this chapter. I'll cover cursors in more detail too, but hopefully you get the idea. Snowflake is always using cursors when you execute a query, but you can choose whether the cursor is created *implicitly* (see Figure 15-3) or *explicitly*, as in this example.

You can also use `let` to define a `resultset` variable, which is a variable that holds the result set from a query. Figure 15-7 shows an example using a two-row result set.

Figure 15-7. Creating a result set using `let`

This example executes a query and captures the result set into the `v_rslt` variable, then uses the `table()` function to return the rows of the result set. Stored procedures that return result sets are called *table functions* and will be covered in Chapter 17, but this should give you a small taste of what is possible.

if

The `if` statement facilitates *conditional logic* and can be found in just about any programming language ever invented. The simplest form looks as follows:

```
if (<condition>) then
  <statement(s)>;
end if;
```

If the condition resolves to `true`, then the statement (or statements) is executed. You can also place your statements within a block if desired:

```
let v_bool boolean := true;
if (v_bool) then
```

```
  declare
    v_int number;
  begin
    v_int := 20;
    return v_int;
  end;
end if;
```

You can also add an `else` clause to an `if` statement, which allows you to specify what should be done if the condition does *not* hold true:

```
if (<condition>) then
  <statement(s)>;
else
  <statement(s)>;
end if;
```

Figure 15-8 demonstrates a simple script that returns one of two strings depending on the evaluation of a condition.

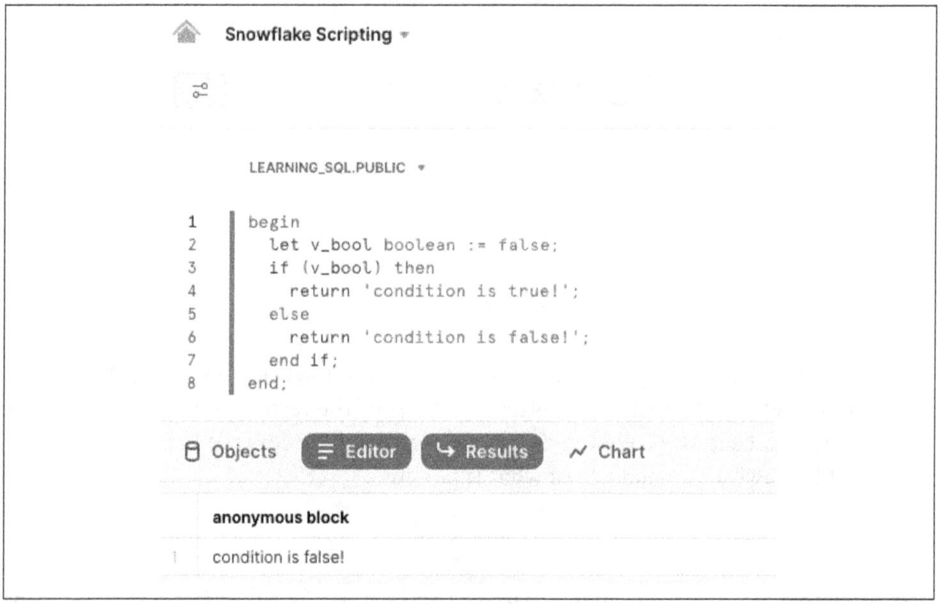

Figure 15-8. Simple if-then-else

There is also an `elseif` clause that can be used if you have multiple conditions to be evaluated, but I suggest that you instead use the `case` statement, which is explored in the next section.

case

The **case** statement is also used for conditional logic, but it is most useful when there are multiple conditions to be evaluated. The structure looks as follows:

```
case
  when <condition1> then
    <statement(s)1>;
  when <condition2> then
    <statement(s)2>;
  ...
  when <conditionN> then
    <statement(s)N>;
  else
    <statement(s)>;
end case;
```

Figure 15-9 shows a simple script to demonstrate how **case** works.

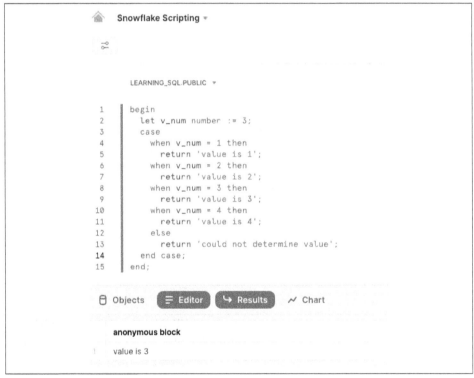

```
1   begin
2     let v_num number := 3;
3     case
4       when v_num = 1 then
5         return 'value is 1';
6       when v_num = 2 then
7         return 'value is 2';
8       when v_num = 3 then
9         return 'value is 3';
10      when v_num = 4 then
11        return 'value is 4';
12      else
13        return 'could not determine value';
14    end case;
15  end;
```

anonymous block

value is 3

Figure 15-9. Case statement

Case statements are evaluated from top to bottom; once a **when** clause evaluates as **true**, the corresponding statements are executed and the **case** statement execution completes. There are actually two flavors of **case**; the one shown in Figure 15-9 is called a *searched case* statement, and there is another flavor called a *simple case* statement. Figure 15-10 demonstrates a modified version of the previous example but reformatted as a simple case statement.

```
     LEARNING_SQL.PUBLIC ▼        Settings ▼

1    declare
2      v_num number := 3;
3    begin
4      case v_num
5        when 1 then
6          return 'value is 1';
7        when 2 then
8          return 'value is 2';
9        when 3 then
10         return 'value is 3';
11       when 4 then
12         return 'value is 4';
13       else
14         return 'could not determine value';
15     end case;
16   end;
```

	anonymous block
1	value is 3

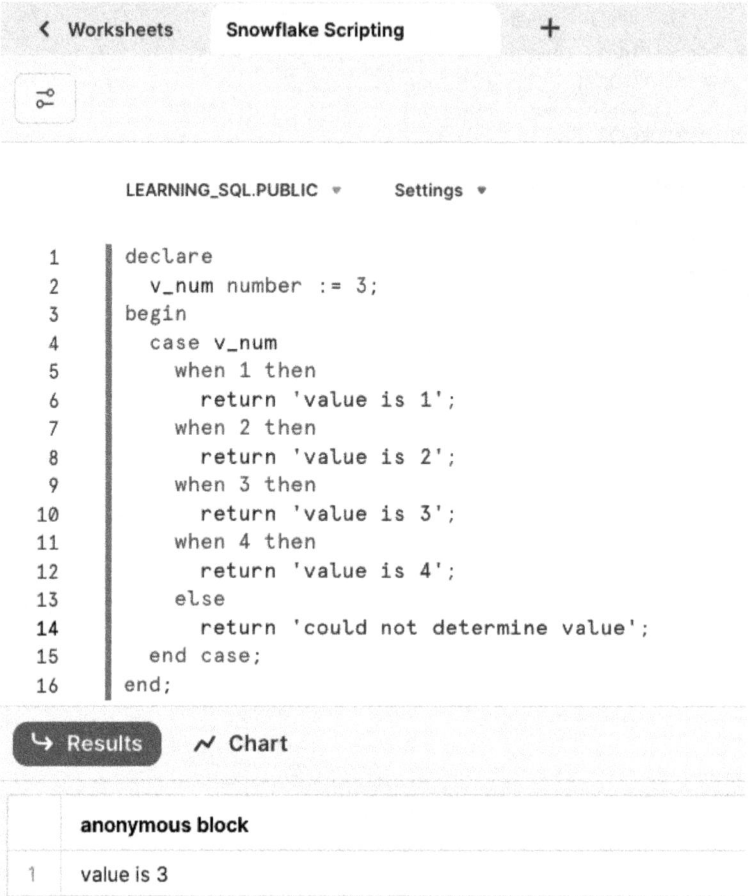

Figure 15-10. Simple case statement

Did you spot the difference? The when clauses in a simple `case` statement don't contain conditions; they have expressions to be compared to the expression at the top of the statement. Here's the structure:

```
case <expression>
  when <expression1> then
    <statement(s)1>;
  when <expression2> then
    <statement(s)2>;
  ...
  when <expressionN> then
```

```
      <statement(s)N>;
    else
      <statement(s)>;
  end case;
```

Again, the when clauses are evaluated from top to bottom, and once a match is found the case statement ends.

Case Expressions Versus Statements

In Chapter 10, you learned about case *expressions*, which are used within SQL statements for evaluating conditional logic. Snowflake Scripting includes the case *statement*, which works in much the same way as a case expression, but is a standalone statement similar to if-then-else. You can use case expressions in your scripts, as shown in Figure 15-11.

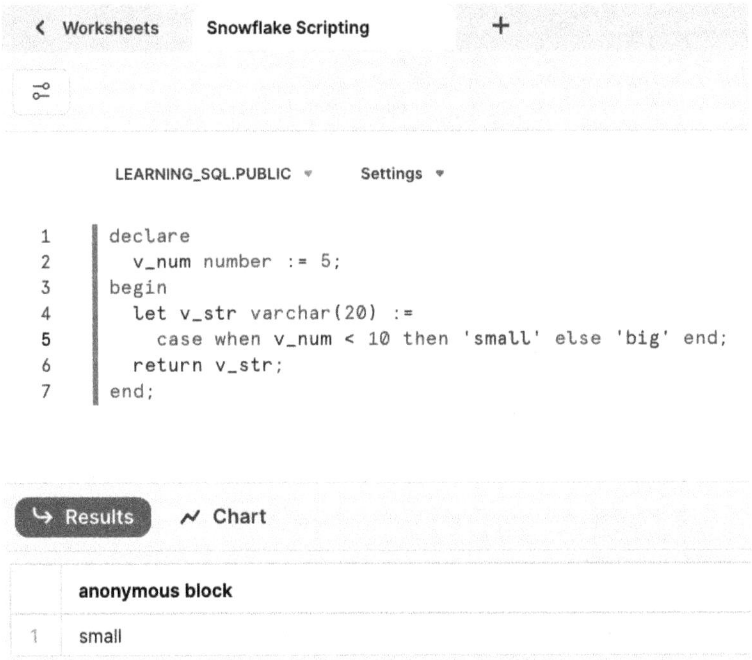

```
1  declare
2    v_num number := 5;
3  begin
4    let v_str varchar(20) :=
5      case when v_num < 10 then 'small' else 'big' end;
6    return v_str;
7  end;
```

	anonymous block
1	small

Figure 15-11. Script using case expression

This script assigns one of two values to a variable and returns the variable value. Figure 15-12 shows the same logic using a case statement instead of an expression.

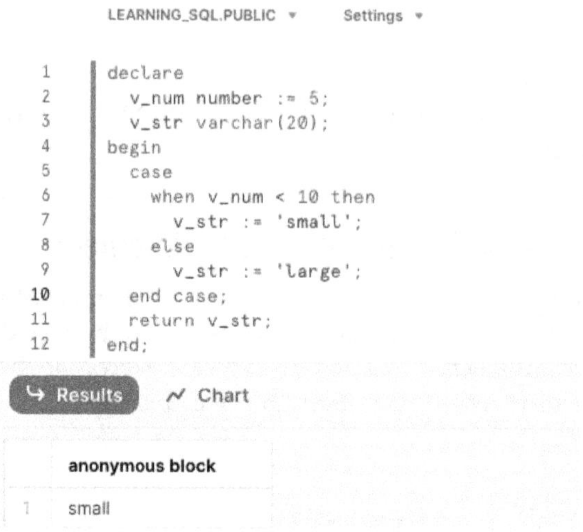

```
1    declare
2      v_num number := 5;
3      v_str varchar(20);
4    begin
5      case
6        when v_num < 10 then
7          v_str := 'small';
8        else
9          v_str := 'large';
10     end case;
11     return v_str;
12   end;
```

↳ **Results**   ∿ **Chart**

anonymous block
1   small

Figure 15-12. Script using case statement

Cursors

A cursor is an object that allows you to execute a query and then step through the result set. All relational database servers use cursors, and a cursor is opened by the server for every SQL statement. You can choose to let Snowflake open and manage the cursor for you, which is known as an *implicit cursor*, or you can take control of the cursor yourself, which is an *explicit cursor*. The life cycle of a cursor is shown in Table 15-2.

Table 15-2. Cursor life cycle

Cursor step	Definition
Declare	Create a cursor variable and assign it a select statement.
Open	Execute the query and move to first row of result set.
Fetch	Retrieve the current row from result set and move to next row.
Close	Stop query execution and close the cursor.

These four steps always occur, but depending on the situation you may only explicitly perform zero, one, or all four steps. Let's start with the first case demonstrated in Figure 15-13, where a cursor is created and used implicitly for you by the server.

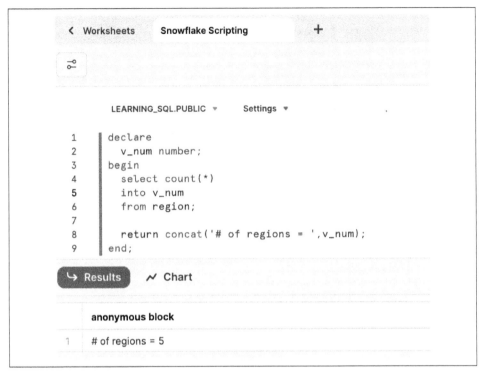

Figure 15-13. Implicit cursor

When this script is executed, the server defines a cursor for the select statement, opens the cursor (executes the query), fetches the results from the single row returned by the query, assigns the value 5 to the v_num variable, and then closes the cursor. This is all done for you behind the scenes. The next example shown in Figure 15-14 executes the same query but using an *explicit* cursor.

As you can see, it takes a lot more work to explicitly manage the cursor, which probably leaves you wondering why you would do so. The short answer is that you should generally leave it up to the server unless you need more control of the process. One such situation would be iterating over the rows in a result set, which will require multiple fetch statements. This will be demonstrated later in this chapter using the for loop.

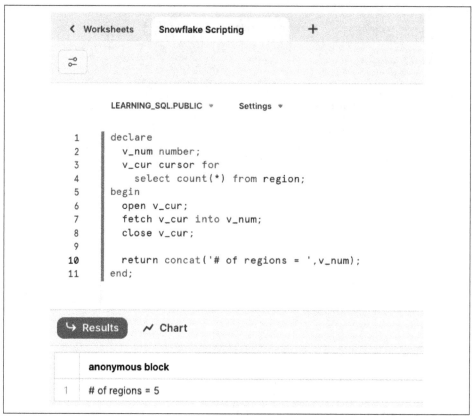

```
     Worksheets     Snowflake Scripting          +


    LEARNING_SQL.PUBLIC  ▾        Settings ▾
 1   declare
 2     v_num number;
 3     v_cur cursor for
 4       select count(*) from region;
 5   begin
 6     open v_cur;
 7     fetch v_cur into v_num;
 8     close v_cur;
 9
10     return concat('# of regions = ',v_num);
11   end;
```

↳ Results   ∿ Chart

anonymous block
1   # of regions = 5

Figure 15-14. Explicit cursor

Loops

Loops are used for *iterative processing*, which allows the same set of statements to be executed multiple times. While iterative processing is a powerful tool, it is important to understand either how many iterations should occur or what condition needs to be met in order to stop the execution of the loop. Otherwise, you could end up launching an *infinite loop*, which would continue iterating until your script is killed. There are four basic types of loops in Snowflake Scripting, all of which include mechanisms for loop termination.

loop

The simplest of the looping statements is simply called loop. The loop statement runs one or more statements iteratively until a break command is executed. Here's the structure:

```
loop
  <statement(s)>;
end loop;
```

It is up to you to ensure that at least one of the statements executed inside the loop contains the break command. Figure 15-15 shows a simple example.

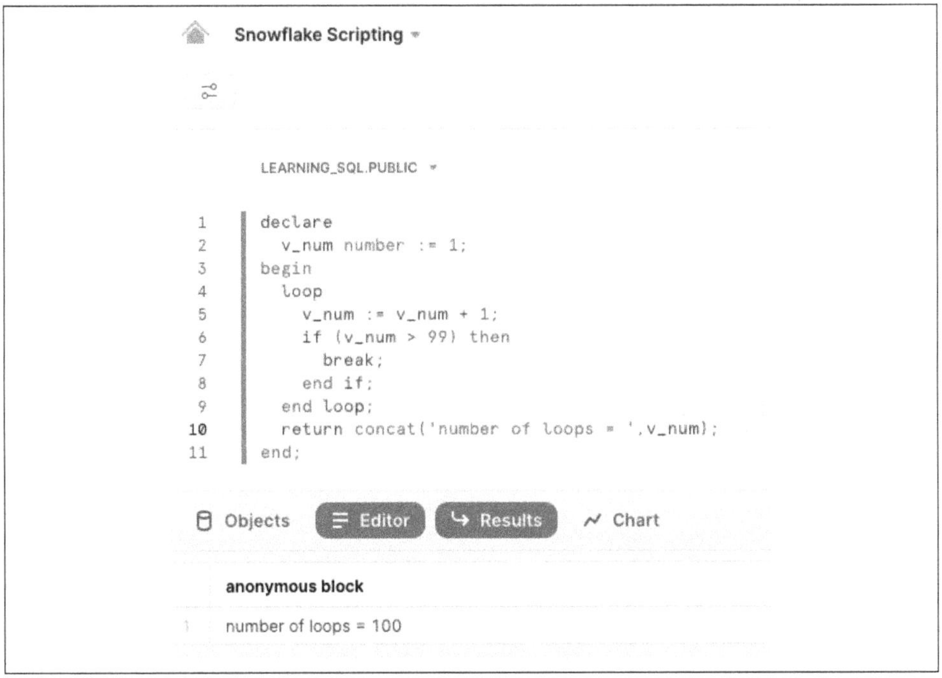

```
        Snowflake Scripting ▾

    ⸦⸧

        LEARNING_SQL.PUBLIC  ▾

    1   declare
    2     v_num number := 1;
    3   begin
    4     loop
    5       v_num := v_num + 1;
    6       if (v_num > 99) then
    7         break;
    8       end if;
    9     end loop;
    10    return concat('number of loops = ',v_num);
    11  end;


    🗄 Objects   ☰ Editor   ↳ Results   ∿ Chart


    anonymous block

    number of loops = 100
```

Figure 15-15. loop statement with break

In this example, the v_num variable is incremented by 1 until the value reaches 100, at which point the break command is issued and the loop is exited. Personally, I prefer to use a loop statement that includes the exit condition as part of the statement definition, which is why I suggest you use repeat, while, or for instead.

repeat

The next looping statement, which is the repeat statement, includes an until clause which specifies the condition by which the loop will terminate. Figure 15-16 demonstrates the previous example again, but this time using repeat.

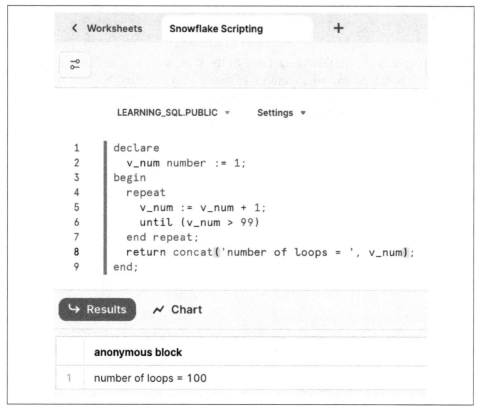

Figure 15-16. repeat statement

This version is less wordy than the loop example, and it doesn't require a break command to be issued in order for the loop to terminate. Keep in mind, however, that you can optionally use the break command to stop loop iteration at any time.

while

Like the repeat command, while includes the loop termination condition, but it is situated at the beginning of the statement, as shown in Figure 15-17.

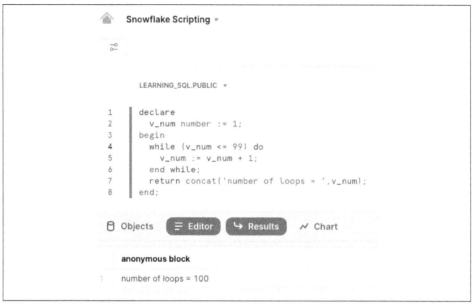

Figure 15-17. while statement

Personally, I like using `while` over `repeat` because you can see the termination condition at the top of the statement. However, I have saved my favorite and most flexible looping statement for last (see next section).

for

The `for` loop comes in two flavors: counter based and cursor based. Counter based `for` loops allow you to specify a counter variable used for iteration, without the need to declare the variable first. Figure 15-18 shows a simple example.

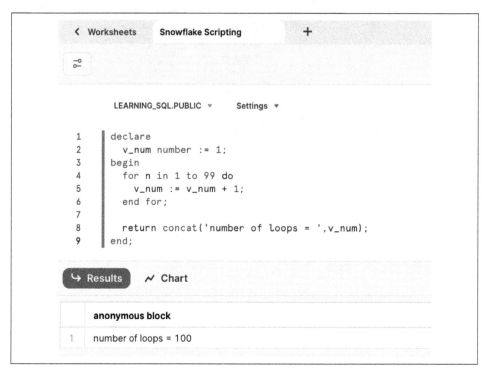

```
1    declare
2      v_num number := 1;
3    begin
4      for n in 1 to 99 do
5        v_num := v_num + 1;
6      end for;
7
8      return concat('number of loops = ',v_num);
9    end;
```

	anonymous block
1	number of loops = 100

Figure 15-18. for counter-based statement

In this example, I chose the variable n to be used as the counter variable, and then specified that the value of n should start at 1 and end at 99. You can also iterate in the opposite direction by adding the reverse keyword, as shown in Figure 15-19.

In Figure 15-19, I am specifying that the counter variable n starts at 10 and completes at 1, as shown by the 'Countdown' output.

Figure 15-19. for counter-based reverse statement

Next, let's look at the cursor-based form of the for statement, which allows you to iterate over the results of a query. Figure 15-20 demonstrates a simple example that loops through all of the rows in the Region table.

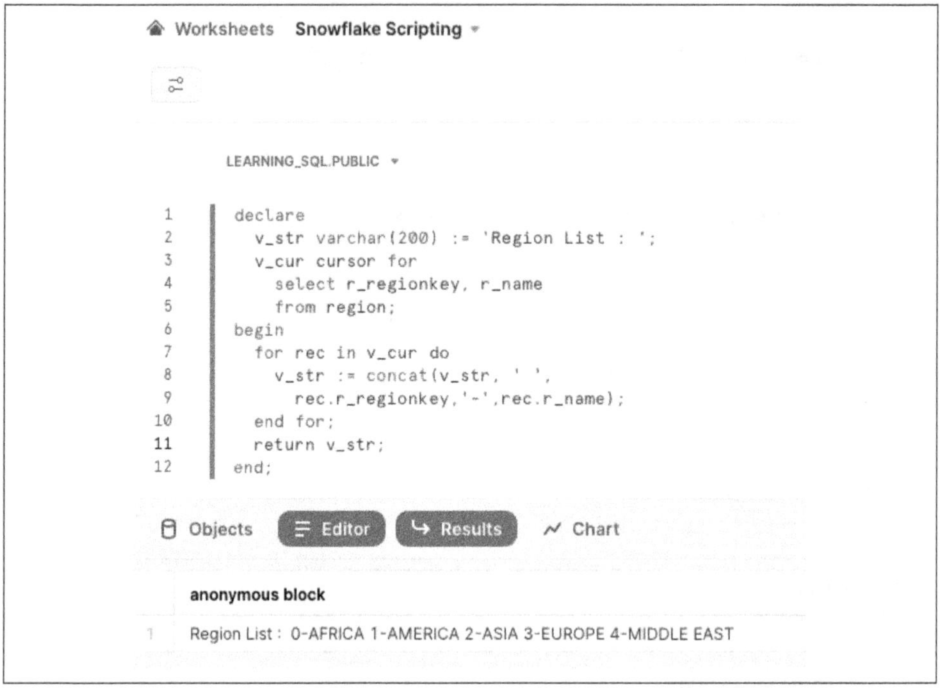

Figure 15-20. for cursor-based statement

In this example, I declare a cursor variable (v_cur) and assign it a query against the Region table that retrieves the r_regionkey and r_name columns. The for loop then executes the query and iterates over the result set, which contains five rows. The columns are made available using a *row variable* which I named rec, so within the for loop I can access the two columns returned by the query using rec.r_regionkey and rec.r_name.

One interesting aspect of cursor-based for loops is that you define the cursor variable, but you don't need to issue open, fetch, or close statements. This is all done implicitly for you as part of the for loop execution. Therefore, this is one case where you will only need to perform one step of the cursor life cycle and Snowflake does the rest for you.

Exceptions

When you write code, the tendency, at least initially, is to expect that everything will work flawlessly. No matter how carefully you code or how much testing you may do, however, there are bound to be issues that arise during script execution. Therefore, you should strive to anticipate and handle errors, and this is the purpose of the exception section in a scripting block. The following sections will discuss how to catch and handle exceptions, as well as how to raise your own exceptions.

Catching exceptions

If you don't include an exception block to catch exceptions, any errors encountered during the execution of your script will be passed on to the caller. This can be problematic for the caller since the error message returned by Snowflake may not be specific enough to pinpoint the problem. Also, if there is an open transaction, it may not be apparent to the caller whether to issue a rollback or a commit. At the very least, you should use the catchall exception when other, which will give you the ability to capture any exception thrown by Snowflake.

Before we start catching exceptions, however, let's look at the components of an exception, shown in Table 15-3.

Table 15-3. Exception components

Component	Description
SQLCODE	A signed integer unique for each exception
SQLERRM	An error message
SQLSTATE	A five-character string indicating an exception type

While the third component, sqlstate, may not be especially useful, the error number (sqlcode) and message (sqlerrm) are critical pieces of information for troubleshooting. It would be great to send all three components to the caller, and Snowflake includes a very useful function called object_construct() that is perfect for generating a document containing related information. Figure 15-21 shows how you could use object_construct() to return all three exception components to the caller as a document.

This script has a single statement, which is an attempt to divide a number by zero, which causes an exception to be thrown. There is a single exception handler, when other, that catches this (or any) exception. A document is then constructed with the three exception components, and then the document is returned to the caller.

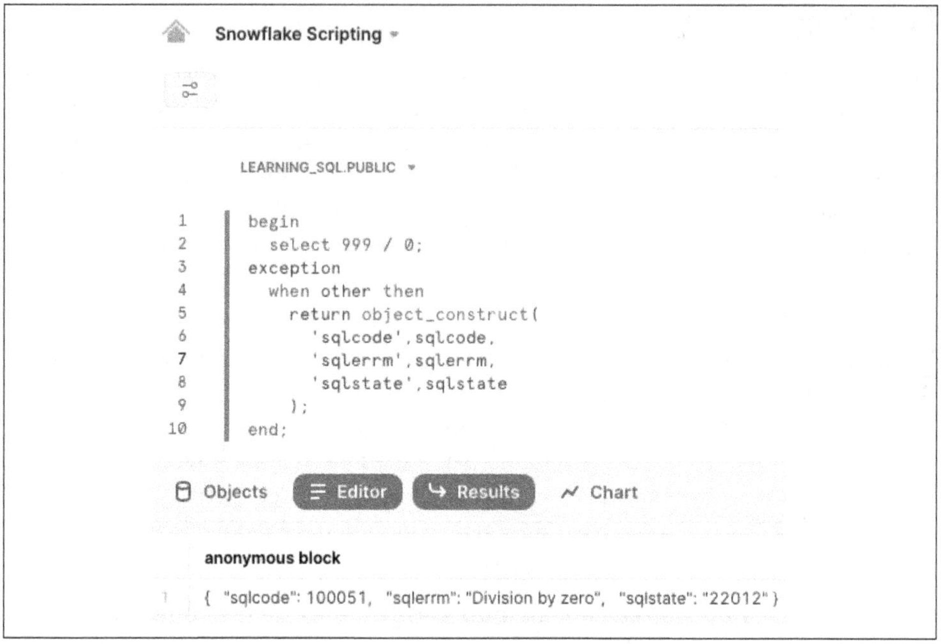

Figure 15-21. Exception catching other and returning document

Along with the when other exception handler, Snowflake supplies two more specific handlers: statement_error and expression_error. The first one, statement_error, will catch any errors related to the execution of an SQL statement, while the second, expression_error, will catch any errors related to the evaluation of an expression. Figure 15-22 expands on the previous example with the addition of these two exception handlers.

Since there are now three exception handlers, I added the type tag to the document, which in this case has the value 'statement' because the exception occurred during the execution of a select statement.

Snowflake also lets you declare your own exceptions in the range –20999 to –20000. This range is reserved for your use, and you can use it to throw very specific exceptions. The next section will discuss how to declare and raise your own exceptions.

Figure 15-22. Snowflake's built-in exception handlers

Declaring and raising exceptions

Let's expand on the previous example one more time and imagine that you need to calculate the average daily balance of a bank account using the total balance divided by the number of days in the month. If, for some reason, the number of days has been set to 0, your calculation will fail with the "Division by zero" error as before, but in this case you would like to return the more specific error "Number of days cannot be zero!" Figure 15-23 demonstrates how you can declare that exception and then raise it from inside your script.

```
Snowflake Scripting ▾

LEARNING_SQL.PUBLIC ▾
1    declare
2      e_num_days_invalid exception (-20115,'Number of days cannot be zero!');
3    begin
4      let v_total_bal number := 24332;
5      let v_num_days number := 0;
6      if (v_num_days = 0) then
7        raise e_num_days_invalid;
8      else
9        select v_total_bal / v_num_days;
10     end if;
11   exception
12     when other then
13       return object_construct(
14          'type','other',
15          'sqlcode',sqlcode,
16          'sqlerrm',sqlerrm,
17          'sqlstate',sqlstate
18       );
19   end;
```

Objects   ≡ Editor   ↳ Results   ∿ Chart

anonymous block

{ "sqlcode": -20115, "sqlerrm": "Number of days cannot be zero!", "sqlstate": "P0001", "type": "other" }

Figure 15-23. Declaring and raising your own exception

In the declare section of the script, a variable of type exception is created and assigned the number -20115 and the message 'Number of days cannot be zero!' The script then checks to see if the value of the v_num_days variable equals 0; if so, the e_num_days_invalid exception is raised, and otherwise the calculation proceeds.

The script raises the e_num_days_invalid exception and then catches it in the when other exception handler. If you prefer to let the exception propagate up to the caller, you can build your own exception handler for your exception, and then issue the raise statement, as shown in Figure 15-24.

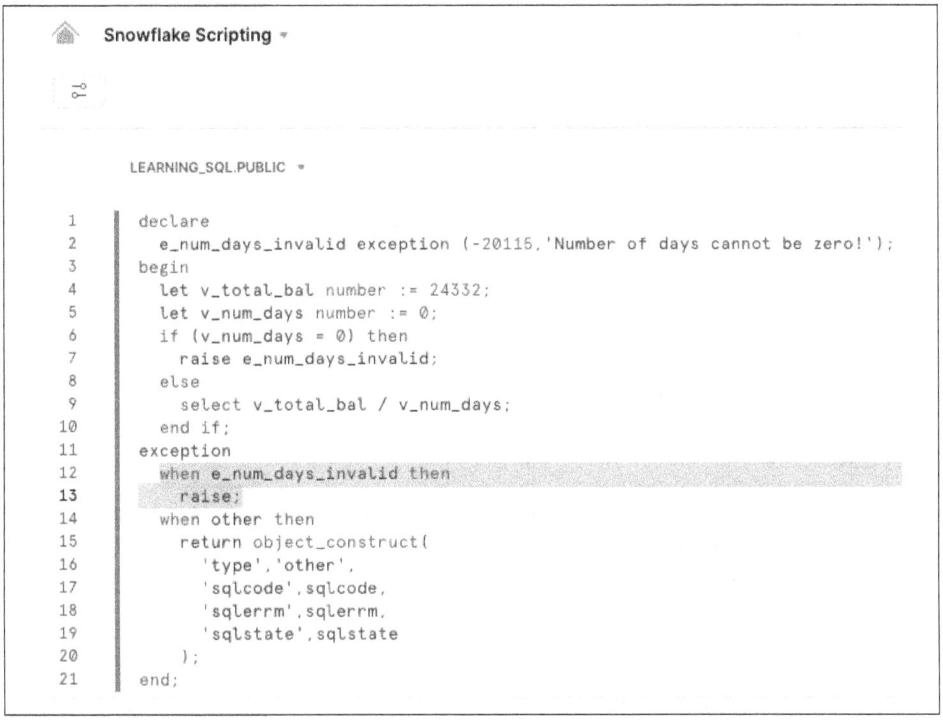

LEARNING_SQL.PUBLIC ▾

```
1    declare
2      e_num_days_invalid exception (-20115,'Number of days cannot be zero!');
3    begin
4      let v_total_bal number := 24332;
5      let v_num_days number := 0;
6      if (v_num_days = 0) then
7        raise e_num_days_invalid;
8      else
9        select v_total_bal / v_num_days;
10     end if;
11   exception
12     when e_num_days_invalid then
13       raise;
14     when other then
15       return object_construct(
16         'type','other',
17         'sqlcode',sqlcode,
18         'sqlerrm',sqlerrm,
19         'sqlstate',sqlstate
20       );
21   end;
```

Figure 15-24. Reraising an exception

With this change, instead of receiving a document with the error details, the exception will flow through to the caller, as shown in Figure 15-25.

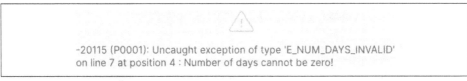

-20115 (P0001): Uncaught exception of type 'E_NUM_DAYS_INVALID'
on line 7 at position 4 : Number of days cannot be zero!

Figure 15-25. Uncaught exception message

As you can see, Snowflake Scripting's exception handling is quite robust, and you should be able to put together a strategy so that upstream applications receive the proper level of diagnostic information to facilitate troubleshooting.

Wrap-Up

In this chapter, you learned about the various components of Snowflake's Scripting language, including the basic block structure along with the commands used for conditional logic, looping, exception handling, and query execution. While you can write and execute anonymous blocks, Chapters 16 and 17 will show you how to create named scripts, which are known as stored procedures.

Test Your Knowledge

The following exercises are designed to test your understanding of Snowflake's Scripting language. Please see "Chapter 15" in Appendix B for solutions.

Exercise 15-1

Write a script that declares a cursor for the query `select max(o_totalprice) from orders`, opens the cursor, fetches the results into a numeric variable, closes the cursor, and returns the value fetched from the query.

Exercise 15-2

Write a script that uses a counter-based `for` loop to iterate over the range 1 to 100. Break out of the loop after the 60th iteration.

Exercise 15-3

Write a script that declares an exception with number -20200 and the string 'The sky is falling!', raises the exception, catches it, and reraises it.

Exercise 15-4

Write a script that uses a cursor-based `for` loop to iterate through all n_name values in the Nation table. Break out of the loop when 'EGYPT' is retrieved.

Building Stored Procedures

Now that you've learned the various components of the Snowflake Scripting language, it's time to learn how to build *stored procedures*, which are compiled programs written using Snowflake Scripting and residing in Snowflake.

Why Use Stored Procedures?

There are a number of reasons you may want to use Snowflake Scripting to build stored procedures, such as:

- Scripts that are used repeatedly can be stored in the database for ease of use and sharing with others.
- Stored procedures allow for one or more *parameter values* to be passed in, enhancing the flexibility of your scripts.
- Stored procedure names can be *overloaded*, meaning that multiple stored procedures may have the same name as long as the parameter types differ.
- Stored procedures facilitate code reuse and hide complex logic from end users.

These are just a few of the advantages of stored procedures, and I'm sure you'll discover more as you progress.

Turning a Script into a Stored Procedure

Let's start with the final script from the previous chapter and walk through the steps needed to turn it into a stored procedure. Figure 16-1 shows the script.

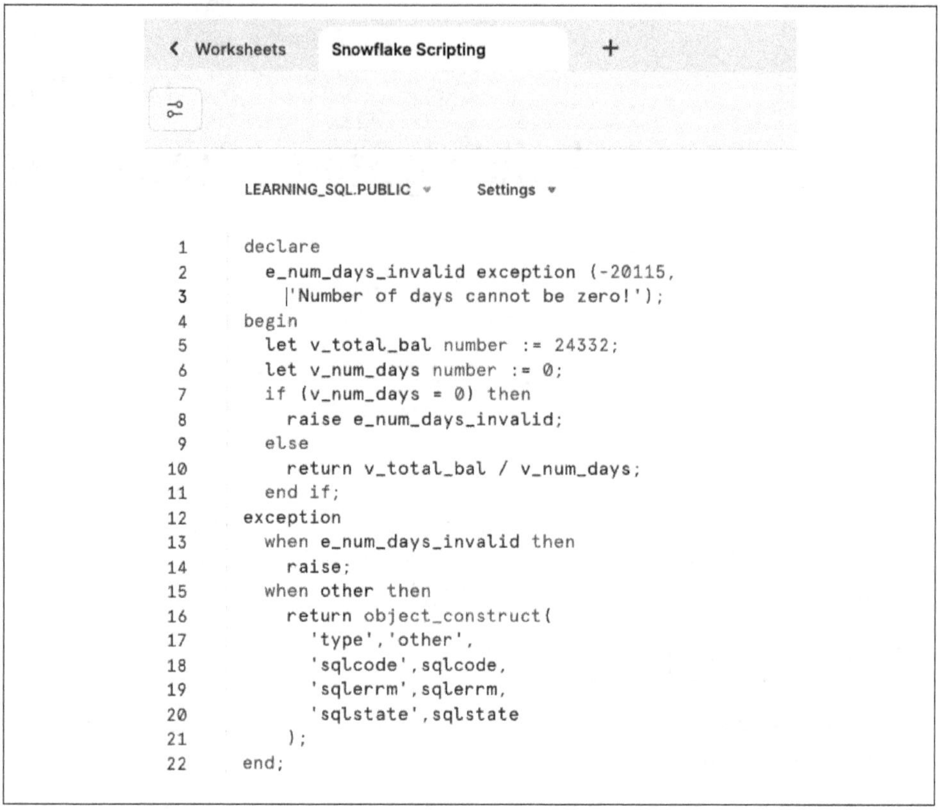

LEARNING_SQL.PUBLIC ▾   Settings ▾

```
1    declare
2      e_num_days_invalid exception (-20115,
3        |'Number of days cannot be zero!');
4    begin
5      let v_total_bal number := 24332;
6      let v_num_days number := 0;
7      if (v_num_days = 0) then
8        raise e_num_days_invalid;
9      else
10        return v_total_bal / v_num_days;
11      end if;
12    exception
13      when e_num_days_invalid then
14        raise;
15      when other then
16        return object_construct(
17          'type','other',
18          'sqlcode',sqlcode,
19          'sqlerrm',sqlerrm,
20          'sqlstate',sqlstate
21        );
22    end;
```

Figure 16-1. Script to return average balance

This script divides the number of days in a month into the total balance and returns the average daily balance. Turning it into a stored procedure requires the following changes:

- Adding the `create procedure` statement and providing a procedure name, which will be `get_avg_balance`
- Providing two parameters (`p_total_bal` and `p_num_days`) for the total balance and number of days
- Defining that the stored procedure returns a number
- Specifying that the stored procedure is built using Snowflake Scripting

Figure 16-2 shows the previous script with the additional components.

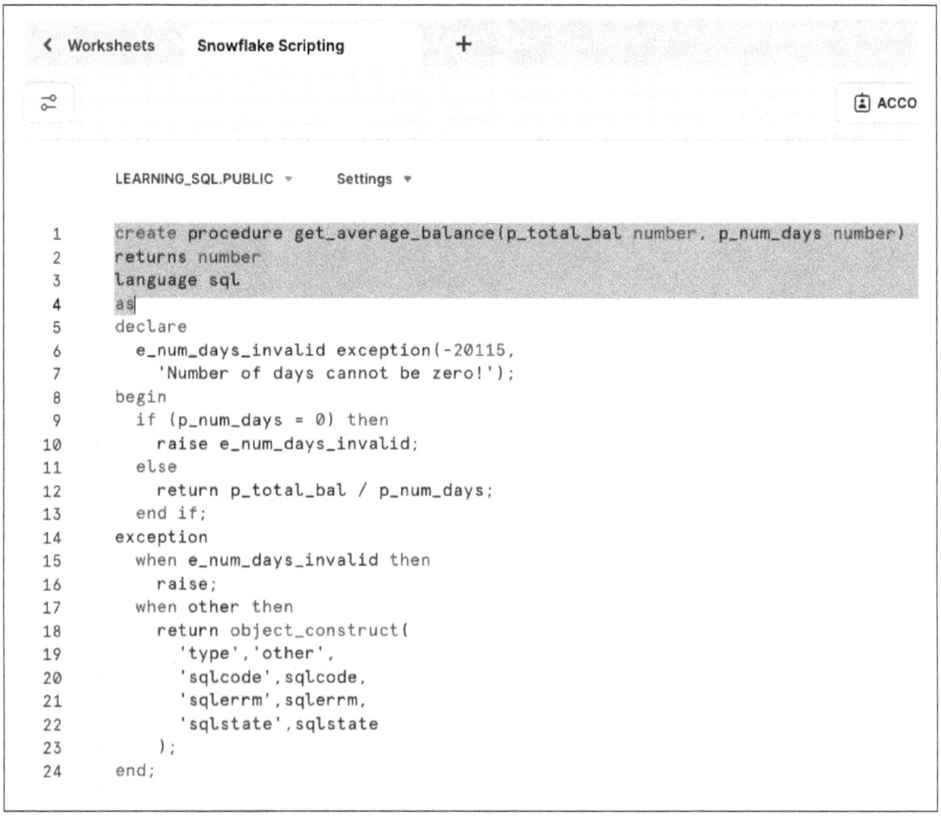

⊶   ⬆ ACCO

LEARNING_SQL.PUBLIC ▾   Settings ▾

```
 1  create procedure get_average_balance(p_total_bal number, p_num_days number)
 2  returns number
 3  language sql
 4  as
 5  declare
 6    e_num_days_invalid exception(-20115,
 7      'Number of days cannot be zero!');
 8  begin
 9    if (p_num_days = 0) then
10      raise e_num_days_invalid;
11    else
12      return p_total_bal / p_num_days;
13    end if;
14  exception
15    when e_num_days_invalid then
16      raise;
17    when other then
18      return object_construct(
19        'type','other',
20        'sqlcode',sqlcode,
21        'sqlerrm',sqlerrm,
22        'sqlstate',sqlstate
23      );
24  end;
```

Figure 16-2. Stored procedure to return average balance

All of the changes needed to change the script into a stored procedure are at the top, and the rest of the script is essentially the same. Snowflake stored procedures are required to return something, but if you don't have anything to return explicitly to the caller you could just return the string 'Success', or return the number of rows modified by the stored procedure. Also, I have specified language sql at the top of the procedure to indicate that the procedure is written using Snowflake Scripting, but this is not required in this case since the default is sql.

I created the script while in the learning_sql.public schema, and you can see it in Snowsight listed under the Procedures section, as shown in Figure 16-3.

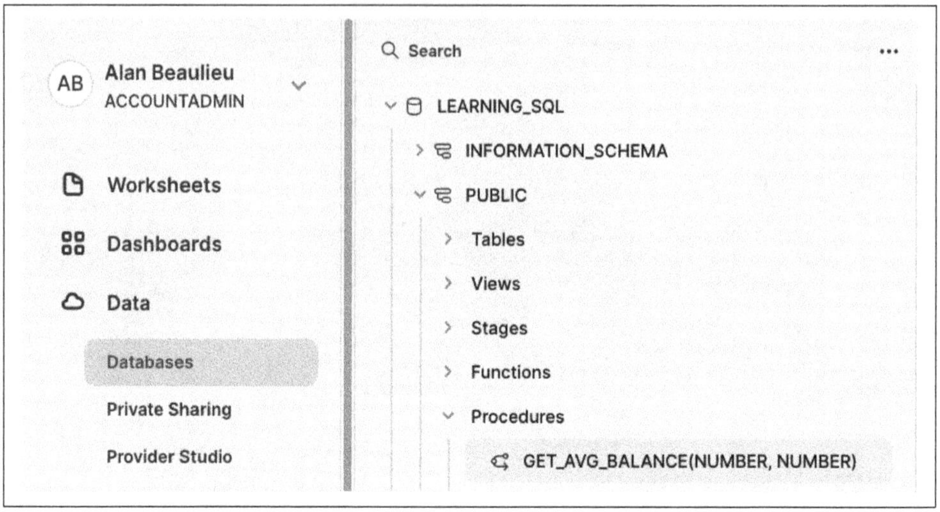

Figure 16-3. Snowsight procedure listing

Stored Procedure Execution

Now that we have created our first procedure, let's discuss the different ways it can be executed. The first and simplest method is to use the `call` command, as shown in Figure 16-4.

Figure 16-4. Stored procedure execution using `call`

In this simple example, the `call` command is used to execute the `get_avg_balance()` stored procedure with parameter values `12000` and `30`, and the result (`400`) is displayed in the *Results* section. Figure 16-5 demonstrates how you can also use the `call` command inside a script and capture the results into a variable.

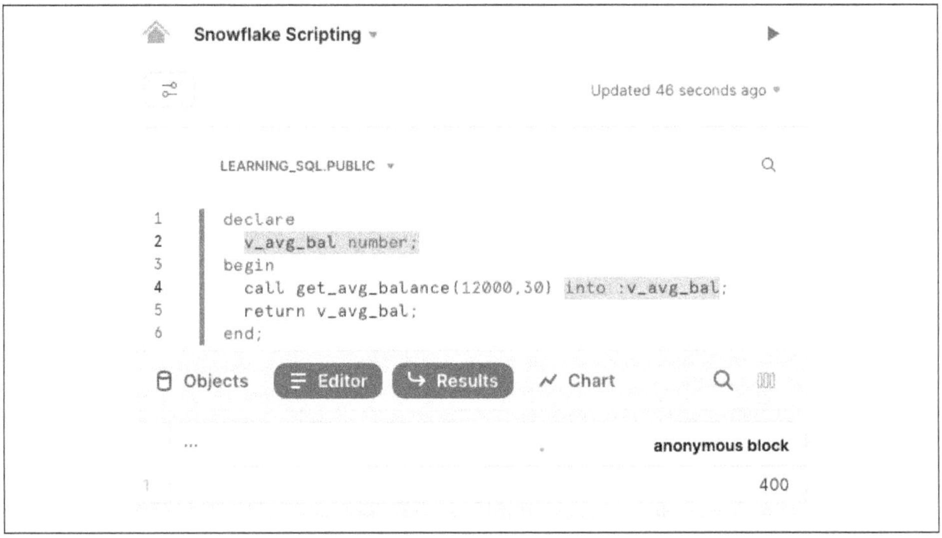

Figure 16-5. Stored procedure execution using `call` and `into`

This version uses the `into` clause of the `call` command to put the results into variable `v_avg_bal`. Lastly, it would be useful to call the stored procedure from an SQL statement, such as the following:

```
declare
  v_avg_bal number;
begin
  select get_avg_balance(12000,30) into v_avg_bal;
  return v_avg_bal;
end;
```

However, executing the script above results in the following error:

```
Unknown function GET_AVG_BALANCE
```

It seems that stored procedures cannot be called from queries, but it is possible to call *user-defined functions*, which are discussed in the next chapter.

Stored Procedures in Action

Now that we have the mechanics out of the way, let's write a stored procedure that does something a little more interesting. First, I will build a data warehouse table to store aggregated sales data across countries, years, and months. Here's the table definition:

```
create table wh_country_monthly_sales
  (sales_year number,
   sales_month number,
   region_name varchar(20),
   country_name varchar(30),
   total_sales number
  );
```

Next, I'll create a stored procedure to populate the new table, and the procedure should do the following things:

- Begin a transaction.
- Delete any existing data for the given region and year.
- Insert rows for the given region and year.
- Commit the transaction, or rollback if error raised.
- Return the number of rows deleted and inserted as a document.

The new stored procedure will be named ins_country_monthly_sales() and will accept two parameters, region_name and year. Here's the stored procedure definition:

```
create procedure ins_country_monthly_sales(
  p_region_name varchar, p_year number)
returns object
language sql
as
begin
  begin transaction;

  delete from wh_country_monthly_sales
  where region_name = :p_region_name
    and sales_year = :p_year;

  let v_num_del number := sqlrowcount;

  insert into wh_country_monthly_sales
    (sales_year, sales_month, region_name,
     country_name, total_sales)
  select date_part(year, o.o_orderdate) as sales_year,
    date_part(month, o_orderdate) as sales_month,
    r.r_name as region_name,
```

```
      n.n_name as country_name,
        sum(o.o_totalprice) as total_sales
    from orders as o
    inner join customer as c
      on o.o_custkey = c.c_custkey
    inner join nation as n
      on c.c_nationkey = n.n_nationkey
    inner join region as r
      on n.n_regionkey = r.r_regionkey
    where r.r_name = :p_region_name
      and date_part(year, o.o_orderdate) = :p_year
    group by date_part(year, o.o_orderdate),
      date_part(month, o_orderdate),
      r.r_name,
      n.n_name;

    let v_num_ins number := sqlrowcount;

    commit;

    return object_construct('rows deleted',v_num_del,
      'rows inserted',v_num_ins);
  exception
    when other then
      rollback;
      raise;
  end;
```

Before executing the procedure, let me describe a couple things highlighted in the procedure logic that may be new to you:

- The procedure returns the type `object`, which is a semistructured data type. The `object_construct()` function returns type `object`, so the stored procedure's return type must be `object` as well.

- Both the `delete` and `insert` statements utilize the two procedure parameters `p_region_name` and `p_year`. When you reference parameters or variables in SQL statements, you must prefix them with `:`. This is known as a *bind variable*, meaning that the variable's value is bound to the statement at execution.

- Snowflake provides the `sqlrowcount` variable, which holds the number of rows modified by the prior SQL statement. I access it twice: once to get the number of rows deleted, and again to get the number of rows inserted.

The next step is to run the procedure, as shown in Figure 16-6.

```
1    │ call ins_country_monthly_sales('EUROPE',1997);
```

🗄 Objects   ≡ Editor   ↳ Results   ⁓ Chart

INS_COUNTRY_MONTHLY_SALES

1   { "rows deleted": 0, "rows inserted": 60 }

Figure 16-6. Execution of `ins_country_monthly_sales` *procedure*

I ran the procedure for the Europe region for the year 1997, and the document returned by the procedure shows that no rows were deleted (which is to be expected, since the table was empty) and 60 rows were inserted. There are 5 countries in the Europe region and 12 months of data, so 60 rows is the expected number.

Next, let's say you put this procedure out for other people on your team to use, but some of them would rather pass in the numeric `regionkey` instead of the region's name. No problem; Snowflake allows stored procedures to be *overloaded*, meaning that two procedures can share the same name as long as the parameter types differ. Here's the definition for the new variation of `ins_country_monthly_sales()`:

```
ins_country_monthly_sales(p_regionkey number, p_year number)
```

While you could simply copy the entire procedure and just change how the parameters are used, you could bypass the need for duplicate code by having the new version simply convert the `regionkey` into a `name`, and then call the original version of the procedure:

```
create procedure ins_country_monthly_sales(
  p_regionkey number, p_year number)
returns object
language sql
as
declare
  v_region_name varchar(20);
  v_document object;
begin
  select r.r_name
  into :v_region_name
  from region as r
  where r.r_regionkey = :p_regionkey;

  call ins_country_monthly_sales(:v_region_name, :p_year)
  into :v_document;
```

```
    return v_document;
end;
```

Since I know that the `regionkey` value for Europe is 3, I can call the new procedure and have it regenerate the results for 1997, as shown in Figure 16-7.

Figure 16-7. Execution of overloaded procedure

This time, the procedure deleted the 60 original rows, and then inserted 60 more.

Stored Procedures and Transactions

There are some rules you should be aware of regarding how stored procedures can take part in transactions. If a transaction has been started prior to calling a stored procedure, the stored procedure can contribute to the transaction but cannot end the transaction via a `commit` or `rollback`. Also, if a transaction is started within a stored procedure, it must be completed (again via `commit` or `rollback`) within the same stored procedure.

Returning Result Sets

While it is certainly helpful to have stored procedures return a scalar value (such as a `varchar` or `number` or `date`) or a more complex type such as `object`, one of the things that brings Snowflake stored procedures to the next level is the ability to return result sets. To do so, the `returns` clause of your stored procedure needs to specify `table(a, b, c)`, where *a/b/c* are the column names returned by the stored procedure.

Snowflake provides the resultset data type to make this process as simple as possible. Here's an example:

```
create procedure get_country_names(p_regionkey number)
returns table(key number, name varchar)
language sql
as
declare
  v_results resultset;
begin
  v_results :=
    (select n_nationkey, n_name
      from nation
      where n_regionkey = :p_regionkey);

  return table(v_results);
end;
```

The get_country_names() procedure returns a result set consisting of a numeric field (key) and a character field (name). The procedure defines a variable of type resultset, associates it with a query, then returns it using the built-in table() function. Figure 16-8 shows the output when I call it for regionkey of 3 (Europe).

Figure 16-8. Stored procedure returning result set

As you can see, the stored procedure returned a result set with column names key and name, which is what was specified in the returns clause of the stored procedure.

Passing Arrays as Parameters

If you recall from Chapter 5, Snowflake provides the array, variant, and object data types along with the usual types such as date, number, and varchar. You are free to use any of these data types in your stored procedures, including as parameters. To illustrate, I have created the get_rgn_country_names() stored procedure that accepts an array of region names as a parameter and returns the region name and the nation's key and name values. Here's the code:

```
create procedure get_rgn_country_name(p_region_names array)
returns table(rgn varchar, key number, name varchar)
language sql
as
declare
  v_results resultset;
begin
  v_results :=
    (select r.r_name, n.n_nationkey, n.n_name
     from nation n
     inner join region r on r.r_regionkey = n.n_regionkey
     where array_contains(r.r_name::variant, :p_region_names));

  return table(v_results);
end;
```

The get_rgn_country_names() procedure will return a list of nations for one or more regions, based on the array that is passed in. Here are the results when called with a two-element array:

```
PUBLIC>call get_rgn_country_name(
        ['EUROPE'::variant, 'ASIA'::variant]);
+--------+-----+----------------+
| RGN    | KEY | NAME           |
|--------+-----+----------------|
| EUROPE |   6 | FRANCE         |
| EUROPE |   7 | GERMANY        |
| ASIA   |   8 | INDIA          |
| ASIA   |   9 | INDONESIA      |
| ASIA   |  12 | JAPAN          |
| ASIA   |  18 | CHINA          |
| EUROPE |  19 | ROMANIA        |
| ASIA   |  21 | VIETNAM        |
| EUROPE |  22 | RUSSIA         |
| EUROPE |  23 | UNITED KINGDOM |
+--------+-----+----------------+
```

While calling stored procedures that return result sets is certainly a useful feature, it would be even better if the result set returned by a stored procedure could be queried, and Snowflake provides two different mechanisms for doing so. The first mechanism, when executed immediately after a stored procedure that returns a result set, allows the result set to be queried. Figure 16-9 demonstrates how this works.

Figure 16-9. Retrieving result set using `result_scan` *function*

This odd-looking query gets the identifier of the latest executed query using `last_query_id()`, calls the `result_scan()` function to retrieve the result set associated with that query identifier, and then sends it through the `table()` function to allow it to be referenced in the `from` clause of a query. Using the `result_scan()` function isn't limited to stored procedures; it can be called after a number of different commands. For example, Figure 16-10 shows the results after running the `show tables` command.

While the `result_scan()` function is a convenient way to retrieve a prior result set, it would be even better if there were a more direct way to query the results of a stored procedure, and I did promise you a second mechanism for doing so. The answer is to use *table functions*, which are the focus of the next chapter.

Figure 16-10. `result_scan` function after show tables command

Dynamic SQL

As mentioned in Chapter 15, Snowflake's Scripting grammar includes statements used for conditional logic, looping, and exception handling, and it also includes the `select`, `update`, `insert`, `delete`, and `merge` statements. However, you may want to execute a `create table` statement, which is *not* part of the Snowflake Scripting language grammar, or you may want to execute a query that needs to be constructed within your script using parameter values passed in by the caller. For these purposes, Snowflake includes the `execute immediate` statement, which lets you execute a string containing a valid SQL statement or scripting block.

To illustrate, let's expand on a stored procedure from earlier in this chapter, `get_country_names()`, which returns the key (`n_nationkey`) and name (`n_name`) values from the `Nation` table. Along with `Nation`, there are four other tables in the sample database that have key/name columns, as shown in Table 16-1.

Table 16-1. Sample database tables with key/name columns

Table name	Key column	Name column
Part	p_partkey	p_name
Supplier	s_suppkey	s_name
Region	r_regionkey	r_name
Customer	c_custkey	c_name

Let's write a stored procedure that will return key/name values from any of these tables by generating a query *dynamically* using the parameter values, and then executing the query using execute immediate. Here's the new procedure's definition:

```
create procedure get_key_name_values(p_table_nm varchar,
                                     key_start number,
                                     key_end number)
returns table(key number, name varchar)
```

The first parameter, p_table_nm, would contain one of the five tables listed previously, and the key_start and key_end parameters would allow the caller to retrieve a subset of rows from the table. For example, executing get_key_name_values ('supplier', 1, 100) would return rows with s_suppkey values between 1 and 100. Here are the steps that need to be taken in the stored procedure:

- Identify the names of the columns that need to be returned using information_schema.columns. The key column is always the first column, and the name column is always the second column.

- Build a string containing the query.

- Execute the query using execute immediate and retrieve result set.

- Return result set to caller.

Here's the stored procedure logic:

```
create procedure get_key_name_values(p_table_nm varchar,
  p_key_start number, p_key_end number)
returns table(key number, name varchar)
language sql
as
declare
  v_results resultset;
  v_query varchar(200);
  v_keycol varchar(20);
  v_namecol varchar(20);
begin
  -- determine names of key/name columns
  select max(case when ordinal_position = 1 then column_name
               else null end) key_col,
    max(case when ordinal_position = 2 then column_name
```

```
            else null end) name_col
    into v_keycol, v_namecol
    from information_schema.columns
    where table_schema = 'PUBLIC'
      and table_name = upper(:p_table_nm)
      and ordinal_position < 3;

    -- build query string
    v_query := concat('select ', v_keycol,', ',v_namecol,
      ' from ', p_table_nm,
      ' where ', v_keycol,' between ',
      case when p_key_start is null then '0' else p_key_start end,
      ' and ',
      case when p_key_end is null then '999999' else p_key_end end);

    v_results := (execute immediate :v_query);

    return table(v_results);
  end;
```

When executed, the stored procedure builds a string that might look like the following:

```
"select p_partkey, p_name from part
where p_partkey between 1 and 50"
```

The string is then executed using execute immediate, and the result set is captured and returned to the caller. Here are some results using each of the five tables:

```
PUBLIC>call get_key_name_values('region',null,null);
+-----+-------------+
| KEY | NAME        |
|-----+-------------|
|   0 | AFRICA      |
|   1 | AMERICA     |
|   2 | ASIA        |
|   3 | EUROPE      |
|   4 | MIDDLE EAST |
+-----+-------------+

PUBLIC>call get_key_name_values('nation',5,10);
+-----+-----------+
| KEY | NAME      |
|-----+-----------|
|   5 | ETHIOPIA  |
|   6 | FRANCE    |
|   7 | GERMANY   |
|   8 | INDIA     |
|   9 | INDONESIA |
|  10 | IRAN      |
+-----+-----------+

PUBLIC>call get_key_name_values('part',100,300);
```

```
+-----+-------------------------------------+
| KEY | NAME                                |
|-----+-------------------------------------|
| 108 | bisque peach magenta tomato yellow  |
| 158 | magenta light misty navy honeydew   |
| 208 | medium pink metallic honeydew ghost |
| 258 | royal frosted blue pale dim         |
+-----+-------------------------------------+

PUBLIC>call get_key_name_values('supplier',700,710);
+-----+--------------------+
| KEY | NAME               |
|-----+--------------------|
| 701 | Supplier#000000701 |
| 704 | Supplier#000000704 |
| 707 | Supplier#000000707 |
| 709 | Supplier#000000709 |
| 710 | Supplier#000000710 |
+-----+--------------------+

PUBLIC>call get_key_name_values('customer',1000,1020);
+------+--------------------+
| KEY  | NAME               |
|------+--------------------|
| 1000 | Customer#000001000 |
| 1007 | Customer#000001007 |
| 1009 | Customer#000001009 |
| 1012 | Customer#000001012 |
| 1015 | Customer#000001015 |
| 1018 | Customer#000001018 |
| 1019 | Customer#000001019 |
+------+--------------------+
```

As you might imagine, having the ability to construct and execute SQL statements dynamically at execution time opens up many possibilities.

Wrap-Up

This chapter introduced you to stored procedures written using Snowflake's Scripting language. You learned how to turn anonymous scripts into stored procedures, how to call stored procedures, and how to return result sets. Chapter 17 will expand on this last feature by introducing table functions.

Test Your Knowledge

The following exercises are designed to test your understanding of stored procedures. Please see "Chapter 16" in Appendix B for solutions.

Exercise 16-1

Turn the following anonymous script into a stored procedure named `rectangle_area()` with numeric parameters `p_width` and `p_length`:

```
declare
  v_width number := 5;
  v_height number := 8;
begin
  return v_width * v_height;
end;
```

Exercise 16-2

Write a stored procedure named `get_parts_by_type()` with a single parameter `p_type_name` (type `varchar`). The stored procedure should return a result set consisting of the `p_partkey` and `p_name` columns from the `Part` table, for rows whose `p_type` column matches the parameter value. Call the procedure with parameter value `'SMALL PLATED NICKEL'` or `'PROMO BRUSHED STEEL'`, both of which should return 23 rows.

Table Functions

This chapter explores the *table function*, which offers a flexible way to provide access to your Snowflake data.

User-Defined Functions

In Chapter 16, you learned how to create stored procedures using Snowflake Scripting, and I pointed out that even though stored procedures can return result sets, they can't be called from SQL statements. Fortunately, Snowflake also allows you to create *user-defined functions* using the create function statement. Also known as UDFs, user-defined functions can be called from SQL statements, but unlike stored procedures they are limited to returning a single expression and cannot take full advantage of the Snowflake Scripting language. UDFs can be written in Python, Java, JavaScript, Scala, and SQL, and this chapter will focus on SQL-based UDFs.

To start, I'll take the simple stored procedure rectangle_area(), which was the focus of one of the exercises in Chapter 16, and turn it into a stored function. Here's the stored procedure:

```
create procedure rectangle_area(p_width number, p_length number)
returns number
language sql
as
begin
  return p_width * p_length;
end;
```

This stored procedure simply returns the product of two numeric parameters. Here's what it looks like as a UDF named fn_rectangle_area():

```
create function fn_rectangle_area(p_width number, p_length number)
returns number
```

```
language sql
as
'p_width * p_length';
```

The function specifies an expression, which in this case is p_width * p_length. There is no looping, conditional logic, or exception handling allowed. However, the function can be called from a query:

```
PUBLIC>select rect.x as width, rect.y as length,
         fn_rectangle_area(rect.x, rect.y) as area
       from (values (2, 6), (4, 7), (8, 12)) as rect(x,y);
+-------+--------+------+
| WIDTH | LENGTH | AREA |
|-------+--------+------|
|     2 |      6 |   12 |
|     4 |      7 |   28 |
|     8 |     12 |   96 |
+-------+--------+------+
```

A UDF such as this one is called a *scalar user-defined function*, in that it returns a single value. Snowflake also allows you to build *tabular user-defined functions* that return result sets, which will be the focus of the remainder of this chapter.

What Is a Table Function?

A table function is a user-defined function that returns a result set and can therefore be included in the from clause of a query and joined to other tables or even other table functions. Table functions must be generated using the create function command and must include a returns table clause specifying the names and types of the columns being returned. Also, the body of the table function must contain a single query and cannot make use of the other features of Snowflake Scripting language, such as scripting blocks and loops.

While this might seem like a serious limitation, table functions can play a critical role in your data access strategy. For example, if there are many people in your organization creating reports and dashboards from Snowflake data, you can build a set of table functions to shield them from complex SQL statements and possibly avoid costly performance issues in the process. Taking it to the extreme, you can force all database users to interact with your databases through a set of stored procedures and table functions, otherwise known as a data-access layer, rather than allowing direct access to tables.

Writing Your Own Table Functions

To get started, let's build a table function using the select statement from the ins_country_monthly_sales() procedure from the previous chapter. Here's what the query looks like:

```
select date_part(year, o.o_orderdate) as sales_year,
  date_part(month, o_orderdate) as sales_month,
  r.r_name as region_name,
  n.n_name as country_name,
  sum(o.o_totalprice) as total_sales
from snowflake_sample_data.tpch_sf1.orders as o
  inner join snowflake_sample_data.tpch_sf1.customer as c
    on o.o_custkey = c.c_custkey
  inner join snowflake_sample_data.tpch_sf1.nation as n
    on c.c_nationkey = n.n_nationkey
  inner join snowflake_sample_data.tpch_sf1.region as r
    on n.n_regionkey = r.r_regionkey
where r.r_name = :p_region_name
  and date_part(year, o.o_orderdate) = :p_year
group by date_part(year, o.o_orderdate),
  date_part(month, o_orderdate),
  r.r_name,
  n.n_name
```

Turning this query into a table function is just a matter of describing the names and types of the columns in the returns clause and wrapping the query in quotes:

```
create function get_country_monthly_sales(
  p_region_name varchar, p_year number)
returns table(
  sales_year number,
  sales_month number,
  region_name varchar,
  country_name varchar,
  total_sales number)
language sql
as
'select date_part(year, o.o_orderdate) as sales_year,
  date_part(month, o_orderdate) as sales_month,
  r.r_name as region_name,
  n.n_name as country_name,
  sum(o.o_totalprice) as total_sales
from snowflake_sample_data.tpch_sf1.orders as o
  inner join snowflake_sample_data.tpch_sf1.customer as c
    on o.o_custkey = c.c_custkey
  inner join snowflake_sample_data.tpch_sf1.nation as n
    on c.c_nationkey = n.n_nationkey
  inner join snowflake_sample_data.tpch_sf1.region as r
    on n.n_regionkey = r.r_regionkey
where r.r_name = p_region_name
  and date_part(year, o.o_orderdate) = p_year
group by date_part(year, o.o_orderdate),
  date_part(month, o_orderdate),
  r.r_name,
  n.n_name';
```

One minor change from the query used in the stored procedure is that you don't specify bind variables (using prefix :) when referencing variables in a table function. Here's a simple query using the `get_country_monthly_sales()` table function:

```
PUBLIC>select sales_month, country_name, total_sales
       from table(get_country_monthly_sales('EUROPE',1997));
+-------------+----------------+-------------+
| SALES_MONTH | COUNTRY_NAME   | TOTAL_SALES |
|-------------+----------------+-------------|
|          11 | GERMANY        |    98033670 |
|           7 | ROMANIA        |   116342292 |
|           6 | UNITED KINGDOM |   108143171 |
|           2 | UNITED KINGDOM |   107067404 |
|           2 | RUSSIA         |   105272625 |
|          10 | FRANCE         |   117884280 |
|           8 | GERMANY        |   106333217 |
|          12 | RUSSIA         |   117657079 |
... 45 rows omitted
|           5 | ROMANIA        |   110093370 |
|           6 | RUSSIA         |   116585712 |
|           6 | ROMANIA        |   119433165 |
|           3 | ROMANIA        |   120104796 |
|          11 | UNITED KINGDOM |   112680947 |
|           1 | ROMANIA        |   123156412 |
|          10 | ROMANIA        |   118360369 |
+-------------+----------------+-------------+
```

You can add `where`, `group by`, `order by`, and any other clauses used in `select` statements, which means that table functions act just like tables. Here's a slightly more complicated query, with the addition of a table alias (`cms`), a `where` clause, and an `order by` clause:

```
PUBLIC>select cms.sales_month, cms.country_name, cms.total_sales
       from table(get_country_monthly_sales('EUROPE',1997)) as cms
       where cms.sales_month = 8
       order by 2;
+-------------+----------------+-------------+
| SALES_MONTH | COUNTRY_NAME   | TOTAL_SALES |
|-------------+----------------+-------------|
|           8 | FRANCE         |   125059627 |
|           8 | GERMANY        |   106333217 |
|           8 | ROMANIA        |   119066485 |
|           8 | RUSSIA         |   118034351 |
|           8 | UNITED KINGDOM |   109899097 |
+-------------+----------------+-------------+
```

You can also join the table function's result set with other tables. The following query includes a join to the `Nation` table in order to include the `nationkey` value:

```
PUBLIC>select cms.sales_month, cms.country_name, cms.total_sales,
         n.n_nationkey
       from table(get_country_monthly_sales('EUROPE',1997)) as cms
```

```
inner join nation n on cms.country_name = n.n_name
where cms.sales_month = 8
order by 2;
```

```
+-------------+----------------+-------------+-------------+
| SALES_MONTH | COUNTRY_NAME   | TOTAL_SALES | N_NATIONKEY |
|-------------+----------------+-------------+-------------|
|           8 | FRANCE         |   125059627 |           6 |
|           8 | GERMANY        |   106333217 |           7 |
|           8 | ROMANIA        |   119066485 |          19 |
|           8 | RUSSIA         |   118034351 |          22 |
|           8 | UNITED KINGDOM |   109899097 |          23 |
+-------------+----------------+-------------+-------------+
```

Table functions can act just like tables, but what makes table functions even more interesting is that they can also act like correlated subqueries, meaning that they can be executed multiple times using inputs from another table. To illustrate, the next query shows how rows from the Region table can be used to pass parameter values to the get_country_monthly_sales() table function:

```
PUBLIC>select cms.sales_month, cms.country_name, cms.total_sales,
         r.r_name as region_name
     from region r
     cross join
       table(get_country_monthly_sales(r.r_name,1997)) as cms
     order by 2;
```

```
+-------------+--------------+-------------+-------------+
| SALES_MONTH | COUNTRY_NAME | TOTAL_SALES | REGION_NAME |
|-------------+--------------+-------------+-------------|
|           4 | ALGERIA      |   114709091 | AFRICA      |
|           3 | ALGERIA      |   111769639 | AFRICA      |
|           1 | ALGERIA      |   112621466 | AFRICA      |
|           8 | ALGERIA      |   122789085 | AFRICA      |
|           7 | ALGERIA      |   105171743 | AFRICA      |
|           9 | ALGERIA      |   110396345 | AFRICA      |
|          12 | ALGERIA      |   118305298 | AFRICA      |
|           5 | ALGERIA      |   129927011 | AFRICA      |
... 284 rows omitted
|           9 | VIETNAM      |   111210164 | ASIA        |
|          12 | VIETNAM      |   122431346 | ASIA        |
|           2 | VIETNAM      |   109812362 | ASIA        |
|           6 | VIETNAM      |   118923739 | ASIA        |
|           5 | VIETNAM      |   114240789 | ASIA        |
|           7 | VIETNAM      |   118306908 | ASIA        |
|           8 | VIETNAM      |   116167259 | ASIA        |
|           1 | VIETNAM      |   111268444 | ASIA        |
+-------------+--------------+-------------+-------------+
```

There are 5 rows in the Region table, so in this example the table function is called 5 times, once for each region name. There are a total of 25 countries across the 5 regions, each with 12 months of data, for a total of 300 rows in the result set. One of the benefits to this approach is that you can build a table function to return data for a specific parameter value, but then join to another table to facilitate iterative calls to the table function.

If that seems impressive, it even gets better; you can pass in values to *both* of the table function's parameters, as shown in the next query:

```
PUBLIC>select yrs.x as year, cms.sales_month as month,
         cms.country_name, cms.total_sales,
         r.r_name as region_name
     from (values (1996), (1997)) as yrs(x)
     cross join region r
     cross join
        table(get_country_monthly_sales(r.r_name, yrs.x)) as cms
     order by 1,2,3;
+------+-------+----------------+-------------+-------------+
| YEAR | MONTH | COUNTRY_NAME   | TOTAL_SALES | REGION_NAME |
|------+-------+----------------+-------------+-------------|
| 1996 |     1 | ALGERIA        |   108656678 | AFRICA      |
| 1996 |     1 | ARGENTINA      |   116520640 | AMERICA     |
| 1996 |     1 | BRAZIL         |   117552027 | AMERICA     |
| 1996 |     1 | CANADA         |   124967892 | AMERICA     |
| 1996 |     1 | CHINA          |   116776832 | ASIA        |
| 1996 |     1 | EGYPT          |   110055251 | MIDDLE EAST |
| 1996 |     1 | ETHIOPIA       |   109986427 | AFRICA      |
| 1996 |     1 | FRANCE         |   112707147 | EUROPE      |
... 584 rows omitted
| 1997 |    12 | MOZAMBIQUE     |   112472614 | AFRICA      |
| 1997 |    12 | PERU           |   114520412 | AMERICA     |
| 1997 |    12 | ROMANIA        |   123820321 | EUROPE      |
| 1997 |    12 | RUSSIA         |   117657079 | EUROPE      |
| 1997 |    12 | SAUDI ARABIA   |   115587404 | MIDDLE EAST |
| 1997 |    12 | UNITED KINGDOM |   107355709 | EUROPE      |
| 1997 |    12 | UNITED STATES  |   124561392 | AMERICA     |
| 1997 |    12 | VIETNAM        |   122431346 | ASIA        |
+------+-------+----------------+-------------+-------------+
```

There are 2 years in the yrs data set, and 5 rows in the Region table, so the table function is being called 10 times and returns a total of 600 rows.

Using Built-In Table Functions

If you're a fan of table functions by now, you'll be happy to know that Snowflake provides dozens of built-in table functions for you to use. While some of them, such as materialized_view_refresh_history(), are used for very specific purposes, others are more general purpose and useful for various programming tasks. This section demonstrates the utility of some of Snowflake's built-in table functions.

Data Generation

There are situations when you will want to fabricate data sets, perhaps to construct a set of test data, or to construct a specific set of data such as a row for every day of a year. The generator() function is perfect for these situations, and it allows you either to create a certain number of rows (using the rowcount parameter) or create rows for a certain number of seconds (using the timelimit parameter). This function is a bit odd because it will generate rows without columns, so it is up to you to specify the columns to be returned.

For example, let's say that you want to generate a row for every day in 2023. The next query shows how you could use generator() to return 365 rows, which you can then use to generate 365 dates from a starting date of 31-Dec-2022:

```
PUBLIC>select dateadd(day, seq4() + 1,
                      '31-DEC-2022'::date) cal_date
    from table(generator(rowcount => 365));
+-------------+
| CAL_DATE    |
|-------------|
| 2023-01-01 |
| 2023-01-02 |
| 2023-01-03 |
| 2023-01-04 |
| 2023-01-05 |
... 355 rows omitted
| 2023-12-27 |
| 2023-12-28 |
| 2023-12-29 |
| 2023-12-30 |
| 2023-12-31 |
+-------------+
```

This example uses the seq4() function to generate a sequence of numbers starting at zero, and the resulting numbers are used to generate a set of dates from 01-Jan-2023 to 31-Dec-2023.

If you need to construct a set of test data, you can use the uniform(), random(), and randstr() functions to create random data values:

```
PUBLIC>select uniform(1, 9999, random()) rnd_num,
       randstr(10, random()) rnd_str
    from table(generator(rowcount => 10));
+---------+------------+
| RND_NUM | RND_STR    |
|---------+------------|
|    8400 | pz88zsz2Ei |
|    2022 | 2vzaRO8qUa |
|    1423 | 0NRc8kQ912 |
|    5532 | ozTxWqmgUY |
```

```
|    2031 | hELDW2dUru |
|    7658 | kPpt4EijzS |
|    1626 | qdEepOXwUW |
|    4019 | E8FWlvCMsD |
|    2783 | a9Cr3jdLAA |
|    8341 | pGzsAHp6wN |
+---------+------------+
```

This example generates 10 random numbers between 1 and 9999, along with random 10-character strings.

Flattening Rows

Snowflake provides several table functions that can be used to flatten a set of values contained in a string or document into a set of rows. Here's how you could use the `split_to_table()` function to flatten a set of pipe-delimited strings:

```
PUBLIC>select index, value
       from table(split_to_table('a1|b2|c3', '|'));
+-------+-------+
| INDEX | VALUE |
|-------+-------|
|     1 | a1    |
|     2 | b2    |
|     3 | c3    |
+-------+-------+
```

While the `split_to_table()` function is handy if you need to parse a string, if you are working with documents you will need something a bit more sophisticated. First, let's generate a simple JSON document containing the contents of the `Employee` table by combining Snowflake's `object_construct()` and `array_agg()` functions:

```
PUBLIC>select object_construct(
         'employees', array_agg(
           object_construct(
             'empid', empid,
             'name', emp_name))) emp_doc
       from employee;
+--------------------------------+
| EMP_DOC                        |
|--------------------------------|
| {                              |
|   "employees": [               |
|     {                          |
|       "empid": 1001,           |
|       "name": "Bob Smith"      |
|     },                         |
|     {                          |
|       "empid": 1002,           |
|       "name": "Susan Jackson"  |
|     },                         |
```

```
|     {                          |
|       "empid": 1003,           |
|       "name": "Greg Carpenter" |
|     },                         |
|     {                          |
|       "empid": 1004,           |
|       "name": "Robert Butler"  |
|     },                         |
|     {                          |
|       "empid": 1005,           |
|       "name": "Kim Josephs"    |
|     },                         |
|     {                          |
|       "empid": 1006,           |
|       "name": "John Tyler"     |
|     },                         |
|     {                          |
|       "empid": 1007,           |
|       "name": "John Sanford"   |
|     }                          |
|   ]                            |
| }                              |
+--------------------------------+
```

This query generates a single document containing each employee's ID and name for all members of the Employee table. If you need to turn this document back into a set of rows and columns, you can use Snowflake's flatten() table function. I can use this document as the input to the flatten() function, which when used with the table() function will return seven rows, one for each employee:

```
PUBLIC>select value
         from table(flatten(input => parse_json(
         '{"employees": [
               {"empid": 1001, "name": "Bob Smith"},
               {"empid": 1002, "name": "Susan Jackson"},
               {"empid": 1003, "name": "Greg Carpenter"},
               {"empid": 1004, "name": "Robert Butler"},
               {"empid": 1005, "name": "Kim Josephs"},
               {"empid": 1006, "name": "John Tyler"},
               {"empid": 1007, "name": "John Sanford"}
             ]}'), path => 'employees'));
+---------------------------+
| VALUE                     |
|---------------------------|
| {                         |
|   "empid": 1001,          |
|   "name": "Bob Smith"     |
| }                         |
| {                         |
|   "empid": 1002,          |
|   "name": "Susan Jackson" |
| }                         |
```

```
| {                              |
|    "empid": 1003,              |
|    "name": "Greg Carpenter"    |
| }                              |
| {                              |
|    "empid": 1004,              |
|    "name": "Robert Butler"     |
| }                              |
| {                              |
|    "empid": 1005,              |
|    "name": "Kim Josephs"       |
| }                              |
| {                              |
|    "empid": 1006,              |
|    "name": "John Tyler"        |
| }                              |
| {                              |
|    "empid": 1007,              |
|    "name": "John Sanford"      |
| }                              |
+----------------------------+
```

The `flatten()` function returns multiple columns, but the actual field values are
found in the `value` column. If you want to retrieve the individual fields, you can sim‐
ply specify the names of the fields you wish to extract:

```
PUBLIC>select value:empid::number as emp_id,
       value:name::varchar as emp_name
    from table(flatten(input => parse_json(
    '{"employees": [
          {"empid": 1001, "name": "Bob Smith"},
          {"empid": 1002, "name": "Susan Jackson"},
          {"empid": 1003, "name": "Greg Carpenter"},
          {"empid": 1004, "name": "Robert Butler"},
          {"empid": 1005, "name": "Kim Josephs"},
          {"empid": 1006, "name": "John Tyler"},
          {"empid": 1007, "name": "John Sanford"}
        ]}'), path => 'employees'));
+--------+----------------+
| EMP_ID | EMP_NAME       |
|--------+----------------|
|   1001 | Bob Smith      |
|   1002 | Susan Jackson  |
|   1003 | Greg Carpenter |
|   1004 | Robert Butler  |
|   1005 | Kim Josephs    |
|   1006 | John Tyler     |
|   1007 | John Sanford   |
+--------+----------------+
```

This version of the query extracts the empid and name fields from the value column by specifying value:empid and value:name. You will learn more about creating and querying JSON documents in Chapter 18.

Finding and Retrieving Query Results

Let's say you've been experimenting with a number of different queries, and you'd like to retrieve and re-execute a recent query. Here's a query that uses the query_history() function in information_schema to retrieve the last 10 queries run in your session:

```
PUBLIC>select query_id,
          substr(query_text, 1, 23) partial_query_text
       from table(information_schema.query_history(
                                    result_limit => 10));
+-----------------------------------------+--------------------------+
| QUERY_ID                                | PARTIAL_QUERY_TEXT       |
|-----------------------------------------+--------------------------|
| 01accfd6-0d04-96b3-0002-9fde0023f1aa    | select query_id, substr(|
| 01accfd2-0d04-96b8-0002-9fde0024507e    | select query_id, substr(|
| 01accfd1-0d04-96b8-0002-9fde0024507a    | select *                 |
|                                         | from table(infor         |
| 01accfc8-0d04-96b8-0002-9fde00245076    | select value:empid::numb|
| 01accfc8-0d04-96b3-0002-9fde0023f1a6    | select value:empid::numb|
| 01accfc5-0d04-96b8-0002-9fde00245072    | select value from table(|
| 01accfc1-0d04-96b3-0002-9fde0023f1a2    | select value from table(|
| 01accfc0-0d04-96b3-0002-9fde0023f19e    | select * from table(flat|
| 01accfbf-0d04-96b3-0002-9fde0023f19a    | select * from table(flat|
| 01accfb7-0d04-96b8-0002-9fde0024506e    | select object_construct(|
+-----------------------------------------+--------------------------+
```

If you find the query you are interested in running, you can feed the query_id value into the result_scan() table function to retrieve the result set:

```
PUBLIC>select *
       from table(result_scan(
          '01accfc8-0d04-96b8-0002-9fde00245076'));
+--------+-----------------+
| EMP_ID | EMP_NAME        |
|--------+-----------------|
|   1001 | Bob Smith       |
|   1002 | Susan Jackson   |
|   1003 | Greg Carpenter  |
|   1004 | Robert Butler   |
|   1005 | Kim Josephs     |
|   1006 | John Tyler      |
|   1007 | John Sanford    |
+--------+-----------------+
```

This happens to be a query from the previous section in this chapter. If you are a database administrator and have the Monitor privilege, you can also retrieve queries run by other users, which can be very helpful for performance monitoring and tuning.

Wrap-Up

This chapter explored tabular user-defined functions, also known as table functions. You first learned about user-defined functions and how they can be called from queries, and then saw how table functions can be queried just like a table or view. Finally, you saw examples using some of Snowflake's built-in table functions.

Test Your Knowledge

The following exercises are designed to test your understanding of table functions. Please see "Chapter 17" in Appendix B for solutions.

Exercise 17-1

Write a scalar UDF named fn_circle_area() that takes a single numeric parameter p_radius and returns the area of a circle ($\pi * p\_radius^2$). The UDF should return type float.

Exercise 17-2

Write a table function named fn_get_parts_by_type() with a single parameter p_type_name (type varchar). The table function should return a result set consisting of the p_partkey and p_name columns from the Part table, for rows whose p_type column matches the parameter value. Call the function with parameter value 'SMALL PLATED NICKEL' or 'PROMO BRUSHED STEEL', both of which should return 23 rows.

Exercise 17-3

Query the fn_get_parts_by_type() table function created in Exercise 17-2, but instead of passing in a string (i.e., 'SMALL PLATED NICKEL'), join the table function to a query against the Part table that retrieves the distinct set of values where p_type is like 'STANDARD % STEEL'. Retrieve only the columns returned by the table function.

Exercise 17-4

Execute the query select 23 * 75. Run another query to find the query_id of the query you just executed.

Semistructured Data

Relational databases are adept at handling complex concepts and relationships, but not all data is easily expressed as rows and columns. Semistructured data formats such as XML, Parquet, Avro, and JSON allow for flexible data storage without the need to conform to a predefined schema. Unlike some database servers, where support for semistructured data was added as an afterthought, Snowflake's architecture was designed from the very beginning to support both structured and semistructured data. This chapter will explore the creation, storage, and retrieval of JSON documents in Snowflake.

Generating JSON from Relational Data

JSON (JavaScript Object Notation) has evolved into the standard format for data interchange. It is easy for both humans and machines to read and write, and while similar to XML it is less verbose and thus more compact. JSON stores data as key-value pairs, so the data is self-describing and there is no need for an external schema. JSON documents can be generated from relational tables, stored in tables using the `variant` data type and queried using built-in functions such as `flatten()`.

Let's start by creating a JSON document from relational tables in Snowflake. There are many built-in functions available for generating XML or JSON documents, but Table 18-1 defines the functions that are used in this chapter.

Table 18-1. Commonly used JSON functions

object_construct()	Returns a set of key-value pairs as type `object`
array_agg()	Pivots a set of values and returns type `array`
parse_json()	Parses a JSON document and returns type `variant`
try_parse_json()	Parses a JSON document and returns either `null` if not a valid JSON document, or `variant` otherwise

To begin, I'll use the `array_agg()` and `object_construct()` functions to build a simple document containing all rows from the `Region` table:

```
PUBLIC>select object_construct('Regions',
           array_agg(
             object_construct('Region_Key', r_regionkey,
                              'Region_Name', r_name))) as my_doc
       from region;
+------------------------------------+
| MY_DOC                             |
|------------------------------------|
| {                                  |
|    "Regions": [                    |
|      {                             |
|        "Region_Key": 0,            |
|        "Region_Name": "AFRICA"     |
|      },                            |
|      {                             |
|        "Region_Key": 1,            |
|        "Region_Name": "AMERICA"    |
|      },                            |
|      {                             |
|        "Region_Key": 2,            |
|        "Region_Name": "ASIA"       |
|      },                            |
|      {                             |
|        "Region_Key": 3,            |
|        "Region_Name": "EUROPE"     |
|      },                            |
|      {                             |
|        "Region_Key": 4,            |
|        "Region_Name": "MIDDLE EAST" |
|      }                             |
|    ]                               |
| }                                  |
+------------------------------------+
```

This query creates an object consisting of two key-value pairs (with keys of `Region_Key` and `Region_Name`), and then pivots them into an array. The net result is a single row of output containing a JSON document.

Next, let's turn this up a notch (or two) and generate a document consisting of an array of objects for each row in the `Region` table, including the region's name and array of associated `Nation` rows. Additionally, total sales will be computed for each `Region` and `Nation` row. Here's what the query looks like:

```
PUBLIC>with
       ntn_tot as
       (select n.n_regionkey, n.n_nationkey,
          sum(o.o_totalprice) as tot_ntn_sales,
          sum(sum(o.o_totalprice))
            over (partition by n.n_regionkey) as tot_rgn_sales
```

```
      from orders o
        inner join customer c
          on c.c_custkey = o.o_custkey
        inner join nation n
          on c.c_nationkey = n.n_nationkey
      group by n.n_regionkey, n.n_nationkey
    ),
    ntn as
    (select n.n_regionkey,
      array_agg(
        object_construct(
          'Nation_Name', n.n_name,
          'Tot_Nation_Sales', ntn_tot.tot_ntn_sales
        )) as nation_list
      from nation n
      inner join ntn_tot
        on n.n_nationkey = ntn_tot.n_nationkey
      group by n.n_regionkey
    )
    select object_construct('Regions',
      array_agg(
        object_construct(
          'Region_Name', r.r_name,
          'Tot_Region_Sales', rgn_tot.tot_rgn_sales,
          'Nations', ntn.nation_list
        ))) as region_summary_doc
    from region r
      inner join ntn on r.r_regionkey = ntn.n_regionkey
      inner join
      (select distinct n_regionkey, tot_rgn_sales
        from ntn_tot) rgn_tot
        on rgn_tot.n_regionkey = r.r_regionkey;
```

The output is a document consisting of an array of regions, each one containing an array of nations:

```
+--------------------------------------------+
| REGION_SUMMARY_DOC                         |
|--------------------------------------------|
| {                                          |
|   "Regions": [                             |
|     {                                      |
|       "Nations": [                         |
|         {                                  |
|           "Nation_Name": "ALGERIA",        |
|           "Tot_Nation_Sales": 867701407.69 |
|         },                                 |
|         {                                  |
|           "Nation_Name": "ETHIOPIA",       |
|           "Tot_Nation_Sales": 840736933.79 |
|         },                                 |
|         {                                  |
|           "Nation_Name": "KENYA",          |
```

```
          "Tot_Nation_Sales": 830403434.37 |
        },                                   |
        {                                    |
          "Nation_Name": "MOROCCO",          |
          "Tot_Nation_Sales": 851082088.95  |
        },                                   |
        {                                    |
          "Nation_Name": "MOZAMBIQUE",       |
          "Tot_Nation_Sales": 849301460.62  |
        }                                    |
      ],                                     |
      "Region_Name": "AFRICA",               |
      "Tot_Region_Sales": 4239225325.42     |
    },                                       |
    {                                        |
      "Nations": [                           |
        {                                    |
          "Nation_Name": "ARGENTINA",        |
          "Tot_Nation_Sales": 858702151.88  |
        },                                   |
        {                                    |
                                             |
          "Nation_Name": "BRAZIL",           |
          "Tot_Nation_Sales": 844227359.85  |
        },                                   |
        {                                    |
                                             |
          "Nation_Name": "CANADA",           |
          "Tot_Nation_Sales": 879554386.21  |
        },                                   |
        {                                    |
          "Nation_Name": "PERU",             |
          "Tot_Nation_Sales": 866428592.22  |
        },                                   |
        {                                    |
          "Nation_Name": "UNITED STATES",    |
          "Tot_Nation_Sales": 872163195.11  |
        }                                    |
      ],                                     |
      "Region_Name": "AMERICA",              |
      "Tot_Region_Sales": 4321075685.27     |
    },                                       |
    {                                        |
      "Nations": [                           |
        {                                    |
          "Nation_Name": "INDIA",            |
          "Tot_Nation_Sales": 867300065.32  |
        },                                   |
        {                                    |
          "Nation_Name": "INDONESIA",        |
          "Tot_Nation_Sales": 866176066.72  |
        },                                   |
        {                                    |
          "Nation_Name": "JAPAN",            |
```

```
        "Tot_Nation_Sales": 867419738.09
      },
      {
        "Nation_Name": "CHINA",
        "Tot_Nation_Sales": 901661903.78
      },
      {
        "Nation_Name": "VIETNAM",
        "Tot_Nation_Sales": 876033401.99
      }
    ],
    "Region_Name": "ASIA",
    "Tot_Region_Sales": 4378591175.9
  },
  {
    "Nations": [
      {
        "Nation_Name": "FRANCE",
        "Tot_Nation_Sales": 900059400.28
      },
      {
        "Nation_Name": "GERMANY",
        "Tot_Nation_Sales": 884705812.34
      },
      {
        "Nation_Name": "ROMANIA",
        "Tot_Nation_Sales": 880243089.92
      },
      {
        "Nation_Name": "RUSSIA",
        "Tot_Nation_Sales": 862689505.23
      },
      {
        "Nation_Name": "UNITED KINGDOM",
        "Tot_Nation_Sales": 864015030.26
      }
    ],
    "Region_Name": "EUROPE",
    "Tot_Region_Sales": 4391712838.03
  },
  {
    "Nations": [
      {
        "Nation_Name": "EGYPT",
        "Tot_Nation_Sales": 862118149.8
      },
      {
        "Nation_Name": "IRAN",
        "Tot_Nation_Sales": 876878109.19
      },
      {
        "Nation_Name": "IRAQ",
```

```
|                     "Tot_Nation_Sales": 865003574.74  |
|                  },                                    |
|                  {                                     |
|                     "Nation_Name": "JORDAN",           |
|                     "Tot_Nation_Sales": 890186225.44  |
|                  },                                    |
|                  {                                     |
|                     "Nation_Name": "SAUDI ARABIA",     |
|                     "Tot_Nation_Sales": 828012176.23  |
|                  }                                     |
|              ],                                        |
|              "Region_Name": "MIDDLE EAST",             |
|              "Tot_Region_Sales": 4322198235.4          |
|          }                                             |
|      ]                                                 |
|  }                                                     |
+-------------------------------------------------+
```

This document is lengthy, so for the rest of the chapter I will omit three of the regions from the output. The next section discusses how to store these types of documents in Snowflake.

Storing JSON Documents

If you recall from Chapter 5, the variant data type can be used to store any kind of data, and that includes JSON documents. Before trying to store the previous document in a table, I want to make sure it is a properly formatted JSON document, so I'm going to call the try_parse_json() function, which takes a string as an argument and returns either null if the string is not a proper JSON document, or else a variant containing the document. Here are the results:

```
select try_parse_json('{
  "Regions": [
    {
      "Nations": [
        {
          "Nation_Name": "ALGERIA",
          "Tot_Nation_Sales": 867701407.69
        },
        {
          "Nation_Name": "ETHIOPIA",
          "Tot_Nation_Sales": 840736933.79
        },
        {
          "Nation_Name": "KENYA",
          "Tot_Nation_Sales": 830403434.37
        },
        {
          "Nation_Name": "MOROCCO",
          "Tot_Nation_Sales": 851082088.95
```

```
        },
        {
          "Nation_Name": "MOZAMBIQUE",
          "Tot_Nation_Sales": 849301460.62
        }
      ],
      "Region_Name": "AFRICA",
      "Tot_Region_Sales": 4239225325.42
    },
... three regions omitted
    {
      "Nations": [
        {
          "Nation_Name": "EGYPT",
          "Tot_Nation_Sales": 862118149.8
        },
        {
          "Nation_Name": "IRAN",
          "Tot_Nation_Sales": 876878109.19
        },
        {
          "Nation_Name": "IRAQ",
          "Tot_Nation_Sales": 865003574.74
        },
        {
          "Nation_Name": "JORDAN",
          "Tot_Nation_Sales": 890186225.44
        },
        {
          "Nation_Name": "SAUDI ARABIA",
          "Tot_Nation_Sales": 828012176.23
        }
      ],
      "Region_Name": "MIDDLE EAST",
      "Tot_Region_Sales": 4322198235.4
    }
  ]
}') as check_json_doc;
+-------------------------------------------+
| CHECK_JSON_DOC                            |
|-------------------------------------------|
| {                                         |
|   "Regions": [                            |
|     {                                     |
|       "Nations": [                        |
|         {                                 |
|           "Nation_Name": "ALGERIA",       |
|           "Tot_Nation_Sales": 867701407.69 |
|         },                                |
|         {                                 |
|           "Nation_Name": "ETHIOPIA",      |
|           "Tot_Nation_Sales": 840736933.79 |
```

```
|          },                                  |
|          {                                   |
|            "Nation_Name": "KENYA",           |
|            "Tot_Nation_Sales": 830403434.37  |
|          },                                  |
|          {                                   |
|            "Nation_Name": "MOROCCO",         |
|            "Tot_Nation_Sales": 851082088.95  |
|          },                                  |
|          {                                   |
|            "Nation_Name": "MOZAMBIQUE",      |
|            "Tot_Nation_Sales": 849301460.62  |
|          }                                   |
|        ],                                    |
|        "Region_Name": "AFRICA",             |
|        "Tot_Region_Sales": 4239225325.42    |
|      },                                      |
... three regions omitted
|      {                                       |
|        "Nations": [                          |
|          {                                   |
|            "Nation_Name": "EGYPT",           |
|            "Tot_Nation_Sales": 862118149.8   |
|          },                                  |
|          {                                   |
|            "Nation_Name": "IRAN",            |
|            "Tot_Nation_Sales": 876878109.19  |
|          },                                  |
|          {                                   |
|            "Nation_Name": "IRAQ",            |
|            "Tot_Nation_Sales": 865003574.74  |
|          },                                  |
|          {                                   |
|            "Nation_Name": "JORDAN",          |
|            "Tot_Nation_Sales": 890186225.44  |
|          },                                  |
|          {                                   |
|            "Nation_Name": "SAUDI ARABIA",    |
|            "Tot_Nation_Sales": 828012176.23  |
|          }                                   |
|        ],                                    |
|        "Region_Name": "MIDDLE EAST",        |
|        "Tot_Region_Sales": 4322198235.4     |
|      }                                       |
|    ]                                         |
|  }                                           |
+---------------------------------------------+
```

The same document was returned, so it's a valid JSON document. If I remove the square brackets from near the top and bottom, however, the document is no longer valid, and try_parse_json() returns null:

```
PUBLIC>select try_parse_json('{
    "Regions":
      {
        "Nations": [
          {
            "Nation_Name": "ALGERIA",
            "Tot_Nation_Sales": 867701407.69
          },
          {
            "Nation_Name": "ETHIOPIA",
            "Tot_Nation_Sales": 840736933.79
          },
          {
            "Nation_Name": "KENYA",
            "Tot_Nation_Sales": 830403434.37
          },
          {
            "Nation_Name": "MOROCCO",
            "Tot_Nation_Sales": 851082088.95
          },
          {
            "Nation_Name": "MOZAMBIQUE",
            "Tot_Nation_Sales": 849301460.62
          }
        ],
        "Region_Name": "AFRICA",
        "Tot_Region_Sales": 4239225325.42
      },
  ... three regions omitted
      {
        "Nations": [
          {
            "Nation_Name": "EGYPT",
            "Tot_Nation_Sales": 862118149.8
          },
          {
            "Nation_Name": "IRAN",
            "Tot_Nation_Sales": 876878109.19
          },
          {
            "Nation_Name": "IRAQ",
            "Tot_Nation_Sales": 865003574.74
          },
          {
            "Nation_Name": "JORDAN",
            "Tot_Nation_Sales": 890186225.44
          },
          {
            "Nation_Name": "SAUDI ARABIA",
            "Tot_Nation_Sales": 828012176.23
          }
        ],
```

```
              "Region_Name": "MIDDLE EAST",
              "Tot_Region_Sales": 4322198235.4
            }
        }') as check_json_doc;
+-----------------+
| CHECK_JSON_DOC |
|-----------------|
| NULL            |
+-----------------+
```

You can use `try_parse_json()` any time you need to validate a JSON document, whether it's one you created yourself, or one obtained from a third party.

I don't currently have any place to store documents, so here's a simple table with a single column of type `variant`:

```
PUBLIC>create table my_docs (doc variant);
+-------------------------------------+
| status                              |
|-------------------------------------|
| Table MY_DOCS successfully created. |
+-------------------------------------+
```

Next, I can combine an `insert` statement with the query from earlier in the chapter:

```
PUBLIC>insert into my_docs
        with
        ntn_tot as
        (select n.n_regionkey, n.n_nationkey,
           sum(o.o_totalprice) as tot_ntn_sales,
           sum(sum(o.o_totalprice))
             over (partition by n.n_regionkey) as tot_rgn_sales
         from orders o
           inner join customer c
             on c.c_custkey = o.o_custkey
           inner join nation n
             on c.c_nationkey = n.n_nationkey
         group by n.n_regionkey, n.n_nationkey
        ),
        ntn as
        (select n.n_regionkey,
           array_agg(
             object_construct(
               'Nation_Name', n.n_name,
               'Tot_Nation_Sales', ntn_tot.tot_ntn_sales
             )) as nation_list
         from nation n
         inner join ntn_tot
           on n.n_nationkey = ntn_tot.n_nationkey
         group by n.n_regionkey
         )
        select object_construct('Regions',array_agg(
```

```
       object_construct(
         'Region_Name', r.r_name,
         'Tot_Region_Sales', rgn_tot.tot_rgn_sales,
         'Nations', ntn.nation_list
     ))) as region_summary_doc
   from region r
     inner join ntn on r.r_regionkey = ntn.n_regionkey
     inner join
     (select distinct n_regionkey, tot_rgn_sales
       from ntn_tot) rgn_tot
       on rgn_tot.n_regionkey = r.r_regionkey;
+--------------------------+
| number of rows inserted  |
|--------------------------|
|                        1 |
+--------------------------+
```

The outermost function call in the query is object_construct(), so the data type of the column returned by the query is object. Snowflake can store anything in a column of type variant, so there is no conversion needed.

If you want to load a JSON document from a string, rather than generating it using a query, you can use the parse_json() function, which accepts a string as an argument and returns type variant:

```
PUBLIC>insert into my_docs
       select parse_json('{
  "Regions": [
    {
      "Nations": [
        {
          "Nation_Name": "ALGERIA",
          "Tot_Nation_Sales": 867701407.69
        },
        {
          "Nation_Name": "ETHIOPIA",
          "Tot_Nation_Sales": 840736933.79
        },
        {
          "Nation_Name": "KENYA",
          "Tot_Nation_Sales": 830403434.37
        },
        {
          "Nation_Name": "MOROCCO",
          "Tot_Nation_Sales": 851082088.95
        },
        {
          "Nation_Name": "MOZAMBIQUE",
          "Tot_Nation_Sales": 849301460.62
        }
      ],
      "Region_Name": "AFRICA",
```

```
        "Tot_Region_Sales": 4239225325.42
      },
... three regions omitted
      {
        "Nations": [
          {
            "Nation_Name": "EGYPT",
            "Tot_Nation_Sales": 862118149.8
          },
          {
            "Nation_Name": "IRAN",
            "Tot_Nation_Sales": 876878109.19
          },
          {
            "Nation_Name": "IRAQ",
            "Tot_Nation_Sales": 865003574.74
          },
          {
            "Nation_Name": "JORDAN",
            "Tot_Nation_Sales": 890186225.44
          },
          {
            "Nation_Name": "SAUDI ARABIA",
            "Tot_Nation_Sales": 828012176.23
          }
        ],
        "Region_Name": "MIDDLE EAST",
        "Tot_Region_Sales": 4322198235.4
      }
    ]
}');
+-------------------------+
| number of rows inserted |
|-------------------------|
|                       1 |
+-------------------------+
```

That's all there is to it; you can store JSON documents in Snowflake as is, without the need to transform or decompose the document. The next section discusses how you can retrieve data from your JSON documents.

Limitations When Storing JSON Documents in Variant Columns

While using variant columns to store documents is certainly easy, there are some limitations to consider. First, variant columns are limited to 16MB, so you won't be able to store very large documents in a single column. Second, temporal data (date, time, and timestamp) fields are stored as strings, so performance can be an issue when performing operations such as add_month() or date diff().

Querying JSON Documents

So far, you've seen SQL statements that generate and store JSON documents, but what if you need to retrieve data from your documents and possibly join this data to other tables? The first step is to understand what fields (the names of the keys in the key-value pairs) are available in the document. I happen to know the field names for the document created earlier in the chapter, since I created it, but let's say you have a different JSON document and want to extract the names of the fields. Here's a query that uses the `flatten()` table function, which was discussed in Chapter 17, along with the `lateral` join discussed in Chapter 9 to retrieve the distinct set of fields from the document:

```
PUBLIC>select distinct d.key, typeof(d.value) as data_type
        from my_docs
          inner join lateral flatten(doc, recursive=>true) d
        where typeof(d.value) <> 'OBJECT'
        order by 1;
+-------------------+-----------+
| KEY               | DATA_TYPE |
|-------------------+-----------|
| Nation_Name       | VARCHAR   |
| Nations           | ARRAY     |
| Region_Name       | VARCHAR   |
| Regions           | ARRAY     |
| Tot_Nation_Sales  | DECIMAL   |
| Tot_Region_Sales  | DECIMAL   |
+-------------------+-----------+
```

The `flatten()` function returns several columns, including `key` and `value` used in this example, and for this query I use the `typeof()` function to determine the data type of each field.

I see that the `Regions` field has type `array`, so I can use the `array_size()` function to determine how many elements are in the array:

```
PUBLIC>select array_size(doc:Regions)
        from my_docs;
+------------------------+
| ARRAY_SIZE(DOC:REGIONS) |
|------------------------|
|                      5 |
+------------------------+
```

Using this information, I can write a query to retrieve the `Region_Name` values from each of the five elements in the `Regions` array:

```
PUBLIC>select
          doc:Regions[0].Region_Name as R0_Name,
          doc:Regions[1].Region_Name as R1_Name,
          doc:Regions[2].Region_Name as R2_Name,
```

```
        doc:Regions[3].Region_Name as R3_Name,
        doc:Regions[4].Region_Name as R4_Name
    from my_docs;
+-----------+-----------+----------+-----------+---------------+
| R0_NAME   | R1_NAME   | R2_NAME  | R3_NAME   | R4_NAME       |
|-----------+-----------+----------+-----------+---------------|
| "AFRICA"  | "AMERICA" | "ASIA"   | "EUROPE"  | "MIDDLE EAST" |
+-----------+-----------+----------+-----------+---------------|
```

While this certainly works, there are two problems with this approach: first, I want to be able to write the query to return an arbitrary number of rows without having to know the size of the array; and second, I would like the data pivoted to have five rows instead of five columns. Once again, the flatten() table function comes to the rescue:

```
PUBLIC>select
        r.value:Region_Name::string as region_name
    from my_docs
        inner join lateral flatten(input => doc:Regions) r;
+--------------+
| REGION_NAME  |
|--------------|
| AFRICA       |
| AMERICA      |
| ASIA         |
| EUROPE       |
| MIDDLE EAST  |
+--------------+
```

This solves both problems mentioned earlier, and I also took the liberty of casting the Region_Name value as a string, which removes the double quotes from around the values.

The next step is to move down another layer and retrieve the values from the Nations array, which will require a second call to the flatten() table function:

```
PUBLIC>select
        r.value:Region_Name::string as region_name,
        r.value:Tot_Region_Sales::decimal as tot_rgn_sales,
        n.value:Nation_Name::string as nation_name,
        n.value:Tot_Nation_Sales::decimal as tot_ntn_sales
    from my_docs
        inner join lateral flatten(input => doc:Regions) r
        inner join lateral flatten(input => r.value:Nations) n;
+-------------+---------------+---------------+---------------+
| REGION_NAME | TOT_RGN_SALES | NATION_NAME   | TOT_NTN_SALES |
|-------------+---------------+---------------+---------------|
| AFRICA      |    4239225325 | ALGERIA       |     867701408 |
| AFRICA      |    4239225325 | ETHIOPIA      |     840736934 |
| AFRICA      |    4239225325 | KENYA         |     830403434 |
| AFRICA      |    4239225325 | MOROCCO       |     851082089 |
| AFRICA      |    4239225325 | MOZAMBIQUE    |     849301461 |
```

```
| AMERICA     |   4321075685 | ARGENTINA      |   858702152 |
| AMERICA     |   4321075685 | BRAZIL         |   844227360 |
| AMERICA     |   4321075685 | CANADA         |   879554386 |
| AMERICA     |   4321075685 | PERU           |   866428592 |
| AMERICA     |   4321075685 | UNITED STATES  |   872163195 |
| ASIA        |   4378591176 | INDIA          |   867300065 |
| ASIA        |   4378591176 | INDONESIA      |   866176067 |
| ASIA        |   4378591176 | JAPAN          |   867419738 |
| ASIA        |   4378591176 | CHINA          |   901661904 |
| ASIA        |   4378591176 | VIETNAM        |   876033402 |
| EUROPE      |   4391712838 | FRANCE         |   900059400 |
| EUROPE      |   4391712838 | GERMANY        |   884705812 |
| EUROPE      |   4391712838 | ROMANIA        |   880243090 |
| EUROPE      |   4391712838 | RUSSIA         |   862689505 |
| EUROPE      |   4391712838 | UNITED KINGDOM |   864015030 |
| MIDDLE EAST |   4322198235 | EGYPT          |   862118150 |
| MIDDLE EAST |   4322198235 | IRAN           |   876878109 |
| MIDDLE EAST |   4322198235 | IRAQ           |   865003575 |
| MIDDLE EAST |   4322198235 | JORDAN         |   890186225 |
| MIDDLE EAST |   4322198235 | SAUDI ARABIA   |   828012176 |
+-------------+--------------+----------------+-------------+
```

The first call to flatten() pivots the array of Regions, and the second call pivots the array of Nations inside of each row generated by the first pivot.

Now that the document has been decomposed into individual fields, you can join the flattened data sets to other tables, as shown in the next query:

```
PUBLIC>select rgn.r_regionkey,
        r.value:Region_Name::string as region_name,
        ntn.n_nationkey,
        n.value:Nation_Name::string as nation_name
    from my_docs
    inner join lateral flatten(input => doc:Regions) r
    inner join region rgn on r.value:Region_Name = rgn.r_name
    inner join lateral flatten(input => r.value:Nations) n
    inner join nation ntn on n.value:Nation_Name = ntn.n_name
    order by 1,3;
+-------------+-------------+-------------+----------------+
| R_REGIONKEY | REGION_NAME | N_NATIONKEY | NATION_NAME    |
|-------------+-------------+-------------+----------------|
|           0 | AFRICA      |           0 | ALGERIA        |
|           0 | AFRICA      |           5 | ETHIOPIA       |
|           0 | AFRICA      |          14 | KENYA          |
|           0 | AFRICA      |          15 | MOROCCO        |
|           0 | AFRICA      |          16 | MOZAMBIQUE     |
|           1 | AMERICA     |           1 | ARGENTINA      |
|           1 | AMERICA     |           2 | BRAZIL         |
|           1 | AMERICA     |           3 | CANADA         |
|           1 | AMERICA     |          17 | PERU           |
|           1 | AMERICA     |          24 | UNITED STATES  |
|           2 | ASIA        |           8 | INDIA          |
|           2 | ASIA        |           9 | INDONESIA      |
```

```
|         2 | ASIA        |     12 | JAPAN          |
|         2 | ASIA        |     18 | CHINA          |
|         2 | ASIA        |     21 | VIETNAM        |
|         3 | EUROPE      |      6 | FRANCE         |
|         3 | EUROPE      |      7 | GERMANY        |
|         3 | EUROPE      |     19 | ROMANIA        |
|         3 | EUROPE      |     22 | RUSSIA         |
|         3 | EUROPE      |     23 | UNITED KINGDOM |
|         4 | MIDDLE EAST |      4 | EGYPT          |
|         4 | MIDDLE EAST |     10 | IRAN           |
|         4 | MIDDLE EAST |     11 | IRAQ           |
|         4 | MIDDLE EAST |     13 | JORDAN         |
|         4 | MIDDLE EAST |     20 | SAUDI ARABIA   |
+-------------+-------------+--------------+----------------+
```

This query joins the `Region_Name` and `Nation_Name` fields from the JSON document to the `Region` and `Nation` table in order to retrieve the unique identifiers.

Wrap-Up

This chapter introduced you to semistructured data, and showed you how to construct, store, and query JSON documents in Snowflake. You were also introduced to several of Snowflake's built-in functions for working with semistructured data, including `parse_json()`, `flatten()`, and `array_agg()`.

Test Your Knowledge

The following exercises are designed to test your understanding of working with JSON documents. Please see "Chapter 18" in Appendix B for solutions.

Exercise 18-1

Given the following query against the `Part` table:

```
PUBLIC>select p_partkey, p_name, p_brand
       from part
       where p_mfgr = 'Manufacturer#1'
         and p_type = 'ECONOMY POLISHED STEEL';
+-----------+-----------------------------------------+----------+
| P_PARTKEY | P_NAME                                  | P_BRAND  |
|-----------+-----------------------------------------+----------|
|     95608 | royal thistle floral frosted midnight   | Brand#12 |
|    100308 | azure honeydew grey aquamarine black    | Brand#11 |
|    103808 | steel lemon tomato brown blush          | Brand#13 |
|     68458 | spring white lime dim peru              | Brand#14 |
|     70808 | gainsboro chiffon papaya green khaki     | Brand#12 |
|    112758 | turquoise saddle moccasin magenta pink  | Brand#14 |
+-----------+-----------------------------------------+----------+
```

Write a query that generates a JSON document containing the same results. The document should consist of an object named `Parts` containing an array of six entries with tags `Partkey`, `Name`, and `Brand`.

Exercise 18-2

Write an `insert` statement that adds the JSON document generated by Exercise 18-1 to the `my_docs` table. (Use the JSON document returned by the query, not the query itself).

Exercise 18-3

Given the following subquery named `city_doc`:

```
with city_doc as
 (select parse_json(
  '{
    "Major_Cities": [
      {
        "Country": "USA",
        "Cities" : [
          {
            "City_Name": "Chicago",
            "Region_Name": "Illinois"
          },
          {
            "City_Name": "New York City",
            "Region_Name": "New York"
          },
          {
            "City_Name": "Los Angeles",
            "Region_Name": "California"
          }
        ]
      },
      {
        "Country": "Canada",
        "Cities" : [
          {
            "City_Name": "Vancouver",
            "Region_Name": "British Columbia"
          },
          {
            "City_Name": "Toronto",
            "Region_Name": "Ontario"
          }
        ]
      }
    ]
```

```
    }') as d
  )
```

Write a query against `city_doc` that will generate the following output:

```
+--------------+---------------+------------------+
| COUNTRY_NAME | CITY_NAME     | REGION_NAME      |
|--------------+---------------+------------------|
| USA          | Chicago       | Illinois         |
| USA          | New York City | New York         |
| USA          | Los Angeles   | California       |
| Canada       | Vancouver     | British Columbia |
| Canada       | Toronto       | Ontario          |
+--------------+---------------+------------------+
```

Sample Database

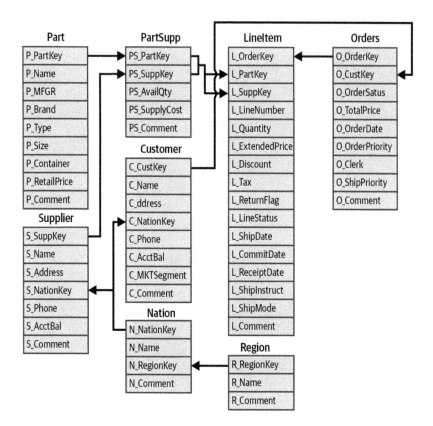

Solutions to Exercises

This appendix contains answers to the set of exercises at the end of each chapter. Keep in mind that there are often several ways to arrive at the correct answer, so if your answer doesn't exactly match what is listed, you may have created an equally correct alternate solution.

Chapter 1

See "Test Your Knowledge" on page 19.

Solution to Exercise 1-1

Write a query to retrieve the n_nationkey and n_name columns from the Nation table. Sort the rows by n_name values.

```
PUBLIC>select n_nationkey, n_name
       from nation
       order by n_name;
+-------------+----------------+
| N_NATIONKEY | N_NAME         |
|-------------+----------------|
|           0 | ALGERIA        |
|           1 | ARGENTINA      |
|           2 | BRAZIL         |
|           3 | CANADA         |
|          18 | CHINA          |
|           4 | EGYPT          |
|           5 | ETHIOPIA       |
|           6 | FRANCE         |
|           7 | GERMANY        |
|           8 | INDIA          |
|           9 | INDONESIA      |
|          10 | IRAN           |
```

```
|    11 | IRAQ           |
|    12 | JAPAN          |
|    13 | JORDAN         |
|    14 | KENYA          |
|    15 | MOROCCO        |
|    16 | MOZAMBIQUE     |
|    17 | PERU           |
|    19 | ROMANIA        |
|    22 | RUSSIA         |
|    20 | SAUDI ARABIA   |
|    23 | UNITED KINGDOM |
|    24 | UNITED STATES  |
|    21 | VIETNAM        |
+-------------+----------------+
```

Solution to Exercise 1-2

Write a query to retrieve the n_nationkey and n_name columns from the Nation table, but only for those rows with a value of 3 for n_regionkey.

```
PUBLIC>select n_nationkey, n_name
       from nation
       where n_regionkey = 3;
+-------------+----------------+
| N_NATIONKEY | N_NAME         |
|-------------+----------------|
|           6 | FRANCE         |
|           7 | GERMANY        |
|          19 | ROMANIA        |
|          22 | RUSSIA         |
|          23 | UNITED KINGDOM |
+-------------+----------------+
```

Solution to Exercise 1-3

Write a query to retrieve the n_nationkey and n_name columns from the Nation table and join to the Region table (using the r_regionkey column) to retrieve only those nations belonging to the Africa region (r_name = 'AFRICA').

```
PUBLIC>select n_nationkey, n_name
       from nation as n
       inner join region as r
       on n.n_regionkey = r.r_regionkey
       where r.r_name = 'AFRICA';
+-------------+------------+
| N_NATIONKEY | N_NAME     |
|-------------+------------|
|           0 | ALGERIA    |
|           5 | ETHIOPIA   |
|          14 | KENYA      |
|          15 | MOROCCO    |
```

```
|       16 | MOZAMBIQUE |
+-------------+-----------+
```

Solution to Exercise 1-4

Retrieve the s_name and s_acctbal columns from the Supplier table. Sort by s_acctbal in descending order and retrieve only the first 10 rows (which will be the 10 suppliers with the highest s_acctbal values).

```
PUBLIC>select s_name, s_acctbal
       from supplier
       order by s_acctbal desc
       limit 10;
+--------------------+-----------+
| S_NAME             | S_ACCTBAL |
|--------------------+-----------|
| Supplier#000006343 |   9998.20 |
| Supplier#000002522 |   9997.04 |
| Supplier#000000892 |   9993.46 |
| Supplier#000002543 |   9992.70 |
| Supplier#000001833 |   9992.26 |
| Supplier#000009966 |   9991.00 |
| Supplier#000002892 |   9989.02 |
| Supplier#000008875 |   9984.69 |
| Supplier#000002331 |   9984.20 |
| Supplier#000007895 |   9977.32 |
+--------------------+-----------+
```

Chapter 2

See "Test Your Knowledge" on page 39.

Solution to Exercise 2-1

Retrieve the c_name and c_acctbal (account balance) columns from the Customer table, but only for those rows in the Machinery segment (c_mktsegment = 'MACHINERY') and with an account balance greater than 9998.

```
PUBLIC>select c_name, c_acctbal
       from customer
       where c_mktsegment = 'MACHINERY'
       and c_acctbal > 9998;
```

```
+--------------------+----------+
| C_NAME             | C_ACCTBAL |
|--------------------+----------|
| Customer#000057166 |  9998.69 |
| Customer#000023828 |  9999.64 |
| Customer#000028474 |  9998.05 |
| Customer#000102296 |  9998.04 |
| Customer#000119437 |  9998.43 |
+--------------------+----------+
```

Solution to Exercise 2-2

Retrieve the c_name, c_mktsegment (market segment), and c_acctbal (account balance) columns from the Customer table, but only for those rows in either the Machinery or Furniture market segments with an account balance between -1 and 1.

```
PUBLIC>select c_name, c_mktsegment, c_acctbal
       from customer
       where c_mktsegment in ('MACHINERY','FURNITURE')
       and c_acctbal between -1 and 1;
+--------------------+--------------+----------+
| C_NAME             | C_MKTSEGMENT | C_ACCTBAL |
|--------------------+--------------+----------|
| Customer#000038476 | FURNITURE    |    -0.72 |
| Customer#000136930 | MACHINERY    |    -0.56 |
| Customer#000146548 | MACHINERY    |    -0.98 |
| Customer#000103441 | MACHINERY    |    -0.74 |
| Customer#000001141 | MACHINERY    |     0.97 |
| Customer#000001327 | MACHINERY    |     0.97 |
+--------------------+--------------+----------+
```

Solution to Exercise 2-3

Retrieve the c_name, c_mktsegment (market segment), and c_acctbal (account balance) columns from the Customer table, but only for those rows where *either* the market segment is Machinery and the account balance is 20, *or* the market segment is Furniture and the account balance is 334.

```
PUBLIC>select c_name, c_mktsegment, c_acctbal
       from customer
       where (c_mktsegment = 'MACHINERY' and c_acctbal = 20)
          or (c_mktsegment = 'FURNITURE' and c_acctbal = 334);
+--------------------+--------------+----------+
| C_NAME             | C_MKTSEGMENT | C_ACCTBAL |
|--------------------+--------------+----------|
| Customer#000007300 | FURNITURE    |   334.00 |
| Customer#000096163 | MACHINERY    |    20.00 |
+--------------------+--------------+----------+
```

Solution to Exercise 2-4

Given a table named `Balances` with the following data:

```
Acct_Num    Acct_Bal
--------    --------
1234        342.22
3498          9.00
3887        (null)
6277         28.33
```

Write a query that retrieves all rows that do *not* have a value of 9 for the `acct_bal` column.

```
select acct_num, acct_bal
from balances
where acct_bal <> 9 or acct_bal is null;
+----------+----------+
| Acct_Num | Acct_Bal |
+----------+----------+
| 1234     |   342.22 |
| 3887     |   (null) |
| 6277     |    28.33 |
+----------+----------+
```

Chapter 3

See "Test Your Knowledge" on page 54.

Solution to Exercise 3-1

Fill in the blanks (denoted by ❶ and ❷) in the query below to obtain the results that follow:

```
PUBLIC>select r.r_name as region_name, n.n_name as nation_name
       from region as r
       inner join nation ❶
         on ❷ = n.n_regionkey
       where n.n_name like 'A%';
+-------------+-------------+
| REGION_NAME | NATION_NAME |
|-------------+-------------|
| AFRICA      | ALGERIA     |
| AMERICA     | ARGENTINA   |
+-------------+-------------+

PUBLIC>select r.r_name as region_name, n.n_name as nation_name
       from region as r
       inner join nation as n
         on r.r_regionkey = n.n_regionkey
       where n.n_name like 'A%';
```

Solution to Exercise 3-2

Given the following data for the Pet_Owner and Pet tables, write a query that returns the owner_name and pet_name of every owner/pet match (same value for owner_id column). Don't include owners with no pets or pets with no owner.

```
Pet_Owner                          Pet
+----------+------------+          +--------+----------+----------+
| OWNER_ID | OWNER_NAME |          | PET_ID | OWNER_ID | PET_NAME |
|----------+------------|          +--------+----------+----------+
|        1 | John       |          |    101 |        1 | Fluffy   |
|        2 | Cindy      |          |    102 |        3 | Spot     |
|        3 | Laura      |          |    103 |        4 | Rover    |
|        4 | Mark       |          |    104 |     NULL | Rosco    |
+----------+------------+          +--------+----------+----------+
```

```
select po.owner_name, p.pet_name
from pet_owner as po
inner join pet as p
  on po.owner_id = p.owner_id;
+------------+----------+
| OWNER_NAME | PET_NAME |
|------------+----------|
| John       | Fluffy   |
| Laura      | Spot     |
| Mark       | Rover    |
+------------+----------+
```

Solution to Exercise 3-3

Using the same data set from Exercise 3-2, write a query that returns every pet owner's name along with the name of the matching pet if one exists. Results should include every row from Pet_Owner.

```
select po.owner_name, p.pet_name
from pet_owner as po
left outer join pet as p
  on po.owner_id = p.owner_id;
+------------+----------+
| OWNER_NAME | PET_NAME |
|------------+----------|
| John       | Fluffy   |
| Laura      | Spot     |
| Mark       | Rover    |
| Cindy      | NULL     |
+------------+----------+
```

Solution to Exercise 3-4

Expanding on the owner/pet exercises, let's say that pets can have zero, one, or two owners:

```
Pet_Owner
+----------+------------+
| OWNER_ID | OWNER_NAME |
|----------+------------|
|        1 | John       |
|        2 | Cindy      |
|        3 | Laura      |
|        4 | Mark       |
+----------+------------+
Pet
+--------+-----------+-----------+----------+
| PET_ID | OWNER_ID1 | OWNER_ID2 | PET_NAME |
|--------+-----------+-----------+----------|
|    101 |         1 |      NULL | Fluffy   |
|    102 |         3 |         2 | Spot     |
|    103 |         4 |         1 | Rover    |
|    104 |      NULL |      NULL | Rosco    |
+--------+-----------+-----------+----------+
```

Return the name of each pet, along with the names of Owner #1 and Owner #2. The result set should have one row for each pet (4 total). Some of the owner names will be null.

```
select p.pet_name,
  po1.owner_name as owner_1, po2.owner_name as owner_2
from pet as p
left outer join pet_owner as po1
  on po1.owner_id = p.owner_id1
left outer join pet_owner as po2
  on po2.owner_id = p.owner_id2;
+----------+---------+---------+
| PET_NAME | OWNER_1 | OWNER_2 |
|----------+---------+---------|
| Rover    | Mark    | John    |
| Spot     | Laura   | Cindy   |
| Fluffy   | John    | NULL    |
| Rosco    | NULL    | NULL    |
+----------+---------+---------+
```

Chapter 4

See "Test Your Knowledge" on page 68.

Solution to Exercise 4-1

Given the following two sets:

```
A = {3, 5, 7, 9}
B = {4, 5, 6, 7, 8}
```

Which sets are generated by each of the following operations?

- A union B
- A union all B
- A intersect B

- A except B
- B except A

- {3, 4, 5, 6, 7, 8, 9}
- {3, 4, 5, 5, 6, 7, 7, 8, 9}
- {5, 7}

- {3, 9}
- {4, 6, 8}

Solution to Exercise 4-2

Write a compound query that returns the names of all regions (`Region.r_name`) and nations (`Nation.n_name`) that start with the letter A.

```
PUBLIC>select r_name from region where r_name like 'A%'
       union
       select n_name from nation where n_name like 'A%';
+-----------+
| R_NAME    |
|-----------|
| AFRICA    |
| AMERICA   |
| ASIA      |
| ALGERIA   |
| ARGENTINA |
+-----------+
```

Solution to Exercise 4-3

Modify the query from Exercise 4-2 to sort by name.

```
PUBLIC>select r_name from region where r_name like 'A%'
       union
       select n_name from nation where n_name like 'A%'
       order by 1;
```

```
+-----------+
| R_NAME    |
|-----------|
| AFRICA    |
| ALGERIA   |
| AMERICA   |
| ARGENTINA |
| ASIA      |
+-----------+
```

Solution to Exercise 4-4

Given the following three sets:

```
A = {3, 5, 7, 9}
B = {4, 5, 6, 7, 8}
C = {8, 9, 10}
```

Which set is returned by the following operation?

```
(A except B) intersect C
{9}
```

Chapter 5

See "Test Your Knowledge" on page 90.

Solution to Exercise 5-1

Write a query that returns the string 'you can't always get what you want'.

```
PUBLIC>select 'you cant always get what you want';
+---------------------------------------+
| 'YOU CANT ALWAYS GET WHAT YOU WANT'   |
|---------------------------------------|
| you can't always get what you want    |
+---------------------------------------+
```

Solution to Exercise 5-2

Write a query that returns an array containing the number 985, the string 'hello there', and the boolean value true.

```
PUBLIC>select [985, 'hello there', true];
+---------------------------+
| [985, 'HELLO THERE', TRUE] |
|---------------------------|
| [                         |
|    985,                   |
|    "hello there",         |
```

```
|   true                  |
|  ]                      |
+-------------------------+
```

Solution to Exercise 5-3

Write a query that uses the array generated in Exercise 5-2 as an input, and then flattens the array into three rows.

```
PUBLIC>select value
       from table(flatten(input => [985, 'hello there', true]));
+---------------+
| VALUE         |
|---------------|
| 985           |
| "hello there" |
| true          |
+---------------+
```

Solution to Exercise 5-4

Given the following data for the Pet_Owner and Pet tables, write an update statement that sets the Pet.Owner column to the name of the associated owner in the Pet_Owner.Owner_Name column.

```
Pet_Owner                      Pet
+----------+------------+  +--------+----------+----------+-------+
| OWNER_ID | OWNER_NAME |  | PET_ID | OWNER_ID | PET_NAME | OWNER |
|----------+------------|  +--------+----------+----------+-------+
|        1 | John       |  |    101 |        1 | Fluffy   | NULL  |
|        2 | Cindy      |  |    102 |        3 | Spot     | NULL  |
|        3 | Laura      |  |    103 |        4 | Rover    | NULL  |
|        4 | Mark       |  |    104 |     NULL | Rosco    | NULL  |
+----------+------------+  +--------+----------+----------+-------+
```

```
update pet as p
set p.owner = po.owner_name
from pet_owner as po
where p.owner_id = po.owner_id;
```

```
select * from pet;
+--------+----------+----------+-------+
| PET_ID | OWNER_ID | PET_NAME | OWNER |
|--------+----------+----------+-------|
|    101 |        1 | Fluffy   | John  |
|    102 |        3 | Spot     | Laura |
|    103 |        4 | Rover    | Mark  |
|    104 |     NULL | Rosco    | NULL  |
+--------+----------+----------+-------+
```

Chapter 6

See "Test Your Knowledge" on page 107.

Solution to Exercise 6-1

Write a query that uses a function to alter the string 'cow it maked dende' by changing all occurrences of c to n, and all occurrences of d to s.

```
PUBLIC>select translate('cow it maked dende','cd','ns');
+-------------------------------------------+
| TRANSLATE('COW IT MAKED DENDE','CD','NS') |
|-------------------------------------------|
| now it makes sense                        |
+-------------------------------------------+
```

Solution to Exercise 6-2

Write a query that returns the numbers 1 through 10, one per row.

```
PUBLIC>select seq1() + 1
        from table(generator(rowcount => 10));
+------------+
| SEQ1() + 1 |
|------------|
|          1 |
|          2 |
|          3 |
|          4 |
|          5 |
|          6 |
|          7 |
|          8 |
|          9 |
|         10 |
+------------+
```

Solution to Exercise 6-3

Write a query that returns the number of days between the dates 01-JAN-2024 and 15-AUG-2025.

```
PUBLIC>select datediff(day, '01-JAN-2024', '15-AUG-2025');
+-----------------------------------------+
| DATEDIFF(DAY, '01-JAN-2024', '15-AUG-2025') |
|-----------------------------------------|
|                                     592 |
+-----------------------------------------+
```

Solution to Exercise 6-4

Write a query that sums the numeric year, month, and day for the date 27-SEP-2025.

```
PUBLIC>select date_part(year, dt.val)
        + date_part(month, dt.val)
        + date_part(day, dt.val)
     from (values ('27-SEP-2025'::date)) as dt(val);
+----------------------------------------------------+
| DATE_PART(YEAR, DT.VAL) + DATE_PART(MONTH, DT.VAL) |
|                          + DATE_PART(DAY, DT.VAL)  |
|----------------------------------------------------|
|                                              2061  |
+----------------------------------------------------+
```

Chapter 7

See "Test Your Knowledge" on page 128.

Solution to Exercise 7-1

Write a query to count the number of rows in the Supplier table, along with determining the minimum and maximum values of the s_acctbal column.

```
PUBLIC>select count(*), min(s_acctbal), max(s_acctbal)
     from supplier;
+----------+----------------+----------------+
| COUNT(*) | MIN(S_ACCTBAL) | MAX(S_ACCTBAL) |
|----------+----------------+----------------|
|     7400 |        -998.22 |        9998.20 |
+----------+----------------+----------------+
```

Solution to Exercise 7-2

Modify the query from Exercise 7-1 to perform the calculations, but for each value of s_nationkey rather than for the entire table.

```
PUBLIC>select s_nationkey,
        count(*), min(s_acctbal), max(s_acctbal)
     from supplier
     group by s_nationkey;
+-------------+----------+----------------+----------------+
| S_NATIONKEY | COUNT(*) | MIN(S_ACCTBAL) | MAX(S_ACCTBAL) |
|-------------+----------+----------------+----------------|
|          17 |      325 |        -990.13 |        9895.02 |
|          15 |      265 |        -980.44 |        9965.05 |
|          23 |      291 |        -970.73 |        9955.05 |
|          10 |      306 |        -997.61 |        9991.00 |
|          24 |      295 |        -967.88 |        9977.19 |
|          18 |      310 |        -939.25 |        9925.41 |
|           8 |      301 |        -941.38 |        9993.46 |
```

```
|         3 |       307 |      -989.86 |       9984.20 |
|        22 |       296 |      -963.79 |       9852.52 |
|         2 |       293 |      -990.16 |       9973.98 |
|         4 |       297 |      -966.20 |       9998.20 |
|         9 |       286 |      -964.32 |       9940.38 |
|        21 |       287 |      -900.49 |       9636.13 |
|        12 |       275 |      -989.05 |       9989.02 |
|         5 |       283 |      -974.42 |       9934.49 |
|         6 |       299 |      -986.14 |       9893.40 |
|        20 |       307 |      -987.45 |       9975.89 |
|        11 |       309 |      -935.13 |       9895.96 |
|         0 |       318 |      -995.53 |       9879.83 |
|         1 |       312 |      -951.70 |       9821.11 |
|        14 |       280 |      -979.44 |       9992.70 |
|        19 |       290 |      -845.44 |       9984.69 |
|         7 |       298 |      -954.24 |       9934.44 |
|        13 |       272 |      -998.22 |       9895.14 |
|        16 |       298 |      -983.40 |       9997.04 |
+-----------+-----------+-------------+---------------+
```

Solution to Exercise 7-3

Modify the query from Exercise 7-2 to return only those rows with more than 300 suppliers per s_nationkey value.

```
PUBLIC>select s_nationkey,
       count(*), min(s_acctbal), max(s_acctbal)
    from supplier
    group by s_nationkey
    having count(*) > 300;
+-------------+----------+-----------------+-----------------+
| S_NATIONKEY | COUNT(*) | MIN(S_ACCTBAL)  | MAX(S_ACCTBAL)  |
|-------------+----------+-----------------+-----------------|
|          17 |      325 |         -990.13 |         9895.02 |
|          10 |      306 |         -997.61 |         9991.00 |
|          18 |      310 |         -939.25 |         9925.41 |
|           8 |      301 |         -941.38 |         9993.46 |
|           3 |      307 |         -989.86 |         9984.20 |
|          20 |      307 |         -987.45 |         9975.89 |
|          11 |      309 |         -935.13 |         9895.96 |
|           0 |      318 |         -995.53 |         9879.83 |
|           1 |      312 |         -951.70 |         9821.11 |
+-------------+----------+-----------------+-----------------+
```

Solution to Exercise 7-4

Using the query from Exercise 7-2, I can join to the Nation table using s_nationkey, and add Nation.n_regionkey to the group by clause, as in:

```
PUBLIC>select n.n_regionkey, s.s_nationkey,
       count(*), min(s.s_acctbal), max(s.s_acctbal)
    from supplier as s
```

```
      inner join nation n
        on s.s_nationkey = n.n_nationkey
      group by n.n_regionkey, s.s_nationkey;
```

Modify this query to generate rows for rollups for each n_regionkey value, rollups for each s_nationkey value, and a single rollup across all rows.

```
PUBLIC>select n.n_regionkey, s.s_nationkey,
          count(*), min(s.s_acctbal), max(s.s_acctbal)
      from supplier as s
      inner join nation n
        on s.s_nationkey = n.n_nationkey
      group by cube(n.n_regionkey, s.s_nationkey);
```

Chapter 8

See "Test Your Knowledge" on page 145.

Solution to Exercise 8-1

Write a query against the Nation table that uses an uncorrelated subquery on the Region table to return the names of all nations except those in the America and Asia regions.

```
PUBLIC>select n_nationkey, n_name
      from nation
      where n_regionkey not in
        (select r_regionkey from region
         where r_name in ('AMERICA', 'ASIA'));
+-------------+----------------+
| N_NATIONKEY | N_NAME         |
|-------------+----------------|
|           0 | ALGERIA        |
|           4 | EGYPT          |
|           5 | ETHIOPIA       |
|           6 | FRANCE         |
|           7 | GERMANY        |
|          10 | IRAN           |
|          11 | IRAQ           |
|          13 | JORDAN         |
|          14 | KENYA          |
|          15 | MOROCCO        |
|          16 | MOZAMBIQUE     |
|          19 | ROMANIA        |
|          20 | SAUDI ARABIA   |
|          22 | RUSSIA         |
|          23 | UNITED KINGDOM |
+-------------+----------------+
```

Solution to Exercise 8-2

Generate the same results as Exercise 8-1, but using a correlated subquery against the Region table.

```
PUBLIC>select n_nationkey, n_name
     from nation n
     where not exists
       (select 1 from region r
        where r.r_regionkey = n.n_regionkey
           and r_name in ('AMERICA', 'ASIA'));
+-------------+----------------+
| N_NATIONKEY | N_NAME         |
|-------------+----------------|
|           0 | ALGERIA        |
|           4 | EGYPT          |
|           5 | ETHIOPIA       |
|           6 | FRANCE         |
|           7 | GERMANY        |
|          10 | IRAN           |
|          11 | IRAQ           |
|          13 | JORDAN         |
|          14 | KENYA          |
|          15 | MOROCCO        |
|          16 | MOZAMBIQUE     |
|          19 | ROMANIA        |
|          20 | SAUDI ARABIA   |
|          22 | RUSSIA         |
|          23 | UNITED KINGDOM |
+-------------+----------------+
```

Solution to Exercise 8-3

Write a query against the Customer table that returns the c_custkey and c_name columns for all customers who placed exactly four orders in 1997. Use an uncorrelated subquery against the Orders table.

```
PUBLIC>select c_custkey, c_name
     from customer
     where c_custkey in
       (select o_custkey
        from orders
        where date_part(year, o_orderdate) = 1997
             group by o_custkey
             having count(*) = 4);
+-----------+--------------------+
| C_CUSTKEY | C_NAME             |
|-----------+--------------------|
|     76729 | Customer#000076729 |
|     81835 | Customer#000081835 |
|     82210 | Customer#000082210 |
```

```
|     83722 | Customer#000083722 |
|    141352 | Customer#000141352 |
|     94282 | Customer#000094282 |
|     48652 | Customer#000048652 |
|    129988 | Customer#000129988 |
+-----------+--------------------+
```

Solution to Exercise 8-4

Modify the query from Exercise 8-3 to return the same results, but with a correlated subquery.

```
PUBLIC>select c_custkey, c_name
      from customer c
      where 4 =
        (select count(*)
         from orders o
         where date_part(year, o_orderdate) = 1997
           and o.o_custkey = c.c_custkey);
+-----------+--------------------+
| C_CUSTKEY | C_NAME             |
|-----------+--------------------|
|    129988 | Customer#000129988 |
|     48652 | Customer#000048652 |
|     76729 | Customer#000076729 |
|     81835 | Customer#000081835 |
|     82210 | Customer#000082210 |
|     83722 | Customer#000083722 |
|    141352 | Customer#000141352 |
|     94282 | Customer#000094282 |
+-----------+--------------------+
```

Chapter 9

See "Test Your Knowledge" on page 159.

Solution to Exercise 9-1

The following query returns the number of customers in each market segment:

```
PUBLIC>select c_mktsegment as mktseg, count(*) tot_custs
      from customer
      group by c_mktsegment;
+------------+-----------+
| MKTSEG     | TOT_CUSTS |
|------------+-----------|
| AUTOMOBILE |     13192 |
| MACHINERY  |     13185 |
| BUILDING   |     13360 |
| FURNITURE  |     13125 |
```

```
| HOUSEHOLD   |      13214 |
+-------------+------------+
```

Use this query as the basis for a pivot query so that there is a single row with 5 columns, with each column having the name of a market segment.

```
PUBLIC>select automobile, machinery, building,
        furniture, household
     from
       (select c_mktsegment as mktseg, count(*) as tot_custs
        from customer
        group by c_mktsegment
        )
     pivot (max(tot_custs)
     for mktseg in ('AUTOMOBILE','MACHINERY','BUILDING',
                    'FURNITURE','HOUSEHOLD'))
     as pvt(automobile, machinery, building,
            furniture, household);
+------------+-----------+-----------+-----------+-----------+
| AUTOMOBILE | MACHINERY | BUILDING  | FURNITURE | HOUSEHOLD |
|------------+-----------+-----------+-----------+-----------|
|      13192 |     13185 |     13360 |     13125 |     13214 |
+------------+-----------+-----------+-----------+-----------+
```

Solution to Exercise 9-2

The following query counts the number of suppliers in each nation:

```
PUBLIC>select s_nationkey, count(*) as supplier_count
     from supplier
     group by s_nationkey;
+-------------+----------------+
| S_NATIONKEY | SUPPLIER_COUNT |
|-------------+----------------|
|          17 |            325 |
|          23 |            291 |
|          10 |            306 |
|          24 |            295 |
|          18 |            310 |
|           8 |            301 |
|           3 |            307 |
|          22 |            296 |
|          19 |            290 |
|          16 |            298 |
|           1 |            312 |
|           7 |            298 |
|          13 |            272 |
|          12 |            275 |
|           5 |            283 |
|          20 |            307 |
|          11 |            309 |
|           2 |            293 |
|           9 |            286 |
```

```
|          21 |              287 |
|           6 |              299 |
|          14 |              280 |
|          15 |              265 |
|           4 |              297 |
|           0 |              318 |
+-------------+------------------+
```

Modify this query to add the Nation.n_name column using a lateral join to the
Nation table.

```
PUBLIC>select s_nationkey, names.n_name,
         count(*) as supplier_count
       from supplier s
       inner join lateral
        (select n.n_name from nation n
         where n.n_nationkey = s.s_nationkey) as names
       group by s_nationkey, names.n_name;
+-------------+------------------+------------------+
| S_NATIONKEY | N_NAME           | SUPPLIER_COUNT |
|-------------+------------------+------------------|
|          17 | PERU             |            325 |
|          15 | MOROCCO          |            265 |
|          10 | IRAN             |            306 |
|          24 | UNITED STATES    |            295 |
|          18 | CHINA            |            310 |
|           8 | INDIA            |            301 |
|           3 | CANADA           |            307 |
|          22 | RUSSIA           |            296 |
|          16 | MOZAMBIQUE       |            298 |
|           2 | BRAZIL           |            293 |
|           4 | EGYPT            |            297 |
|          13 | JORDAN           |            272 |
|          14 | KENYA            |            280 |
|           5 | ETHIOPIA         |            283 |
|          20 | SAUDI ARABIA     |            307 |
|          11 | IRAQ             |            309 |
|          23 | UNITED KINGDOM   |            291 |
|           1 | ARGENTINA        |            312 |
|           6 | FRANCE           |            299 |
|          19 | ROMANIA          |            290 |
|           9 | INDONESIA        |            286 |
|           0 | ALGERIA          |            318 |
|          21 | VIETNAM          |            287 |
|           7 | GERMANY          |            298 |
|          12 | JAPAN            |            275 |
+-------------+------------------+------------------+
```

Solution to Exercise 9-3

The Smith_History table holds genealogy information for the Smith family:

```
Person_ID  Name        Father_Person_ID
---------  ----------  ----------------
    1      Thomas      (null)
    2      Clara       (null)
    3      Samuel      1
    4      Charles     1
    5      Beth        3
    6      Steven      4
    7      Sarah       6
    8      Robert      4
    9      Dorothy     8
    10     George      8
```

Thomas and Clara's parents are unknown at this point, so they have a null value for the father_person_id column. Write a query to walk the Smith family tree starting with Thomas, using the sys_connect_by_path() function to show the full ancestry. You can use the following with clause as a starter:

```
with smith_history as
  (select person_id, name, father_person_id
   from (values
           (1,'Thomas',null),
           (2,'Clara',null),
           (3,'Samuel',1),
           (4,'Charles',1),
           (5,'Beth',3),
           (6,'Steven',4),
           (7,'Sarah',6),
           (8,'Robert',4),
           (9,'Dorothy',8),
           (10,'George',8))
         as smith(person_id, name, father_person_id)
  )

PUBLIC>with smith_history as
        (select person_id, name, father_person_id
         from (values
         (1,'Thomas',null),
         (2,'Clara',null),
         (3,'Samuel',1),
         (4,'Charles',1),
         (5,'Beth',3),
         (6,'Steven',4),
         (7,'Sarah',6),
         (8,'Robert',4),
         (9,'Dorothy',8),
         (10,'George',8))
           as smith(person_id, name, father_person_id)
```

```
     )
  select name, sys_connect_by_path(name, '->') lineage
  from smith_history
    start with name = 'Thomas'
    connect by father_person_id = prior person_id;
+---------+-----------------------------------+
| NAME    | LINEAGE                           |
|---------|-----------------------------------|
| Thomas  | ->Thomas                          |
| Samuel  | ->Thomas->Samuel                  |
| Charles | ->Thomas->Charles                 |
| Beth    | ->Thomas->Samuel->Beth            |
| Steven  | ->Thomas->Charles->Steven         |
| Robert  | ->Thomas->Charles->Robert         |
| Sarah   | ->Thomas->Charles->Steven->Sarah  |
| Dorothy | ->Thomas->Charles->Robert->Dorothy |
| George  | ->Thomas->Charles->Robert->George |
+---------+-----------------------------------+
```

Chapter 10

See "Test Your Knowledge" on page 174.

Solution to Exercise 10-1

Add a column named order_status to the following query that will use a case expression to return the value 'order now' if the ps_availqty value is less than 100, 'order soon' if the ps_availqty value is between 101 and 1000, and 'plenty in stock' otherwise.

```
PUBLIC>select ps_partkey, ps_suppkey, ps_availqty
       from partsupp
       where ps_partkey between 148300 and 148450;
+------------+------------+-------------+
| PS_PARTKEY | PS_SUPPKEY | PS_AVAILQTY |
|------------+------------+-------------|
|    148308  |     8309   |     9570    |
|    148308  |      823   |     7201    |
|    148308  |     3337   |     7917    |
|    148308  |     5851   |     8257    |
|    148358  |     8359   |     9839    |
|    148358  |      873   |     6917    |
|    148358  |     3387   |     1203    |
|    148358  |     5901   |        1    |
|    148408  |     8409   |       74    |
|    148408  |      923   |      341    |
|    148408  |     3437   |     4847    |
|    148408  |     5951   |     1985    |
+------------+------------+-------------+
```

```
PUBLIC>select ps_partkey, ps_suppkey, ps_availqty,
        case
          when ps_availqty <= 100 then 'order now'
          when ps_availqty <= 1000 then 'order soon'
          else 'plenty in stock'
        end as order_status
      from partsupp
      where ps_partkey between 148300 and 148450;
+------------+------------+-------------+----------------+
| PS_PARTKEY | PS_SUPPKEY | PS_AVAILQTY | ORDER_STATUS   |
|------------+------------+-------------+----------------|
|     148308 |       8309 |        9570 | plenty in stock |
|     148308 |        823 |        7201 | plenty in stock |
|     148308 |       3337 |        7917 | plenty in stock |
|     148308 |       5851 |        8257 | plenty in stock |
|     148358 |       8359 |        9839 | plenty in stock |
|     148358 |        873 |        6917 | plenty in stock |
|     148358 |       3387 |        1203 | plenty in stock |
|     148358 |       5901 |           1 | order now       |
|     148408 |       8409 |          74 | order now       |
|     148408 |        923 |         341 | order soon      |
|     148408 |       3437 |        4847 | plenty in stock |
|     148408 |       5951 |        1985 | plenty in stock |
+------------+------------+-------------+----------------+
```

Solution to Exercise 10-2

Rewrite the following query to use a searched case expression instead of a simple case
expression.

```
PUBLIC>select o_orderdate, o_custkey,
        case o_orderstatus
          when 'P' then 'Partial'
          when 'F' then 'Filled'
          when 'O' then 'Open'
        end status
      from orders
      where o_orderkey > 5999500;
+-------------+-----------+---------+
| O_ORDERDATE | O_CUSTKEY | STATUS  |
|-------------+-----------+---------|
| 1993-02-24  |     80807 | Filled  |
| 1995-05-06  |    124231 | Partial |
| 1995-06-03  |    141032 | Partial |
| 1994-07-20  |     30140 | Filled  |
| 1998-02-16  |     86125 | Open    |
| 1996-09-14  |    108310 | Open    |
| 1994-01-09  |     40673 | Filled  |
| 1995-11-19  |    124754 | Open    |
+-------------+-----------+---------+
```

```
PUBLIC>select o_orderdate, o_custkey,
         case
            when o_orderstatus = 'P' then 'Partial'
            when o_orderstatus = 'F' then 'Filled'
            when o_orderstatus = 'O' then 'Open'
         end status
      from orders
      where o_orderkey > 5999500;
+------------+----------+---------+
| O_ORDERDATE | O_CUSTKEY | STATUS  |
|------------+----------+---------|
| 1993-02-24 |     80807 | Filled  |
| 1995-05-06 |    124231 | Partial |
| 1995-06-03 |    141032 | Partial |
| 1994-07-20 |     30140 | Filled  |
| 1998-02-16 |     86125 | Open    |
| 1996-09-14 |    108310 | Open    |
| 1994-01-09 |     40673 | Filled  |
| 1995-11-19 |    124754 | Open    |
+------------+----------+---------+
```

Solution to Exercise 10-3

The following query returns the number of suppliers in each region:

```
PUBLIC>select r_name, count(*)
      from nation n
      inner join region r on r.r_regionkey = n.n_regionkey
      inner join supplier s on s.s_nationkey = n.n_nationkey
      group by r_name;
+-------------+----------+
| R_NAME      | COUNT(*) |
|-------------+----------|
| AMERICA     |     1532 |
| AFRICA      |     1444 |
| EUROPE      |     1474 |
| MIDDLE EAST |     1491 |
| ASIA        |     1459 |
+-------------+----------+
```

Modify this query to use **case** expressions to pivot this data so that it looks as follows:

```
+---------+--------+--------+-------------+------+
| AMERICA | AFRICA | EUROPE | MIDDLE_EAST | ASIA |
|---------+--------+--------+-------------+------|
|    1532 |   1444 |   1474 |        1491 | 1459 |
+---------+--------+--------+-------------+------+

PUBLIC>select
         sum(case when r_name = 'AMERICA' then 1
               else 0 end) as America,
         sum(case when r_name = 'AFRICA' then 1
               else 0 end) as Africa,
```

```
            sum(case when r_name = 'EUROPE' then 1
                    else 0 end) as Europe,
            sum(case when r_name = 'MIDDLE EAST' then 1
                    else 0 end) as Middle_East,
            sum(case when r_name = 'ASIA' then 1
                    else 0 end) as Asia
        from nation n
        inner join region r on r.r_regionkey = n.n_regionkey
        inner join supplier s on s.s_nationkey = n.n_nationkey ;
+---------+--------+--------+-------------+------+
| AMERICA | AFRICA | EUROPE | MIDDLE_EAST | ASIA |
|---------+--------+--------+-------------+------|
|    1532 |   1444 |   1474 |        1491 | 1459 |
+---------+--------+--------+-------------+------+
```

Chapter 11

See "Test Your Knowledge" on page 183.

Solution to Exercise 11-1

Generate a unit of work to transfer $50 from account 123 to account 789. You will need to insert two rows into the transactions table and update two rows in the account table. Use the following table definitions/data:

```
                Account:
account_id avail_balance last_activity_date
---------- ------------- --------------------
123        500           2023-07-10 20:53:27
789        75            2023-06-22 15:18:35


                Transactions:
txn_id txn_date    account_id txn_type_cd amount
------ ----------- ---------- ----------- --------
1001   2023-05-15  123        C           500
1002   2023-06-01  789        C           75
```

Use txn_type_cd = 'C' to indicate a credit (addition), and txn_type_cd = 'D' to indicate a debit (subtraction).

```
begin transaction;

insert into transactions
  (txn_id, txn_date, account_id, txn_type_cd, amount)
values (1003, current_timestamp(), 123, 'D', 50);

insert into transactions
  (txn_id, txn_date, account_id, txn_type_cd, amount)
values (1004, current_timestamp(), 789, 'C', 50);

update account
```

```
set avail_balance = available_balance - 50,
  last_activity_date = current_timestamp()
where account_id = 123;

update account
set avail_balance = available_balance + 50,
  last_activity_date = current_timestamp()
where account_id = 789;

commit;
```

Chapter 12

See "Test Your Knowledge" on page 197.

Solution to Exercise 12-1

Consider the following query and result set against a view:

```
PUBLIC>select * from region_totalsales_vw;
+-------------+----------------+
| REGION_NAME | SUM_TOTALPRICE |
|-------------+----------------|
| ASIA        |  4378591175.90 |
| AMERICA     |  4321075685.27 |
| EUROPE      |  4391712838.03 |
| AFRICA      |  4239225325.42 |
| MIDDLE EAST |  4322198235.40 |
+-------------+----------------+
```

Write the view definition for `region_totalsales_vw`. You will need to join the `Region`, `Nation`, `Customer`, and `Orders` tables. Your column names should match what is shown in the result set.

```
create view region_totalsales_vw as
select r.r_name as region_name,
  sum(o.o_totalprice) as sum_totalprice
from region r
inner join nation n on r.r_regionkey = n.n_regionkey
inner join customer c on c.c_nationkey = n.n_nationkey
inner join orders o on o.o_custkey = c.c_custkey
group by r.r_name;
```

Solution to Exercise 12-2

The `Supplier` table looks as follows:

```
PUBLIC>desc supplier;

+-------------+---------------+--------+-------+
| name        | type          | kind   | null? |
```

```
| ------------+---------------+--------+------- |
| S_SUPPKEY   | NUMBER(38,0)  | COLUMN | Y      |
| S_NAME      | VARCHAR(25)   | COLUMN | Y      |
| S_ADDRESS   | VARCHAR(40)   | COLUMN | Y      |
| S_NATIONKEY | NUMBER(38,0)  | COLUMN | Y      |
| S_PHONE     | VARCHAR(15)   | COLUMN | Y      |
| S_ACCTBAL   | NUMBER(12,2)  | COLUMN | Y      |
| S_COMMENT   | VARCHAR(101)  | COLUMN | Y      |
+-------------+---------------+--------+-------+
```

Create a view called `supplier_vw` that includes the following fields:

- `s_suppkey` as `keyval`

- `s_name` as `supplier_name`

- `partial_phone` (obscure all but last 4 digits of `s_phone`)

- `acct_status` (`'negative'` if `s_acctbal` < 0, `'positive'` otherwise)

For testing, you can work with `s_suppkey` between 1 and 50. To obscure the phone number, replace any digit (except the last four) with a `*`. There are many possible Snowflake functions that could be used to obscure part of the phone number, including `substr()`, `right()`, `length()`, `translate()`, `regexp_replace()`, etc. Results should look like:

```
PUBLIC>select * from supplier_vw
        where keyval between 1 and 50;
+--------+--------------------+------------------+-------------|
| KEYVAL | SUPPLIER_NAME      | PARTIAL_PHONE    | ACCT_STATUS |
|--------+--------------------+------------------+-------------|
|      1 | Supplier#000000001 | **-***-***-1736  | positive    |
|      4 | Supplier#000000004 | **-***-***-7479  | positive    |
|      7 | Supplier#000000007 | **-***-***-2201  | positive    |
|      9 | Supplier#000000009 | **-***-***-8662  | positive    |
|     10 | Supplier#000000010 | **-***-***-8585  | positive    |
|     11 | Supplier#000000011 | **-***-***-1505  | positive    |
|     12 | Supplier#000000012 | **-***-***-7181  | positive    |
|     13 | Supplier#000000013 | **-***-***-7813  | positive    |
|     14 | Supplier#000000014 | **-***-***-5058  | positive    |
|     15 | Supplier#000000015 | **-***-***-6394  | positive    |
|     16 | Supplier#000000016 | **-***-***-4215  | positive    |
|     17 | Supplier#000000017 | **-***-***-9219  | positive    |
|     18 | Supplier#000000018 | **-***-***-1115  | positive    |
|     19 | Supplier#000000019 | **-***-***-2731  | positive    |
|     20 | Supplier#000000020 | **-***-***-6730  | positive    |
|     21 | Supplier#000000021 | **-***-***-5816  | positive    |
|     22 | Supplier#000000022 | **-***-***-2814  | negative    |
|     23 | Supplier#000000023 | **-***-***-5776  | positive    |
|     24 | Supplier#000000024 | **-***-***-2254  | positive    |
|     25 | Supplier#000000025 | **-***-***-3541  | positive    |
|     26 | Supplier#000000026 | **-***-***-4436  | positive    |
```

```
|    27 | Supplier#000000027 | **-***-***-2028 | positive   |
|    28 | Supplier#000000028 | **-***-***-8460 | negative   |
|    29 | Supplier#000000029 | **-***-***-5922 | negative   |
|    30 | Supplier#000000030 | **-***-***-4852 | positive   |
|    31 | Supplier#000000031 | **-***-***-4159 | positive   |
|    33 | Supplier#000000033 | **-***-***-9374 | positive   |
|    35 | Supplier#000000035 | **-***-***-5245 | positive   |
|    36 | Supplier#000000036 | **-***-***-3679 | positive   |
|    37 | Supplier#000000037 | **-***-***-1330 | positive   |
|    39 | Supplier#000000039 | **-***-***-5633 | positive   |
|    41 | Supplier#000000041 | **-***-***-2525 | positive   |
|    42 | Supplier#000000042 | **-***-***-6317 | positive   |
|    43 | Supplier#000000043 | **-***-***-4862 | positive   |
|    45 | Supplier#000000045 | **-***-***-8862 | positive   |
|    47 | Supplier#000000047 | **-***-***-4471 | positive   |
|    48 | Supplier#000000048 | **-***-***-9498 | positive   |
+---------+--------------------+------------------+------------+

create view supplier_vw as
select s_suppkey as supplier_key, s_name as supplier_name,
  concat(translate(substr(s_phone,1,length(s_phone) - 4),
    '0123456789','**********'),
    right(s_phone,4)) as partial_phone,
  case
    when s_acctbal < 0 then 'negative'
    else 'positive'
  end as account_status
from supplier;
```

Chapter 13

See "Test Your Knowledge" on page 217.

Solution to Exercise 13-1

Retrieve the names of all tables along with their row counts using the `informa
tion_schema.tables` view. Retrieve only tables having more than 1000 rows.

```
PUBLIC>select table_name, row_count
      from information_schema.tables
      where row_count > 1000;
+------------+-----------+
| TABLE_NAME | ROW_COUNT |
|------------+-----------|
| CUSTOMER   |     66076 |
| PART       |      4000 |
| SUPPLIER   |      7400 |
| LINEITEM   |    119989 |
| PARTSUPP   |     16000 |
| ORDERS     |    115269 |
+------------+-----------+
```

Solution to Exercise 13-2

Write a query against `account_usage.views` that returns the name of any view that has been created more than once.

```
PUBLIC>select table_name
       from snowflake.account_usage.views
       group by table_name
       having count(*) > 1;
+----------------------+
| TABLE_NAME           |
|----------------------|
| ORDER_CALCULATION_VW |
| SUPPLIER_VW          |
| YEARLY_PART_SALES_VW |
+----------------------+
```

Chapter 14

See "Test Your Knowledge" on page 241.

Solution to Exercise 14-1

Add two columns to generate rankings for `num_orders` and `tot_sales`. The highest value should receive a ranking of 1.

```
PUBLIC>select date_part(year, o_orderdate) as order_year,
       count(*) as num_orders, sum(o_totalprice) as tot_sales,
       rank() over (order by count(*) desc) as ordr_rnk,
       rank() over (order by sum(o_totalprice) desc) as sls_rnk
    from orders
    group by date_part(year, o_orderdate);
+------------+------------+----------------+----------+---------+
| ORDER_YEAR | NUM_ORDERS |      TOT_SALES | ORDR_RNK | SLS_RNK |
|------------+------------+----------------+----------+---------|
|       1995 |      17637 | 3317521810.43  |        2 |       1 |
|       1992 |      17506 | 3309734764.39  |        3 |       2 |
|       1996 |      17657 | 3296373352.79  |        1 |       3 |
|       1994 |      17479 | 3278473892.67  |        4 |       4 |
|       1993 |      17392 | 3270416270.14  |        6 |       5 |
|       1997 |      17408 | 3255086721.08  |        5 |       6 |
|       1998 |      10190 | 1925196448.52  |        7 |       7 |
+------------+------------+----------------+----------+---------+
```

Solution to Exercise 14-2

Add a `qualify` clause to the query in Exercise 14-1 to return only rows where either ranking is 2 or 6.

```
PUBLIC>select date_part(year, o_orderdate) as order_year,
       count(*) as num_orders, sum(o_totalprice) as tot_sales,
       rank() over (order by count(*) desc) ordr_rnk,
       rank() over (order by sum(o_totalprice) desc) sls_rnk
    from orders
    group by date_part(year, o_orderdate)
    qualify ordr_rnk in (2,6)  or sls_rnk in (2,6);
+------------+------------+----------------+----------+----------+
| ORDER_YEAR | NUM_ORDERS |     TOT_SALES  | ORDR_RNK | SLS_RNK  |
|------------+------------+----------------+----------+----------|
|       1995 |      17637 | 3317521810.43  |       2  |       1  |
|       1992 |      17506 | 3309734764.39  |       3  |       2  |
|       1993 |      17392 | 3270416270.14  |       6  |       5  |
|       1997 |      17408 | 3255086721.08  |       5  |       6  |
+------------+------------+----------------+----------+----------+
```

Solution to Exercise 14-3

Starting again with the original query, add a column to compute the total sales across all years (grand total). The value will be the same for each row.

```
PUBLIC>select date_part(year, o_orderdate) as order_year,
       count(*) as num_orders, sum(o_totalprice) as tot_sales,
       sum(sum(o_totalprice)) over () grnd_tot_sales
    from orders
    group by date_part(year, o_orderdate);
+------------+------------+----------------+-----------------+
| ORDER_YEAR | NUM_ORDERS |     TOT_SALES  | GRND_TOT_SALES  |
|------------+------------+----------------+-----------------|
|       1997 |      17408 | 3255086721.08  | 21652803260.02  |
|       1998 |      10190 | 1925196448.52  | 21652803260.02  |
|       1994 |      17479 | 3278473892.67  | 21652803260.02  |
|       1992 |      17506 | 3309734764.39  | 21652803260.02  |
|       1995 |      17637 | 3317521810.43  | 21652803260.02  |
|       1993 |      17392 | 3270416270.14  | 21652803260.02  |
|       1996 |      17657 | 3296373352.79  | 21652803260.02  |
+------------+------------+----------------+-----------------+
```

Solution to Exercise 14-4

Modify the window function from Exercise 14-3 to generate a running sum instead of a grand total. Each row's value should be the sum of itself and all prior years.

```
PUBLIC>select date_part(year, o_orderdate) as order_year,
       count(*) as num_orders, sum(o_totalprice) as tot_sales,
       sum(sum(o_totalprice))
         over (order by date_part(year, o_orderdate)
         rows unbounded preceding) rng_tot_sales
    from orders
    group by date_part(year, o_orderdate);
+------------+------------+----------------+-----------------+
| ORDER_YEAR | NUM_ORDERS |     TOT_SALES  | RNG_TOT_SALES   |
```

```
|------------+------------+----------------+----------------|
|       1992 |      17506 |  3309734764.39 |   3309734764.39 |
|       1993 |      17392 |  3270416270.14 |   6580151034.53 |
|       1994 |      17479 |  3278473892.67 |   9858624927.20 |
|       1995 |      17637 |  3317521810.43 |  13176146737.63 |
|       1996 |      17657 |  3296373352.79 |  16472520090.42 |
|       1997 |      17408 |  3255086721.08 |  19727606811.50 |
|       1998 |      10190 |  1925196448.52 |  21652803260.02 |
+------------+------------+----------------+----------------+
```

Chapter 15

See "Test Your Knowledge" on page 268.

Solution to Exercise 15-1

Write a script that declares a cursor for the query select max(o_totalprice) from orders, opens the cursor, fetches the results into a numeric variable, closes the cursor, and returns the value fetched from the query.

```
declare
  v_prc number;
  v_cur cursor for select max(o_totalprice) from orders;
begin
  open v_cur;
  fetch v_cur into v_prc;
  close v_cur;
  return v_prc;
end;
```

Solution to Exercise 15-2

Write a script that uses a counter-based for loop to iterate over the range 1 to 100. Break out of the loop after the 60th iteration.

```
begin
  for n in 1 to 100 do
    if (n > 60) then
      break;
    end if;
  end for;
end;
```

Solution to Exercise 15-3

Write a script that declares an exception with number -20200 and the string 'The sky is falling!', raises the exception, catches it, and reraises it.

```
declare
  e_my_excptn exception (-20200, 'The sky is falling!');
```

```
begin
  raise e_my_excptn;
exception
  when e_my_excptn then
    raise;
end;
```

Solution to Exercise 15-4

Write a script that uses a cursor-based for loop to iterate through all n_name values in the Nation table. Break out of the loop when 'EGYPT' is retrieved.

```
declare
  v_cur cursor for select n_name from nation;
begin
  for rec in v_cur do
    if (rec.n_name = 'EGYPT') then
      break;
    end if;
  end for;
end;
```

Chapter 16

See "Test Your Knowledge" on page 284.

Solution to Exercise 16-1

Turn the following anonymous script into a stored procedure named rectangle_area() with numeric parameters p_width and p_length:

```
declare
  v_width number := 5;
  v_height number := 8;
begin
  return v_width * v_height;
end;

create procedure rectangle_area(p_width number, p_length number)
returns number
language sql
as
begin
  return p_width * p_length;
end;
```

Solution to Exercise 16-2

Write a stored procedure named `get_parts_by_type()` with a single parameter `p_type_name` (type varchar). The stored procedure should return a result set consisting of the `p_partkey` and `p_name` columns from the `Part` table, for rows whose `p_type` column matches the parameter value. Call the procedure with parameter value `'SMALL PLATED NICKEL'` or `'PROMO BRUSHED STEEL'`, both of which should return 23 rows:

```
create procedure get_parts_by_type(p_type_name varchar)
returns table(partkey number, name varchar)
language sql
as
declare
  v_results resultset;
begin
  v_results :=
    (select p_partkey, p_name from part
     where p_type = :p_type_name);
  return table(v_results);
end;

PUBLIC>call get_parts_by_type('PROMO BRUSHED STEEL');
+---------+-------------------------------------------+
| PARTKEY | NAME                                      |
|---------+-------------------------------------------|
|  181158 | pink grey navy khaki drab                 |
|  125808 | wheat chocolate chartreuse deep beige     |
|    5858 | beige green sienna lemon firebrick        |
|  134908 | turquoise dodger almond bisque medium     |
|  198808 | magenta cornflower forest azure light     |
|  199058 | metallic violet slate khaki thistle       |
|   19758 | dark lemon black red sienna               |
|   86008 | dodger cyan royal midnight drab           |
|   54108 | orchid black spring forest antique        |
|   88058 | lawn midnight frosted maroon light        |
|   54858 | orchid lime black orange burnished        |
|   90158 | lawn green honeydew smoke linen           |
|   60408 | chartreuse magenta lawn aquamarine medium |
|   67958 | tan azure linen mint honeydew             |
|   71008 | orchid floral beige blue turquoise        |
|  145758 | hot chartreuse tan dim steel              |
|  152808 | papaya blue deep white red                |
|  155308 | blanched red bisque lemon spring          |
|  157508 | goldenrod orange navy tomato medium       |
|  159158 | blanched dark cornsilk cyan goldenrod     |
|  162058 | magenta honeydew hot burlywood lavender   |
|  166708 | smoke navajo maroon brown plum            |
|  174108 | goldenrod rose peru forest antique        |
+---------+-------------------------------------------+
```

Chapter 17

See "Test Your Knowledge" on page 298.

Solution to Exercise 17-1

Write a scalar UDF named `fn_circle_area()` that takes a single numeric parameter `p_radius` and returns the area of a circle (π * p_radius^2). The UDF should return type `float`.

```
PUBLIC>create function fn_circle_area(p_radius number)
      returns float
      language sql
      as
      'pi() * square(p_radius)';
+-----------------------------------------------+
| status                                        |
|-----------------------------------------------|
| Function FN_CIRCLE_AREA successfully created. |
+-----------------------------------------------+

PUBLIC>select fn_circle_area(5);
+-------------------+
| FN_CIRCLE_AREA(5) |
|-------------------|
|       78.53981634 |
+-------------------+
```

Solution to Exercise 17-2

Write a table function named `fn_get_parts_by_type()` with a single parameter `p_type_name` (type varchar). The table function should return a result set consisting of the `p_partkey` and `p_name` columns from the `Part` table, for rows whose `p_type` column matches the parameter value. Call the function with parameter value `'SMALL PLATED NICKEL'` or `'PROMO BRUSHED STEEL'`, both of which should return 23 rows.

```
PUBLIC>create function fn_get_parts_by_type(p_type_name varchar)
      returns table(
        p_partkey number,
        p_name varchar)
      language sql
      as
      'select p_partkey, p_name from part
       where p_type = p_type_name';
+--------------------------------------------------------+
| status                                                 |
|--------------------------------------------------------|
| Function FN_GET_PARTS_BY_TYPE successfully created.    |
```

```
+-------------------------------------------------------+

PUBLIC>select *
       from table(fn_get_parts_by_type('SMALL PLATED NICKEL'));
+-----------+-------------------------------------------+
| P_PARTKEY | P_NAME                                    |
|-----------+-------------------------------------------|
|    121458 | maroon dark burnished cyan dim            |
|    125608 | khaki rose gainsboro violet black         |
|      2658 | burnished royal lemon steel drab          |
|    135608 | cyan sandy navy floral black              |
|    139208 | wheat dark khaki tomato azure             |
|     13808 | black cyan burlywood chocolate forest     |
|     16358 | navy purple chartreuse plum aquamarine    |
|     17158 | antique burnished light metallic blush    |
|     18708 | aquamarine steel turquoise slate olive    |
|     80208 | slate lavender violet indian floral       |
|     94108 | wheat lace green cream rosy               |
|    101808 | sienna royal floral rosy thistle          |
|     67258 | honeydew maroon firebrick steel seashell  |
|     69858 | turquoise aquamarine brown green antique  |
|     71758 | puff white salmon lawn seashell           |
|     74308 | tan aquamarine powder steel rosy          |
|     78608 | snow tomato tan indian navy               |
|    145808 | papaya misty medium green lawn            |
|     21658 | maroon spring azure light almond          |
|     30008 | almond forest mint midnight violet        |
|     39808 | cyan firebrick salmon drab red            |
|    170408 | smoke bisque chocolate antique cyan       |
|    111108 | salmon peru cornsilk beige hot            |
+-----------+-------------------------------------------+
```

Solution to Exercise 17-3

Query the fn_get_parts_by_type() table function created in Exercise 17-2, but instead of passing in a string (i.e., 'SMALL PLATED NICKEL'), join the table function to a query against the Part table that retrieves the distinct set of values where p_type is like 'STANDARD % STEEL'. Retrieve only the columns returned by the table function.

```
PUBLIC>select gpt.*
       from (select distinct p_type from part
             where p_type like 'STANDARD % STEEL') p
       cross join table(fn_get_parts_by_type(p.p_type)) as gpt;
+-----------+-------------------------------------------+
| P_PARTKEY | P_NAME                                    |
|-----------+-------------------------------------------|
|    120258 | floral medium seashell hot grey           |
|    122958 | navy papaya honeydew rose tan             |
|    127008 | sky blanched dark orange salmon           |
|    130358 | peach azure lace sandy navy               |
|    130858 | cyan magenta lace chocolate black         |
```

```
|    184908 | seashell chartreuse peach peru khaki    |
|    195058 | spring violet pale puff indian          |
|     40708 | rosy ivory maroon peach sienna          |
|     47908 | honeydew pink maroon steel cream        |
|     80358 | turquoise orchid sandy dodger rosy      |
|     28358 | puff cream ivory antique almond         |
... 106 rows omitted
|     33208 | almond drab medium chartreuse salmon    |
|     34108 | metallic grey misty beige orchid        |
|    165958 | cyan rosy papaya cream white            |
|    166558 | chiffon pale frosted chocolate dark     |
|    166858 | tan firebrick pink chiffon peru         |
|    107258 | frosted tan pale burlywood rosy         |
|    172408 | azure blue gainsboro light white        |
|    175208 | navy grey floral tomato goldenrod       |
|    117308 | rose rosy lavender floral mint          |
+-----------+-----------------------------------------+
```

Solution to Exercise 17-4

Execute the query `select 23 * 75`. Run another query to find the `query_id` of the query you just executed.

```
PUBLIC>select 23 * 75;
+---------+
| 23 * 75 |
|---------|
|    1725 |
+---------+

PUBLIC>select query_id,
         substr(query_text, 1, 23) partial_query_text
       from table(information_schema.query_history(
                                     result_limit => 10))
       where query_text like '%75%';

+--------------------------------------+--------------------+
| QUERY_ID                             | PARTIAL_QUERY_TEXT |
|--------------------------------------+--------------------|
| 01acd01d-0d04-96b8-0002-9fde002450ea | select query_id,   |
| 01acd01c-0d04-96b8-0002-9fde002450e6 | select 23 * 75;    |
+--------------------------------------+--------------------+
(your query_id value will be different)
```

Chapter 18

See "Test Your Knowledge" on page 314.

Solution to Exercise 18-1

Given the following query against the Part table:

```
PUBLIC>select p_partkey, p_name, p_brand
       from part
       where p_mfgr = 'Manufacturer#1'
         and p_type = 'ECONOMY POLISHED STEEL';
+-----------+-------------------------------------------+---------+
| P_PARTKEY | P_NAME                                    | P_BRAND |
|-----------+-------------------------------------------+---------|
|     95608 | royal thistle floral frosted midnight     | Brand#12 |
|    100308 | azure honeydew grey aquamarine black      | Brand#11 |
|    103808 | steel lemon tomato brown blush            | Brand#13 |
|     68458 | spring white lime dim peru                | Brand#14 |
|     70808 | gainsboro chiffon papaya green khaki      | Brand#12 |
|    112758 | turquoise saddle moccasin magenta pink    | Brand#14 |
+-----------+-------------------------------------------+---------+
```

Write a query that generates a JSON document containing the same results. The document should consist of an object named Parts containing an array of 6 entries with tags Partkey, Name, and Brand.

```
PUBLIC>select object_construct('Parts',
         array_agg(
           object_construct(
             'Partkey', p_partkey,
             'Name', p_name,
             'Brand', p_brand
       ))) as part_doc
       from part
       where p_mfgr = 'Manufacturer#1'
         and p_type = 'ECONOMY POLISHED STEEL';
+----------------------------------------------------------+
| PART_DOC                                                 |
|----------------------------------------------------------|
| {                                                        |
|   "Parts": [                                             |
|     {                                                    |
|       "Brand": "Brand#12",                               |
|       "Name": "royal thistle floral frosted midnight",   |
|       "Partkey": 95608                                   |
|     },                                                   |
|     {                                                    |
|       "Brand": "Brand#11",                               |
|       "Name": "azure honeydew grey aquamarine black",    |
|       "Partkey": 100308                                  |
|     },                                                   |
```

```
|   {                                                     |
|       "Brand": "Brand#13",                              |
|       "Name": "steel lemon tomato brown blush",         |
|       "Partkey": 103808                                 |
|   },                                                    |
|   {                                                     |
|       "Brand": "Brand#14",                              |
|       "Name": "spring white lime dim peru",             |
|       "Partkey": 68458                                  |
|   },                                                    |
|   {                                                     |
|       "Brand": "Brand#12",                              |
|       "Name": "gainsboro chiffon papaya green khaki",   |
|       "Partkey": 70808                                  |
|   },                                                    |
|   {                                                     |
|       "Brand": "Brand#14",                              |
|       "Name": "turquoise saddle moccasin magenta pink", |
|       "Partkey": 112758                                 |
|   }                                                     |
| ]                                                       |
| }                                                       |
+---------------------------------------------------------+
```

Solution to Exercise 18-2

Write an insert statement that adds the JSON document generated by Exercise 18-1 to the my_docs table. (Use the JSON document returned by the query, not the query itself).

```
PUBLIC>insert into my_docs
       select parse_json(
       '{
         "Parts": [
           {
             "Brand": "Brand#12",
             "Name": "royal thistle floral frosted midnight",
             "Partkey": 95608
           },
           {
             "Brand": "Brand#11",
             "Name": "azure honeydew grey aquamarine black",
             "Partkey": 100308
           },
           {
             "Brand": "Brand#13",
             "Name": "steel lemon tomato brown blush",
             "Partkey": 103808
           },
           {
             "Brand": "Brand#14",
             "Name": "spring white lime dim peru",
```

```
          "Partkey": 68458
        },
        {
          "Brand": "Brand#12",
          "Name": "gainsboro chiffon papaya green khaki",
          "Partkey": 70808
        },
        {
          "Brand": "Brand#14",
          "Name": "turquoise saddle moccasin magenta pink",
          "Partkey": 112758
        }
      ]
    }');
+------------------------+
| number of rows inserted |
|------------------------|
|                      1 |
+------------------------+
```

Solution to Exercise 18-3

Given the following subquery named `city_doc`:

```
with city_doc as
 (select parse_json(
  '{
    "Major_Cities": [
      {
        "Country": "USA",
        "Cities" : [
          {
            "City_Name": "Chicago",
            "Region_Name": "Illinois"
          },
          {
            "City_Name": "New York City",
            "Region_Name": "New York"
          },
          {
            "City_Name": "Los Angeles",
            "Region_Name": "California"
          }
        ]
      },
      {
        "Country": "Canada",
        "Cities" : [
          {
            "City_Name": "Vancouver",
            "Region_Name": "British Columbia"
          },
```

```
        {
          "City_Name": "Toronto",
          "Region_Name": "Ontario"
        }
      ]
    }
  ]
}') as d
)
```

Write a query against `city_doc` that will generate the following output:

```
+--------------+---------------+------------------+
| COUNTRY_NAME | CITY_NAME     | REGION_NAME      |
|--------------+---------------+------------------|
| USA          | Chicago       | Illinois         |
| USA          | New York City | New York         |
| USA          | Los Angeles   | California       |
| Canada       | Vancouver     | British Columbia |
| Canada       | Toronto       | Ontario          |
+--------------+---------------+------------------+

PUBLIC>with city_doc as
        (select parse_json(
         '{
           "Major_Cities": [
             {
               "Country": "USA",
               "Cities" : [
                 {
                   "City_Name": "Chicago",
                   "Region_Name": "Illinois"
                 },
                 {
                   "City_Name": "New York City",
                   "Region_Name": "New York"
                 },
                 {
                   "City_Name": "Los Angeles",
                   "Region_Name": "California"
                 }
               ]
             },
             {
               "Country": "Canada",
               "Cities" : [
                 {
                   "City_Name": "Vancouver",
                   "Region_Name": "British Columbia"
                 },
                 {
                   "City_Name": "Toronto",
                   "Region_Name": "Ontario"
```

```
                }
              ]
            }
          ]
        }') as d
      )
    select cntry.value:Country::varchar as country_name,
      cty.value:City_Name::varchar as city_name,
      cty.value:Region_Name::varchar as region_name
    from city_doc
    inner join lateral
      flatten(input => d:Major_Cities) cntry
    inner join lateral
      flatten(input => cntry.value:Cities) cty;
+--------------+----------------+------------------+
| COUNTRY_NAME | CITY_NAME      | REGION_NAME      |
|--------------+----------------+------------------|
| USA          | Chicago        | Illinois         |
| USA          | New York City  | New York         |
| USA          | Los Angeles    | California       |
| Canada       | Vancouver      | British Columbia |
| Canada       | Toronto        | Ontario          |
+--------------+----------------+------------------+
```

Index

Symbols

!= (not equal) operator, 25

$$ (dollar signs) delimiting complex strings, 72

% (percent sign), matching 0, 1, or more characters, 28

' ' (single quotes)
  enclosing values for character columns, 72
  strings containing, delimiting, 72

() (parentheses)
  using for calculation precedence, 95
  using for grouping set operations, 67
  using in condition evaluation, 22
    with not operator, 23

: (colon)
  preceding bind variables, 275
  separating keys from values, 78

:: (cast) operator, 77, 97, 106

< (less than) operator, 25, 132

<= (less than or equal to) operator, 132

= (equality) operator, 132

> (greater than) operator, 25, 132

>= (greater than or equal to) operator, 132

[] (square brackets), delimiting array literals, 77

_ (underscore), matching a single character, 28

{} (curly braces), creating object literals with, 78

|| string concatenation operator, 92

A

abs function, 96

accounts, setting up with Snowflake, xiii

account_usage schema, 212-217
  query showing all SQL statements issued
    from an account, 216
  views in

advantages over views in information-
    tion_schema, 215
  disadvantage of using, 216

administrative scripts
  generating using get_ddl function and
    information_schema, 210-212
  generating using information_schema
    metadata, 209

aggregate functions, 97, 110, 111-115
  count, 113
  count and max functions, use in correlated
    subquery, 157
  group by clause and, 112
  listagg, 114
  min, max, avg, and sum functions, 113
  use with partition by and/or order by clau-
    ses, 232

aggregation of data, using views, 193-195

aliases
  column, 7, 231
    in compound queries with set opera-
      tions, 66
  subquery, 141
  table, 43, 142, 290
    in join of table to itself, 51

all operator, 135

alter account command, 74

alter session command
  changing time zone in your session, 74
  changing timestamp output format, 101
  enabling or disabling autocommit, 179

Amazon Web Services (AWS), xi

and operator, 21
  using between each condition, 23

About the Author

Alan Beaulieu has been designing, building, and implementing custom database applications for over 25 years. He is the author of *Learning SQL* and *Mastering Oracle SQL* and has written an online course on SQL for the University of California. He currently runs his own consulting company that specializes in database design and development in the fields of financial services and telecommunications. Alan has a Bachelor of Science degree in operations research from Cornell University School of Engineering.

Colophon

The animal on the cover of *Learning Snowflake SQL and Scripting* is a Rocky Mountain goat (*Oreamnos americanus*), also known as a mountain goat. Rocky Mountain goats live in the mountainous regions of western North American at elevations as high as 13,000 feet and temperatures as low as –51°F.

Their ability to survive at high altitudes provides defense against predators, such as bears and wolves, but they migrate to lower elevations as well. These goats have outer coats of white fur that camouflages them in the snow, which they molt in the spring. Rocky Mountain goats also have distinctive horns and beards, as well as hooves that are particularly suited for rock climbing. Goats are herbivores and have a lifespan of 12–15 years in the wild, limited primarily by the dulling of their teeth.

Males fight each other for show during mating season. Females (or nannies) usually have multiple partners in a mating season and form groups with other females known as *nursery bands*. Kids are able to walk within hours of birth and stay close to mothers for about a year.

The current IUCN conservation status of the mountain goat is "Least Concern." Many of the animals on O'Reilly covers are endangered; all of them are important to the world.

The cover illustration is by Karen Montgomery, based on an antique line engraving from the Museum of Natural History. The cover fonts are Gilroy Semibold and Guardian Sans. The text font is Adobe Minion Pro; the heading font is Adobe Myriad Condensed; and the code font is Dalton Maag's Ubuntu Mono.

O'REILLY®

Learn from experts.
Become one yourself.

Books | Live online courses
Instant answers | Virtual events
Videos | Interactive learning

Get started at oreilly.com.

Printed in the USA
CPSIA information can be obtained
at www.ICGtesting.com
JSHW051344041223
53222JS00012B/128

9 781098 140328